ORGANISATIONAL
BEHAVIOUR

ANDREW CREED

CASE STUDIES BY
PAUL PHILLIPS

ORGANISATIONAL BEHAVIOUR

OXFORD
UNIVERSITY PRESS
AUSTRALIA & NEW ZEALAND

OXFORD
UNIVERSITY PRESS

Oxford University Press is a department of the University of Oxford.
It furthers the University's objective of excellence in research,
scholarship, and education by publishing worldwide. Oxford is a registered
trademark of Oxford University Press in the UK and in certain other
countries.

Published in Australia by
Oxford University Press
253 Normanby Road, South Melbourne, Victoria 3205, Australia

National Library of Australia Cataloguing-in-Publication data

Creed, Andrew.
Organisational behaviour / Andrew Creed, Paul Phillips.

9780195572308 (pbk.)

Includes index.
Organisational behaviour.
Phillips, Paul Stuart, 1948-

658.3

Reproduction and communication for educational purposes

For details of the CAL licence for educational institutions contact:

Copyright Agency Limited
Level 15, 233 Castlereagh Street
Sydney NSW 2000
Telephone: (02) 9394 7600
Facsimile: (02) 9394 7601
Email: info@copyright.com.au

Edited by Venetia Somerset
Typeset by Denise Lane
Proofread by Tim Fullerton
Indexed by Russell Brooks
Printed by Sheck Wah Tong Printing Press Ltd

*Links to third party websites are provided by Oxford in good faith and for information only.
Oxford disclaims any responsibility for the materials contained in any third party website
referenced in this work.*

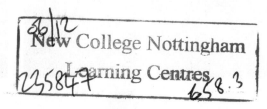

BRIEF CONTENTS

List of Figures   xii

List of Tables   xii

List of Case Studies   xiii

Case Study Mapping Grid   xiv

List of Practitioner Insights   xvi

Guided Tour   xviii

About the Authors   xx

Preface   xxii

Acknowledgments   xxv

PART ONE: MANAGEMENT STRATEGIES

1 The Atmosphere and the Architecture: Organisational Strategy and Structure 3

PART TWO: INDIVIDUAL FACTORS

2 Learning: The Pathway to Constructive People Management 35

3 Modern Diversity: The Adaptation of Values, Attitudes and Personality 67

4 Motivation and Job Satisfaction 95

PART THREE: RELATIONAL FACTORS

5 Groups and Teams 125

6 The Leadership Function 153

7 Power, Control and Influence 179

PART FOUR: ORGANISATIONAL FACTORS

8 Culture 205

9 Equitable Design and Negotiation of Work Arrangements 231

10 Stability and Change 257

Glossary   280

Index   286

EXPANDED CONTENTS

List of Figures	xii
List of Tables	xii
List of Case Studies	xiii
Case Study Mapping Grid	xiv
List of Practitioner Insights	xvi
Guided Tour	xviii
About the Authors	xx
Preface	xxii
Acknowledgments	xxv

PART ONE: MANAGEMENT STRATEGIES

1 The Atmosphere and the Architecture: Organisational Strategy and Structure	3
Introduction	3
Overview	4
Defining the human relations field	4
Management	4
Organisation	5
Organisational behaviour	5
Communication, decision-making, conflict and negotiation, and ethics	6
The atmosphere of work	7
External factors: Diversity of people and perceptions	7
Internal factors: Changes to the employee–employer relationship	10
Job security	10
Outsourcing	10
Pay and discrimination	11
Work–family balance (maternity, paternity and caring)	13
Effectively managing in the atmosphere of globalisation	13
Trust, ethics and agreement	13
Task versus relationship	14
Absenteeism and turnover	14
Job satisfaction and productive work	15
The architecture of work	17
Organisational structure basics	17
Technology and scale	17
Control and coordination	18
Departments, the matrix and networks	20

EXPANDED CONTENTS

Effectively managing the strategic architecture   22

Organisations and the neural network metaphor   22

Conclusion   25

PART TWO: INDIVIDUAL FACTORS

2   Learning: The Pathway to Constructive People Management 35

   Introduction   35

   Overview   36

   A definition   37

   The relativity of perception   39

   An aspect of diversity   41

   Learning and attention   42

     Focus on what is critical   43

     Attention and motivation to learn   43

   Learning and expectations   45

   Reinforcement and behaviour modification   46

     Classical and operant conditioning   48

     Behaviour modification   50

     Reinforcement as a management tool   51

   Social learning and the complex workplace   52

     Individual and organisational learning: The neural network   52

     Culture and learning   53

     Learning to change   55

     The challenge of power and politics   57

     Constructive leadership   59

   Conclusion   59

3   Modern Diversity: The Adaptation of Values, Attitudes and Personality 67

   Introduction   67

   Overview   68

   Attitudes and values   68

     The formation of attitudes and values and their influence on personality   68

     Job satisfaction   71

   Personality   72

     Environment or heredity?   73

     Foundational ideas   75

Freud and Jung	75
Myers-Briggs	76
The Big 5	78
Self-efficacy	79
Locus of control	79
Emotional intelligence	79
Socialisation	81
Culture, diversity and equity	82
Hofstede	83
Developing respect and trust in the workplace	85
Conclusion	88
4 Motivation and Job Satisfaction	**95**
Introduction	95
Overview	96
Does satisfaction limit motivation?	96
Needs-based motivation: The content theorists	97
Maslow and the needs hierarchy	97
Alderfer and ERG	100
Herzberg's two-factor theory	101
McClelland and acquired needs	104
Situation-based motivation: The process theorists	105
Locke: Goal-setting theory	105
Vroom: Expectancy theory	106
Adams: Equity theory	108
Empowerment	111
Work–family balance and relational factors at work	113
Learning and reinforcement through leadership	113
Conclusion	116

PART THREE: RELATIONAL FACTORS

5 Groups and Teams	**125**
Introduction	125
Overview	126
Groups versus teams	126
Group types and the team development sequence	128
Punctuated equilibrium in team performance	130

Groupthink 131

Synergy 132

Social loafing 133

Capitalising on group energy: Getting to a decision 135

The architecture and atmosphere of high-performance teams 140

Belbin's team roles 141

Cohesiveness and team spirit 141

Team leadership and control 142

Conclusion 145

6 The Leadership Function 153

Introduction 153

Overview 154

Leadership traits 154

Are there universal traits? 155

Leadership styles (behavioural theories) 158

The Michigan and Ohio State studies 158

The managerial grid 158

Situational leadership theories 160

Path-goal theory 160

Fred Fiedler 161

Hersey & Blanchard 163

Contemporary leadership 165

Emotional (social) intelligence 166

Ethical leadership 168

Charisma and the leadership of change 169

Leadership in the neural network 171

Conclusion 172

7 Power, Control and Influence 179

Introduction 179

Overview 180

The sources of power 180

Potential power 181

Actualised power 181

Individual versus organisational power: The basis of industrial relations 182

How to get power 183

Personal power 183

Referent factors 183

Expert factors   184

Position power   184

Reward factors   184

Legitimacy factors   185

The exercise of power   186

Ethics and evil in organisations   187

Organisational power and politics   192

Techniques of influence   195

Conclusion   197

PART FOUR: ORGANISATIONAL FACTORS

8 Culture 205

Introduction   205

Overview   206

Implicit cultural factors: Shared values and attitudes   206

Explicit cultural factors: Observable culture   209

Language and stories   209

Norms and rituals   209

Innovation—Conservatism   210

Precision—Imprecision   210

Relationship orientation—Task orientation   211

Aggression—Calmness   212

Growth—Stability   213

Design   213

Global culture   215

Culture and ethics: Competition and collaboration   219

Work–life balance   220

Leadership of cultural learning and change   221

Conclusion   229

9 Equitable Design and Negotiation of Work Arrangements 231

Introduction   231

Overview   232

Designing work   232

Different approaches to the design of work   236

Integrated job design   237

Performance appraisal, negotiation and equity   242

The functions and challenges of performance appraisal 242
Work–life balance, health and flexible work design 245
    Space design 245
    Time design 246
    Relationship design 249
The link with learning 249
Conclusion 250

10 Stability and Change 257
  Introduction 257
  Overview 258
  Forces for change 258
  Forces for stability 258
  Planned change 259
  Unplanned change 260
  Cycles of change and learning 260
  Change management models 262
    The cultural web 262
    The Pettigrew model 264
    Force field analysis 265
    Unfreezing, changing, refreezing 267
  Competitive advantages, innovation and change 270
  Work–life balance in the midst of change 272
  Conclusion 275

Glossary 280
Index 286

LIST OF FIGURES

1.1: Themes affecting the atmosphere of organisational behaviour 7

1.2: Hierarchy and span of control 18

1.3: Sample matrix organisational structure 20

2.1: Learning involves thinking, relating and behaving 38

2.2: Perception is unique for each individual 39

2.3: Perceptual paradoxes 40

3.1: The factors of personality 72

3.2: Example of a personality test 77

4.1: Maslow's hierarchy of needs 98

4.2: Expectancy theory 107

5.1: A team is a special type of group 127

5.2: Tuckman's group development sequence 129

5.3: Punctuated equilibrium: The realities of teamwork when deadlines loom 130

6.1: Blake & Mouton's managerial grid 159

6.2: Situational favourability and the LPC score 162

6.3: Hersey & Blanchard's situational leadership 163

7.1: A continuum of ethics: Self and others 188

8.1: People, groups and culture have common heritage 215

8.2: One cultural continuum: Compete or collaborate? 219

10.1: Diverging forces of change 265

LIST OF TABLES

2.1: The philosophers on the nature of learning 36

3.2: The features and effects of the Big 5 at work 78

7.1: How to increase influence under each power source 195

10.1: Pettigrew's model of organisational change 264

LIST OF CASE STUDIES

Underlying racism upsets equilibrium in a call centre 8

Using Facebook: Appearances can be misleading 16

Too much friendliness in the Customer Service staff 47

Competition from overseas means that the old hands need to change 56

Older staff find Sally's unconventional appearance irksome 84

Speaking up for yourself or being aggressive? 87

Avoiding staff turnover in boring jobs 110

Two different kinds of motivation 114

Staff leave in spite of excellent team performance 139

Tom's team resist meetings as a waste of time: A team or a group? 143

Problems with the new immigrants in Shirley's dispatch team 165

When the main customer disappears, more of the same won't do 170

The manager learns from an unlikely worker 191

Can too much power steamroll ethics? 196

Culture and the manager's style 213

In practice: Managing culture during change 222

Benefits Officers denied the satisfaction of full responsibility 234

Being a mother and working from home is possible 244

Genuine interpersonal conflict or simply resistance to change? 266

Applying strategy to change: A book industry example 274

CASE STUDY MAPPING GRID

The grid below identifies the chapter in which each case sits (*) and also shows other chapters for which the case applies due to integration of ideas (✓).

CASES	CH 1	CH 2	CH 3	CH 4	CH 5	CH 6	CH 7	CH 8	CH 9	CH 10
Underlying racism upsets equilibrium in a call centre	* ✓						✓	✓	✓	
Using Facebook: Appearances can be misleading	* ✓	✓	✓							
Too much friendliness in the customer service staff		* ✓							✓	
Competition from overseas means that the old hands need to change		* ✓		✓						
Older staff find Sally's unconventional appearance irksome			* ✓					✓		
Speaking up for yourself or being aggressive?			* ✓			✓	✓	✓		
Avoiding staff turnover in boring jobs				* ✓					✓	
Two different kinds of motivation		✓		* ✓		✓				
Staff leave in spite of excellent team performance				✓	* ✓				✓	
Tom's team resist meetings as a waste of time: A team or a group?					* ✓	✓			✓	

CASE STUDY MAPPING GRID

CASES	CH 1	CH 2	CH 3	CH 4	CH 5	CH 6	CH 7	CH 8	CH 9	CH 10
Problems with the new immigrants in Shirley's dispatch team			✓		✓	* ✓		✓		
When the main customer disappears, more of the same won't do				✓	✓	* ✓	✓			
The manager learns from an unlikely worker			✓				* ✓			✓
Can too much power steamroll ethics?						✓	* ✓			✓
Culture and the manager's style				✓	✓			* ✓	✓	
In practice: Managing culture during change				✓				* ✓	✓	✓
Benefits Officers denied the satisfaction of full responsibility				✓					* ✓	✓
Being a mother and working from home is possible	✓		✓						* ✓	
Genuine interpersonal conflict or simply resistance to change?		✓								* ✓
Applying strategy to change: A book industry example	✓		✓						✓	* ✓

LIST OF PRACTITIONER INSIGHTS

1. **Camilla Britton**, *Human Capital Team Manager, PwC* 30

2. **Jessica Harrison**, *Head of Talent, KPMG Australia* 64

3. **Leanne Klahsen**, *Senior Consultant, Human Resources Division, Deakin University* 92

4. **Louise Jensen**, *Director, HR, Grant Thornton Australia Limited* 120

5. **Rebecca Woodward**, *Human Resources Manager, Madgwicks* 150

LIST OF PRACTITIONER INSIGHTS

6. Rita D'Arcy, *HR, Particularly People* 176

7. Tom Hutchinson, *Principal Consultant, Hassett People Solutions* 200

8. Vin Lucas, *HR Director, Schweppes Australia* 228

9. Wendy Cooper, *Executive Director, Human Resources Division, Deakin University* 254

How to use this book

Organisational Behaviour is enriched with a range of features designed to help support and reinforce your learning. This guided tour shows you how to best utilise your textbook and get the most out of your study.

LEARNING OBJECTIVES

Each chapter begins with a bulleted list of learning objectives outlining the main concepts and ideas that you will encounter in the chapter.

LEARNING OBJECTIVE REINFORCEMENT

Learning objectives are reinforced in blue margin notes at critical points throughout the text. These serve as helpful signposts for learning and revision.

KEY TERMS AND GLOSSARY

Key terms are highlighted where they first appear in the text and the definition appears in red in the margin notes. The definitions are also collated at the end of each chapter and in a complete Glossary at the back of the book for easy reference.

THOUGHT PATHWAY

These pathways give you the opportunity to stop and reflect on the material at various points throughout the text, either on your own or in a group.

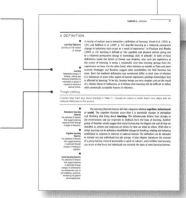

CASE STUDIES

Case studies apply the theory being discussed in each chapter to real-life business situations. Each chapter is supplemented by two case studies which include questions that help you to assess your understanding of the material covered in the chapter.

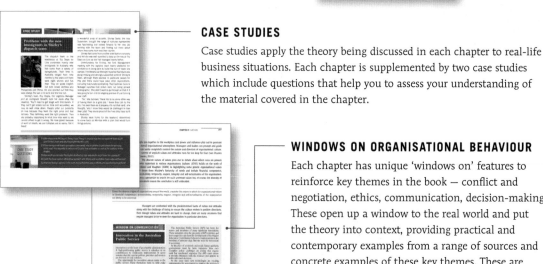

WINDOWS ON ORGANISATIONAL BEHAVIOUR

Each chapter has unique 'windows on' features to reinforce key themes in the book — conflict and negotiation, ethics, communication, decision-making. These open up a window to the real world and put the theory into context, providing practical and contemporary examples from a range of sources and concrete examples of these key themes. These are taken from the local and global setting.

KEY POINTS

A summary of key points is listed at the end of every chapter to reinforce your comprehension of the learning objectives and the central themes of the chapter.

STUDY AND REVISION QUESTIONS

Carefully designed questions have been provided at the end of every chapter. You can use these to check your understanding of the key topics before moving on to the next chapter, or for group discussion or revision.

PRACTITIONER INSIGHTS

In these short interviews, the practitioners explain how their understanding of Organisational Behaviour has enhanced their career, and explore how this continues to be an important aspect of their working lives.

REFERENCES

References have been provided as a guide to help broaden your understanding of the topics covered in each chapter.

Oxford Business Hub

Please visit the Oxford Business Hub for further digital resources for students and lecturers.

Hub (noun): a central point of interest, activity etc...

To get the most from your study, come and explore the Oxford Business Hub oup.com.au/obh.

The OBH includes a rich selection of resources, including:

Author audio explaining key issues from each chapter.

Flashcard glossary to test yourself on the key terms from the text.

Weblinks to give quick access to the further reading and resources.

OXFORD BUSINESS HUB

ABOUT THE AUTHORS

Andrew Creed was born in Davenport, Iowa, USA, and raised in Warrnambool, Victoria, Australia, Andrew Creed fondly recalls his early working life spent on a reception desk in his family's rural and regional health care clinic. This is the place where he learned much about human relationships, service and a basic respect for the predicaments of others. Subsequent career opportunities helped Andrew to build on his early learning about people management. Starting his own businesses in bookselling, publishing and business consulting contributed to a genuine pragmatism in his understanding of management. Later work in non-profit organisations and managing government contract implementation in the field of micro-enterprises through the New Enterprise Incentive Scheme (NEIS) merged in Andrew a sentiment of altruism with a focus on the bottom line, plus an interest in the entrepreneurial mindset. A friend and mentor encouraged Andrew into the field of vocational education in the TAFE sector in the early 1990s, which launched a prolonged experience of professional development combined with frenetic business operations and management consulting. By 2001, Andrew was involved in instructional design, writing and project management for online industrial training toolboxes in the fields of food and meat processing, and office administration, and also stepping into academia in Australia and globally as the natural extension of a decade and a half immersed in adult education.

With an MBA from University of Maryland University College (UMUC) and a PhD from University of Exeter (UK), Andrew Creed has rounded out a global experience of management and education. He has been a Lecturer at Deakin University and an Adjunct Associate Professor at UMUC. Drawing always on experience, Andrew's applied research is in the vibrant discipline of organisational behaviour. Online education and relational ethics are among his main interests. He is published in the journals *European Business Review, Journal of Electronic Commerce in Organizations, Team Performance Management, International Journal of Learning, International Journal of Business Governance and Ethics* and *Journal of Knowledge Globalization*, among others. He has book chapters published with Studentlitteratur in Sweden, Information Science Reference and IGI Publishing in the USA, and NAISIT in Canada. He is also co-author of *Organisational Behaviour: Core Concepts and Applications* (2nd Australasian edition) with John Wiley & Sons, Australia. You will find Andrew's name on textbook supplements including Instructor Guides, Lecture Notes, and Test Banks for a variety of publishers indicative of the fact that, as he puts it, 'Writing is my hobby'. As an accomplished and experienced manager and author, Andrew Creed presents in this current book an original, engaging treatise covering the rich field of group human endeavour.

ABOUT THE AUTHORS

Paul Phillips contributed to this book by writing the case studies. His human resources management career extends over 35 years covering both corporate and consulting roles. The early part of his life was spent in New Zealand and he later worked for an international telecommunications company in the UK with various assignments internationally.

Since moving to Australia he has held senior roles in the private and public sectors and has worked as a consultant providing HRM services to a range of local and international organisations. He has a passion for making a difference in the workplace through better understanding and application of practical concepts.

Soma Pillay contributed online resources to this book. She is a lecturer in Human Resource Management and Organisation Studies at Swinburne University of Technology, Hawthorn campus, Melbourne. Soma teaches undergraduate and postgraduate programs in the subject areas of Organisational Behaviour and Change, Management and Organisations, and International Management. Before joining academia, Soma spent many years in the public service. Her qualifications are cross-disciplinary and include public sector governance. Soma is an active researcher in the Faculty of Business. Her teaching interests contribute and complement her research into issues associated with work and family, cross-cultural studies, ethics and public sector governance. She is also actively involved in management education and has worked closely with the Australian Institute of Human Resource Management in accreditation matters.

It is with great pleasure that this book is presented as the crystallisation of experiences gained in genuine pursuit of a better understanding of human relationships. Have I succeeded? I hope that you think so. I believe I can offer a special insight into organisational behaviour (OB) from a multidisciplinary background. I have worked with micro, small, medium and large organisations. I have pursued profits but also altruistic organisational objectives. Always I have been focused on what makes people work well together. Organisations are driven by people. A collection of machines does nothing without the directives of human beings. Even the promise of full automation and artificial intelligence is at best a long way off. Organisational sustainability and the attainment of real work–life balance require adaptive, interactive strategy formulation and responses by people actively engaged with purpose and motivation. Every organisation has its own architecture (structure and processes) and a unique atmosphere (culture). This book pays respect to these fundamental facts and explores OB using an integrated approach. You will discover connections between chapters and theories at regular intervals. The learning objectives are interrelated. The key definitions and theories are all included to cater for the introductory reader, but there is plenty here for advanced knowledge of OB to be explored and challenged. It is a brave new world in the global workplace for managers and staff in Australia and beyond. This book is designed as an innovative and thoughtful exploration of OB concepts through chapters presented in the following spirit:

Chapter 1 connects immediately with organisational strategy and makes a salute to organisational structure. This is an original and essential way to make clear the relevance of organisational behaviour.

Chapter 2 breaks from the common sequence in OB and elevates the function of learning. Professional development and the management of organisational change are intrinsically linked with theories of learning, so it is crucial for managers to get an early view of this topic. The formation of individual perceptions is one part of this field. I hope you can appreciate this innovation in the curriculum for OB. Whether you are a student or a teacher in this subject, learning and continuous improvement for competitive advantage should be highly relevant.

Chapter 3 is an acknowledgment of globalisation, socio-technical change and the individualism that lies at the heart of the diversity within organisations large and small. Diversity is a real and confronting challenge for managers. The people who work for organisations are unique individuals with their own personalities and deserve a level of respect at all times. Managers are often guilty of discrimination and insensitivity. This chapter is a must-read for anyone hoping to have a better relationship with staff at all levels of their organisation.

Chapter 4 completes the section on individual factors in the workplace. It summarises the main theories of motivation in the workplace, from needs theories through to process theories. Why do people turn up to work at all? This is a valid question and one that needs a well-researched answer if managers are to be successful in the longer term. This chapter covers the main theories in an integrative way.

Chapter 5 introduces the foundations of group dynamics with an emphasis on team functioning as an essential relational factor in modern organisations. There is, perhaps, nothing more self-evident in OB than the fact that people have to work well together to achieve significant things in life. This chapter brings together the key concepts in this area, giving managers a toolkit for creating high-performing teams and improving organisational performance as a result.

Chapter 6 flows naturally from the fact that leaders emerge from group and team dynamics. The prominent ideas about leadership are traced from past through to present trait theories. The details of behavioural and situational theories are also covered. An idea is proposed that the function of leadership is constant even where leaders themselves may move on. This has obvious implications indicating that the quest for consolidating a leadership role in times of change is perennial.

Chapter 7 is a pivotal reality check for managers and educators. Power and control are at the heart of human relationships whether we are prepared to admit it or not. There is idealism in OB and this chapter is the antidote to that. A better understanding of power and control gives people the tools to express respect, manage diversity and handle change.

Chapter 8 is the culminating thesis about organisational atmosphere. The collective expression of individual personalities, group and team dynamics, leadership initiatives, and executions of power and control make up the complex thing we refer to as organisational culture. We know it when we experience it, but culture can be hard to explain. This chapter presents the main ideas about organisational culture on the premise that a better understanding of it is essential for normal functioning, improved performance, management of change, and motivation of workers.

Chapter 9 draws all of the theoretical threads together for the pragmatic manager. It is through the design of jobs that most of the theories of OB come into practice. Staff will either flourish or die by their job descriptions and the expectations inherent in their roles. Work–life balance, motivation, absenteeism, turnover, satisfaction and any other relevant measure of success in OB are largely a result of the way that work is designed and implemented. Inequities have their roots in job design. If you are busy and need to read one chapter above others to inform your work as manager, this is the one.

Chapter 10 closes the learning circle for organisational behaviour. Change is a type of learning, and organisational strategy and structure depend on good management of the dynamic situations of today. A poor understanding of the management of change and stability in organisations leads to all kinds of problems with motivation, satisfaction, turnover, absenteeism and other key indicators. People don't like to change, and yet the essence of competitive advantage rests with the embrace of change. This paradox is at the heart of organisational strategy and structure, thus taking us back to the very start so that a new perspective on organisational behaviour can move us forward again. The integrated nature of the chapter sequence is graphically displayed. It shows individual, relational and organisational factors in reciprocal interactions within the broader field of organisational strategy and structure. Chapters for each variable are listed:

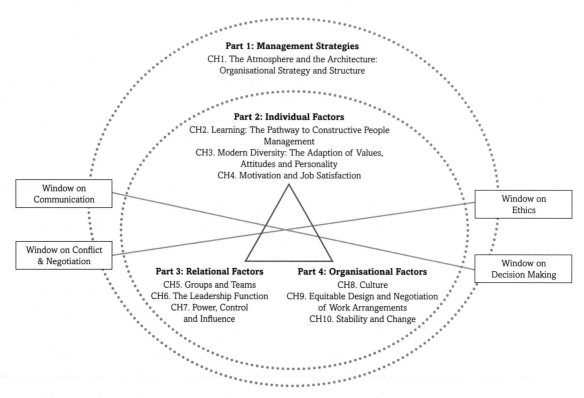

I hope you appreciate the book. It is based on experience as a practising manager, a practising educator, and a continually developing author. Your feedback about the text from the perspective of student, educator or management practitioner is always welcome. Even I can learn from feedback and I aim to emulate the concepts at the heart of this book by including responses to feedback in future editions.

ACKNOWLEDGMENTS

How a senior publisher can know when an author is going to deliver on a book concept, I cannot fully explain. I sincerely appreciate the foresight of Karen Hildebrandt, who, while travelling one day in southwestern Victoria, found me at work in my teaching territory and was able to discern that I could offer a new and accessible perspective on organisational behaviour. The professional support and guidance that ensued from Karen is one of the key factors behind the completion of this project.

My life is filled with mentors who should know that I appreciate them. Mr Peter Lewis Young (dec.), Dr Wilf Backhaus (dec.), Dr Jane Ross, Dr Ambika Zutshi, Professor Patrick Dillon, Mr Don Swanson, Mr Ken Howell, Mr Michael Callaghan, Mr Peter Costello and Professor Greg Wood are the most prominent, but there are many more today and from my past who are not forgotten. For example, the TRENDS team who once worked at SWTAFE helped my writing immensely. If you are not already listed, please take me up on it after you read this and I will probably accede and buy you a drink.

I have immediate family who learned to adapt to having an author around. The odd hours of inspiration and the need for me to travel for added perspective are among the challenges for family and I truly value the tolerance they have had to express. Thank you to Gemma Creed (who was there the day I met Karen Hildebrandt), Ethan Creed, Janet Creed, Nita Creed, Trevor Creed and Gloria Howard because you are the ones who have given the most for projects such as this one.

Readers should know that I also have a wealth of global and online experience of management education. I have been mentored by Dr Jack Ross, Mr Maurice Hladik, Professor James Stewart, Professor Mike Evanchik and others at University of Maryland University College. All experience is valued and some are the type that should never be underestimated.

A big thank-you to my co-contributors, Paul Phillips and Soma Pillay, who added the extra perspectives and flavours that fine-tuned this book to be both professional and enjoyable for students and teachers alike.

Finally, the team at OUP are the real champions of a book like this. Good people with great skills have contributed along the way, including Jessica Hambridge, Natalie Davall, Venetia Somerset, Jen Butler, Estelle Tang, Michelle Cottrill, Regine Abos and Ana Cosma.

Thank-you all.

Andrew Creed

ACKNOWLEDGMENTS

I would like to thank the numerous colleagues and clients who, over the years, have provided a range of interesting experiences and challenges on which many of these case studies are based. I would also like to thank my wife and business partner, Chris, for keeping me in touch with reality.

Paul Phillips

The authors and Oxford University Press would like to thank the following reviewers, who provided incisive and helpful feedback:
Alan Burton-Jones, Bond University, Griffith University and the University of New South Wales
Bill Harley, The University of Melbourne
Alick Kay, The University of South Australia
Monica Kennedy, University of Canberra
Darren Lee-Ross, James Cook University
Bernadette Lynch, University of Southern Queensland
Kerrie Unsworth, University of Western Australia

We would also like to thank the professionals who provided interviews for the Practitioner Insights:
Camilla Britton, Human Capital Team Manager, PwC
Jessica Harrison, Head of Talent, KPMG Australia
Leanne Klahsen, Senior Consultant, Human Resources Division, Deakin University
Louise Jensen, Director, HR, Grant Thornton Australia Limited
Rebecca Woodward, Human Resources Manager, Madgwicks
Rita D'Arcy, HR, Particularly People
Tom Hutchinson, Principal Consultant, Hassett People Solutions
Vin Lucas, HR Director, Schweppes Australia
Wendy Cooper, Executive Director, Human Resources Division, Deakin University

01
Management
Strategies

1 The Atmosphere and the Architecture:
Organisational Strategy and Structure 3

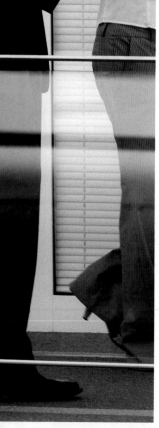

The Atmosphere and the Architecture: Organisational Strategy and Structure

INTRODUCTION

■

Organisation
An organisation comprises people and other resources brought together with a design and strategy directed towards a common purpose.

■

Atmosphere
The collective manifestation of people and resources for a purposeful strategy is expressed as an atmosphere.

■

Architecture
The structure of an organisation—the way that work is arranged, departments are established and processes are articulated—collectively represent the architecture of the workplace.

■

Organisational behaviour
The study of individual and group characteristics and behaviour in the context of workplace structures and strategies.

The workplace is changing. The structures and processes of **organisations** are evolving through the vast forces imposed by history, society and technology. People working in organisations today are communicating, interacting and responding in order to achieve objectives just as workers have done before them, but those objectives are markedly different from the past and the tools of activity have also transformed the ways that people fulfil their organisational functions. Internal and external factors combine to affect and generate an **atmosphere** within which communication, culture and relationships manifest. The strategy of an organisation affects and responds to the available structures, tools, processes and resources that are aspects of the organisational **architecture**. This book surveys the contemporary factors that make **organisational behaviour** a useful field of study.

Chapter 1 defines organisational behaviour within the global context of changed and continuously transforming organisational design and strategy. It establishes a basis upon which subsequent chapters integrate all the key elements of organisational behaviour, including individual, relational and organisational factors.

LEARNING
OBJECTIVES

Understanding this chapter will help you to
- define key concepts in the field of organisational behaviour
- describe the key concepts that historically underpin the study of organisational behaviour
- identify strategy as a determinant of organisational atmosphere

- explain the design and structure elements of organisations as a kind of architecture that influences strategy and people at work
- articulate the neural network metaphor and its implications for the future of organisational behaviour.

OVERVIEW

Management
Planning, organising, leading and controlling the variables of time, money, physical resources and people (human resources).

People are fundamentally important for creating, participating in and maintaining organisational design and structure (Follett, 1918; Drucker, 1977). It is also clear that organisational strategy inevitably fails unless the majority of human resources of an organisation give it meaning, direction and support (Denis et al., 2010). The field of organisational behaviour exists in order to study the influence and interaction of people within organisational structure and strategy. The effect of human relational interactions on the inputs, processes and outcomes of daily work is ubiquitous and equally challenging for workers and managers. This has applied throughout the history of **management** and it is surely still relevant today. The first step is to establish some key definitions, explore some consistent themes, and develop some initial concepts to assist understanding.

Defining the human relations field

Learning Objective
Key concepts in the field of organisational behaviour

The opening discussion suggests that the field of organisational behaviour is broadly defined by foundational concepts in the study of human relations in the management discipline. In order to arrive at a useful and agreeable definition of organisational behaviour, an understanding of key terms, such as management and organisation, is helpful.

MANAGEMENT

Time, money, physical resources and people (human resources) compose the inventory of variables normally at a manager's discretion. Management involves planning, organising, leading and controlling these variables. Although an ancient requirement for human organisation, management as a formalised field of study emerged relatively recently, largely in response to the convergence of the industrial and scientific revolutions. The energy released by large-scale mechanisation, combined with the new understanding that a scientific approach to all kinds of disciplines, including mass production, brought to the world, gave the impetus for early industrialists to develop and document procedures and principles to distinguish the field of management. Subsequent development of theories of management and schools dedicated to its study consolidated the management discipline.

ORGANISATION

The prolific management writer Peter Drucker, while acknowledging the pioneering work of Mary Parker Follett in the field of management (Follett & Graham, 1995) agrees that we are a society of organisations, and primarily social organisations at that. An organisation comprises people and other resources brought together with a design and strategy directed towards a common purpose. It is effectively through the efforts of a group of managers to plan, organise, lead and control that an organisation develops and operates to assist these ends. In many legal frameworks an organisation retains a separate legal identity; it is recognised in its own right (Kleinberger & Bishop, 2010). An organisation can have a kind of synergy that expresses more than its individual parts. Like a swarm of bees, a school of fish or a flock of birds, an organisation comprises individuals who all work together to achieve a common purpose. It is social design and strategy that creates the binds that tie staff into synchronisation for the organisation (Hatchuel et al., 2010). The coordinated functioning of the unit would begin to disintegrate if it were not for a singular mission and a clearly communicated set of strategies and design principles. Integrity of an organisation is also highly dependent on the interpersonal relationships of the people within it. Whether the organisation exists to make profit, complete a government function or fulfil some other purpose, without the people working cohesively on the task, it would not work.

ORGANISATIONAL BEHAVIOUR

Organisational behaviour is the study of individual and group characteristics and behaviour in the context of workplace structures and strategies. Continuing the comparison with a swarm, school or flock, if people start to disagree, fight or retreat from responsibility in an organisation, these are the beginnings of problems that could break down the synchronisation of the whole formation. It is human nature to cooperate but also to compete (Gnyawali & Madhavan, 2001), so we have a troublesome dichotomy that has to be carefully managed if an integrated organisation is to be sustainable. This is why an understanding of organisational behaviour is so important for managers.

■

Learning Objective
Key concepts that
historically underpin the
study of organisational
behaviour

In fact, organisational behaviour is a hybrid discipline that draws in part from psychological, sociological and anthropological bases (Judge & Robbins, 2011). If you have studied in such fields you will notice some cross-referencing of theories and concepts from those areas. Managers operate in a social setting dealing with issues ranging from personality, friendship, power, status and intelligence, to relationships and more. This ensures that a diversity of solutions needs to be explored for the variety of problems that can emerge. For this reason, the study of organisational behaviour is eclectic, realistic and relevant; however, it is not at all simple. Those who yearn for one best way to handle the issues arising from human relationships are not very pragmatic. Being a good people manager takes energy and application, openness to diverse theories and frameworks, and a penchant for navigating through complexity.

Communication, decision-making, conflict and negotiation, and ethics

There are recurring themes in the daily interaction of managers with staff. Communication is an ongoing concern; it is as much the lifeblood of an organisation as finance. Good communication flows are critical for relaying data for organisational responsiveness and overall efficiency and effectiveness. Poor communication is a frequently cited cause of problems, including interpersonal conflict, among people in the workplace (Belbin, 2010). It appears to be the nature of human beings to get into conflict with each other and it is a common function of managers to have to deal with and respond to staff in the midst of such disagreements. The skills of negotiation must be coordinated with communication to ensure conflicts do not escalate and impede the functioning of the organisation (de Reuver & van Woerkom, 2010). At a fundamental level, acceptable ideas and behaviours in the workplace are underpinned by individual and collective values. The expression of values determines the culture of the organisation as well as the general ethical tone. Legal and regulatory frameworks guide managers, but the values, attitudes and behaviours of people during the conduct of daily work give the clearest expression of the ethics and the culture of the organisation (Bresman et al., 2010). Individual managers must also continually assess their ethical stance when making key decisions. Figure 1.1 builds on the notion that an organisation is composed of an atmosphere (design and strategy) as well as an architecture (structure). Each chapter in this book includes windows on the four recurring management themes: Communication, Decision-making, Conflict and Negotiation, and Ethics. These themes contribute to the atmosphere of the workplace.

Figure 1.1 Themes affecting the atmosphere of organisational behaviour

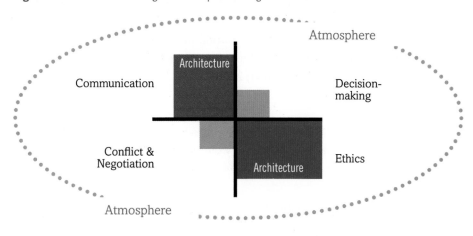

There are many themes affecting the atmosphere of organisational behaviour.

The next sections explain more about the distinction between atmosphere and architecture and the relevance of this to the study of organisational behaviour.

THE ATMOSPHERE OF WORK

The way things are designed creates a purpose as well as an aesthetic quality. This dual aspect of design contributes to what is ultimately a kind of atmosphere in the workplace (Creed et al., 2006). The aim or purpose of an organisation is expressed most articulately in its strategic plan. It is from the strategic plan that resources are funded and arranged, and people are, ideally, empowered to act. The collective manifestation of people and resources for a purposeful strategy is expressed as an atmosphere or, alternatively, a climate. When underlying factors in the environment drive a need for organisational climate change, as is increasingly occurring in today's complex and interrelated world, people have to take steps to cope, strategies must be changed and behaviours altered in order for individuals and organisations to survive. There are external and internal factors that affect the atmosphere of an organisation.

■
Learning Objective
Strategy as a determinant of organisational atmosphere

External factors: Diversity of people and perceptions

The inexorable march of globalisation is continuing. Information and transportation technologies have brought the world into close connection. Goods can be rapidly moved around, and information can be transmitted and copied exponentially faster than before. This has happened despite the fact that people continue to be born into distinct geographic and cultural environments. Each human being still takes a couple of decades to mature and does so with quite unique perspectives built into their thinking and behaviours. When it comes time to enter the workforce, people can do so increasingly at any location on earth and may bring into that position a widely diverse and quite entrenched background in comparison to others. It is an exciting time for cultural mingling, but one of some tension as rigid expectations based on cultural influences imbued over time are not always easy to overcome (Syed & Kramar, 2008).

Thought pathway

Can you truly live and let live? Be honest with yourself about your level of tolerance for the 'quirky' beliefs and behaviours of other people, especially those from markedly different cultural backgrounds to your own. Think about steps you could take to improve your tolerance for people's differences.

With the rapidity of technological developments enabling so much human movement, communication and change, the cultural and perceptual clash is continuing. Diversity management in complex environments has become the quintessential management skill.

CASE STUDY

Underlying racism upsets equilibrium in a call centre

James Scott is the Operations Manager at Trident Support, a call centre that provides customer support to some major home appliance manufacturers and distributors. The service provided covers delivery and service calls as well as technical support and trouble shooting. Trident Support employs 300 people and 250 of these work two shifts in a large open-plan area that is very modern and has well-designed workstations for each operator.

James has two shift managers reporting to him and they each have three supervisors reporting to them. The three areas they are responsible for are Transport, Service and Technical Support. Each supervisor is responsible for four teams of about ten operators, each headed by a Team Leader. These teams are usually built around product groups such as types of white goods and electronic appliances.

The Company provides excellent conditions for the staff. There is a small gym, a fully equipped lunchroom where people can warm up or cook food, and a bank of vending machines to provide a wide range of refreshments.

James is proud of his operation and receives good feedback from customers. Unfortunately he has trouble recruiting good staff. There are always plenty of applicants but many do not speak English well or do not have the temperament to handle customers who are annoyed at having problems with their new purchases.

The call centre workforce tends to be made up of three major groups: young people who are on a working holiday who are usually English or New Zealanders; Indians, many of whom are recent immigrants; and Anglo-Australians, who tend to be longer serving.

James has been in his job for three years and with Trident for seven. He worked his way up through the organisation after returning from a few years travelling overseas. He had spent some time travelling in Asia and Europe and felt he had developed a reasonable understanding of different cultures and a tolerance for the various traits they demonstrated. For this reason he had no problem considering all types of people for the jobs in the call centre and put up with the jibes of his peers about the range of nationalities he employed.

The training to be become an effective call centre operator took about two weeks and James was continually improving this process by obtaining feedback on performance after training.

He found the Indians the best workers by far. They were reliable, polite and very productive. As he introduced new systems they were keen to take on the changes and were very good with the new technology. Many had worked in call centres in India and were familiar with some of the new systems. Because of this their numbers had grown and so had the performance of the business.

The problem that James faced was that he had started to pick up some negative comments from the Anglo-Australian group. These had included comments about the smell of the food they prepared in the kitchen and sometimes ate at their desks, the way they dressed and their accents, and some of them were even referred to as 'boat people'. James was quite sickened by these attitudes but didn't want to get into a debate about any underlying racism. He wanted to focus on the business issues.

He invited a few of the longer serving Anglo-Aust-ralians to a meeting to discuss business performance and relationships among the staff.

Len King and Joan Ford had been with Trident for over five years and had seen a number of trends over that time. At first there were young people joining the company but they became bored and left. Then new immigrants would join but struggled because of the language. The Company had provided English training to some but the others found it too hard and had to leave. The young travellers were good but rarely stayed more than a year. They agreed that the Indians were more stable and worked well but said they did not mix with the Anglos and 'were different'. 'I've got nothing against Indians,' said Len, 'but they don't fit in with the way we do things here.' 'No,' thought James, 'they turn up on time, work all day and don't give me any strife.'

Joan said, 'I don't mind them really but the people in my team don't like the smell of their food and they don't really mix in very well. And another thing—they don't let us know what's happening with some of the delivery delays where installation is required so we have trouble rescheduling service technicians. Sometimes I think they don't want to help.'

To try and get a balanced view, James met with some of the longer serving Indians. Sandeep Singh was a supervisor and was worried about the feedback James gave him and assured him that most of his colleagues wanted to fit in, not only with Trident, but wanted to become good Australians as well. He was aware of some of the comments but assured James that Indians were used to these and he half jokingly suggested if he had a few Aussies in his team he would show them what Indian culture was all about. James then realised he had let, even encouraged, supervisors to pick their own teams. As a result they were grouped along racial lines.

James asked Sandeep about the communications issue that Joan had raised. 'I think I know what happened,' he said, 'and it only happened twice. It was Meena who hadn't been here long and was embarrassed about letting Joan's team know about the delays because she felt responsible. It wasn't her fault at all; the transport company had let us down. It is all fixed now and shouldn't happen again. I explained that to Joan and apologised for not letting them know.'

'Why don't these people just talk to each other,' James thought, 'rather than just save up points to win an argument or hide problems because they are afraid of the consequences?'

The other issue that James was worried about was the soon-to-be-introduced paid parental leave. He was concerned that, due to the larger percentage of younger females in the Indian group, there would be more people going on parental leave. He was sure that their other attributes would outweigh these extra costs but didn't want the figures to provide ammunition for some of the more xenophobic people in the Company.

James knew what he wanted as an outcome: a high-performing business where people enjoyed coming to work. He just wasn't sure how to get it.

CASE STUDY QUESTIONS

1 If James had read Chapter 1 when he started in his job, what three factors do you think he should have taken into account when planning his call centre and why?

2 Referring to the section 'External Factors: Diversity of people and perceptions', list some of the reasons you feel the Anglo-Australians may feel antagonistic towards the Indians.

3 If James's concerns about parental leave are justified, how do you think he could reduce the risk of criticism about his recruiting practices?

4 Why do you think the Indians are more reliable and more productive than the Anglo-Australians?

5 Referring to the section 'The Architecture of Work', describe how James might reorganise his workforce to overcome some of his problems.

Internal factors: Changes to the employee–employer relationship

As time passes, different organisational concerns fill the minds of managers and staff. The wider social environment filters through to daily work practices. In recent years some of the internal organisational issues have been related to job security, **outsourcing**, pay, discrimination and the balance between work and life.

Outsourcing
The decision taken to contract some aspect of an operation out to an external organisation, often offshore.

JOB SECURITY

The history of management includes many changes and crises that have affected the sense of job security workers develop. There have only been relatively brief periods at the peak of economic cycles in developed nations where people could realistically expect to have a choice of employment, let alone a sense of a job for life. The great depression, the recessions of the 1970s and 1980s and, of course, the most recent global financial crisis have been different manifestations of the same basic economic cycles. While such events affect organisations in different ways, it is clear that organisations cannot prosper constantly; there must be periods of contraction and realignment (Koutenakis, 2010). The impact of this lack of job security on the people who work in organisations should be at the forefront of a manager's mind when the cycles change.

OUTSOURCING

It is not only the big economic cycles that affect job security. Strategic decisions driven by the need for efficiency and by opportunities emerging from national deregulation, global trade agreements and technological developments also play a role. These forces have converged in recent decades and allowed the proliferation of outsourcing. Outsourcing is the decision taken to contract some aspect of an operation out to an external organisation, often offshore. This has created change and uncertainty in the workforces of those organisations that choose to outsource. It has also imposed immense social and cultural change on the nations (such as India and China) that have allowed large-scale manufacturing and information processing facilities to become established within their borders to service international outsourcers (Naghavi & Ottaviano, 2010). There has been a large redistribution of the labour force from key sectors of some of the developed nations that dominated in the 20th century to rising nations in the 21st century. People have also become more mobile across national borders, both physically and virtually (via telecommunications technology) as they service the outsourcing industry with its diverse human resources needs (Oster & Millett, 2010).

PAY AND DISCRIMINATION

Economic development and the desire for better living standards may be at the heart of the drivers of global workforce changes, but it is through the mechanisms of pay and reward for work completed that the daily evidence of progress is gauged by people. The fact is that large differentials continue to infest the relationships of staff with their organisations. This discrimination can happen on the basis of age, gender, ethnicity, religion, mental health and competency differences (Petit, 2007; Syed & Kramar, 2009).

Paid parental leave at the national level was introduced for the first time in Australia in 2011, but not without a fiery debate revealing a convergence of discrimination, equitable pay and work–family balance issues (Dunkerley, 2011). For one thing, no males and not every female can have babies, so a divide is immediately created by the scheme. It is one of those social dialogues where an ethical line is difficult to completely discern. It may be so that the legal line is not clear because of the prevalence of cases where individual workers feel aggrieved by not being paid enough, not getting the leave they need, or not being able to balance workload effectively with family demands. It is certainly so that regulators, managers and individual staff need to constantly monitor their actions and decisions so that the internal atmospheres of organisations are conducive to satisfaction and productivity.

There is a very subtle trap hidden in the relationships between managers and staff. Sometimes discrimination can occur almost unconsciously when hidden values and assumptions influence decisions that perpetuate inequalities. Sometimes the discrimination emerges blatantly, as in males being paid more than females for the same kinds of jobs, or people of a certain ethnic background being employed in preference to another.

WINDOW ON ETHICS

Virgin rejects pregnancy discrimination

BY ANDREA HAYWARD

Virgin Blue has rejected claims two of its executives were discriminated against and forced out for being pregnant or taking parental leave. Action will be launched in the Federal Magistrates Court by Terri Butler, the principal of legal firm Maurice Blackburn, who is representing the pair after mediation through Fair Work Australia failed to resolve the claims.

Ms Butler said the two women were part of the airline's eight-person PR team until mid-last year. 'They and another woman, for whom parental leave was imminent, were made redundant,' Ms Butler said.

Virgin Blue had failed to adhere to its own redundancy policy which requires the airline speak with affected employees before making a decision about their redundancy, Ms Butler said. Both eventually were forced to take redundancies, she said.

'My clients' skills, extensive experience and good performance remained relevant to Virgin Blue.

'They were discriminated against for being pregnant and on maternity leave.'

The department the pair worked for was restructured and their roles renamed but essentially still existed, Ms Butler said.

A Virgin Blue spokeswoman said the company completely rejected the allegations.

'Virgin Blue is an industry leader in supporting working mothers,' she said.

More than half of the airline's workforce was female and 28 per cent of the total workforce had flexible arrangements in the last 12 months.

'We are one of the only companies in Australia with 50 per cent female representation in our executive team.'

Ms Butler said the first woman was told a month after she informed Virgin she was pregnant she could not work outside business hours and was denied the earlier flexibility she enjoyed to drop an older child at school.

Soon after, the airline's general public affairs manager and human resources told the woman her role was redundant and there were no suitable positions to suit her skills.

Ms Butler said the woman was entitled to return to the same role or have the first opportunity at the new role, which performed exactly the same job.

The second woman claims she returned from maternity leave on a part-time basis and agreed to increase her work hours to 35 before being told part-time work was no longer available.

After taking two months leave at the request of the company, the woman was then told her position was no longer required and her position was redundant, Ms Butler said.

'Someone actually moved to her desk the day she was dismissed and picked up her role,' she said.

'So, she doesn't really accept that it was redundant because redundancy means the role's no longer required to be done by anyone. That's the definition of redundancy.'

The job title was changed but required the same work, Ms Butler said.

'That suggests to me that there is, at least from the surface, quite a problematic attitude to people who need to go on parental leave.'

A human resources manager had been heard saying 'all females should be on contracts so that when they get pregnant it is easy for the company to get rid of them,' Ms Butler said.

'So, if that's the attitude of HR, you wonder about the attitude that is being promulgated by the balance of the company.'

One of the women had also been subject to inappropriate comments about her pregnant belly and her constant eating, Ms Butler alleged.

Source: <http://au.news.yahoo.com/queensland/a/-/mp/8888076/virgin-rejects-pregnancy-discrimination/7>

This Window on Ethics demonstrates how the emergence of inequity is one of the greatest challenges we face in managing issues in the workplace. The letter of the law is one thing but the actions of managers who in all other respects observe the law are another. Respectfulness, clear communication, and reward of appropriate skill and competency are the ideals. The reality in the workplace is that the relationship between individuals and the factors of group dynamics tend to determine who gets employed and at which rates of pay. When matters of tension between work and family arise there is a need for reasonableness and flexibility on all sides.

WORK–FAMILY BALANCE (MATERNITY, PATERNITY AND CARING)

The success of industrialisation and the subsequent rise of living standards have delivered lifestyle choices to large numbers of people. The rise of a materialistic society in many parts of the globe has coincided with a lot of reflection about what is really important. Escaping the rat race, having a sea or a tree change, and trying to get a balance between work and life have become common topics of conversation among workers everywhere.

Thought pathway

Some organisations still seem to be clustered in large population centres, thus limiting the ability of workers to choose a genuine sea or tree change. Rising debt levels create a need to keep working. Technology also has us well connected with work and family. In the light of these factors, consider how realistic is a concept of work–family balance?

At certain levels of prosperity, people want more time to spend with their families, or to pursue personal interests (Michel et al., 2010). The issue of finding time is further exacerbated where full-time work is being progressively supplanted by part-time and casual employment.

Effectively managing in the atmosphere of globalisation

Some things have stayed constant in organisational behaviour: people must be motivated to work; a fair pay for a fair day's work is generally expected; abuses of power and authority must be carefully guarded against; the culture of the workplace has an effect on productivity; leadership is a vital function; and changes to structure and strategy have to be carefully managed with the people involved. But many things have also changed about organisational behaviour: globally mobile and diverse labour pools; increased labour force protections; significant technological impacts on speed and types of work; a stronger environmental conscience; and changing expectations about work–life balance. Common themes are emerging in organisational behaviour literature as people demand more trust and ethical behaviour from leaders and colleagues, a better balance between task and relationship emphases by managers, and greater levels of engagement and motivation to work translating to higher job satisfaction and better productivity. These demands are testing managers and making an understanding of organisational behaviour concepts increasingly relevant.

TRUST, ETHICS AND AGREEMENTS

The contract between an organisation and a staff member comes with obligations and expectations on both sides, some of which may be implied rather than explicit. Each individual agrees to work based upon the expectation that a level of recompense, monetary and otherwise, will be supplied in return. Likewise, the organisation knows it is giving pay and other benefits to staff on the understanding that a range of rewards, from productivity to quality, contribution to culture and team spirit, creative ideas and more will come from staff in return (Coyle-Shapiro & Neuman, 2004; Restubog & Bordia, 2007). There may be a written employment contract (but not always) and there are certainly legal frameworks that protect and compensate individuals and organisations where there are acts such as discrimination, abuses of power, and employment contracts established below the basic awards.

A series of business failures, frauds and corporate collapses in recent decades, accentuated by the financial losses of recent global financial crises, have elevated concern about the overall honesty and ethical behaviour of managers as well as general staff (Smallman et al., 2010). People are more educated, more connected to information, and more able to discern their rights and obligations. This places the imperative on managers to behave in trustworthy ways, to respect the rights of individuals and to generally behave ethically. Organisations that want to retain good people as a means for ensuring competitive advantage will often establish and promote a code of conduct, or build ethical imperatives into strategic plans (Singh et al., 2005). People are increasingly able to identify organisations that behave ethically as good places to work. There are examples of rhetoric in this emerging field, but the relevance and economic sense that building trust through ethical practices imparts is, perhaps, gradually turning the tide of cynicism.

TASK VERSUS RELATIONSHIP

A recurring theme in organisational behaviour is recognition of two types of personality and behaviour in managers and staff alike. Some people are more comfortable focusing on tasks, getting the job done, and knowing as much as they can about specifications, facts and processes. Other people are more comfortable focusing on relationships, fitting in with the social scene, being liked and sensitive to the concerns of others (Blake & Mouton, 1964; Salleh et al., 2010). You will see this continuum emerge throughout this book. Most of us find a balance somewhere between the two extremes, but we also will be able to identify leaders or friends we know who are either mostly task-focused or mostly relationship-focused. The former type is quite good for productivity, efficiency and achieving strategic plans. The latter type is suitable for building team morale, fostering goodwill and a sense of belonging, thereby minimising absenteeism and staff turnover.

ABSENTEEISM AND TURNOVER

What motivated you to read this chapter right through until this point? Why did you not lose interest in an earlier section and put this book away? The answer to these questions will help you to understand why someone would not turn up to work one day (absenteeism), or even choose to quit work altogether (turnover).

They are different scenarios but the same underlying factors of motivation and satisfaction are at play. If you feel dissatisfied with something, you will want to quit it. If you cannot find the motivation to enjoy something, you will prefer to stop doing it. The reasons for these feelings relate back to your needs as an individual in various situations, and also your thinking and feeling processes as your experiences are unfolding. Your health is also a determining factor and it relates in many ways to your working conditions and the levels of stress associated with any detrimental conditions (Holden et al., 2010). As managers, we should pay attention to health and safety of our workers and ourselves.

JOB SATISFACTION AND PRODUCTIVE WORK

One of the significant dilemmas of managing staff and self is the relationship of job satisfaction to overall productivity. It is reasonable to consider the promise of job satisfaction to be quite motivating for many people. Any expectation that getting involved with a job and doing the job well will lead to one feeling satisfied is sure to contribute to the motivation to get out of bed and start the working day with some enthusiasm. The problem is that once a level of satisfaction is achieved then what is left to motivate an individual to keep working hard? On the other hand, to consistently not achieve the things that you believe will make you satisfied could ultimately lead to disillusion and a lack of motivation. The manager is confronted with quite a delicate balancing act which relates to the previous section about task versus relationship factors. Being too relationship-focused, too giving and supportive, might be satisfying for staff but ultimately diminish overall drive and motivation. Being too task-focused, too impersonal and centred on goals and output, might be very motivating at first but lead to diminished job satisfaction and higher absenteeism and turnover in future. Labour market factors also play a role in job satisfaction. For instance, the increasing trend to part-time and casual work affects the general sense of job security and this has been shown to affect overall job satisfaction (Brown et al., 2010).

Thought pathway

Whenever you have finished a meal and feel satisfied are you especially motivated to eat more? Thinking of going to work as a similar kind of human need, consider the implications for how our work tasks ought to be organised.

To this point we have been outlining the factors that affect the atmosphere and overall culture of an organisation. Subsequent chapters will provide further detail about theories of motivation, culture, leadership, work–life balance and the range of interacting influences these bring to bear on the strategy of an organisation. Now we should turn to the structure of organisations on the understanding that strategy and structure are closely related.

Using Facebook: Appearances can be misleading

Gail Young was excited about her new job as a Marketing Assistant at BSI Pty Ltd, an events management business that organised the logistics for corporate functions. The services provided included booking venues, organising catering, printing and mailing invitations and providing suitable staff through contractors. Each project was quite profitable and clients were pleased with the value they received.

Gail was a new graduate and considered herself very lucky to have secured the job, which involved identifying organisations that may need the services of BSI. She was very adept at accessing and manipulating data and was rapidly developing her skills in communicating with prospective clients as well as networking with existing contacts.

Working alongside Elaine Ponsonby was very useful to Gail. Elaine was a mature-age woman who had been with BSI for over 15 years and was willing to pass on what she knew.

Both Gail and Elaine reported to David Miller, the Marketing Manager. He was very pleased about the way Gail was fitting in to the business so was surprised when Elaine came into his office and shut the door. 'I just wanted a few words about Gail,' she said. 'She seems to spend a lot of time on Facebook and messaging her friends on her mobile phone. She also sits around with some of the other young people chatting. They even sit on each other's desks while they're talking! Then there's the going out for coffees together. I'm not sure she is really committed.'

David was surprised at Elaine's comments but took them on board because she was a good solid employee and he was reasonably happy with her work. He really didn't know why young people spent hours on Facebook and other social media. He had read about this new fad but didn't really understand it. He decided to talk to Gail about it.

After waiting for a reasonable time so she would not suspect it was Elaine who had told him, he called her into his office and said 'Gail, I'm really pleased with your work but I'm a bit concerned that you seem to spend a fair bit of time on Facebook. Have you not got enough to do?'

Gail went red and spluttered a bit. 'I've got plenty to do, why do you think I'm here 'til six or seven every night? Last week I spent Sunday preparing the proposal for Carters and two weeks ago I spent the whole weekend at the Exhibition Centre event to make sure it went smoothly. If you're not happy with my work please let me know.'

David was puzzled. Elaine seemed to keep fairly normal hours, 8.30am to 5.00pm. He assumed Gail would work similar hours.

'Well, if your job is taking that much time, why do you spend time on Facebook?'

'The last three clients I got for BSI came from my Facebook "friends". I have a lot of contacts in business and also social friends. They know what I do and I know what they do. Elaine keeps on plodding through the Yellow Pages but I think my way is better. She only uses her computer for email. If you'd rather I did it the old way I can but we won't get as much business.'

David thanked her for her openness and went away to think about what he had learned.

1 Which elements of Chapter 1 would explain some of the differences between the way Elaine and Gail work?

2 How could David best explain Gail's way of working to Elaine so they could build a better working relationship?

3 If David is convinced by Gail that her way of operating is better, how could he best try and get Elaine to work the same way?

4 By referring to the section 'Organisations and the Neural Network Metaphor', as well as other sections if necessary, explain how David could take some of Gail's methods and have the rest of the Company be more creative?

5 What could go wrong if David ended up with all the employees at BSI behaving like Gail?

THE ARCHITECTURE OF WORK

The structure of an organisation, including the way that work is arranged, departments are established and processes are articulated, collectively represent the architecture of the workplace (Augier & Knudson, 2004; Creed et al., 2006). This is the space within which an organisational atmosphere is able to develop. The structure of organisation has been studied quite intensively. From the early days of industrialisation through the development of bureaucracies and the more recent eras of downsizing and decentralisation, the importance of structure has been recognised and identified to be in a symbiotic relationship with strategy (Loorbach et al., 2010).

Organisational structure basics

Learning Objective
The design and structure elements of organisations as a kind of architecture that influences strategy and people at work

The objectives of an organisation can determine how organisational structure should be arranged. Likewise, the way an organisation is linked together can determine the strategy that could best be used to capitalise on its structure. To understand this relationship we can consider the basics of structure from size and scope, to technology and control, and the common structures that organisational charts are able to display.

TECHNOLOGY AND SCALE

The Industrial Revolution unleashed the first really broad application of technology that enabled managers to harness economies of scale (Mokyr, 2001; Jeremy, 2005). Among others, Frederick Taylor and Henry Ford are examples of industrialists who recognised how technology could help to grow a production facility and realise efficiencies that were previously thought impossible. Scientific management was itself a field of study borne of new technology combined with an objective understanding of job design and organisational structure. The development of the factory production line was an alignment of technology and organisational scale. Of course, technological development has continued into the current times and organisations have continued to be influenced and defined by technology and process innovations (such as Toyota, see Ohno, 1988; Shingo, 1989). A different wave, the information revolution, is continuing to filter through the global economy and managers have at their fingertips a world of interconnected and fast knowledge management devices (Šmihula, 2010). Robotics and artificial intelligence applications are proliferating. Once more there are opportunities for finding efficiencies in goods and services operations. There are also implications for the optimal size of organisational units since the very nature of work is under revision.

Thought pathway

Consider whether a large organisation can ever be flexible enough to be competitive in changing times, and what role technology plays in your thinking on this matter.

This is where the human impact of strategy and structure is most apparent. If jobs are changing or disappearing, managers have to be mindful of how people feel about such changes. Strategy is reciprocally linked with structure even in the midst of transformation.

CONTROL AND COORDINATION

Every organisation has a power structure that can be mapped for a better understanding of the way things are controlled and coordinated. The lines of authority and communication represent a hierarchy with a span of control. Some organisations have a deeper hierarchy, some flatter. Some have a wide span of control, others a narrow span. Figure 1.2 illustrates the concept of hierarchy and span of control. While some larger organisations today have many levels in their hierarchy, there has been a general trend towards flattening, or minimising middle management hierarchy, as increasing competition demands more flexibility and responsiveness in organisational structure (Rajan & Wulf, 2006).

Figure 1.2 Hierarchy and span of control

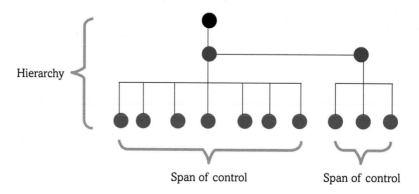

Hierarchy and span of control are vital.

Note that the top manager in Figure 1.2 has the widest span of control due to overseeing the spans covered by each of the managers next down in the hierarchy. The lines between positions represent formal reporting authority. A more realistic picture would form if we overlaid informal communication connections. Someone in the bottom of the hierarchy might regularly communicate with someone higher up even if there were no formal reporting lines. This is the reality of the workplace: informal connections can sometimes facilitate organisational activity more readily than formal ones.

Thought pathway

Consider the informal communication connections in an organisation that you know well. Can you estimate how important such relationships are to the success of that organisation? How important are the formal lines of authority?

Both positive and negative outcomes could arise from informal communication connections, depending on your perspective, which is a significant challenge for managers trying to achieve objectives without upsetting perceptions of equity.

WINDOW ON DECISION-MAKING

Unions welcome overtime decision

BEN SCHNEIDERS
April 16, 2010

Unions have welcomed an important Fair Work Australia test case backing the principle that workers should be paid overtime when they request to work flexible hours.

ACTU secretary Jeff Lawrence said the full bench decision in the case involving aged care provider Bupa Care Services 'confirms when employees volunteer to work overtime, they should not be disadvantaged'.

'It reinforces our view that long-established conditions and community standards remain protected under the new Fair Work laws,' he said.

'Workers spent many years campaigning for the 38-hour week, and those who volunteer to work overtime should be properly compensated.'

Employers had appealed the Fair Work decision that rejected a deal between Bupa and two unions that would have allowed the more flexible hours without paid overtime. The deal sought to remove overtime payments where staff asked to work extra hours for personal reasons.

Australian Chamber of Commerce and Industry workplace policy director David Gregory said it was disappointing that the tribunal could not approve the Bupa agreement and another case it decided. 'We believe that these arrangements can provide mutual benefit to both employers and employees,' he said.

Source: <www.smh.com.au/small-business/managing/unions-welcome-overtime-decision-20100416-sjew.html>

This window highlights the opportunities that can come from clever communication and ideas for improving productivity, but also the pitfalls of making decisions that test the boundaries of established legal and social expectations.

DEPARTMENTS, THE MATRIX AND NETWORKS

During the 20th century many organisations grew to have large hierarchies and spans of control. Management as a kind of command-and-control approach was common, and it was the larger of the structures in commercial and non-commercial organisations that warranted separate attention and their own identification as bureaucracies. Administrative theorists such as Fayol (1917) and Mills, Gerth and Weber (1947) studied and gave a vocabulary to the field of bureaucracy. It was in the first bureaucracies that people and systems were arranged in a pattern that was a blueprint for things to come.

A matrix of connections represents the essence of bureaucratic structure. The early theorists were very optimistic about the potential of bureaucracies to deliver powerful benefits to society. Of course, we all know the cynical undertone that has become linked with the term bureaucracy, especially those with tall hierarchies built into their structure. Popular culture has portrayed bureaucracy as mostly dehumanising and mechanical (Lang, 1926). In fact, it is the systematic structuring and labelling of departments and the recognition and harnessing of matrices of structural interconnections to which some of the great achievements of organisations can be attributed (Galbraith, 1971). Where a relatively flat hierarchy can be maintained, it appears the network of connections in a matrix structure can be a practical way to engage interdepartmental collaboration. Figure 1.3 is an example of a matrix structure. It effectively splits managerial duties in two directions. This structure can be a source of uncertainty and bureaucratic red tape, but it also allows operational tasks to be completed interdepartmentally, which is sometimes positive for innovation and interpersonal communication within the organisation.

Figure 1.3 Sample matrix organisational structure

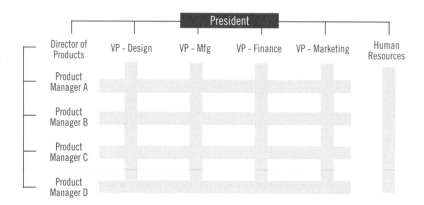

Source: <www.vertex42.com/ExcelTemplates/Images/orgcharts/matrix-organizational-structure.gif>

A new variation of the matrix structure is showing promise for the demands of a turbulent, competitive global environment. Collaborative communities or networks are being trialled and debated for their flexible and responsive structure that can capitalise on the creative skills and talents of the best people in the organisational network (Miles et al., 2010).

WINDOW ON CONFLICT AND NEGOTIATION

ASBEC says Australia needs a Minister for Cities

Australia needs a federal Minister and Department for Cities and Urban Development to ensure the nation meets its urban challenges, the Australian Sustainable Built Environment Council (ASBEC) claims.

ASBEC made the call to action yesterday at the Green Cities 2011 conference in Melbourne.

'We have developed this call to action to highlight the urgent need for bold leadership and a streamlined, coordinated approach to urban management policy,' says ASBEC president Tom Roper.

'We are facing a future of transport gridlock, rising greenhouse gas emissions and eroded quality of life unless we take decisive action. An integrated and collaborative approach is mandatory if we are to foster a culture of innovation and excellence, and ensure our cities are liveable, affordable and sustainable,' Roper says.

ASBEC's list of urgent actions includes:

A Federal Minister for Cities & Urban Development to drive the reforms needed to better connect urban built environment policies and programs across all levels of government.

A Cities & Urban Development Cabinet Committee of federal ministers whose portfolios involve decisions or activities pertaining to urban centres.

A COAG Cities & Urban Development Ministerial Council involving representation by state and territory treasurers and planning ministers, and local government.

A Cities & Urban Development NGO Roundtable to ensure business and community groups have a direct voice to government on issues involving our cities.

A Department of Cities & Urban Development tasked with developing and co-ordinating policy which involves urban outcomes.

According to Romilly Madew, chief executive of the Green Building Council Australia and chair of the Cities task group, the ASBEC call to action includes a matrix which plots 45 Australian Government programs, strategies and initiatives which impact the built environment.

'While the Australian Government's commitment to national urban policy is welcome, we are particularly concerned by the lack of coordination between the three levels of government in Australia, resulting in inconsistently-managed programs and policies across eight state and territory governments, and more than 500 local governments,' Ms Madew says.

The chief executive of the Property Council of Australia, Peter Verwer, says: 'Business and the community are looking to the Federal Government to join up their forthcoming policies on population, cities, regional Australia and sustainability.'

Australian Institute of Architects' chief executive David Parken added: 'Cities—of all shapes and sizes—are the centre of action. A linked up, coordinated approach is needed to meet the challenges of managing growth, improving quality and liveability and transitioning to a low-carbon economy while maintaining wealth creation.'

Chairman of the Facility Management Association of Australia, Steve Taylor, said: 'With industry work- ing together like never before across the design, development, operation and management of Australia's built environments, it is essential that our governments match this initiative and fully support our call to action.'

Roper concluded: 'It is clear that a coordinated approach to urban policy development is required to meet Australians' desire for sustainable and liveable cities, to make our cities more resilient to climate change and environmental disasters and to maximise the opportunities of our cities as drivers of Australia's productivity and innovation.'

Source: <www.sustainablebuildingproducts.com. au/news/asbec-says-australia-needs-a-minister-for-cities>

This Window shows that the definition of an organisation can sometimes be stretched to include a whole country. In this case, the cut and thrust of politics in the midst of turbulent and challenging events results in some interesting suggestions. The Australian nation is a complex matrix of businesses, associations, authorities and regulatory frameworks, but the principles of good management in a complex structure persist. When a social movement as compelling as the drive for sustainability goes to work, our leaders have to step up to the mark and work on some innovative solutions. Of course, the leaders argue that it is the groundswell of laypeople pushing up through the network of connections that makes the real difference: in practice, it is quite a bit of both.

Effectively managing the strategic architecture

Organisations must be controlled and coordinated; however, the modern environment is one of immense uncertainty, diversity and transformation. Pervasive technological innovations are converging with social and demographic shifts to stretch the traditional view of organisational strategy and structure. As subsequent chapters in this book will affirm, some important people management issues arise from structural factors:

- Technology alters the way communication flows in, through and out of the organisation's structure, which upsets the status quo in terms of power, control and obedience to authority.

- People are less likely today to conform to rigid hierarchical structures; instead they are more likely to engage with loose networks of connections internal and external to the organisation, thus impacting on leadership styles which must be carefully applied if productivity and other organisational goals are to be achieved.

- Smaller units of organisation are more common, although the connections between units are far more frequent. Groups of groups must often be coordinated on a global scale which makes the management of diversity, and adherence to cross-cultural variations in laws and ethics, far more complex than in the past.

ORGANISATIONS AND THE NEURAL NETWORK METAPHOR

Neural network
A metaphor of the contemporary workplace in which the individuals, groups and organisations simulate the way a brain and nervous system operate.

With the development of flexible, collaborative networks, contemporary organisational atmosphere and architecture have emerged with the assistance of advanced information technology. As databases of digitised information have systematically become networked all around the globe, something resembling a **neural network** has been established. Organisations have new opportunities to participate in and build upon the neurology of the global network (Mukherjee, 2009). Not all parts of the network are completely open (though hackers may argue otherwise), but they are mostly connected and resemble the structures of nerve cells in a brain. It is increasingly possible for entire arrays of computers in intranets and across the internet to be harnessed for collective information-processing tasks. Information system managers have a new tool at their disposal—a virtual brain—that is growing in power by the day (Morgan, 2008; Sawhney & Nambisan, 2010). People, however, are still in charge of the brain. Information is created and input by people as a crucial aspect of the neural network, but the combined power of multiple-machine processing centres working in collaboration across the network is a simulation of a supercomputer and can be articulated to operate well beyond the capabilities of humans working alone or even in groups. The boundaries of each organisation and the role of organisations in such an environment are under scrutiny. It is a new world, a technology-centric world, and new possibilities are emerging from these information-processing powers.

■
Learning Objective
The neural network metaphor and its implications for the future of organisational behaviour

The challenge for people managers is how to work with the advantages of vast networks of connected people and machines while minimising the potential disadvantages of complexity and possible loss of identity in such a system (Atwater et al., 2008). From within the ferment of network theory emerges the concept of Six Degrees of Separation (once jokingly referred to as the Six Degrees of Kevin Bacon). This is the idea that we are all connected to each other (even to the actor Kevin Bacon) within only six separate points of acquaintance (Milgram, 1967; Urry, 2003). Experiments are continuing to demonstrate the reality of this phenomenon, especially as communication technology via mobile devices is interlacing each of us with multiple layers of contact points. As the individual and organisational network infrastructure intensifies globally, the image of a neural network integrally connecting us all within close proximity to every other point in the system is increasingly relevant. What this unfolding situation means for organisations and the engagement of people in contemporary work is one of the primary exploration facets of this book.

Thought pathway

How would you locate one person in a crowd of one hundred thousand? The answer to this problem rests in how you arrange the crowd. If everybody was randomly standing around, you would have little hope of locating a particular person unless luck had positioned you near to them. However, if you were seated in a football stadium and the person could wave their hand while everyone else was relatively still, your chances would be much improved; even more so if they had a flag to wave and you had some binoculars in the stadium. This is the equivalent of what is happening globally with mobile information and communication devices; everyone is being positioned in an array that makes directly locating another person exponentially easier. We can connect and share ideas as if we are neurons in a network.

WINDOW ON COMMUNICATION

Networking at a business lunch

KIM MCGUINNESS

INVOLVE OTHERS

Don't be afraid to say hello to a stranger—that is, after all, why you are there! It is also likely that the person you meet is just as nervous as you are! If you see someone standing alone looking like a nervous first-timer, make the effort to draw them into your conversation and they will be thankful for the helping hand.

At sit-down business lunches with open seating, try to sit with people you haven't met before and invite the person you met in the foyer to join you if he or she is alone. Try to get the whole table involved in a discussion rather than just the person next to you.

Robyn Henderson, a master networker, says to 'act like the host' and invite those at the table to introduce themselves in turn. You could begin by asking everyone what brought them to the business lunch. This is a great way to learn more about the motivation of each guest at your table and what they hope to achieve by attending. Take it a step further by asking what each person does. I guarantee there will be some form of synergy around the table between at least two of the guests. There really is just six degrees of separation!

LOOK BEFORE YOU LUNCH

Evaluate the opportunities for networking around you. Look at industry associations, business networking groups, special interest groups and so on. Also look at networking groups that your typical client may belong to. The web is a great place to begin your search and the phone book also lists industry associations and networks.

Choose networks that fit with your interests and area of business. Create a short list of networks that you can attend regularly and that realistically fit into your monthly calendar. If your time is limited it is preferable to attend one network regularly, rather than try to spread yourself over a few networks every so often.

Remember that networking is not only about meeting people. By attending business lunches with guest speakers you'll get a regular motivational injection and learn something too. A ticket to a networking event makes a cost-effective and unusual thank-you gift for a client.

FOLLOW UP SOONER RATHER THAN LATER

Use the afternoon to complete your follow-up activity for guests you met at the business lunch. Maybe even carry on for a coffee after the lunch with a few new contacts. Guests leaving the function will go straight back to their daily activities and the normality of life and, unless you establish the connection, your foundation on which to build a relationship will be very weak. Take the time to nurture your new contacts and who knows where they may lead.

The key to success at any networking event is in preparing for a networking function. That way you will arrive relaxed and receptive to the new opportunities that await you.

Source: <http://money.ninemsn.com.au/article.aspx?id=327156>

So organisations today can construct an information architecture that simulates a neural network (Bailey, 2007; Jacobs, 2010) and this is supported by the strategic concepts of knowledge management (Polanyi, 1966; Nonaka, 2007) and the learning organisation (Senge, 1990). To remain competitive, we need our organisations to be flexible, able to move rapidly when new information is received and processed, and to express a kind of intelligence. Organisations can be smart (Matheson & Matheson, 1998; Deiser, 2009). Of course, people continue to be the heart of organisations. The emphasis on technology cannot be allowed to obscure the fact that emotional sensitivity is just as important as hard competitive intelligence (Goleman, 2006; Abrahams, 2007; Creed, 2011). When it comes to organisational atmosphere, the maintenance of a culture, team spirit, motivation and inspiring leadership, managers must pay attention to the full suite of theories and frameworks covered in the chapters of this book.

CONCLUSION

This opening chapter defined organisations, management and organisational behaviour. While acknowledging the history of the management discipline, contemporary factors that are affecting the role of people managers were also introduced. Most broadly, the strategy and structure of an organisation were aligned respectively with the concepts of atmosphere and architecture. There is a constant interplay between the atmospherics of an organisation, such as job security, diversity, pay, changes to workloads and perceptions of work–family balance. This places management emphasis on trust and ethics, managing turnover and absenteeism and effectively managing morale and motivation. A reciprocal link exists between the architecture (structure) of an organisation and many of the issues dealing with atmospherics (strategy). Technological change continues to alter the hierarchies, spans of control and extent and types of communication flows inside and outside organisations. The networked environment is delivering new ways of thinking about structure. Loosely coupled networks and organisational connections that resemble neurons in a brain-like structure suggest possibilities that at once emphasise the role of individuals at work, but can also threaten to lose the identity of individuals in the midst of the turbulence created by change. People managers have their work cut out ensuring that all of the usual organisational outcomes—productivity, job satisfaction, low turnover, low absenteeism and general loyalty—can be achieved through people as these transformations continue. Four key recurring themes were identified for exploration in the windows throughout the book: Communication, Decision-making, Conflict and Negotiation, and Ethics.

KEY POINTS

This chapter has

- defined key concepts in the field of organisational behaviour
- described the key concepts that historically underpin the study of organisational behaviour
- identified strategy as a determinant of organisational atmosphere
- explained the design and structure elements of organisations as a kind of architecture that influences strategy and people at work
- articulated the neural network metaphor and its implications for the future of organisational behaviour.

KEY TERMS

ARCHITECTURE
The structure of an organisation—the way that work is arranged, departments are established and processes are articulated—collectively represent the architecture of the workplace.

ATMOSPHERE
The collective manifestation of people and resources for a purposeful strategy is expressed as an atmosphere.

MANAGEMENT
Planning, organising, leading and controlling the variables of time, money, physical resources and people (human resources).

NEURAL NETWORK
A metaphor of the contemporary workplace in which the individuals, groups and organisations simulate the way a brain and nervous system operate.

ORGANISATION
An organisation comprises people and other resources brought together with a design and strategy directed towards a common purpose.

ORGANISATIONAL BEHAVIOUR
The study of individual and group characteristics and behaviour in the context of workplace structures and strategies.

OUTSOURCING
The decision taken to contract some aspect of an operation out to an external organisation, often offshore.

STUDY AND REVISION QUESTIONS

Q   *The letter of the law is one thing but the actions of managers who in all other respects observe the law are another. Review the Window on Ethics and identify the actions or decisions in the example that, in your view, are probably legal but unethical.*

Q   *Communication, Decision-making, Conflict and Negotiation, and Ethics are described as recurring themes in people management. Explain four different work situations you have experienced or know about that you believe would demonstrate one of the four themes.*

Q   *'Managing people is nothing new; the techniques for keeping people happy at work have been the same all along.' Discuss the extent to which this statement is true.*

Q   *'The integrity of an organisation is highly dependent upon the interpersonal relationships of the people within it.' Explain the extent to which you agree or disagree with this statement.*

REFERENCES

Abrahams, D. (2007). Emotional intelligence and army leadership: Give it to me straight! *Military Review*, 87(2), 86–93.

Atwater, J., Kannan, V. & Stephens, A. (2008). Cultivating systematic thinking in the next generation of business leaders. *Academy of Management Learning and Education*, 7(1), 9–25.

Augier, M., & Knudsen, T. (2004). The architecture and design of the knowledge organization. *Journal of Knowledge Management*, 8(4), 6–20.

Bailey, C. (2007). Cognitive accuracy and intelligent executive function in the brain and in business. *Annals of the New York Academy of Sciences*, 1118(1), 122–41.

Belbin, R. M. (2010). *Management teams: Why they succeed or fail.* Amsterdam: Butterworth-Heinemann.

Bresman, H., Birkinshaw, J. & Nobel, R. (2010). Knowledge transfer in international acquisition. *Journal of International Business Studies*, 41(1), 5–20.

Brown, T., Goodman, J. & Yasukawa, K. (2010). Academic casualization in Australia: Class divisions in the university. *Journal of Industrial Relations*, 52(2), 169–82.

Coyle-Shapiro J., & Neuman, J. (2004). The psychological contract and individual differences: The role of exchange and creditor ideologies. *Journal of Vocational Behavior*, 64(1), 150–64.

Creed, A. (2011). Smart Organizations: Should Emotion Play a Role? In M. Sarlak (ed.) *The new faces of organizations in the 21st century.* Toronto: NAISIT.

Creed, A., Ross, J., Stewart, J., Bolesta, M., Hladik, M. & Backhaus, W. (2006). Tapping global human resources in an MBA teaching team: Insights with implications for management education worldwide. In J. Kennedy & L. Di Milia (eds), *ANZAM 2006: Proceedings of the 20th Annual Conference of the Australian and New Zealand Academy of Management 2006*, pp. 1–21.

Deiser, R. (2009). *Designing the smart organization: How breakthrough corporate learning initiatives drive strategic change and innovation*, Mobipocket Edition. London: John Wiley & Sons.

Denis, J., Langley, A. & Rouleau, L. (2010). The practice of leadership in the messy world of organizations. *Leadership*, 6(1), 67–88.

de Reuver, R., & van Woerkom, M. (2010). Can conflict management be an antidote to subordinate absenteeism? *Journal of Managerial Psychology*, 25(5), 479–94.

Drucker, P. F. (1977). *People and performance: The best of Peter Drucker on management.* New York: Harper's College Press.

Dunkerley, S. (2011). Libs say no plan to dump parental leave. *Sydney Morning Herald*, 8 February. <http://news.smh.com.au/breaking-news-national/libs-say-no-plan-to-dump-parental-leave-20110208-1albw.html>

Fayol, H. (1917). *Administration industrielle et générale: Prévoyance, organisation, commandement, coordination, contrôle.* Paris: Dunod & Pinat.

Follett, M. P. (1918). *The new State: Group organization: The solution for popular government.* New York: Longman, Green and Company.

Follett, M. P., & Graham, P. (1995). *Mary Parker Follett—prophet of management: A celebration of writings from the 1920s.* Boston: Harvard Business School Press.

Galbraith, J. (1971). Matrix organization designs: How to combine functional and project forms. *Business Horizons*, 14(1), 29–40.

Gnyawali, D., & Madhavan, R. (2001). Cooperative networks and competitive dynamics: A structural embeddedness perspective. *Academy of Management Review*, 26(3), 431–45.

Goleman, D. (2006). The socially intelligent leader. *Educational Leadership*, 64(1), 76–81.

Hatchuel, A., Starkey, K., Tempest, S. & Le Masson, P. (2010). Strategy as innovative design: An emerging perspective. In J. Baum (ed.) *The globalization of strategy research* (*Advances in Strategic Management*, vol. 27). Bingley, UK: Emerald Group Publishing Limited, pp. 3–28.

Holden, L., Scuffham, P., Hilton, M., Vecchio, N. & Whiteford, H. (2010). Work performance decrements are associated with Australian working conditions, particularly the demand to work longer hours. *Journal of Occupational & Environmental Medicine*, 52(3), 281–90.

Jacobs, C. S. (2010). *Management rewired: Why feedback doesn't work and other surprising lessons from the latest brain science.* New York: Portfolio.

Jeremy, D. J. (2005). *Transatlantic industrial revolution: The diffusion of textile technologies between Britain and America, 1790–1830s.* New York: ACLS History E-Book Project.

Judge, T., & Robbins, S. P. (2011). *Organizational behavior.* Upper Saddle River, NJ: Prentice Hall.

Kleinberger, D., & Bishop, C. (2010). The single member limited liability company as disregarded entity: Now you see it, now you don't. *William Mitchell Legal Studies Research Paper No. 2010-04*, SSRN: <http://ssrn.com/abstract=1559401>

Koutenakis, F. (2010). The effect of temporary contracts on job security of permanent workers. *Economics Letters*, 101(2008), 220–2.

Lang, F. (1926). *Metropolis.* Berlin: UFA Films.

Loorbach, D., van Bakel, J., Whiteman, G. & Rotmans, J. (2010). Business strategies for transitions towards sustainable systems. *Business Strategy and the Environment*, 19(2), 133–46.

Matheson, D., & Matheson, J. E. (1998). *The smart organization: Creating value through strategic R&D.* Boston: Harvard Business School Press.

Michel, J., Mitchelson, J., Pichler, S. & Cullen, K. (2010). Clarifying relationships among work and family social support, stressors, and work–family conflict. *Journal of Vocational Behavior,* 76(2010), 91–104.

Miles, R., Snow, C., Fjeldstadt, O., Miles, G. & Lettl, C. (2010). Designing organizations to meet 21st-century opportunities and challenges. *Organizational Dynamics,* 39(4), 1–11.

Milgram, S. (1967). The small world problem. *Psychology Today,* 1(5), 61–7

Mills, C. W., Gerth, H. H. & Weber, M. (1947). *From Max Weber: Essays in sociology.* International Library of Sociology and Social Reconstruction (Routledge & Kegan Paul). London: Kegan Paul, Trench & Co.

Mokyr, J. (2001). The rise and fall of the factory system: Technology, firms, and households since the industrial revolution. *Carnegie-Rochester Conference Series on Public Policy,* 55(1), 1–45.

Morgan, G. (2008). *Images of organization.* Thousand Oaks, CA: Sage.

Blake, R. R., & Mouton, J. S. (1964). *The managerial grid: Key orientations for achieving production through people.* Houston: Gulf Publishing Company.

Mukherjee, A. (2009). Leading the networked organization. *Leader to Leader,* 2009(52), 23–9.

Naghavi, A., & Ottaviano. G. (2010). Outsourcing, complementary innovations, and growth. *Industrial and Corporate Change,* 19(4), 1009–35.

Nonaka, I. (2007). The knowledge-creating company. *Harvard Business Review,* 85(7/8), 162–71.

Ohno, T. (1988). *Toyota production system: Beyond large scale production.* Cambridge, MA: Productivity Press.

Oster, E., & Millett, B. (2010). *Do call centers promote school enrollment? Evidence from India.* NBER Working Paper Series, vol. w15922, pp. 1–39.

Pedler, M. (2008). *Action learning for managers.* Aldershot: Ashgate.

Petit, P. (2007). The effects of age and family constraints on gender hiring discrimination: A field experiment in the French financial sector. *Labour Economics,* 14(3), 371–91.

Polanyi, M. (1966). *Tacit knowledge.* London: Routledge & Kegan Paul.

Rajan, R., & Wulf, J. (2010). The flattening firm: Evidence from Panel Data on the changing nature of corporate hierarchies. *Review of Economics and Statistics,* 88(4), 759–73.

Restubog, S. L., & Bordia, P. (2007). One big happy family: Understanding the role of workplace familism in the psychological contract dynamics. In I. A. Glendon, B. M. Thompson & B. Myors (eds), *Advances in organisational psychology,* 1st edn, Australia: Australian Academic Press, pp. 371–87.

Salleh, A., Lee, K. & Raida, A. (2010). The impingement of managerial supervision on employees' satisfaction: The Malaysian case. *International Journal of Learning and Intellectual Capital,* 7(1), 1–22.

Sawhney, M., & Nambisan, S. (2010). *The global brain: Your roadmap for innovating faster and smarter in a networked world.* Upper Saddle River, NJ: Wharton School.

Senge, P. M. (1990). *The fifth discipline fieldbook: Strategies and tools for building a learning organization.* New York: A Currency Book , published by Doubleday.

Shingo, S. (1989). *A study of the Toyota production system from an industrial viewpoint,* transl. A. P. Dillon. Portland, OH: Productivity Press.

Šmihula, D. (2010). Waves of technological innovations and the end of the information revolution. *Journal of Economics and International Finance,* 2(4), 58–67.

Singh, J., Carasco, E., Svensson, G., Wood, G. & Callaghan, M. (2005). A comparative study of the contents of corporate codes of ethics in Australia, Canada and Sweden. *Journal of World Business,* 40, 91–109.

Smallman, C., McDonald, G. & Meuller, J. (2010). Governing the corporation: Structure, process and behaviour. *Journal of Management & Organization* 16, 194–8.

Syed, J., & Kramar, R. (2008). What is the Australian model for managing cultural diversity? *Personnel Review,* 39(1), 96–115.

Syed, J., & Kramar, R. (2009). Socially responsible diversity management. *Journal of Management & Organization,* 15(5), 639–51.

Urry, J. (2003). Social networks, travel and talk. *British Journal of Sociology,* 54(2), 155–75.

PRACTITIONER INSIGHT

CAMILLA BRITTON

HUMAN CAPITAL
TEAM MANAGER, PWC

Camilla Britton joined PwC in 2006 as the Recruitment Manager. After managing the Resourcing team in Melbourne, Camilla worked on a strategic recruitment project before an internal agility move into an HR generalist role. In 2009, Camilla was appointed as National HC Team Manager for Specialist Tax.

Camilla has recently completed her Masters in Commerce (HRM) while also being selected to be part of PwC's Young Leadership Team. Before PwC, Camilla worked in external recruitment and also as an Auditor at KPMG.

INTERVIEW

What was your first job?

After finishing school I gained a scholarship to University in Japan for a year. During my time there I taught English as a part-time job. My first real job though after graduating with a Commerce/Asian Studies degree from ANU, was as a graduate at KMPG Melbourne in Audit. I still find it strange saying that I was an Accountant, however this experience has put me in good stead to understand the commercial aspects of a business.

What has been your career highlight so far?

On reflection there have been many great moments that I am truly appreciative of throughout my career. I think one of the highlights has been moving into the role I am in now. I get to work with a fantastic team at PwC in Tax & Legal Human Capital (HC); I have a wonderful coach who is a truly inspiring leader, and PwC Partners who challenge me in a positive way every day to really help them drive the People agenda in their teams. A recent highlight has been selection to be on the Young Leadership Team (YLT). The program is teaching me to have greater self-awareness around who I am as an individual, my leadership style and ultimately what kind of leader I want to be.

In your current role, what does a typical day involve?

It can really change from day to day as you juggle many different balls in the air from operational to strategic HR work – that is what I love about my role. If I look at my day yesterday as an example of 'a day in the life of', it went something like this:

- Discussing our Diversity & Talent Strategy with one of my Partners on our Talent Council
- Reviewing our succession planning & leverage of the business
- Spending time over a coffee with one of my team members in a coaching conversation
- Planning for the next six months ahead for what is on the horizon for the business unit I support
- Reading the December financial results to understand the commercial status of the business (yes, it must be my Audit background as to why I still enjoy numbers).

What's the best part of your job?

What I enjoy the most about my job, is the fact that my day can be so varied and keeps me mentally challenged. Above all, the thing that really keeps me passionate and working at PwC are relationships. To me, relationships are the key to truly being a successful HR business Partner. Being able to influence behaviours and actions in the workplace through these relationships is also rewarding.

What are the current challenges facing you, in your role?

With the market gradually returning to pre GFC times of 'war for talent', I think the biggest challenge ahead is around supporting my Partners to retain and engage our talent. Part of this also includes ensuring we have a diverse, flexible & agile workforce to really maximise business performance while providing individuals with a range of experiences throughout their career.

Do you regularly apply the principles or theories you learnt (when studying organisational behaviour) into your everyday work? In what way?

Yes, but more broadly around human resource management theories, not just OB theories. These come into play around leadership, coaching, diversity (particularly around unconscious bias), our Pulse surveys and performance review time. The focus on behaviours and how people interact and have conversations with each other is all part of what we call the PwC Experience – it's how we interact, behave and treat each other and our clients.

How important is an understanding of 'organisational behaviour' in today's workplace?

Organisational behaviour is very relevant as behaviours underpin everything we do in the workplace. Understanding how people, individuals and groups act is crucial to understanding and shaping a culture. We strive for a high-performing, inclusive culture at PwC.

What strategies do you implement in your workplace to help employees achieve an appropriate work–life balance?

We have a flexible work arrangement policy which supports our diversity strategy. This covers areas such as part-time, flexible hours, job sharing, working from home, paid parental leave, leave of absence (for example some people take time off to travel overseas, work for a charity, compete in sporting events, study etc), accelerated study and the option to purchase additional annual leave. We also provide subsidised gym and other health and well-being options. I think as an organisation this is a key priority for the firm and its people, and we continually strive to improve our strategies to achieve this.

Has technology impacted on work–life balance? Is it harder to achieve with constant access to the 'office', for example?

Technology can have both positive and negative impacts on your work–life balance. I think it is how you set your own personal boundaries and choose to work with technology and this access to the 'office'. Technology can have such positive

impacts on work–life balance or flexibility especially for those working from home or part-time or travelling a lot. It is how you chose to work with technology that best suits you and your lifestyle.

Are there greater expectations (on you or your workplace) to help motivate and engage employees in their work than ever before?

I do believe there are greater expectations from our people and an appreciation for loyalty. As an organisation we focus on our Pulse results (measuring engagement) to constantly try and improve our motivation and engagement of our people by delivering on what our people want. This will continue to evolve as generations have different expectations, but will always remain a focus particularly over the next 12 months to ensure we retain and engage our talent.

What do you believe makes a good manager or decision maker? How would you describe your own management style?

I believe both Managers and decision-makers (Leaders) should have the same type of behaviours and attributes, encouraging others to succeed, and inspiring the team through their own behaviours and actions. I believe my leadership style is one of honesty and openness and I encourage the heart of others. My strengths are my courage, relationship-building skills and commerciality. The YLT program has built my awareness around leadership, and also my development opportunities as a leader.

How do you communicate company strategy with staff at all levels?

Our internal communications have many different ways of connecting with our people on topical firm and market issues across all of our offices. One of the main tools that is used to communicate the firm's Market Growth Strategy is the CEO's Annual Roadshow, which is run across all our offices.

A significant part of our strategy is based around behaviours, so our CEO and his leadership team also lead by example in their own way, and share stories to help bring the strategy to life.

What do you believe is the best way for a manager to avoid conflict in the workplace? And is this an easy approach to take?

I don't believe avoiding conflict is healthy in the workplace. It is more effective for a Manager to face conflict, but in a constructive, open and honest way. Having a robust conversation, challenging each other and providing honest feedback, can also lead to greater innovation and solutions to a problem if you have more of a growth mindset to the situation.

02
Individual
Factors

2 Learning: The Pathway to Constructive
People Management 35

3 Modern Diversity: The Adaptation
of Values, Attitudes and Personality 67

4 Motivation and Job Satisfaction 95

Learning: The Pathway to Constructive People Management

INTRODUCTION

Being open to change is essential in a dynamic organisational environment. Getting stuck in one's ways, while sometimes good for certain aspects of quality, is less useful for being adaptive and responsive in the hyper-connected landscape of work today. This situation elevates learning to the pivotal position for individual and organisational performance. It is our predisposition to learn that enables us to change thoughts, feelings and behaviours in appropriate ways at work. The psychological foundations of Organisational Behaviour (OB) look first at individual differences. Perception and perceptual illusion are informative starting points but the weight of discussion and examples moves to learning as a means for minimising dissonance and improving job and organisational performance. The learning process followed appropriately enables us to deal better with the current global environment and the particular challenges confronted by individuals and groups. Learning is linked to individual differences and the organisation as a whole. Learning theories are central to managing self, managing change, and making constructive efforts to redirect power, politics, culture and leadership in an organisation. There are behavioural, cognitive and social influences on learning that are introduced and developed in this chapter. The field of learning is an essential foundation for individuals and organisations and builds on themes emerging from Chapter 1. Learning can lead to constructive people management, the understanding of which establishes the groundwork for the next chapter on diversity, values and personality.

<table>
<tr><td>LEARNING OBJECTIVES</td><td>Understanding this chapter will help you to
<ul><li>define learning in the context of change</li><li>explain the relevance of individual and organisational learning for the workplace</li></ul></td><td><ul><li>describe key cognitive, behavioural and social learning theories</li><li>explain the link between learning and key OB topics, including organisational culture, leadership, and power and politics.</li></ul></td></tr>
</table>

OVERVIEW

Learning is a complex thing. We seem to know what it is by experiencing it, but it can be quite difficult to explain. This section examines the kinds of definitions that make sense and leads into subsequent sections about perception, attention, expectations and the various categories of learning theories that have been developed over time. Learning normally occurs as the result of a process. But there is conjecture about what goes into the process and whether the outcomes measure up to the definition of the concept of learning. Learning has been described by a wide range of intelligent people through the ages. Table 2.1 presents some adapted and notable examples of efforts to pin down the nature of learning.

Table 2.1   The philosophers on the nature of learning

THEORIST	PERSPECTIVE ON LEARNING
Plato	Learning is recollection (Jowett & Plato, 1914)
Aristotle	Learning is gained through experience and not recollection (Aristotle & Apostle, 1966)
Immanuel Kant	Though all our knowledge begins with experience, it by no means follows that all arises out of experience (Kant, 1958)
Martin Heidegger	Learning is essentially relearning the essential (Heidegger, 1962)
John Dewey	The student's task is to do and learn; an activity that is often painful (Dewey, 1916)
Jean Piaget	Knowledge is not merely transmitted verbally but must be constructed and reconstructed by the learner (Inhelder & Piaget, 1958)
Jerome Bruner	Learning is, most often, figuring out how to use what you already know in order to go beyond what you currently think (Bruner, 1983)
Albert Bandura	Most human behavior is learned observationally through modeling: from observing others one forms an idea of how new behaviors are performed, and on later occasions this coded information serves as a guide for action (Bandura, 1977)
Benjamin Bloom	It will be the responsibility of the school to seek learning conditions that enable each individual to reach the highest level of learning possible for her or him (Bloom et al., 1971, p. 6)

A DEFINITION

A variety of authors aim to formalise a definition of learning. Wood et al. (2010, p. 121) and Robbins et al. (2009, p. 54) describe learning as a 'relatively permanent change in behaviour that occurs as a result of experience'. In Fincham and Rhodes (2005, p. 22) learning is defined as 'the cognitive and physical activity giving rise to a relatively permanent change in knowledge, skill, or attitude'. In both of these definitions nestle the beliefs of Dewey and Aristotle, who each put experience at the centre of learning. It seems a reasonable view that learning springs from the experiences we have. On the other hand, when thinkers as notable as Plato and more recently Heidegger and Bandura suggest other possibilities, the field becomes less clear. Even the textbook definitions just mentioned differ in their view of whether it is behaviour or some other aspect of human expression (perhaps knowledge) that is affected by learning. To be fair, human beings are very complex and are the result of a diverse blend of influences, so it follows that learning will be difficult to define with universally acceptable frames of reference.

Thought pathway

Consider what Kant says about learning in Table 2.1. Discuss the extent to which Kant's view aligns with the textbook definitions in this section.

The learning theorists tend to fall into categories labelled **cognitive**, **behavioural** or **social**. The cognitive theorists assert that it is essentially changes in perception and thinking that bring about **learning.** The behaviourists believe that changes in the environment and our responses to feedback form the basis of learning. Another group of theorists would suggest that social factors play the biggest role and all that we manifest as actions and responses are driven by how we relate to others. With this in mind, learning can be defined as identifiable changes in thinking, relating and behaving established in response to internal or external stimuli. The definition can be extended to include not just individuals but also groups. A later chapter introduces the concept of a group having a kind of personality (a spirit or culture), and it follows that learning can occur at that level, but individuals are certainly the basis of most learning theories.

Figure 2.1   Learning involves thinking, relating and behaving

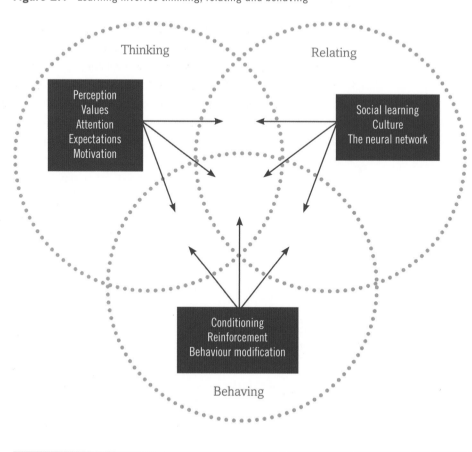

Learning leads to changes in thinking, behaving or relating, which are interrelated factors in individuals and groups. Consider where they occur.

Reinforcement
Any kind of feedback that encourages a certain learned behaviour to be repeated.

Behaviour modification
This is the process of shaping the behaviour of others through positive reinforcement, negative reinforcement, punishment or extinction.

The elements of Figure 2.1 are explained in this chapter and revisited in the final chapter. Thinking involves perception, the formation of values and attitudes, and the development of attention, expectations and motivation. Behaving involves conditioning through **reinforcement** and the possibilities of **behaviour modification**. Relating involves the social factors of learning, including culture and the emerging understanding we have about the organisational structure and strategy implications of the neural network (covered in Chapter 1). The next sections explore the thinking component of learning. As you process these ideas, remember the connections between all of the factors. Subsequent sections discuss the behaving and relating components. Engaging with the complexity of these three broad fields is the daily task of people managers.

THE RELATIVITY OF PERCEPTION

From a cognitive perspective, the relativity of our relationships in the workplace stems from the basic problem of perception (Pocock, 1973; Goldstein, 2009; Marr, 2010). Psychologists, neurologists and philosophers (including many from Table 2.1) have had long discussions in the historical literature about the fact that we all perceive things differently. Something that appears in a certain form for you may not appear the same for me (Vitevitch & Luce, 1998; Marr, 2010).

Figure 2.2 Perception is unique for each individual

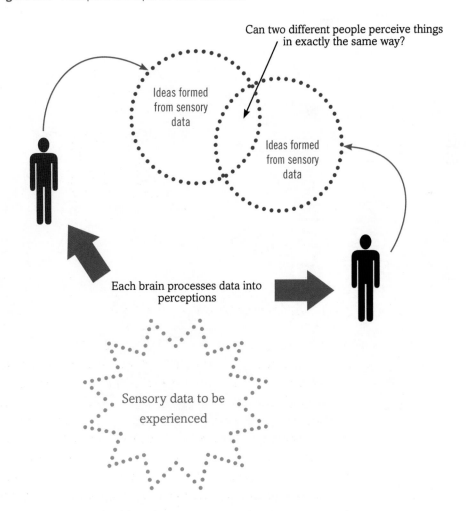

There are many fascinating puzzles and paradoxes that demonstrate this fundamental point. It is important not to be distracted by the fun of these examples but to realise just how relevant this inherent uncertainty is to our daily interactions with people and organisations.

Figure 2.3 Perceptual paradoxes

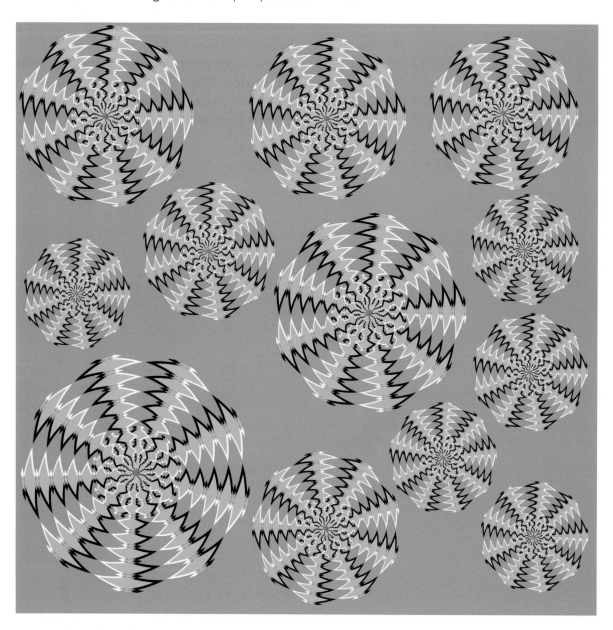

Paradox of perception
The fact that we are each likely to perceive the same situations in sometimes markedly different ways.

Like the uncertainty principle of science (Heisenberg et al., 1930), the **paradox of perception** leaves us with the knowledge that we are each likely to perceive the same situations in sometimes markedly different ways. Attribution theory is one approach that tries to explain how to manage with this reality (Weiner, 1974). The theory suggests that people try to attribute either external or internal causes to the behaviours

■

Fundamental attribution error
People tend to overestimate the control that others have over their behaviours and therefore default to being quite judgmental and discriminatory towards those others.

they observe. With any behaviour, we tend to judge that the person either has internal control of their actions or is at the whim of their circumstances, and we are often more tolerant when we think the environment is to blame. As perception would have it, a **fundamental attribution error** has been observed: we tend to overestimate the control that people have over their behaviours and therefore we default to being quite judgmental and discriminatory. However, just how strong the attribution error is going to be is never clear. As a leader of people, as a manager who needs to get certain tasks accomplished, this uncertainty about how people will perceive the requests we make and the behaviours we express has the potential to be very confusing.

Thought pathway

Is it an impossible task to manage people if you know that everyone perceives things differently?

There are groups of stimuli that we can perceive to be approximately the same and this is how humans manage to work successfully together. For example, performance targets and other quantifiable goals can be generalised on the basis of agreement about numbers being measured; however, desirable qualitative goals such as trust, friendliness, authenticity and so on are more prone to multiple interpretations. Diversity of perception, therefore, makes people management quite complex.

AN ASPECT OF DIVERSITY

In practice, perceptual differences are most apparent where there is a wide diversity of staff with varying backgrounds working in an organisation or workgroup. Groups coming together for the first time, with people having been brought up in very different environments with widely different cultural values, attitudes and norms, are generally more exposed to the effects of misunderstanding the intentions of each other's styles and behaviours. It is important to realise that people with similar backgrounds and upbringings also have different individual perceptions; it is just that the added layers of cultural differences in heterogeneous groups can challenge the perceptual harmonisation between members (Furunes & Mykletun, 2007; Sia & Bhardwaj, 2009). The next chapter draws out this point in detail, thus recognising the role of values and personality formed through the easily refracted lens of perception. The issue of perception also goes to the core of organisational and interpersonal communication. So much angst can be avoided at work by managers understanding the need for repeated cycles of reflection and clear communication in order to overcome the relativity of perception. What seems clear to one person may not be understood at all by another without careful attention to good communication.

WINDOW ON COMMUNICATION

Bullying fines deliver a stern message

PENNY STEVENS
February 9, 2010

A COURT decision yesterday to issue $335,000 in fines arising from workplace behaviour that resulted in a waitress committing suicide highlights the significant risks associated with bullying and harassment in the workplace.

The owner of Cafe Vamp in Hawthorn was one of four workers to plead guilty to failing to take reasonable care for the health and safety of persons.

The owner and his one-man company also pleaded guilty to failing to provide and maintain a safe working environment.

The company was fined $220,000, and magistrate Peter Lauritsen said he would have doubled the penalties had the defendants not pleaded guilty to what he described as 'the most serious case of bullying'.

The decision demonstrates one of the many costs associated with failing to manage bullying and harassment in the workplace appropriately.

According to a recent draft report released by the Productivity Commission, 'psycho-social hazards' such as bullying and harassment in the workplace tend to be more costly on average than claims for less serious physical injuries, both in relation to direct costs and time taken off work.

The report indicates that an estimated 2.5 million Australians experience some form of bullying over the course of their working lives.

It is reported that a high prevalence of stress (including that caused by bullying) translates into direct costs to employers in Australia of about $10 billion a year, and costs to the economy of about $14.8 billion a year.

Research shows these costs are due to increased absenteeism and the loss of productivity that occurs when employees are present at work but not fully functioning.

The figures do not include hidden costs associated with increased turnover of staff and recruitment and retraining costs, the costs of management dealing with internal complaints, and intangible costs associated with decreased trust, loyalty and staff morale.

Workplace bullying and harassment are not given the same attention in occupational health and safety legislation as managing physical hazards—such as manual handling, working at heights and dangerous substances—and this has led to additional uncertainty being placed on businesses about the extent of their duty of care and how to tackle such hazards.

Eliminating workplace bullying and harassment is an integral part of any employer's organisational OH&S commitments.

The Cafe Vamp decision sends a clear message to employers, company directors and employees that allowing or participating in workplace bullying can lead to tragic results and to criminal charges that carry significant penalties.

Source: <www.theage.com.au/business/bullying-fines-deliver-a-stern-message-20100208-nne9.html>

This Window on Communication highlights the continuous battle managers confront against misperception of people's roles and expectations in the workplace. The reversal of people's tendencies towards bullying and discrimination of all kinds requires ongoing learning and relearning.

LEARNING AND ATTENTION

Another important cognitive or psychological phenomenon linked with learning is that of attention. In a large and complex universe of daily tasks, people only have the capacity to pay attention to particular things. These are the things that actually get done. A person's choice to pay attention determines the things that can be achieved. The early work of William James (1890) laid a solid foundation of psychological study in this area. In organisational behaviour today, the issues of motivation and job performance owe much to the fundamental understanding of what makes people pay attention to some things and ignore others (Nadeau, 2005; Carsetti, 2010).

Thought pathway

Are there examples at any workplace you can think of when attention of staff is effectively gained for a task? Consider how and why their attention gained. Also imagine what things are ignored while the focus of attention is held in your examples.

■

Attention
The taking possession by the mind of one out of several simultaneously possible objects or trains of thought. It involves withdrawal from some things in order to deal effectively with the things chosen for attention.

James (1890) summarised **attention** when he said: 'It is the taking possession by the mind, in clear and vivid form, of one out of what seem several simultaneously possible objects or trains of thought. Focalization, concentration, of consciousness are of its essence. It implies withdrawal from some things in order to deal effectively with others' (pp. 403–4). These things, it would seem, go to the core of learning. They also set the stage for many theories of motivation that will be covered in Chapter 4.

■

Learning Objective
The relevance of individual and organisational learning for the workplace

Focus on what is critical

One could argue that learning is essentially about gradually improving the focus on what is important. It is by learning the right things as managers that we arrive at an understanding of priorities. It is clear in introductory management studies that much time and money can be saved by managers knowing what, where, when and how to apply resources. For instance, time management has been considered in various forms ever since work has been around. When you think about it, an understanding of attention and the ways that priorities emerge wherever attention is focused gives some insight into effective time management. Frederick Taylor's famous quest for the 'one best way' to prioritise and organise industrial tasks, and the Gilbreths' well-known and adapted time and motion studies are chief among the legacy of early management theory which, in many ways, was the focusing of organisational and worker attention on critical tasks (Taylor, 1911; Gilbreth & Gilbreth, 1916; Hunt & Collins, 2008). Much was learned during the scientific management period, for instance, that better harnessed time and resources boosted organisational production, and improved worker safety and performance. In modern times, a focus on continuous quality improvement is an ongoing reflection of the cycle of learning and the critical role of paying attention to the right things at work.

Attention and motivation to learn

Another spin on attention is the motivation effect that can occur when a supervisor is seen to be paying attention to workers in a work team, today known as the Hawthorne Effect (Mayo, 1931). As the behavioural theories emerged most strongly in the middle of the 20th century, the task emphasis of scientific management gave way a little to the people and relationships emphasis of theories of motivation, leadership and continual learning and improvement (Hodgetts & Hegar, 2009). Now the new century has proved to be one of immense change and challenge. The question of where to focus attention is a much harder one to answer when the natural environment is threatened, financial and economic structures are transforming, and diversity within local communities and organisations is accelerating. New models for learning about and understanding the nature of organisations and our place within them and the wider community are starting to emerge (Taylor, 2006; Devanna & Tichy, 2008; Rowley & Warner, 2010). In the following Window there is a focus on decision-making in the midst of highly complex variables that can characterise organisations immersed in regulated yet frequently changing situations.

WINDOW ON DECISION-MAKING

Respect the differences

BARRY HANSEN

In his two recent articles in Inquirer, Nicolas Rothwell exposed and demolished the facade of the Northern Territory government and set out the society to which the NT should aspire in 20 to 50 years. How do we achieve such high aspirations?

Reform is not something to be done only for the Aboriginal people of the Territory, nor is it something to be done exclusively by Aborigines. It is our collective society and we need to move forward together.

The process is simple, but the ways in which it is carried out are crucially important. An integrated plan is needed for education, jobs, housing, health, social inclusion and the other key areas of inequality between indigenous and non-indigenous society in the Territory.

The plan needs to show understanding and respect for the differences between the two cultures, avoiding judgments and implied superiority of either culture. It must be understood that there are fundamental differences in perceptions of the world in how knowledge is transmitted, in social etiquette, in interpersonal relationships and reciprocal responsibilities, in who may discuss and decide what and when, and, very significantly, in communication, quantitative measures and language concepts.

Understanding these differences is essential for a non-Aborigine to function effectively in an Aboriginal context. The reverse is also true.

Until its closure in the 1970s, the Australian School of Pacific Administration ran two-year full-time courses for government employees intending to work in Aboriginal communities.

Similarly, missions operating in the Territory up to the 70s required their staff to immerse themselves in local culture. But since then mutuality has deteriorated and miscommunication has increased.

Throw into this mix the high frequency of changes in government policies and programs, and confusion reigns in both the bureaucracy and communities. As one Aboriginal man once said to me: 'As soon as I understand (a program), they (the government) change it', while bureaucrats bemoan the lack of adherence to program guidelines. Consistency and continuity will be important in the way forward.

If things are to change, the plethora of government programs will need to be scrutinised for their contribution to any integrated plan.

Programs appear to be developed in isolation and without reference to any common objectives or structure, so that gaps and overlaps occur.

Training programs without jobs at the end are of little value. Education based on whitefella parameters can only succeed if there is at least a basic comprehension of whitefella society.

Across society, inequality is directly linked to reduced life expectancy, more illness, more violence, more antisocial behaviour and greater mistrust of authority and others. More than 50 studies worldwide have largely confirmed these links.

People don't care what happens to them if they have nothing to lose. That's why 'tough on crime' attitudes directed at the most disadvantaged achieve nothing but reinforce the sense of inequality causing the problems. It is a spiral to the bottom fed by lowest common denominator politics. It is no coincidence that reported alcohol, drug and substance abuse incidents in the remote Territory communities have almost doubled since the federal intervention.

So education and jobs are fundamental to equality in society.

That includes having positions of influence that command respect and the power to make decisions.

But an integrated development plan would recognise the dangers of appointing underqualified people for political correctness and propose a balanced approach.

Formulation of a plan such as I propose would involve a range of indigenous parties, churches, business leaders, non-partisan politicians and bureaucrats.

Firm and measurable progress indicators need to be agreed and progress independently reported annually.

Source: <www.theaustralian.com.au/news/opinion/ respect-the-differences/story-e6frg6zo-1225797512390>

This example illustrates the critical importance of planning in complex situations. It again demonstrates the delicate balance of perceptions among diverse people. It shows how simple decisions in various organisations—to change a focus, to discontinue a program, to reword a policy—can have chaotic effects on different stakeholders. And it implies that learning has to be a process of continual improvement and not necessarily one of replacing completely what went before. The motivation to learn wells up in people from realistic, stepped visions of how to advance and improve. This is not to deny that there can be quite a difference between what people expect and what actually takes place in organisations.

LEARNING AND EXPECTATIONS

Cognitive dissonance
Leon Festinger's theory that a mismatch between expectations and reality will be handled by individuals, changing their behaviour in ways that try to minimise the dissonance.

What does a person do when the dreams they have can simply not be fulfilled? This is a dramatic way of asking how we should reconcile goals against actual achievements. The phenomenon of **cognitive dissonance** noted by Festinger (1957) illustrates how the attention of individuals can become focused on particular things as a way of ensuring a better match between expectations and reality. For example, a new item of clothing may catch your eye in a shop window. It is attractive and unique. You are sure you have not seen it before and you know that you will look great when you wear it around your various social functions. After buying it, you start to notice other people wearing the same item, even though you were sure you had not seen it before. This is an attention effect: because you were previously not paying attention to that item, you were not especially inclined to notice it. It was the new perceptual arrangement in the store window that first got your attention. Once you make the emotional commitment and purchase the item, your cognitive processes are geared towards affirming your decision. You are effectively adjusting your attitude about the item to align with your expectations about it. You actively (often unconsciously) start to look for assurance that the item of clothing is as good as you think. As someone passes by wearing the item, you are fine-tuned to pay attention and feel satisfied that you are not alone in your liking for the fashion. There is a double edge, however, because you may not like the way this clothing looks on others, or those others may not be the kinds of people you expect to be equated with. So, cognitive dissonance suggests you have two courses of action to follow here: you will either adjust your attitude to feel good about your purchase, thus continuing to wear the item and be satisfied, or you will choose to feel bad about your purchase and take steps to return it or wear something else instead. Either course of action is designed to minimise cognitive dissonance. The gap between what you expect and the attitude you develop through experience has to be minimised if you are to feel comfortable. Thus your attitude and behaviour tend towards anything that achieves this end.

The cognitive dissonance phenomenon reveals the importance of setting clear expectations about work, and about learning objectives in relation to professional development. Theories of motivation also expand on this understanding (Vroom, 1964; Law, 2010). If expectations are not clear and if regular reflection about the learning cycle and one's resultant attitudes are not adhered to, there is a risk of dissonance occurring. This can lead to avoidance or resistance to change behaviours becoming a problem. At the very least, managers should be aware of the pervasive and often unconscious nature of cognitive dissonance and consider it among the possible explanations for certain individual attitudes and behaviours.

REINFORCEMENT AND BEHAVIOUR MODIFICATION

To call oneself a manager is to suggest a belief that one can encourage others to follow or conform to one's directives. Parents of children soon learn that human beings can be 'programmed' up to a point before individuality and rebelliousness reassert themselves. People's behaviours are a mixture of social and psychological influences and the best we can hope for in the workplace as managers is to be able to modify or shape other people's behaviours in very specific instances for quite a narrow range of purposes. To try to control people too much and too often will be perceived as abusive management style (Aryee et al., 2008). But to reasonably suggest workplace priorities and provide incentives for appropriate behaviours and disincentives for inappropriate ones is certainly achievable (Dishman et al., 2009). It becomes a process of helping people to learn and reinforcing the desired changes in behaviours. There are well-researched theories of behaviour modification, conditioning and reinforcement that establish a foundation in the literature about learning, from classical and operant conditioning through to well-utilised schedules of reinforcement in the context of pay and other work-related benefits.

CASE STUDY

Too much friendliness in the Customer Service staff

Sleepy Bed Linen imports upmarket bed linen and sells it to retail stores and also directly to hotel and motel chains. The business was started by two women, Sally Martin and Stella Demetriou, who had an interest in fine linen but couldn't find the products they wanted. They slowly built the business by supplying market stalls and local retailers. They also started employing friends on a part-time basis. When they obtained the distribution rights for some quality products from Europe they found that the business grew rapidly.

While they had moved to employing people other than friends, they still maintained a very friendly atmosphere and tended to attract people who were interested in the products and other quality housewares.

They had built a business that employed over 60 people with 12 of these in the customer service department, which was now largely run as a call centre. They had an excellent range of retail and hotel/motel clients who valued the service provided and the quality of the products.

Sally chose to retire from the business as her husband was not well, and sold her share to Stella.

During the valuation of the business by their accountants, a number of areas were flagged as being open to improvement. One area was that the cost of their customer service was increasing rapidly and did not correlate strongly with where the profitable business was coming from.

Now Stella was the sole owner she wanted to ensure first that she had a financially sustainable business, and then grow the business to develop some further security.

Her first focus was the call centre. She realised it was really an order-taking operation and that a growing number of orders were now being placed using their new website.

She noticed that the customer service staff spent a long time on each call. They talked about the products but also chatted about personal issues which they considered as building a relationship with the customer. This was not followed up with accurate data entry, knowledge of inventory or a proactive approach to sales. The result was that customers felt the Sleepy Bed Linen people were friendly but they were frustrated when orders were wrong or they found later that the product they wanted was out of stock.

Stella needed to have the customer service staff be more commercial in their dealings with customers.

She didn't want to damage the relationships that had taken years to build but needed to have them focus on dealing with orders efficiently, being aware of the margins on each product, having deliveries made on time with the right products and, where possible, she wanted them to sell additional product rather than just take orders. She wasn't sure some of the staff she had were up to it but she wanted to give them every opportunity.

Stella also thought that there were some smaller, time-consuming customers who cost the Company money and she would prefer they take their business to one of the retail outlets Sleepy Bed Linen supplied. She couldn't imagine her staff ever being able to tell a customer this.

Stella had to get her customer service staff to maintain great customer relationships but ensure there was a professional service to back it up and build healthy profit margins.

1 How do you think the customer service staff developed their current work culture?

2 What factors have influenced the perceptions of Stella and prompted her to take action?

3 What difficulties do you think Stella will encounter if she tries to change the way the customer service staff behave?

4 After reviewing the various methods of changing behaviour described in the chapter, discuss which ones might be used by Stella to bring about the desired changed and how she might best implement them.

5 If Stella is successful in introducing the change she wants, discuss what methods she might use to sustain it.

Classical and operant conditioning

Learning Objective
Key cognitive, behavioural and social learning theories

Classical conditioning
The first formalised theory of conditioning in which it was discovered by Ivan Pavlov that reflexive responses could be altered with different kinds of stimuli.

Conditioning is a conscious strategy to shape the behaviour of others through repeated signals. Early or **classical conditioning** theory emerged from the work of Russian physiologist Ivan Pavlov, whose experiments on dogs revealed some interesting learning principles (Pavlov, 1929). Looking primarily at reflexive behaviour, Pavlov observed the salivation response of a dog when given meat (or meat powder by some accounts). He also observed the neutral, non-salivating response when some other stimulus, such as a ringing bell, was given to the same dog at a different time. At a later stage, Pavlov began directly associating the ringing bell with the feeding of meat to the dog. The salivation response of the dog over time became linked with the ringing bell. The association became so strong that the mere ringing of the bell would incite salivation in the dog without the meat being present. While this tale of Pavlov's Dog may seem unremarkable, it was the first time various stimulus and response factors had been explicitly observed and labelled. This animal was learning to develop a reflex response that it had never expressed before. Pavlov deduced that an understanding of appropriate stimulus and response mechanisms could lead to an improved understanding of learning in people. The terminology he applied to the factors of classical conditioning help to explain the phenomenon.

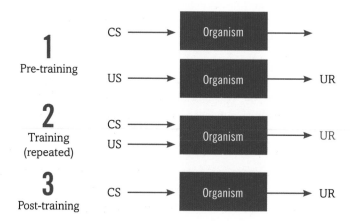

Source: adapted from Principles of Organisational Behaviour, 4th edition, Robin Fincham and Peter Rhodes (2005) by permission of Oxford University Press UK.

■ An **unconditioned stimulus (UCS)** and an **unconditioned response (UCR)** compose the original reflex. In the case of Pavlov's dog, the meat is the UCS and salivation at the smell of it is the UCR. Subsequently, a **conditioned stimulus (CS)** is applied to generate a **conditioned response (CR)**. For Pavlov's dog the bell is the CS and the act of learning to salivate when the bell rings represents the CR. The classical conditioning mechanism explains well the reflexive behaviours of animals. Even people regularly demonstrate conditioned responses from conditioned stimuli such as smells, sounds and sights.

Unconditioned stimulus (UCS)
In conditioning theory an unconditioned stimulus is one that elicits a reflexive response. In the example of Pavlov's dog, the meat is the unconditioned stimulus when in the first instance it creates reflexive salivation in the dog.

Thought pathway

Think through at least one simple reflexive learning situation for people or animals where classical conditioning can be observed.

■ **Operant conditioning** was developed later from the work of Skinner and puts its focus on voluntary rather than reflexive behaviours. Skinner paid special attention to the behaviour-shaping capacity of the environment (Skinner, 1974, 1984). It was noticed that people do consciously change their own behaviours depending on whether they expect to get something good or avoid something bad. Skinner suggested that positive reinforcement, or providing something pleasant as a consequence of behaviour that is desirable, will strengthen that behaviour and increase the chances that it will be adopted more permanently. The inverse is also true; that is, remove any response that is unpleasant and the likelihood of repeating the behaviour also increases. Although operant conditioning can be applied to behaviours that appear voluntary, it was noticed that many of the behaviours and responses occur with limited conscious awareness. People automatically and subconsciously identify what they find pleasant and what they want to avoid and then set about behaving in ways that deliver the reinforcement they desire.

Unconditioned response (UCR)
In conditioning theory an unconditioned response is a reflex in relation to a certain stimulus. In the example of Pavlov's dog, the meat is the unconditioned stimulus which leads to the unconditioned response of salivation in the dog in the first instance.

Thought pathway

Escape and avoidance are types of behaviours where the person tries to get out of completing unpleasant tasks. Locate the definitions from psychology sources and consider which of Skinner's reinforcements (positive or negative) best explains escape and avoidance.

■ The terminology of conditioning theory was expanded by Skinner and the principles are well covered in animal and child psychology classes to this day. This is perhaps the main criticism of conditioning theories—that they work for relatively simple behaviour problems in less complex social situations. The realities of the modern workplace and the learning needs of adults are normally a bit more complex. There are other learning theories that have further insight for managers. However, there remain direct and powerful methods of reinforcement drawn from theories of conditioning that can be used to modify workplace behaviours.

Conditioned stimulus (CS)
In conditioning theory a conditioned stimulus is one that has been linked by experience to the generation of a response. In the example of Pavlov's dog, the ringing sound became the conditioned stimulus once it was able to elicit salivation in the absence of the meat.

Behaviour modification

When a manager understands they may shape the behaviour of others through four simple mechanisms, positive reinforcement, negative reinforcement, punishment and extinction, then a number of practical strategies can be deployed.

Positive reinforcement is the provision of something enjoyed or desired after a person responds in an appropriate way. For instance, working hard on a task and then being told you did a good job is positive reinforcement, especially when you are personally motivated by the idea that your supervisor would notice good work and see fit to comment on it. Other examples of positive reinforcement are receiving a bonus after selling agreed targets of goods or services, getting time off after achieving certain productivity goals, receiving tuition or other fringe benefits after reaching certain performance levels. The thing to remember is that individuals feel differently about various rewards. For best effectiveness, positive reinforcement must be tailored to individual desires. When the required behaviour is consistent with the individual's work values and the reward received is matched with the individual's desires, positive reinforcement is a powerful conditioning and behaviour-shaping tool.

Negative reinforcement is the removal of something perceived as unpleasant after a person responds in an appropriate way. For instance, you may have worked hard on a certain task required at work and always been criticised by your supervisor regardless of whether the task was done well. One day the supervisor stops being critical of you, they don't say anything at all. The removal of their negative response is not replaced by anything positive, but the absence of critique is now a kind of reinforcement to you and you feel a bit more motivated to continue performing the task knowing you won't be attacked. It is not the same as positive reinforcement but it is still quite refreshing to have something negative removed from your stimulus-response loop.

Punishment is all too well understood by most of us as a behaviour-shaping tool. To follow up unwanted behaviour by providing something unpleasant, such as a rebuke, the removal of something valuable, the limitation of privileges, suspension of duties, and so on, is the essence of punishment. Obviously, in a few rare cases, punishment may be the only course of action managers can take in the workplace. However, it is generally better to try out the other reinforcement methods before resorting to punishment due to the loss of mutual trust and respect that can emerge from prioritising this approach in the workplace (Fehr & Falk, 2002). Managers who become known for punishing regularly may achieve certain ends but there can be a cost when it comes to relationships with people at work. Ethics as well as power and control, which are discussed in Chapter 7, are significant workplace issues brought to the fore by the application of punishments.

Extinction is a useful reinforcement tool that involves the removal of any response at all when an inappropriate behaviour occurs. The worker who completes a task and then receives no noticeable feedback about performance inevitably loses interest in the task. This can apply to any kind of positive or negative reinforcement and it may also be a substitute for punishment in some cases. When one's actions go completely

Conditioned response (CR) In conditioning theory a conditioned response is one that has been linked by experience to a certain stimulus. In the example of Pavlov's dog, the occurrence of salivation merely at the ringing sound became the conditioned response.

Operant conditioning A conditioning theory acknowledging the behaviour-shaping capacity of the environment. Skinner suggested that positive reinforcement, or providing something pleasant as a consequence of behaviour that is desirable, will strengthen that behaviour and increase the chances that it will be adopted more permanently. The inverse is also true; that is, remove any response that is unpleasant and the likelihood of repeating the behaviour increases.

unacknowledged, one's motivation for repeating the behaviour tends to diminish. We are social creatures and our behaviours are shaped by the responses of others. No response at all is quite an unnatural feeling for most of us.

Reinforcement as a management tool

Remember from Figure 2.1 that Plato said, 'Learning is recollection', and Heidegger said, 'Learning is essentially relearning the essential'. These evocative quotations raise the question of how do we know what we know? The most practical answer is that feedback tells us what we know. We behave in a certain way and people and objects react to our behaviour; their response is a type of feedback that we can observe and interpret. We are constantly getting information from our environment and developing feelings about that information. Classical conditioning identifies reflexive responses to environmental feedback and operant conditioning gives us a vocabulary to describe the reinforcing feedback that helps us to learn about and shape our behaviour. As managers we have a certain degree of control over feedback and reinforcement for workers. Understanding the available schedules of reinforcement provides useful tools. We can provide pay and other benefits to workers as a type of feedback on continuous, intermittent, fixed or variable schedules depending on organisational resources, legal and ethical boundaries, industry norms, and staff and supervisor preferences (Latham & Dossett, 1978; Twenge & Campbell, 2008).

Continuous reinforcement is intensive and often impractical in all areas of work. Although it would be quite motivating, offering feedback about every task accomplished would be time-consuming and expensive. More practical is intermittent reinforcement, which involves giving people enough feedback (including pay or other benefits) to ensure the appropriate behaviour is worth repeating but is not given every time. For instance, praising someone for a job well done but not doing this every time they do it is a kind of intermittent positive reinforcement. An intermittent schedule is a way to keep people guessing about the reinforcement, still motivated to perform, and it may save the organisation some resources. It is one example of the variable interval approach. Variable interval schedules of reinforcement involve distributing feedback in time to make the reinforcements less predictable.

Fixed interval schedules of reinforcement are also quite practical and involve the spacing of feedback (including pay or other benefits) at regular intervals. For instance, a regular pay packet provided each fortnight represents fixed interval reinforcement. Fixed ratio schedules are another way to arrange the delivery of pay and benefits. Piece rate pay for the completion of a set number of outputs is an example of a fixed ratio approach.

Variable ratio schedules are another way to envisage reinforcement and are evident in commission-based schemes of pay and benefits. Workers know they will receive feedback for measurable aspects of their work; they can know exactly what type and how much to expect, but are not sure exactly when their work will be completed and the reward provided. The variable nature of such schedules has proved to be quite motivating in the shorter term in fields such as sales.

Thought pathway

Think about pay schedules as a special kind of reinforcement. Identify the pros and cons of different kinds of pay and the relative relationship with learning.

Chapter 9 draws the obvious link between reinforcement and job design; however, it soon becomes clear that broader social influences are important when considering the best way to encourage learning and improvement of work practices.

SOCIAL LEARNING AND THE COMPLEX WORKPLACE

Learning Objective
The relevance of individual and organisational learning for the workplace

Albert Bandura is chief among the early exponents of social learning theory, which posits that humans learn primarily through social observation and role modelling (Bandura & Walters, 1963; Bandura, 1977). It is clearly true that supervisors, colleagues and mentors in the workplace play a powerful and practical role in conveying important knowledge about values, attitudes, skills and overall work culture. It might even be argued that while cognitive and behavioural learning mechanisms can be observed, they can also be overridden by more compelling social learning circumstances. People tend to pay more attention to the views and practices of respected others at work than they do to formal training or behaviour modification attempts. The complexity of the modern workplace puts social relationships near the top of our considerations.

Individual and organisational learning: The neural network

As discussed in Chapter 1, some organisational theorists have turned to the image of the brain and neural networks to help describe organisations and the connections between people and organisations that have been established around the world (Garud & Kotha, 1994; Morgan, 2007; Nambisan & Sawhney, 2010). Since we have been discussing in this chapter brain functions such as perception and attention, the image continues to be informative. Can it be that people and their relationships at work are arranged much like the networks of nerves, neurons and nerve centres in the human brain? When a business task needs to be achieved, say, food has to be got to market or an airline has to be coordinated, a certain set of nerve centres (key organisations) fire up and send out signals (contracts and finance) via communication pathways (memos, speeches and documents through various media). If we could see a magnetic resonance image (MRI) of the world when a certain food is being produced and distributed or when a certain airline is conducting its operations, we would likely see a fired-up neural network quite similar to a brain when a particular task is being fulfilled.

Systems theory, network theory and the concept of the intelligent organisation that contributed to and was changed by the knowledge management revolution at the close of the 20th century fit neatly into a metaphor of a brain or neural network structure (uit Beijerse, 1999; Lee, 2000). It is easy to see how organisations are more connected to each other than ever before. Individuals now often work for more than one organisation. Competitors now often collaborate with each other on some projects, thus testing the boundaries of competition laws. Information technology has proliferated to the point where we are all individually connected to a range of communication networks. This makes the workforce a weblike organism that appears to sustain a system of centres, or organisations, in increasingly symbiotic structures (Tetlow, 2007).

Thought pathway

The trend to a casual workforce continues. Part-time and casual jobs continue to appear at a faster rate than full-time jobs. Consider whether this trend helps or hinders the concept of the global workplace being a brain-like web of neural networks.

In practice, managers have to find ways to build professional development into the workplace but with the understanding that the skills transferred may filter through the network into other organisational centres. Attempts to control the flow of workers between organisations will affect worker motivation, morale and turnover, but having completely open systems of information, communication and labour contracting means that the intellectual property of one organisation can be quickly replicated to another. The only way to differentiate one organisation from another in the perception of staff is to emphasise the aspects of the culture that are unique or special; in that way people may choose to stay around.

Culture and learning

■

Learning Objective
The link between learning and organisational culture

The unique way that a person perceives their world and the particular things they choose to pay attention to come together in their relationships with others. When groups of people are relating to each other and negotiating how to behave in an organisation, a novel identity emerges from this mixture that we often call a culture. The processes that lead to this situation can collectively be conceived as a type of learning. To build a culture takes time and a unique set of experiences in the relationships between people. The social settings and relational processes flavour the learning that occurs and the kind of cultural expression that emerges. There is a type of 'personality' that emerges from a group and that may be the culture to which we refer.

Consider again what was just explained. Culture (a kind of group personality) is the result of time spent developing unique perceptions and working through repeated cycles of learning processes, mostly in social settings. This may give pause to anyone considering a career in change management, especially if the brief is ever going to be to create cultural change. There is no quick and painless way to move an organisation from one established cultural pattern to another. You simply have to take the time and energy to work through the learning processes trying to keep everyone on track. This has implications for managing and negotiating through workplace conflicts. The next Window takes a view of such a case.

WINDOW ON CONFLICT AND NEGOTIATION

Massive jump in dismissal claims

EWIN HANNAN
October 28, 2009

DISMISSAL-RELATED claims by employees jumped by an extraordinary 30 per cent during the last year of the Work Choices laws, despite exemptions that prevented millions of workers from successfully making claims.

New figures released by the Australian Industrial Relations Commission show the number of applications by workers contesting their dismissal rose to 7994 last financial year, the highest since 2000–01.

In its annual report tabled in federal parliament, the AIRC attributed the increase to the impact of the global financial crisis. 'Although there is no clear indication of the reason for the increase, it is reasonable to assume that the significant downturn in global financial markets has had an effect and employers are responding to market conditions by reducing labour costs where it is practical to do so,' the commission's overview says.

'It is also likely that the rising unemployment rate is providing an…incentive to challenge a termination of employment which is perceived to be unfair.'

The increase occurred during the last 12 months of Work Choices and before Labor's Fair Work Act came into operation on July 1 this year. Under Work Choices, small and medium-sized businesses with 100 or fewer employees were exempt from unfair dismissal claims, and employers could also dismiss workers for operational reasons.

The significant increase last financial year suggests Labor's changes to the unfair dismissal laws, including the removal of the 100 employee exemption, are not the sole reason for the recent jump in claims during the first three months of the new system.

ACTU secretary Jeff Lawrence said yesterday that unfair dismissal laws assisted in preventing unnecessary sackings and gave workers job security.

'This protection is particularly important in an economic downturn when some unscrupulous employers will use economic conditions as an excuse to sack workers,' he said.

'But it should also be remembered that until the commencement of the Fair Work Act there were also hundreds of thousands of workers who did not have this basic workplace right.'

Employers said the jump in applications could be attributed to economic conditions as well as a change of perceptions among workers. The Australian Chamber of Commerce and Industry said while the laws did not change during the period, there had been a change of government in the lead-up.

'There was probably a sense among employees that they had limited entitlements or limited access to remedies (under the Howard government),' said the chamber's workplace policy director, David Gregory.

'I think with the change in government, there have been some changes to those perceptions…perhaps employees felt they had more options available to them than they had previously,' he said.

Mr Gregory said he was concerned unfair dismissal claims under Labor could reach 11,000 in the first 12 months of the new system. But University of Adelaide law professor Andrew Stewart said the figures were consistent with levels recorded prior to Work Choices.

Source: <www.theaustralian.com.au/ news/massive-jump-in-dismissal-claims/story- e6frg6no-1225791897260>

Despite the internal emphasis of organisational culture, this story shows how large external forces can drive managers to force change. Even in the midst of compulsions like a global financial crisis, there are opportunities to manage staff with compassion and clear communication. The ripples imposed on organisational culture by poorly negotiated changes are long remembered and difficult to reverse (Clegg & Walsh, 2004; Lewis et al., 2010).

Thought pathway

Think about Albert Bandura's perspective on learning from Figure 2.1. Given what you now know about culture and learning, decide on the extent to which you agree or disagree with his perspective.

■

Learning organisation
A kind of ideal culture in which all the people and systems of the organisation are oriented to an open and continuous shared learning cycle as a way to remain competitive and adaptive.

Peter Senge (1990) coined the concept of the **learning organisation**, which has since been identified as a kind of ideal culture (Finger & Brand, 1999) in which all the people and systems of the organisation are oriented to an open and continuous shared learning cycle as a way to remain competitive and adaptive. The reality more than 20 years later is that few organisations can truly claim to be learning organisations in this ideal sense. The adeptness required of managers and the commitment required of all staff to the principle of a culture of continuous learning is significant. Some organisations have achieved it but many have not.

Learning to change

Learning is essentially a process of change. Individuals and organisations may start the day at a certain level of skill and understanding and by the end of the day the environment will have provided events, challenges and objectives that require a new set of skills and understanding. Learning or change must occur in order for individuals or groups to adapt to the dynamic environment (Dibella et al., 2007). Heidegger (1962) views learning as a continuous cyclical process where feedback at each stage helps the individual gain greater understanding. This is a philosophical view, but later learning and organisational theorists adapted Heidegger's theory into well-known quality improvement and change management frameworks (Deming, 1986; Juran & Godfrey, 1999). Lewin (1951) developed the continuously reflective action research process using Heidegger's concepts, and also generated the three-phase process of change—unfreeze, change, refreeze—which explicitly recognises people's inherent resistance to change (discussed in Chapter 10). The important thing according to Lewin is that people don't really like to change, especially when they have established ways of behaving. So there is a paradox for managers every day. The competitive environment demands innovation, change and continuous improvement, but people don't normally find change a comfortable internal experience. This has implications for people management in relation to motivation and leadership in times of change.

CASE STUDY

Competition from overseas means that the old hands need to change

Designer Taps, a successful business started by the Rossini family after the Second World War, had grown by manufacturing taps for domestic use and gradually moving into upmarket designer taps as the more common designs became low-margin commodities.

Many of the 110 employees had been with the business for over 20 years and they considered themselves 'part of the family'. Some of them had older relatives who were employed by the founder, Tony Rossini.

George Jackson had been employed as General Manager a year ago to fill a gap left by Simon Rossini who was retiring but staying on the Board. George had to start learning about the tapware market and what he found was disconcerting.

While Designer Taps had good relationships with upmarket builders, architects and some select retailers, their sector in the market was now being challenged by imports from China. The Chinese products were good quality, lower cost and there was an aggressive local distributor who was starting to build momentum.

Designer Taps had relied heavily on its market dominance and customer relationships, but George thought this might not be enough as the economy became tougher and the building industry looked closely at costs.

He knew that service was an issue at Designer Taps as delivery times were too long and he'd overheard a conversation in the production planning office where an employee had said, 'Don't worry, they'll wait for it, they won't go anywhere else, they've been with us for thirty years. The old man takes them out on his boat every year.'

He had also seen a similar attitude in the customer service department and warehouse where procedures were almost nonexistent and orders were handled on the basis of who knew who and who shouted the loudest. He had noticed the customer service staff spending long periods on the phone chatting to customers. He was told this was to maintain the excellent customer relationships which are what the company is based on.

There seemed to be a similar attitude around other departments: 'We have great products that they can't get anywhere else and they love us.'

He was also aware that there was no disciplined approach to costs. He had seen the costs creep up due to increased labour, maintenance issues and a general lack of planning that had led to inefficient work practices. To cover these costs, they had to increase prices. He was constantly reassured by the Sales Manager that the market would handle it as they had a 'premium product' and loyal customers.

While they took pride in the quality of their products, George thought this was skewed more towards the design than towards technical quality as he had noticed an increase in the number of faulty units returned. When he queried this he was told that 'the new staff don't take care like we used to.'

George knew he had to change things or the imports would eat into their business as the personnel in the 'loyal' customers changed and, they too, started looking at costs. He had a manufacturing background so he knew how to go about improving the production processes which were tending to be short runs in reaction to small orders, but he needed to get everyone onside to make it happen.

He had checked on the local labour market and found his staff were paid in line with similar organisations. While he didn't want to terminate anyone's employment, there were some that were definitely more lax in their work ethic than others.

Over the year he had been there he had come to know most of the employees. He was aware that there was a group of older employees who had been at Designer Taps for over 30 years and they were referred to by others as the 'old gang'. They had plenty of influence over many of the employees and some of them held quite senior positions. He had heard stories that when a new person joined at a management level and tried to change things, they would meet resistance from this group and often left the business out of frustration. It appeared to George that if new ideas didn't win the approval of this group they were unlikely to be implemented.

He knew he had to let people know what the situation was regarding the competition and how this affected the future of the business and hence their job security. He didn't want to scare them but wanted to show them it was possible to change the organisation so they could use their strengths to compete with the imports.

CASE STUDY QUESTIONS

1 Using the sections in the chapter related to learning, discuss how George could let people know about the situation as he understands it?

2 How can he ensure they take it as seriously as he does and that they maintain that view?

3 What options does he have to change the way they work?

4 What can he do to preserve the 'family atmosphere' culture? Is this a good thing?

5 If employees think customer relationships are more important than profit, how can he change their views? Are they right?

Thought pathway

'No pain, no gain' is a well-known cliché. Think whether this could have an explanation according to various learning and change theories.

The challenge of power and politics

Learning Objective
The link between learning and leadership, power and politics

The learned culture of an organisation gives rise to the normal human patterns of control, power and influence. People naturally stand up to be leaders or are prepared to be followers based upon individual characteristics and the social learning that has occurred in the workplace. The natural resistance to change noted by Lewin (1951), and phenomena such as the limited spread of honourable ideals like the learning organisation, may be the outcome of political protection of established authority and protection of limited resources. People do not lightly give up the territory they have obtained. To embark upon a learning program is a promise of making change, and change can be a threat to established controls.

Thought pathway

If change is such a threat to people with established power and control, why do you think change management programs are so widely implemented today? Discuss.

In practice, the need to remain innovative and competitive as an organisation drives leaders to try to change stagnant departments, divisions and workgroups. The market drives the need for change. In addition, most people desire to not be bored and to have some level of novelty and variety in their day. Adept managers of change can harness both of these forces to generate positive motion over time, but it is a delicate balancing act. Every organisation has rules and regulations by which to abide, but there is a vast and fuzzy field of ethics that must also be traversed. This Window on Ethics illustrates such a case.

WINDOW ON ETHICS

Business graduates accept ethics with degrees

University of Ottawa MBAs swear oath in Canadian first

GLEN MCGREGOR, *THE OTTAWA CITIZEN*
October 26, 2009

OTTAWA—About two dozen masters of business administration graduates stood together Sunday and recited an oath of ethics that would draw a gasp of horror from fictional *Wall Street* tycoon Gordon Gekko.

The graduates from the Telfer School of Management at the University of Ottawa became the first MBAs in Canada to sign pledges to conduct their affairs ethically and work toward the well-being of all stakeholders and not just their shareholders.

In their oath, written collaboratively by the students, members of the 2009 graduating class promised to oppose corruption, consider the societal and environmental costs of their actions, and treat public money with the same care and vigilance as they would their own.

'I will allow neither ego nor malice to play a role in my decision-making process,' they recited in unison Sunday.

No mention of 'Greed is good,' the philosophy personified by Gekko in the 1987 film *Wall Street* and by countless other real-life examples among the executive ranks of failed brokerage Lehman Brothers or defunct energy giant Enron.

The student-led drive for an ethics oath followed a similar move by Harvard University's business school, which sought to rehabilitate the image of business leaders damaged by the Bernie Madoff fraud scandal and the avarice in the financial services sector that helped trigger the global economic downturn.

The University of Ottawa is believed to be the third in North America, after Harvard and Thunderbird School of Global Management in Arizona, to mark MBA graduation with an ethics oath.

The oath is entirely voluntarily and in no way binding on anyone who takes it. About half of this year's graduating class were on hand to take the oath and sign a certificate Sunday.

'If even one of them contemplates making a different decision because of this, it's worthwhile,' says Harley Finkelstein, a lawyer and now Telfer graduate who helped lead the oath initiative among his classmates.

MBA graduates will take on responsibility for not just their shareholders, but also their employees' salaries and pensions, Finkelstein says.

'All those are major things professional managers are responsible for, without accountability whatsoever.'

He says he sees the oath as a first step toward certification of MBAs, much like doctors, lawyers and accountants are certified and regulated by their own professional bodies.

Just as their members take oaths pledging to uphold the standards of their professions, so, too, should MBAs vow to raise the ethical bar in the business world, Finkelstein says.

He notes that many MBAs go on to work for non-profit organizations or in the public sector, and those elements are reflected in the oath.

Finkelstein believes that social responsibility and fiduciary duty to shareholders can go hand in hand.

'You can consider a decision that has the most shareholder value and also consider sustainability and environmental issues.'

He points to U.S. business titans like former CEOs Jack Welsh of General Electric and eBay's Meg Whitman who led companies that were financially successful and ethically sound.

'These guys have achieved great success on the basis of the fact they show great shareholder returns. But GE is a pillar of corporate governance and they do amazing stuff for the environment.'

Source: <www.ottawacitizen.com/business/ Business+graduates+accept+ethics+with+ degrees/2144268/story.html>

The global financial crisis helped to spur business schools to defend their educational quality. Oaths may not hold strong legal sway but they are influential where individual and professional ethics are concerned. In times of rapid change, people look for stability and strength of principles. Political moves abound in the midst of tumult. Managers change jobs, staff move on or seek promotion, and organisations seek new market opportunities. The ways that changes to power and control work themselves out are often dependent on the strength of vision and leadership that emerges from those caught up in the change. The role of the leader is vitally important. It is through mechanisms of learning for the purpose of continual improvement that constructive leaders can help organisations succeed.

Constructive leadership

The leader of any group of people sets a tone for learning, establishes the benchmark for cultural responses and further development and, through their style of handling the delicate issues of power and politics, either helps or hinders the cycles of learning (Jones, 2010; Denis et al., 2010). The two key tensions in OB are to manage for task performance or to manage for relationship maintenance and development. For either aspect, professional development for staff can deliver significant benefits.

Thought pathway

New ways of doing things can be imposed by leaders from the top down, or suggested and implemented by the staff from the bottom up. Reflect upon how the organisational leaders may play a positive role in either scenario.

The benefits of good people management flow through to increased job satisfaction, reduced turnover, lower absenteeism and increased productivity, quality and profitability. Finding the balance as a manager so that these benefits can emerge is the real challenge and a continuous learning approach has much to offer in this regard.

CONCLUSION

In this chapter it was found that an effective manager of people is able to understand how learning is linked to individual differences and to the organisation as a whole. Learning theories are central to managing self, managing change, and making constructive efforts to redirect power, politics, culture and leadership in an organisation. The learning process is intertwined with cognitive, behavioural and social factors within and between individuals and groups. The networked nature of modern organisations draws parallels with the functioning of a brain. Web-like structures and systems enable information to be emanated simultaneously. Individuals and teams in this environment have unique learning needs. The feedback cycles necessary to sustain the equivalent of neural networks between people are intense and continuous. There are special challenges for the manager in relation to culture, power, resistance to change, motivation, cognitive dissonance and the relativity of perceptions in each area.

KEY POINTS

This chapter has

- defined learning in the context of change
- explained the relevance of individual and organisational learning for the workplace
- described key cognitive, behavioural and social learning theories
- explained the link between learning and key OB topics, including organisational culture, leadership, and power and politics.

KEY TERMS

ATTENTION
The taking possession by the mind of one out of several simultaneously possible objects or trains of thought. It involves withdrawal from some things in order to deal effectively with the things chosen for attention.

BEHAVIOURAL LEARNING THEORIES
The collection of theories that suggest learning expresses itself through changes in behaviour.

BEHAVIOUR MODIFICATION
This is the process of shaping the behaviour of others through positive reinforcement, negative reinforcement, punishment or extinction.

CLASSICAL CONDITIONING
The first formalised theory of conditioning in which it was discovered by Ivan Pavlov that reflexive responses could be altered with different kinds of stimuli.

COGNITIVE DISSONANCE
Leon Festinger's theory that a mismatch between expectations and reality will be handled by individuals, changing their behaviour in ways that try to minimise the dissonance.

COGNITIVE LEARNING THEORIES
The collection of theories that suggest learning is expressed through changes in thinking or cognition.

CONDITIONED RESPONSE (CR)
In conditioning theory a conditioned response is one that has been linked by experience to a certain stimulus. In the example of Pavlov's dog, the occurrence of salivation merely at the ringing sound became the conditioned response.

CONDITIONED STIMULUS (CS)
In conditioning theory a conditioned stimulus is one that has been linked by experience to the generation of a response. In the example of Pavlov's dog, the ringing sound became the conditioned stimulus once it was able to elicit salivation in the absence of the meat.

FUNDAMENTAL ATTRIBUTION ERROR
People tend to overestimate the control that others have over their behaviours and therefore default to being quite judgmental and discriminatory towards those others.

LEARNING
Identifiable changes in thinking, relating and behaving established by individuals or groups in response to internal or external stimuli.

LEARNING ORGANISATION
A kind of ideal culture in which all the people and systems of the organisation are oriented to an open and continuous shared learning cycle as a way to remain competitive and adaptive.

OPERANT CONDITIONING

A conditioning theory acknowledging the behaviour-shaping capacity of the environment. Skinner suggested that positive reinforcement, or providing something pleasant as a consequence of behaviour that is desirable, will strengthen that behaviour and increase the chances that it will be adopted more permanently. The inverse is also true; that is, remove any response that is unpleasant and the likelihood of repeating the behaviour increases.

PARADOX OF PERCEPTION

The fact that we are each likely to perceive the same situations in sometimes markedly different ways.

REINFORCEMENT

Any kind of feedback that encourages a certain learned behaviour to be repeated.

SOCIAL LEARNING THEORIES

The collection of theories that suggest learning is expressed through changes in relationships via mechanisms such as role modelling, parenting, mentoring and general social experiences.

UNCONDITIONED STIMULUS (UCS)

In conditioning theory an unconditioned stimulus is one that elicits a reflexive response. In the example of Pavlov's dog, the meat is the unconditioned stimulus when in the first instance it creates reflexive salivation in the dog.

UNCONDITIONED RESPONSE (UCR)

In conditioning theory an unconditioned response is a reflex in relation to a certain stimulus. In the example of Pavlov's dog, the meat is the unconditioned stimulus which leads to the unconditioned response of salivation in the dog in the first instance.

STUDY AND REVISION QUESTIONS

Q *Discuss the polarised views on recollection that Aristotle and Plato have in their definitions of learning. Is either definition of learning, therefore, wrong? Why?*

Q *The Window on Communication carries a message about workplace attention and priorities. Describe this message in your own words.*

Q *Proper planning enables the focus of attention on matters of priority or the purpose of learning. Is this view supported by the conclusions emerging from the Window on Decision-making?*

Q *Discuss why the individual and organisational learning imperative fits well with the metaphor of the brain and neural network.*

REFERENCES

Aristotle, & Apostle, H. G. (1966). *Metaphysics*, Bloomington: Indiana University Press.

Aryee, S., Sun, L., Chen, Z. X. G. & Debrah, Y. A. (2008). Abusive supervision and contextual performance: The mediating role of emotional exhaustion and the moderating role of work unit structure. *Management and Organization Review*, 4(3), 393–411.

Bandura, A. (1977). *Social learning theory*. Prentice-Hall series in social learning theory. Englewood Cliffs, NJ: Prentice Hall.

Bandura, A., & Walters, R. (1963). *Social learning and personality development*. New York: Holt, Rinehart & Winston.

Bloom, B. S., Hastings, J. T. & Madaus, G. F. (1971). *Handbook on formative and summative evaluation of student learning*. New York: McGraw-Hill.

Bruner, J. (1983). *In search of mind*. New York, Harper.

Carsetti, A. (2010). *Causality, meaningful complexity and embodied cognition*. Dordrecht: Springer.

Clegg, C., & Walsh, S. (2004). Change management: Time for a change! *European Journal of Work and Organizational Psychology*, 13(2), 217–39.

Deming, W. E. (1986). *Out of the crisis*. Boston: MIT Press.

Denis, J., Langley, A. & Rouleau, L. (2010). The practice of leadership in the messy world of organizations. *Leadership*, 6(1), 67–88.

Devanna, M., & Tichy, N. (2008). Creating the competitive organization of the 21st century: The boundaryless corporation. *Human Resource Management*, 29(4), 455–71.

Dewey, J. (1916). *Democracy and education: An introduction to the philosophy of education*. New York: Macmillan.

Dibella, A., Nevis, E. & Gould, J. (2007). Understanding organizational learning capability. *Journal of Management Studies*, 33(3), 361–79.

Dishman, R., Vandenberg, R., Motl, R., Wilson, M. & DeJoy, D. (2009). Dose relations between goal setting, theory-based correlates of goal setting and increases in physical activity during a workplace trial. *Health Education Research*, Oxford University Press. <http://her.oxfordjournals.org/cgi/reprint/cyp042v1>

Fehr, E., & Falk, A. (2002). Psychological foundations of incentives. *European Economic Review*, 46(4–5), 687–724.

Festinger, L. (1957). *A theory of cognitive dissonance*. London: Tavistock.

Fincham, R., & Rhodes, P. S. (2005). *Principles of organizational behaviour*. Oxford: Oxford University Press.

Finger, M., & Brand, S. B. (1999). The concept of the 'learning organization' applied to the transformation of the public sector. In M. Easterby-Smith, L. Araujo & J. Burgoyne (eds), *Organizational learning and the learning organization*. London: Sage.

Furunes, T., & Mykletun, R. J. (2007). Why diversity management fails: Metaphor analyses unveil manager attitudes. *Hospitality Management*, 26(1), 974–90.

Garud, R., & Kotha, S. (1994). Using the brain as a metaphor to model flexible production systems. *Academy of Management Review*, 19(4), 671–98.

Gilbreth, F. B., & Gilbreth, L. M. (1916). The effect of motion study upon the workers. *Annals of the American Academy of Political and Social Science*, 65(1), 272–6.

Goldstein, E. B. (2009). *Sensation and perception*. London: Wadsworth.

Heidegger, M. (1962). *Being and time: A translation of Sein und Zeit* (1927) by John Macquarrie and Edward Robinson. New York: Harper & Row.

Heisenberg, W., Eckart, C. & Hoyt, F. C. (1930). *The physical principles of the quantum theory*. University of Chicago science series. Chicago.

Hodgetts, R. M., & Hegar, K. W. (2009). Modern human relations at work. Eastbourne, UK: Gardners Books.

Hunt, J., & Collins, R. (2008). Urwick on the pioneers of management. *Australian Journal of Public Administration*, 38(4), 377–82.

Inhelder, B., & Piaget, J. (1958). *The growth of logical thinking from childhood to adolescence*. New York, Basic Books.

James, W. (1890). *The principles of psychology*. New York: Henry Holt.

Jones, J. (2010). Leadership lessons from the fast track programme for teachers in England. *Educational Management Administration & Leadership*, 38(2), 149–63.

Jowett, B., & Plato. (1914). *The dialogs of Plato*. New York: Bigelow, Brown.

Juran, J., & Godfrey, A. (1999). *Juran's quality handbook*, 5th edn. New York: McGraw-Hill.

Kant, I. (1958). *Critique of pure reason*. New York: Modern Library.

Latham, G. P., & Dossett, D. L. (1978). Designing incentive plans for unionized employees: A comparison of continuous and variable ratio reinforcement schedules. *Personnel Psychology*, 31(1), 47–61.

Law, K. M. Y. (2010). How do engineering students differ from students of other disciplines in Taiwan? *International Journal of Management in Education*, 4(2), 120–32.

Lee, J. (2000). Knowledge management: The intellectual revolution. *IIE Solutions* (USA), 32(10), 34–8.

Lewin, K. (1951). *Field theory in social science: Selected theoretical papers*. New York: Harper.

Lewis, E., Romanaggi, D. & Chapple, A. (2010). Successfully managing change during uncertain times. *Strategic HR Review*, 9(2), 12–18.

Marr, D. (2010). Vision: *A computational investigation into the human representation and processing of visual information*. Cambridge, MA: MIT Press.

Mayo, E. (1931). *Industrial research at the Western Electric Co., Inc. (U.S.A.)*. Geneva: International Management Institute.

Morgan, G. (2007). *Images of organization*. Thousand Oaks, CA: Sage Publications.

Nadeau, K. (2005). Career choices and workplace challenges for individuals with ADHD. *Journal of Clinical Psychology*, 61(5), 549–63.

Nambisan, S., & Sawhney, M. (2010). *The global brain*. New York: Wharton School Publishing.

Pavlov, I. P. (1929). Review of lectures on conditioned reflexes. *American Journal of Sociology*, 35(3), 519–20.

Pocock, D. (1973). Environmental perception process and product. *Tijdschrift voor Economische en Sociale Geografie*, 64(4), 251–7.

Robbins, S., Judge, T., Millett, B. & Waters-Marsh, T. (2008). *Organisational behaviour*. Sydney: Pearson Education Australia.

Rowley, C., & Warner, M. (2010). Whither management in South-East Asia? Directions and themes. *Asia Pacific Business Review*, 16(1/2), 1–17.

Senge, P. M. (1990). *The fifth discipline: The art and practice of the learning organization*. New York: Doubleday.

Sia, S. K., & Bhardwaj, G. (2009). Employees' perception of diversity climate: Role of psychological contract. *Journal of the Indian Academy of Applied Psychology*, 35(2), 305–12.

Skinner, B. F. (1974). *About behaviorism*. New York: Knopf, distributed by Random House.

Skinner, B. F. (1984). The phylogeny and ontogeny of behaviour. *Behavioral and Brain Sciences*, 7(1), 669–77.

Taylor, F. W. (1911). *Shop management*. New York: Harper & Brothers.

Taylor, J. (2006). Shifting from a heteronomous to an autonomous worldview of organizational communication: Communication theory on the cusp. *Communication Theory*, 5(1), 1–35.

Tetlow, P. (2007). *The Web's awake: An introduction to the field of Web science and the concept of Web life*. Hoboken, NJ: John Wiley/IEEE Press.

Twenge, J., & Campbell, S. (2008). Generational differences in psychological traits and their impact on the workplace. *Journal of Managerial Psychology*, 23(8), 862–77.

uit Beijerse, R. (1999). Questions in knowledge management: Defining and conceptualising a phenomenon. *Journal of Knowledge Management*, 3(2), 94–110.

Vitevitch, M., & Luce, P. (1998). When words compete: Levels of processing in perception of spoken words. *Psychological Science*, 9(4), 325–29.

Vroom, V. H. (1964). *Work and motivation*. New York: Wiley.

Weiner, B. (1974). *Achievement motivation and attribution theory*. Morristown, NJ: General Learning Press.

Wood, J., Zeffane, R., Fromholtz, M., Wiesner, R. & Creed, A. (2010). *Organisational behaviour: Core concepts and applications*. Milton, Qld: John Wiley & Sons Australia.

PRACTITIONER INSIGHT

JESSICA HARRISON

HEAD OF TALENT,
KPMG AUSTRALIA

Overseeing all aspects of the talent function for KPMG Australia, Jessica is responsible for ensuring that the strategies of the Talent function align with KPMG's strategy of being the Best Firm to Work With. Jessica is responsible for the graduate, experienced hire and global mobility functions and is also responsible for the strategy and implementation of KPMG's Emerging Leader program in Australia. Jessica also sits on both KPMG's regional and global resourcing steering committees.

Before joining KPMG, Jessica was the North American Head of Recruiting with Protiviti in Chicago, where she oversaw all aspects of the graduate and experienced hire recruiting processes as well as developed Protiviti's National Internship Program, which was first ranked in the top 50 Intern programs in the USA in 2008. Before her move into Human Resources, Jessica worked in consulting at both Protiviti and Arthur Andersen. She has a Bachelor of Arts degree with a focus on Communications and Economics from DePauw University.

INTERVIEW

What was your first job?
Consultant at Arthur Andersen

What has been your career highlight so far?
Working abroad in Australia

In your current role, what does a typical day involve?
I typically work across several projects at a time as well as manage a national team. Therefore, I spend a good portion of the day in meetings, managing issues and either designing or executing strategic projects.

What's the best part of your job?
The people I work with! I don't believe you can enjoy work without having a great team.

What is the hardest aspect of your role?
Finding time to complete strategic projects while managing my day-to-day responsibilities.

What are the current challenges facing you, in your role?
Managing expectations from stakeholders when implementing a new process or piece of technology. It's important to get your stakeholder group engaged from the very beginning to ensure change acceptance.

Do you regularly apply the principles or theories you learnt (when studying organisational behaviour) into your everyday work? In what way?
Absolutely! I think it is important to think about your audience – both as a whole as well as the individual – before making decisions and communicating.

How important is an understanding of 'organisational behaviour' in today's workplace?
Knowing your audience and anticipating their views is important to ensuring your ideas and thoughts are communicated effectively.

Is a work–life balance a reasonable expectation in a modern workplace?
Many employers recognise that employees want work–life balance. As such, many companies have implemented formal work–life balance programs. However, outside of formal programs, it is important for employees to manage their work and personal lives by planning ahead and prioritising both personal and professional tasks. As a manager, I spend a lot of time coaching employees on managing their time and learning to prioritise.

Has technology impacted on work–life balance? Is it harder to achieve with constant access to the 'office', for example?

There is no doubt that technology has impacted the workplace. Like anything an employee needs to be sure to disconnect as necessary and use technology as an asset, not as a chain. Personally, I limit the number of times I check my handheld during non-work hours, I don't respond out of hours unless urgent.

How do you communicate company strategy with staff at all levels?

We have several communication forums including the use of our intranet, town hall forums and email communications.

Are you able to find much time to think about the strategic design of work in your organisation?

Prioritising forward-looking activities can be difficult but is of course very important. I schedule large chunks of time in my diary to ensure time for strategic design and delivery.

Modern Diversity: The Adaptation of Values, Attitudes and Personality

INTRODUCTION

Building on the understanding of learning from Chapter 2, this chapter explores what is permanent and what can be changed in individuals at work. Every individual is quite different in their views and capabilities. The psychological perspective of what constitutes **personality** is discussed. The concept of diversity is addressed through differences in personality generated by environment versus heredity, socialisation and cross-cultural perspectives. The process of personality formation is described and relevant personality characteristics for organisational behaviour are presented, along with the means by which change or learning can be achieved in various degrees. The role of equity, respect and trust as contemporary organisation behaviour issues are integrated, and this establishes a solid lead into the motivation theories in Chapter 4.

Personality
The combined expression of individual values and attitudes through the actions and reactions the individual experiences with others.

LEARNING OBJECTIVES

Reading this chapter will help you to

- develop a pragmatic awareness of diversity
- discuss the formation of attitudes and values and their influence on personality
- explain the influence of genetics and environment on the formation of personality
- discuss how personality relates to organisational cultures
- articulate equity, respect and trust as necessary components of the workplace.

OVERVIEW

Just as Chapter 2 establishes that individual perceptions are different for everybody, it follows that the **values**, **attitudes** and entire personalities of each individual are also unique. This brings diversity into the workplace. There have been other developments in the workplace, as highlighted in Chapter 1: globalisation, technological developments in transport and telecommunications, political and trading bloc changes in large portions of the world. All of these make for an increasingly mobile and diverse labour pool. Cross-cultural mingling abounds and managers today, even in the most remote regions, are likely to find astonishing diversity of values, attitudes and personalities in their staff. However, such a milieu creates in people a desire for something more consistent and stable. Even in the study of personality we find a desire to categorise, crystallise and stereotype people. This labelling is often necessary for appropriate allocation of tasks and roles to particular people. So, read the chapter with this warning in mind: giving a name to a personality type is a potential trap despite its usefulness at certain moments in the workplace. The contemporary situation is that the growth of heterogeneity appears inexorable and probably even most desirable for many workplace objectives.

ATTITUDES AND VALUES

Thoughts, feelings and actions combine to indicate a person's attitude. When someone is said to have a positive attitude, for example, this conclusion will be derived from some cognitive factors, such as the person explaining their optimistic point of view, some affective factors, such as the look in their eye, and some behavioural factors, such as the way they walk. A person can have an attitude (a subjective evaluation) about objects, people or events. In organisational behaviour we are most interested in attitudes related to job satisfaction, job involvement and organisational commitment. Wouldn't it be nice as a manager to ensure that people develop productive and positive attitudes at work? Of course, in practice, it is next to impossible to completely control people's thoughts, emotions and behaviours. There is complexity in the way attitudes form and how they can be influenced or changed.

The formation of attitudes and values and their influence on personality

Among the founding factors of attitude and, ultimately, personality are people's values. Values are basic convictions about means and ends. Examples include integrity, accountability, trust, concern for others, and self-interest. There are many possible values and there is considerable debate about the cultural relativity of values.

What one culture holds important may not be the same as what another does. Ferrell et al. (2011) cite the work of Ruhe and Lee (2008) and Sikula (1996) in outlining global values, then go on to highlight the Global Sullivan Principles as an outgrowth of work done at the United Nations to encourage values of social responsibility around the world. The Global Sullivan Principles are core values encapsulated in a pledge available for business managers to aim for tolerance and peace as they go about their operations.

Thought pathway

Read the Global Sullivan Principles and consider the extent to which a manager who has performance objectives related to profit or productivity could follow through on the principles.

The Global Sullivan Principles

The Preamble

The objectives of the Global Sullivan Principles are to support economic, social and political justice by companies where they do business; to support human rights and to encourage equal opportunity at all levels of employment, including racial and gender diversity on decision-making committees and boards; to train and advance disadvantaged workers for technical, supervisory and management opportunities; and to assist with greater tolerance and understanding among peoples; thereby helping to improve the quality of life for communities, workers and children with dignity and equality.

I urge companies large and small in every part of the world to support and follow the Global Sullivan Principles of Corporate Social Responsibility wherever they have operations.

Reverend Leon H. Sullivan (Author and Founder)

The Principles

As a company which endorses the Global Sullivan Principles we will respect the law, and as a responsible member of society we will apply these Principles with integrity consistent with the legitimate role of business. We will develop and implement company policies, procedures, training and internal reporting structures to ensure commitment to these Principles throughout our organisation. We believe the application of these Principles will achieve greater tolerance and better understanding among peoples, and advance the culture of peace.

Accordingly, we will:

- Express our support for universal human rights and, particularly, those of our employees, the communities within which we operate and parties with whom we do business.
- Promote equal opportunity for our employees at all levels of the company with respect to issues such as color, race, gender, age, ethnicity or religious beliefs, and operate without unacceptable worker treatment such as the exploitation of children, physical punishment, female abuse, involuntary servitude or other forms of abuse.
- Respect our employees' voluntary freedom of association.
- Compensate our employees to enable them to meet at least their basic needs and provide the opportunity to improve their skill and capability in order to raise their social and economic opportunities.
- Provide a safe and healthy workplace; protect human health and the environment; and promote sustainable development.
- Promote fair competition including respect for intellectual and other property rights, and not offer, pay or accept bribes.

- Work with governments and communities in which we do business to improve the quality of life in those communities—their educational, cultural, economic and social well-being—and seek to provide training and opportunities for workers from disadvantaged backgrounds.
- Promote the application of these Principles by those with whom we do business.

We will be transparent in our implementation of these Principles and provide information which demonstrates publicly our commitment to them.

Source: <www.thesullivanfoundation.org/gsp/principles/gsp/default.asp>

We are each brought up to believe there is a right way to do certain things and particular goals for which it would be best to aim. For example, someone who is raised to think positively and conditioned to believe that they can change things for the better is likely to continue expressing this value throughout their life. The expression of such a value appears most immediately in attitudes (such as others noticing they have a positive attitude) and, ultimately, in a proactive personality. Naturally, this is but one example of the way values can affect attitude and personality. The fact remains that there is a complex mix of people in any workplace and the expression of different personalities becomes one of the most difficult but possibly most rewarding aspects of management.

WINDOW ON CONFLICT AND NEGOTIATION

Discrimination occurs against older workers

ELIZABETH BRODERICK, *THE NEWCASTLE HERALD*
February 5 2010

As someone fast approaching 50 years of age and in the latter part of my working life, there is one thing that takes on immense importance for me, as it does for many people. And that is choice. But too often, choice is something that mature age workers find they are lacking, often for reasons that are unfair and out of their control.

A great many people look forward to retirement, plan for it and rejoice in its prospects once it comes their way. For them, retirement is the reward at the end of their working lives—a time when they get to do the things that the daily grind of paid work has prevented them from doing.

At the same time, there are other people who, for reasons that are personal to them, would prefer to stay working—some on a full-time basis, others preferring part-time or casual employment. These people don't want to retire.

Still other people have to stay in paid work because of financial and other pressures. For them, retirement is simply not an option.

What I am describing here is choice—the choice to retire, the choice to stay working because you want to, and having the choice to stay in work because you need to.

We all have the right to work, however the reality is not that simple.

On Monday, the federal Treasurer, Wayne Swan, released the Government's 2010 Intergenerational Report. In his speech, he made an extremely important point. He said, 'The choice for older Australians to stay in or leave the workforce should be just that—a choice, not something forced on them by prejudice or bad policy.'

In making his point, Mr Swan rightly acknowledged that ageism and age based prejudice can prevent mature age workers from exercising their choice to stay in work.

We live in a culture that is largely obsessed with appearance and places high value on being 'vital and young'. These values often lead to systematic stereotyping of, and discrimination against, people simply because of their age—in this case, mature age. That is ageism. The unfortunate thing about stereotypes like, 'mature people are slow to pick up technology', is not just that they are untrue, but that they are often accepted as 'truth' or 'reality'. Ageism strongly implies a message of decline and of burden.

In the employment arena, I am talking about people over a certain age being ignored in recruitment processes, people being told by others that they are too old and should move aside to let a younger person have their job, people being overlooked for training and development because they are too old to pick it up and 'are going to retire soon, anyway'.

These sorts of discriminatory practices are not only unfair, they are unlawful and can have profound psychological and social impacts. As a result, mature age workers may no longer feel welcome in the workplace, no longer feel able to compete for jobs or apply for promotions, and they may give up altogether. This is the 'forced' retirement to which Mr Swan alluded.

A woman recently wrote to me, 'I'm currently studying a Master of Human Resource Management…it does not make one scrap of difference in the job market. I have three other degrees that also fit in contemporary markets. I'm 54. No-one wants me. It is very disillusioning.'

In my role as Commissioner for Age Discrimination,

I have met with a host of individuals and community and advocacy groups, and I have spoken on radio shows and taken talkback calls on this issue. I can tell you first-hand of the heartfelt stories of rejection, isolation and lost hope that people tell me when they talk about their experiences as mature age workers. It is one thing to hear that you're not appropriately skilled for a role. That's something you can often fix. But it's quite another thing to feel that you missed out on the job because of your age, despite having all the skills required.

Australia's changing age profile presents us not only with economic opportunity but with opportunity for individuals to live their life as they choose, to secure their financial future, and for all of us to build a socially inclusive community that values the rights and contribution of people of all ages.

But this will not happen unless each one of us is able to recognize ageism—wherever it may exist—and be prepared to stand against it.

Source: <www.hreoc.gov.au/about/media/media_ releases/op_ed/20100205_older_workers.html>

As a manager making daily decisions about recruitment and task allocations, it is important to continuously assess one's own values and the social pressures that influence decisions and actions. Conflicts can emerge from actions that, even done without malice, can have the effect of hurting or discriminating against individuals.

Job satisfaction

In organisational behaviour it is common for people to strive for an attitude of job satisfaction. No one really wants to work in a place without feeling some level of satisfaction, otherwise they start to look elsewhere for work. Managers can potentially minimise turnover and absenteeism and maximise commitment and productivity if they focus on ensuring their staff are experiencing job satisfaction (Saks et al., 2009). The difficulty rests with the ambiguous nature of satisfaction (Locke, 1969). On the one hand, the promise of achieving satisfaction while at work can be quite motivating. You are more likely to climb out of bed and get to the workplace on time and with enthusiasm if you think job satisfaction will be the result of your actions. On the other hand, actually achieving a level of satisfaction might also be argued to diminish motivation. This is the metaphor of the carrot and the stick where the donkey keeps walking as long as the carrot is just out of reach. The promise of satisfaction is motivating. However, upon getting the carrot the donkey stops walking. Hunger is satisfied, the carrot is gone, so why bother to keep spending energy?

Thought pathway

There was once a manager who espoused the philosophy, 'Treat 'em mean to keep 'em keen'. Consider to what extent this may be true, and how your job performance might be affected if your own manager applied this approach.

This appears to be the nature of the balancing act that managers are engaged with. Give staff too much reward at work and their motivation for continuing to improve performance may diminish. Give staff not enough reward and they may seek their fortunes elsewhere. Getting it just right can enhance motivation and make an attitude of job satisfaction, however fleeting, realistically obtainable.

PERSONALITY

Personality is the combined expression of individual values and attitudes through the actions and reactions the individual experiences with others. A key source of one's personality is obviously the environment, such as the sensations and experiences of a unique position in the world, and of course parental influences and other social interactions. Another key source of personality is genetics, which establishes various predispositions which may or may not be developed as one's life proceeds. There is quite a debate about the extent that inborn genes can ultimately determine an adult's personality. The environment can clearly condition people in certain ways, but just how successful that conditioning can be may be determined by genetic predispositions (heredity). Figure 3.1 outlines the factors of personality.

Figure 3.1 The factors of personality

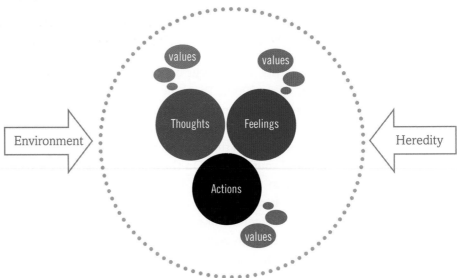

Figure 3.1 shows the broad influence of the environment and heredity in the formation of personality. From this base the individual develops values that underpin and feed their thoughts, feelings and actions in various situations. The combined expression of thoughts, feelings and actions is revealed through individual attitudes, such as job satisfaction, job involvement and organisational commitment.

Environment or heredity?

Learning Objective
The influence of genetics and environment on the formation of personality

There has been a swinging pendulum of opinion ever since the discovery of genes in humans as to how influential those genes may be in determining overall personality. Some extreme views of the past have fuelled science fiction writers and some political dictators to suggest that engineering of workplaces and societies might be possible if only systematic selection of genetic makeup in people could be implemented. In fact, the cat is already out of the bag in relation to human diversity. Today, even with the map of the human genome completed, the complexity of possible combinations means that, despite some promising fields of control in relation to health care (Torgersen, 2010), most of what makes us unique is still up for grabs. The human genome appears to establish predispositions for certain features, skills and abilities, but it by no means predetermines exactly how an individual will turn out. As Chapter 2 indicated, it is through perception and learning that most of our values and attitudes are formed, and it is the environment of our experiences and our own reactions within that environment that play the largest parts in learning. As a result, all individuals turn out with personalities quite different from each other. Studies of sets of identical twins brought up in similar and different environments have tended to support this view. While there can be fascinating similarities in appearances and some behaviours in the twins, there are even more compelling differences due to variances in their experiences and perceptions in those environments (Schulman et al., 1993; Riemann et al., 2006; Bouchard & Hur, 2008). There are also studies of the personalities of first-born versus later-born children that ignite rather than settle the nature (heredity) versus nurture (environment) debate (Hartshorne, 2010).

WINDOW ON DECISION-MAKING

Gene testing exposes us all to discrimination

February 16, 2010

It is 10 years since the human genome was mapped. Genetic testing is big business. However, by 2000, most European countries and American states had enacted laws on the use of such tests for employment and insurance purposes. At the time, *The Age* warned that Australians lacked privacy protection and faced economic and social assessments of their genetic 'stamp'. Despite some legal changes since then, people remain vulnerable to invasive and discriminatory practices.

The issue has been revived by a trial offer of half-price genetic tests made to customers with NIB health cover. Testing would assess their genetic risks of illnesses such as diabetes, cancers and cardiovascular disease. NIB chief executive Mark Fitzgibbon says in a letter that his test was an 'invaluable experience'. Only the small print discloses a downside (aside from the shock of unwanted findings): 'You may be required to disclose genetic test results, including any underlying health risks and conditions which the tests reveal, to life insurance or superannuation providers.' That includes NIB, which also sells life insurance.

While people might regard DNA information as profoundly personal, they can be forced to reveal test results to obtain life, income protection or mortgage insurance and even some superannuation products. If tests indicate a higher risk, a person may be charged more, offered a shorter period or more limited form of cover, or refused cover (but health insurance premiums cannot be adjusted for individual risk). If a customer conceals a test, the insurer may refuse to pay out. A member of the federal government's Human Genetics Advisory Committee, Kristine Barlow-Stewart, studies genetic discrimination in Australia. In one study she found 48 cases, of which 46 people reported adverse treatment by insurers on the basis of genetic tests.

It is wrong, biologically and philosophically, to treat a person as if they are no more than the sum of their DNA, as if it is 'all in the genes'. Geneticists say it is not so simple; a person's genes and environment interact in complex ways. Yet, as early as 2000, job and loan applicants were asked to have genetic tests, with refusal counting against them.

The potential health benefits of DNA science are great. For instance, individuals from families with a history of bowel cancer can improve survival rates through early detection by 50 per cent. However, a Melbourne University study last year found that when told about insurance implications, the number declining testing leapt from 20 per cent to 50 per cent. That is the damaging health impact of laws that enable insurers and employers to use results of genetic testing against people. Last year, the Disability Discrimination Act was amended to cover genetic predispositions to disability, but the definition of a disability is far narrower than the range of genetic conditions that expose people to discrimination.

This is much more than an issue of medical risk and insurance. As *The Age* stated in 2005: 'We all hold information in our DNA that would be of interest to insurers, employers, police, doctors and researchers. That does not mean they have a right to it.' No one should feel pressure to undergo DNA tests when the benefits are offset by often poorly disclosed financial risks and invasions of privacy.

The power of DNA testing invites abuse, and individuals have limited recourse against this. The march of science and markets has outpaced legal and ethical frameworks meant to protect us. Australians hold well-founded fears that DNA test results can be used against them.

Ultimately, the problem is that the privacy most people rightly believe should be safeguarded against corporate or government intrusion has no constitutional protection. The solution might be a bill of rights. Unfortunately, progress in that area has been even slower than government action to uphold individuals' rights to their genetic information.

Source: <www.theage.com.au/opinion/editorial/ gene-testing-exposes-us-all-to-discrimination-20100215-o2ta.html>

Managers need to base decisions in the workplace on all of the factors that are important. People respond due to a complex mix of genetic and environmental inputs. Regardless of debates about the factors of personality, managers are still confronted with organisational performance to be achieved and a diverse workforce with which to achieve it. Some models of personality have been developed to enable categorisation of personality types and features and possibly improve the match between individuals and their tasks at work. The next sections discuss some of the better known models of personality characteristics that are relevant to the workplace.

Foundational ideas

FREUD AND JUNG

Psychoanalysis
Developed originally by Sigmund Freud as a practical tool for exploring aspects of personality, more specifically dysfunctions in personality development at different stages of life.

Sigmund Freud is well known for the development of **psychoanalysis**, a practical tool for exploring aspects of personality, more specifically dysfunctions in personality development at different stages of life. Freud identified personality phenomena and produced a vocabulary to describe them that spawned a wide-ranging application of his ideas for many decades (Freud & Brill, 1938; Freud, 1990). One key component of his approach was in identifying both conscious and unconscious elements of people's behaviours. He also outlined stages of development (oral, anal and phallic) through which people must successfully move in order to develop healthfully. Failure to progress through these stages leads to arrested development and compensatory behaviours that can recur at various times. While psychoanalysis techniques are hotly debated, for organisational behaviour, some of Freud's concepts can assist in understanding people's responses to various work situations. For example, Freud noticed people tend to revert to habitual ways of behaving when situations are difficult. Habit is a way of defending oneself against stress.

Regression
The psychoanalytic term for reverting to behaviours learned in childhood.

Four kinds of behavioural defence mechanisms are **regression** (reverting to behaviours learned in childhood), **fixation** (becoming rigid and inflexible), **rationalisation** (overly complex explaining away to cover up true motives), and **projection** (attribution of one's intentions and feelings to others). Anyone with work experience will recognise these kinds of behaviours in all kinds of people. For instance, even if hard to prove, one can often suspect that certain leaders may rationalise when something does not go according to plan, or that some workers become fixated on old techniques that really ought to be adapted or changed for quality improvement, or managers can sometimes project their own inadequacies on their subordinates when apportioning blame for errors, or that when a disagreement arises some people regress to childlike behaviours rather than seek sensible compromises.

Fixation
The psychoanalytic term for becoming rigid and inflexible.

Rationalisation
The psychoanalytic term for overly complex explaining away to cover up true motives.

Projection
The psychoanalytic term for attribution of one's intentions and feelings to others.

Carl Jung is another famous psychologist who worked in his early career with Freud but later developed his own insights into personality that have added much to the models that are applied in practice today. Jung noticed four archetypal aspects of personality that he suggested could be present in all people: desiring self-actualisation, expressing a dark side, having both masculine and feminine qualities, and engaging a 'persona' or a role for oneself (Fordham & Jung, 1966). As well as agreeing with the Freudian view that people have conscious and unconscious elements to their behaviours, Jung added a fascinating third level called the 'collective unconscious', a kind of evolutionary storehouse of shared human experiences. There are some positive and intuitive aspects of Jung's approach that make practical sense in terms of organisational behaviour. For instance, to have goals and aspirations runs to the heart of any organisation and each individual worker, and this appears to equate with the Jungian idea of self-actualisation. The self-actualisation concept is further developed by motivation theorists, most notably Abraham Maslow (see Chapter 4). Jung's four archetypes have also been used as an underpinning for the Myers-Briggs Type Indicator personality tests.

MYERS-BRIGGS

The Myers-Briggs Type Indicator (MBTI) is widely implemented in organisations and anecdotally supported (Furnham, 2006; Bouchard & Hur, 2008). Building on four continua and enabling the prediction of 16 different personality combinations, MBTI uses Jungian psychology to improve self-awareness of personality traits and has been used for career guidance. The 100-question personality test enables classification of individuals as:

- extroverted (E) or introverted (I)
- sensing (S) or intuitive (N)
- thinking (T) or feeling (F)
- judging (J) or perceiving (P)

As an example, the test might reveal an individual to be ESTJ. This combination of personality traits suggests organised, realistic, logical, analytical and decisive types who may respond positively to roles in business systems or mechanical occupations. You can read all of the 16 types published online: <www.myersbriggs.org/my-mbti-personality-type/mbti-basics/the-16-mbti-types.asp>

While the test is interesting and may accurately characterise people, there is limited evidence that it predicts greatly improved job performance in certain roles. Sometimes introverts can rise to the occasion when a job requires extroversion, or a feeling-type person can do very well when asked to be more thinking. In other words, personality tests such as this carry the risk of stereotyping or pigeonholing people in roles that may not always deliver the best outcome for the individual or the organisation. A more interesting line of thought is around the extent to which MBTI personality traits are inherited or learned. There is evidence that personality stays quite consistent over time, which might suggest a strong genetic component, but the fact that people can be observed to behave contrary to their dominant personality type suggests a significant environmental aspect.

Figure 3.2 gives an example of a personality test.

Figure 3.2 Example of a personality test

1 I like to connect with others.

Very Inaccurate ○ ○ ○ ○ ○ Very Accurate

2 I am messy.

Very Inaccurate ○ ○ ○ ○ ○ Very Accurate

3 I am a brainiac.

Very Inaccurate ○ ○ ○ ○ ○ Very Accurate

4 I don't keep my emotions under control.

Very Inaccurate ○ ○ ○ ○ ○ Very Accurate

5 I get stressed out easily.

Very Inaccurate ○ ○ ○ ○ ○ Very Accurate

6 I talk to many different people at parties.

Very Inaccurate ○ ○ ○ ○ ○ Very Accurate

7 I am more interested in intellectual pursuits than anything else.

Very Inaccurate ○ ○ ○ ○ ○ Very Accurate

8 I am not easily frustrated.

Very Inaccurate ○ ○ ○ ○ ○ Very Accurate

9 I put myself first.

Very Inaccurate ○ ○ ○ ○ ○ Very Accurate

10 I take charge.

Very Inaccurate ○ ○ ○ ○ ○ Very Accurate

THE BIG 5

The five-factor model of personality has been well supported in organisational research of recent years (Caligiuri, 2000; Erdheim et al., 2006; Musek, 2007). The five factors, which have become known as 'the Big 5', are identified as the attribute scales of extraversion, agreeableness, conscientiousness, emotional stability and openness to experience. Compared with other personality tests, the Big 5 features suggest some direct impacts on job performance, especially in the measures of performance ratings, training proficiency, and salary levels. Table 3.2 shows how high and low measures of each of the Big 5 factors can have different effects at work.

Table 3.2 The features and effects of the Big 5 at work

PERSONALITY FACTOR	HIGH	…EFFECT ON WORK	LOW	…EFFECT ON WORK
extraversion	gregarious, sociable, assertive	Happier in their jobs. More inclined to impulsive absence. More disposed to team work. Higher job performance, especially in managerial and sales positions.	quiet, timid, reserved	Less disposed to team work.
agreeableness	accepting, warm, cooperative	Happier in their jobs. Higher job satisfaction.	antagonistic, cold, defensive	Lower job satisfaction.
conscientiousness	dependable, persistent, organised, responsible	Higher job performance in most occupations. Higher levels of job knowledge and organisational citizenship behaviour. More resistant to change.	unreliable, disorganised, distractible	Lower job performance in most organisations. Lower levels of job knowledge and organisational citizenship behaviour. Less resistant to change.
emotional stability	calm, secure, unstressed	Happier in their jobs. Higher job satisfaction. Lower stress levels.	anxious, insecure, depressed, stressed	Sometimes higher and sometimes lower job performance.
openness to experience	curious, creative, accepting of change	Higher training proficiency. Less resistant to change.	conservative, traditional, resistant to rapid change	Lower training proficiency. More resistant to change.

There are some simple tests available online that give an indication of personality factors in the Big 5. EG: <www.similarminds.com/big5.html>.

The research is suggesting the Big 5 could be useful for managers trying to forecast the types of people who would help their organisation achieve its objectives. As with the observations about Myers-Briggs, however, there may be the unexpected individuals who can rise above their labelled personality to perform well in contra-indicated roles. There are also a range of other personality factors that seem to play their part in improving job performance, from self-efficacy to locus of control and emotional intelligence.

SELF-EFFICACY

■
Self-efficacy
A sense of confidence
about one's ability to
complete a task.

Self-efficacy is a sense of confidence about one's ability to complete a task, and it recurs in the work-motivation literature as an indicator of individual job performance (Bandura, 1997; Somech & Drach-Zahavy, 2000; Semadar et al., 2006; Wilson et al., 2007). It is experience of success that enables a person to learn about their ability to control work outcomes. Bandura (1997) is clear about self-efficacy being a feeling of control. It is a feeling that arrives by having experiences of situations where one is able to direct and achieve things.

Thought pathway

Think about whether a newborn baby can have any sense of self-efficacy and what the source of that feeling would be.

There is an internal versus an external perspective that can be considered at this point. The way one person feels internally about their control over work may be quite different to another. There are also external factors imposed on people at work.

LOCUS OF CONTROL

■
Locus of control
The extent of our feelings
about the level of control
we have over the world.

When we go to work each day, stuff happens to us. To a large extent the world exists out there and we did not have a direct hand in creating it. However, some aspects of the world we apparently can control, and parts of it we can even create. The extent of our feelings about the level of control we have over the world determines our locus of control. Psychologists have noted two broad types of personality when it comes to a sense of control over the events in one's life (Rotter, 1966). People with an internal **locus of control** tend to believe they are responsible for their own experiences and achievements. People with an external locus of control tend to believe that the influence of others and the general opportunities provided by their environment are the main determinants of their personal experiences and achievements.

Thought pathway

Consider the locus of control of someone who lives by the motto, 'Seize the day'.

Self-efficacy and locus of control obviously have some connection and one's feelings of control are gradually learned through experience.

EMOTIONAL INTELLIGENCE

■
Learning Objective
How personality relates to
organisational cultures

There is another personality feature that spans the bridge between thoughts and feelings. The absence of this feature has been stereotyped in the labels of 'geek' or 'nerd'. Smart but socially awkward people are certainly not lacking intelligence, and many of the 'nerdiest' people around have risen to be prominent leaders and highly

■
Emotional intelligence
The ability to be sensitive
to the feelings of others
and to pick up on and be
responsive to social cues.

successful. A high intelligence quotient (IQ) is positive for the workforce. When it comes to people management, however, the ability to be sensitive to the feelings of others, to pick up on and be responsive to social cues, become crucial attributes for gaining the trust and cooperation of others, especially in situations of conflict and emotional crisis (Mikolajczak et al., 2007; Goleman, 2010). Emotional intelligence is the term for this kind of social awareness and sensitivity, which can also be called a high emotional quotient (EQ). Leaders with high emotional intelligence are more likely to have loyal staff that respect and trust them over long periods of time. Workers with emotional intelligence are more likely to succeed in team situations and will fit in better long term with the organisational culture.

Some research has suggested that overall job performance can be improved where emotional intelligence is high in the people involved (Semadar et al., 2006; Mayer et al., 2007). Clearly some technical, back-room tasks do not require quite so much socialisation and the need for EQ is less relevant than a high IQ. But most work requires some element of social interaction, and employing staff and managers with good proportions of both EQ and IQ is more likely to deliver positive job outcomes.

Thought pathway

Read the article by Semadar et al. and consider how emotionally intelligent actions by the boss and the worker may have been better. What could those actions have been?

WINDOW ON EMOTIONAL INTELLIGENCE

Workplace gossip turns nasty as woman unfairly sacked for alleged backbiting

A WORKPLACE expert has issued a warning about the pitfalls of office gossip after Fair Work Australia ruled a woman had been illegally sacked over it.

The woman's boss maintains the office policy was there to stamp out malicious 'backbiting' about other staff.

But Fair Work commissioner John Ryan took into account evidence that the woman had previously complained to the centre's director about one of the employees, who was the director's sister, and nothing had been done.

The ruling shows that the exact legal line on sexism and other forms of workplace harassment can be a confusing one to negotiate for both sides.

Melbourne Business School professor Isabel Metz said the decision, which awarded Hippity Hop childcare worker Tara Davies almost $10,000 compensation for her unfair dismissal and put the centre on notice over its handling of policing alleged gossip, shows the ramifications can be costly.

But there are steps within the law to deal to ensure a harmonious workplace.

Ms Metz, an associate professor of Organisational Behaviour, says employers should first allow staff somewhere to speak freely when they are dissatisfied with their job or the performance of other workers and then deal with it sympathetically and effectively.

WHAT RULES DOES YOUR WORKPLACE HAVE? IS AN 'ANTI-GOSSIP' POLICY A GOOD IDEA? TELL US BELOW.

'When an employee is dissatisfied, [they will] backbite and this spreads what we call toxins, which are feelings of unhappiness and strong negative emotions, through the workplace,' she said.

'If they are allowed to spread, all of a sudden you have a negative culture in the workplace which is very unpleasant for everyone.

'What we recommend is that management or the leadership assume a role of what we call a "toxin handler".'

A toxin handler is an obviously sympathetic manager who is able to [empathise] like a good mediator, who will listen to the people with negative feelings and try to resolve the problems, she said.

Fair Work Australia's ruling stated the centre's policy on backbiting instead made 'no distinction between malicious and untrue comments made behind a person's back with the clear intention of destroying the person's reputation and comments made behind a person's back which are true and which would not result in serious damage to the employee's reputation.'

Commissioner Ryan found Ms Davies' conduct was not serious enough to warrant her sacking and awarded her $9480 in compensation.

GET EXPERT ADVICE

Council of Small Businesses of Australia's (COSBOA) executive director Peter Strong said rulings like this one hit members hard.

It was difficult to navigate the legalities around internal staff policies without the resources and expertise of big businesses, Mr Strong said.

'[Fair Work Australia] expects employers of small businesses to have the same expertise as a big business,' he said.

'In small business it's like a family—they sort it out, they solve a problem and sometimes they're sacked.

'An employer has to make a decision at the end of the day in the context of the business and it may be the wrong decision, but why should they be fined $10,000 because they made a mistake?'

Hippity Hop co-owner Ferruccio Baiocchi today said he was considering an appeal.

'We [tell] all our staff that the children come first,' Mr Baiocchi said. 'They come to work happy and the children are the beneficiaries.'

Further comment was being sought from Ms Davies through her legal representative.

Source: <www.news.com.au/business/business-smarts/employee-accused-of-backbiting-unfairly-dismissed/story-e6frfm9r-1226001934261>

This Window highlights the paradox that the burgeoning social software sites that are transforming organisational and personal communication can sometimes lend themselves to less than social outcomes. Emotional intelligence is about understanding when and how to apply social etiquette. Not everybody has high EQ but it happens to be something that can be learned through socialisation and concentration on the needs of others.

SOCIALISATION

Individuals rarely work in isolation in organisations. Coming together in groups or teams is virtually inevitable. The ways that personalities mesh and interact is of great importance to managers because the performance of work and the achievement of organisational objectives require synchronicity between people. Where there is conflict and miscommunication there is likely to be lower organisational performance. The next chapter in this book describes the fundamental importance of human socialisation to worker motivation. It is no coincidence that, in prisons, solitary confinement has been used a form of punishment. This is based on an understanding that human beings require socialisation opportunities for healthy functioning. While some things in the workplace can be achieved by an individual working alone, most things require social interaction as a motivator as well as a source of creativity and synergy that can deliver significant organisational benefits.

The increasingly diverse labour pool contributes to organisational and work team cultures that often need regular maintenance. As globalisation continues there has even been recent work to identify a global mindset or a kind of 'multicultural personality' which may predict if an individual will be a more effective and productive worker in the midst of diversity (Ponterotto, 2010).

Culture, diversity and equity

Learning Objective
Equity, respect and trust as necessary components of the workplace

Managers and organisations can benefit from a workplace culture that embraces and capitalises on the creativity and innovation that diverse perspectives can bring. If the diverse range of staff is also treated equitably in relation to benefits and promotion opportunities, this can minimise conflicts and contribute to a sense of fairness in the work culture. Workplace laws exist in Australia, New Zealand and most of the economically developed countries of the world that protect individuals against discrimination and seek to preserve diversity. The laws also aim to maintain a sense of equity and justice in the workplace. When you think about it there is a tension between diversity, which celebrates the differences in people's experiences, and equity, which focuses on similarities between people's skills and abilities. For example, if you promote a staff member because they stand out on certain criteria, you might be overlooking another staff member with other criteria that may also contribute to success in the role. As a manager, it is possible to treat staff legally in relation to decisions affecting workplace diversity and equity, but still generate conflict based on what they perceive as lack of courtesy or morality. The delicate balance of workplace culture is prone to unexpected changes in dynamics.

WINDOW ON ETHICS

The 2009/10 report *What Women Want* (CPSU, 2010) found the following about women in the public service sector of the Australian workforce:

Summary of Key Findings

1 More pressure on the sandwich generation

- The survey results provide clear evidence that many women caring for children are also caring for others such as parents, adult children and partners.

- Despite these caring responsibilities, nearly a quarter (23.5%) of women reported that taking time away from work for personal matters was frowned upon.
- The majority (83.6%) of full time women reported working additional hours and one in 10 of these said they received no additional compensation for this.
- Compared with the 2008 survey results, the survey shows that more women are being contacted more frequently out of hours.

2 Flexible work arrangements

Flexible working arrangements have never before been more important to women.

- Being able to negotiate part-time work was very important or important to 78.8 per cent of women with dependants.
- The survey results show that while flexible work provisions are important to women, they were rarely able to access them regularly. Nearly 23.5%

of women reported that taking time away from work for personal matters was frowned upon.

3 Superannuation

Superannuation continues to be a big issue for women with many feeling too time-pressed to learn more and gain control of their retirement futures.

- A quarter of respondents did not know how much they currently have in their superannuation accounts.

- Having more than one superannuation account was fairly common with two in five women indicating that they had more than one account. This rate was slightly higher among those aged 34 and below.
- Nearly two-thirds of women had never seen a financial planner about superannuation or their retirement.

Source: <www.cpsu.org.au/multiversions/16808/ FileName/WWW_WEB.pdf>

This report reveals that many decisions might be made by managers about women or, indeed, by women as managers that improve on the ethical foundations of earlier perceptions about this significant component of the workforce. Any labelled group in the workplace can be identified and studied in similar fashion. Managers improve their approach greatly by having a clear and balanced perspective on the diverse range of people they are managing.

HOFSTEDE

Workplace culture can be notionally distinguished from national culture, but in practice there is some overlap. Chapter 8 covers this concept in more detail. Geert Hofstede conducted a large study of organisational culture in a single organisation, IBM, which has offices in many different countries (Hofstede, 1980). This is a cleverly designed study of factors that are linked with individual personality that enabled the drawing of consistencies of organisational culture across different national cultures. For this reason, we include Hofstede's personality factors here for your comparison with other models in this chapter. The scales on which his research was drawn include:

Power distance
Hofstede's term for the extent to which the less powerful members of organisations and institutions accept and expect that power is distributed unequally.

Uncertainty avoidance
Hofstede's term for the extent to which a culture programs its members to feel either uncomfortable or comfortable in unstructured situations.

- **Power distance**—the extent to which the less powerful members of organisations and institutions accept and expect that power is distributed unequally.

- Individualism versus collectivism—the degree to which individuals are integrated into groups.

- Masculinity versus femininity—the distribution of roles between the genders.

- **Uncertainty avoidance**—the extent to which a culture programs its members to feel either uncomfortable or comfortable in unstructured situations.

- Long- versus short-term orientation—the extent to which a culture programs its members to deal with virtue regardless of truth.

You may notice elements of other personality models in these factors. The research is not without criticism (Baskerville, 2003) but it does provide a cross-cultural view of personality that offers some insights for managers. The analysis results in country-by-country rankings enabling comparison.

More about organisational culture is discussed in Chapter 8. Since culture is an outgrowth of individuals amalgamating their personalities through social interaction, it becomes relevant to touch upon issues that hold people together in groups and teams, most importantly, how respect and trust can be propagated in the midst of the uncertainty and diversity of human relations.

CASE STUDY

Older staff find Sally's unconventional appearance irksome

The accounting firm of George Davis and Associates was located in a suburb of Adelaide and employed 30 people. It was established in 1960 by George Davis Snr, who had now retired, and the majority of employees were long serving. Many of the clients were also well established and quite a few elderly people came to the office to discuss their affairs. George Davis Jnr was now the Managing Partner but George Snr still had a share of the business and stayed in touch.

The office was open plan and was behind the reception desk so visitors could see most of the office.

Sally Miller started as the Office Junior straight out of high school. She was keen at first but as her social life developed it was obvious when she'd had a hard night out. Many of the older employees did not really approve of her when she arrived at work looking 'under the weather'.

The surprise for everyone was when she arrived at the office with a rather obvious nose ring and additional piercings in her ears. She was rather proud of these and announced that her new boyfriend was a tattooist and was going to give her some body art!

There was the normal office chatter about her change of appearance but she took it the same way she did when people made comments about clothes, shoes or hairstyles.

The matter escalated when one of the older, well-established clients spoke to George Davis Snr at a golf function and commented that his reputable business was 'going to the dogs' under the management of his son. He specifically mentioned girls that looked like they had been 'target practice' in the office, which he didn't consider very professional.

When one of the older female employees, Betty Kilmore, heard about it she went to George Jnr and volunteered that several of the older employees were also upset about the appearance of Sally and thought it reflected poorly on all of them.

The next week Sally turned up for work with a small tattoo on her neck which was quite visible and she had added a tongue ring.

This was just too much for Betty. She confronted George Jnr and said; 'That Sally is not turning out well. We shouldn't have to work with people like that. This used to be a very professional office. Other employees are not happy and we've had clients comment on her appearance.'

George Jnr was not sure how to react. Sally's work performance was satisfactory and he was aware that young people are a bit different these days. His own daughter had just come home with a belly button ring of which he did not approve.

CASE STUDY
QUESTIONS

1 Is Sally a fair representation of her social group and entitled to conform with her idea of fashion as long as she does her job?

2 If George Jnr and more senior employees wanted to have her conform to their group's norms, could they be accused of discrimination or not allowing diversity in the workplace?

3 If Sally happened to turn up some old Christmas party photos of current staff in the 1970s with girls wearing miniskirts and men with flares and long hair, how would you suggest George Jnr should respond? Discuss how this group may have developed their attitudes in contrast with how Sally developed hers.

4 George Davis and Associates will need to recruit young graduates as trainee accountants in the future. How would you suggest they determine a recruitment policy that takes this issue into account?

5 Referring to the section 'Attitudes and Values', could you defend the older employees' views if they spent time grumbling about Sally while she carried on doing her job?

Developing respect and trust in the workplace

As discussed in Chapter 1, the managerial objective of maintaining human resources often sits diametrically opposed to the equally important objective of ensuring that tasks are completed. The challenge comes in allowing staff to experience sufficient job satisfaction to want to remain loyal to the organisation, but also giving enough clarity and motivation to them to be sure the important measures of work output are achieved. People are clever enough to know that work gives them an opportunity to achieve things they want in their personal lives. They also know why managers sometimes have to crack the whip to get tasks achieved. A good manager–staff relationship depends on respecting each other's intelligence and acting on the basis of mutual trust when communicating about workloads. Everyone at work has a different personality type and a different mix of personal and work objectives. Even where tests like the Big 5 or Myers-Briggs might categorise two people the same, or match one person to a particular task, on an individual basis there remain variations in perception and degrees of intensity in the expression of personality factors. This puts the emphasis back on what Chapter 2 refers to as continuous learning. It is a cycle of repeated communication and reinterpretation of people's relationships in the workplace. Learning and relearning what it means to work individually or in a team and regularly communicating about changes to situations and objectives ensures a dialogue that should be founded on respect and able to build trust over time.

WINDOW ON COMMUNICATION

Toyota chief holds morale-boosting meet in Japan

BY MIWA SUZUKI (AFP)
March 4, 2010

TOKYO—Toyota's president Friday swapped his business jacket for a workman's uniform to address thousands of employees and suppliers in Japan in a bid to boost morale at the crisis-hit car giant.

Akio Toyoda, the grandson of the founder of what is now the world's biggest automaker, admitted it had grown too rapidly, leading to the crisis that has forced it to recall more than eight million vehicles worldwide.

'It was totally against what we intended. Let me apologise for that,' he said at the 'all-Toyota emergency meeting' of 2,000 employees, dealers and parts suppliers at the company headquarters in central Japan.

Toyota executives at the event, which was beamed live to offices nationwide in a video conference, briefed workers and other stakeholders on US congressional hearings where they have recently testified.

'I was feeling lonely as Toyota was being criticised repeatedly on TV and in newspapers and I was being chased by the media,' Toyoda said of his US visit, during which he spoke in Congress, faced Toyota dealers and appeared on CNN.

But the 53-year-old executive—wearing an ash-grey jacket just like the rows of employees standing before him—noted he had felt encouraged by the Toyota factory workers and dealers he met in the United States.

'I had been thinking I was striving to protect those people, but I realised I was actually being protected by them. I was deeply moved and thought I was really lucky to be a member of Toyota,' he said with a choked voice.

Toyota executives in Washington this week ended a third marathon hearing before US lawmakers over their handling of the safety defects. Toyoda has vowed to rebuild shattered global faith in the firm.

Toyota reported an 8.7 percent drop in February US sales amid the series of mass recalls, most of them involving accelerator systems blamed for sudden spikes in speed that have been blamed for more than 50 deaths.

Amid the company's unprecedented crisis, Toyota's leading Japanese labour union said Wednesday it would cancel an annual spring rally for higher wages out of consideration for the automaker's woes.

Japanese media have meanwhile reported that the workers will get their customary annual wage increases, which would be an average 7,100 yen (80 dollars) each per month, in line with the union's demand.

*Source: <www.google.com/hostednews/afp/article/
ALeqM5hkRf5SGx2Nm99s3YiNNjlfV4klew>*

Humility is among the characteristics that may be helpful for building trust in a relationship (Nielsen, 2010). Hofstede's research suggests possible cultural variations in the expression of some characteristics. It has already been suggested that elements of emotional intelligence contribute to the establishment of trust and respect. The fact remains that managing people with diverse personalities found in offices in different regions defined by significant variations in cultural expectation is especially challenging.

Speaking up for yourself or being aggressive?

Michael Khoury had arrived in Australia from Lebanon as a young man of 19 to start a new life. He spoke no English, so set about teaching himself while he worked in a hotel. He later found a job in a manufacturing business and studied business management part-time while he worked on the production line. Within five years he had been made Production Manager. He later moved to another company and headed up their logistics operation where he implemented major changes to introduce new technology and improve their performance.

He was justifiably proud of his achievements and was recognised by others in the industry as a very talented logistics manager. He continually tried to develop his abilities by reading and studying as well as keeping himself fit by regular visits to the gym.

As he was looking for more challenges he responded to the head-hunter's call positively and was soon taking up the role of National Logistics Manager at National Appliances. National Appliances provided household appliances and spare parts to the trade and had a large warehouse operation in Melbourne which was quite complex as there were tens of thousands of different line items. They despatched all orders from there so speed was important, as was ensuring that customers received the right parts.

Michael knew he could redesign the layout to be more effective and he also knew that after this was done he could streamline the picking and packing process; this would ultimately lead to needing less staff. He was aware that if he did a good job here, there would be opportunities for him in a senior management role in the Asia-Pacific region.

His direct reports were mainly women who had been there a long time, between 12 and 20 years. They each had a team of people reporting to them who picked the products, packed them and passed them on to the despatch team.

Michael was making great progress with the layout of the warehouse and was working on the picking and packing process. He felt he knew how it should be done but wanted to include his team so he could benefit from their ideas, and he also knew that selling the final plan would be easier if they had been involved.

He found the team constructive to work with apart from Joyce McGregor who, if she disagreed with something, seemed to attack him in a very aggressive way rather than raise it as an issue that needed to be discussed logically. She didn't seem to want to change anything unless it was her idea. She had been with the Company for 18 years but showed no sign of wanting to further her career. Michael had found out that she had left school at 16 and not had any further education since then. She did not seem to be particularly healthy and was obese, although she didn't take any more personal leave than the average.

The other five in the team either went along with what he suggested or made positive contributions. Either way, they discussed options in a rational way and seemed very professional and well spoken. They all seemed to be keen to see the operations of the business improve.

Michael wasn't going to let Joyce slow the process down so he ploughed on with the other members of the team and let Joyce contribute where she wanted to.

He was surprised one morning to be called into the office of Amy Thompson, the HR Manager. There had been a bullying complaint from Joyce. She had told Amy that she was being excluded and that Michael didn't like dealing with her because she could see where he was making mistakes with the layout plans and told him so. Joyce had told Amy that 'I'm the sort of person who speaks my mind. I've always said what I thought and always will. That's just how I am—I'm honest.'

Michael explained to Amy that he had not bullied Joyce and that he never really intended to exclude her—he just dealt with the people who could work on the project more cooperatively. He felt she had 'an aggressive style' and he was not used to being spoken to the way she did. Although technically he was happy with her work he thought she was very unprofessional and he expected his team to set a better example.

Amy Thompson explained that she would have to investigate the complaint to see if was substantiated.

She had separate discussions with Joyce and the rest of the supervisors who report to Michael as part of the investigation.

Joyce reiterated her views about being the sort of person who spoke up. Other supervisors supported that view and said that Joyce's style obviously upset Michael because he was a different sort of person to them and they had become used to Joyce. They confirmed that at times they had seen him avoid dealing with her if one of them was available instead but he was never rude or raised his voice. They concluded from this that he just preferred not to deal with her if there were other options.

At the end of her investigation Amy spoke to Joyce again who said she didn't want to proceed with the bullying claim but just wanted to bring the situation to someone's attention.

CASE STUDY QUESTIONS

1 Who is in the right? Why might Michael and Joyce both think they are right? Give reasons based on theories or frameworks discussed in the chapter.

2 Is it possible to continue with this situation? Are these are just two people who represent diversity in the workplace or is there a problem to be fixed?

3 Are any of the behaviours described in conflict with what should be a constructive work culture or the Global Sullivan Principles? Does anyone need to change their behaviour and, if so, why?

4 How do you think Michael and Joyce might have developed their current set of behaviours?

5 What do you think gives Michael and Joyce their job satisfaction?

CONCLUSION

Are we genetically predetermined to think, feel and relate in the ways that we do? Or perhaps the ways we are brought up and the experiences we have are most important for defining who we are? This chapter highlighted the diversity of the modern workplace but also introduced values and attitudes, such as job satisfaction, that have implications for job performance. Individual personality was explained as a complex manifestation of values and attitudes based on a blend of heredity and environment. Personality measures such as Myers-Briggs, the Big 5, self-efficacy, locus of control and emotional intelligence were found to explain some things but left questions about their rigid application in all cases where individual and organisational performance is at stake. Ultimately, people mostly have to work together in groups and teams, thus reconciling diversity in order to effectively socialise. The cross-cultural research very clearly shows the need for acceptance and appreciation of differences. There are many opportunities to build trust and respect by bridging differences. Leaders and workers alike can continuously observe, reflect and respond to the complex realities of the workplace.

KEY POINTS

This chapter has

- developed a pragmatic awareness of diversity
- described the reasons for differences between individuals
- discussed the formation of attitudes and values and their influence on personality
- explained the influence of genetics and environment on the formulation of personality
- discussed how personality relates to organisational cultures
- articulated equity, respect and trust as necessary components of the workplace.

KEY TERMS

ATTITUDE
A subjective evaluation about objects, people or events that manifests as a combination of thoughts, feelings and behaviours.

EMOTIONAL INTELLIGENCE
The ability to be sensitive to the feelings of others and to pick up on and be responsive to social cues.

FIXATION
The psychoanalytic term for becoming rigid and inflexible.

LOCUS OF CONTROL
The extent of our feelings about the level of control we have over the world.

PERSONALITY
The combined expression of individual values and attitudes through the actions and reactions the individual experiences with others.

POWER DISTANCE
Hofstede's term for the extent to which the less powerful members of organisations and institutions accept and expect that power is distributed unequally.

PROJECTION
The psychoanalytic term for attribution of one's intentions and feelings to others.

PSYCHOANALYSIS
Developed originally by Sigmund Freud as a practical tool for exploring aspects of personality, more specifically dysfunctions in personality development at different stages of life.

RATIONALISATION
The psychoanalytic term for overly complex explaining away to cover up true motives.

REGRESSION
The psychoanalytic term for reverting to behaviours learned in childhood.

SELF-EFFICACY
A sense of confidence about one's ability to complete a task.

UNCERTAINTY AVOIDANCE
Hofstede's term for the extent to which a culture programs its members to feel either uncomfortable or comfortable in unstructured situations.

VALUES

Basic convictions about means and ends.
The Global Sullivan Principles are examples
of values.

STUDY AND REVISION QUESTIONS

Q *Someone may be said to have an attitude of job commitment. Describe the kinds of observations that would lead to that conclusion.*

Q *Select one of the Global Sullivan Principles and, as a hypothetical, mount a case for its opposite. For example, you might try to argue that employees should never have freedom of association. When you are finished run your case by a good friend or maybe a fellow student and discuss the extent to which any of your argument may be justifiable. To conclude the exercise, jot down the main reasons the principle you chose is included in the Global Sullivan Principles.*

Q *Write a summary of the main values and their effects in the workplace that are described by Elizabeth Broderick in the Window on Conflict and Negotiation.*

Q *How would you feel if your boss made an apology to you and your workmates in a similar fashion to that given by Akio Toyoda in the Window on Communication? Using Hofstede's country comparison charts, explain how the differences between your own country background and that of Toyota's mainly Japanese workers who received the apology may lead to different feelings about Toyoda's apology.*

REFERENCES

Bandura, A. (1997). *Self-efficacy: The exercise of control.* New York: W. H. Freeman.

Baskerville, R. (2003). Hofstede never studied culture. *Accounting, Organizations and Society,* 28(1), 1–14.

Bouchard, T., & Hur, Y. (2008). Genetic and environmental influences on the continuous scales of the Myers-Briggs type indicator: An analysis based on twins reared apart. *Journal of Personality*, 66(2), 135–49.

Caligiuri, P. M. (2000). The Big Five personality characteristics as predictors of expatriates' desire to terminate the assignment and supervisor-rated performance. *Personnel Psychology*, 53(1), 67–88.

CPSU (2010). *What women want: 2009/10 Survey Report.* Community and Public Sector Union, Canberra, p. 4.

Erdheim, J., Wang, M. & Zickar, M. (2006). Linking the Big Five personality constructs to organizational commitment. *Personality and Individual Differences*, 41(5), 959–70.

Ferrell, O., Fraedrich, J. & Ferrell, L. (2011). *Business Ethics: Ethical decision making and cases.* Mason, OH: South-Western Cengage.

Fordham, F., & Jung, C. G. (1966). *An introduction to Jung's psychology.* Pelican Books, A273. Harmondsworth: Penguin Books.

Freud, S. (1990). *The major works of Sigmund Freud.* Chicago: Encyclopædia Britannica.

Freud, S., & Brill, A. A. (1938). *The basic writings of Sigmund Freud.* New York: Modern library.

Furnham, A. (2006). Can people accurately estimate their own personality test scores? *European Journal of Personality*, 4(4), 319–27.

Goleman, D. (2010). *Emotional intelligence: Why it can matter more than IQ.* London: Bloomsbury.

Hofstede, G. (1980). *Culture's consequences: International differences in work-related values.* Beverly Hills, CA: Sage.

Hartshorne, J. (2010). Perspectives: Ruled by birth order? *Scientific American Mind*, January/February, 1.

Locke, E. (1969). What is job satisfaction? *Organizational Behavior and Human Performance*, 4(4), 309–36.

Mayer, J., Roberts, R. & Barsade, S. (2007). Human abilities: Emotional intelligence. *Annual Review of Psychology*, 59(1), 507–36.

Mikolajczak, M., Menila, C. & Luminet, O. (2007). Explaining the protective effect of trait emotional intelligence regarding occupational stress: Exploration of emotional labour processes. *Journal of Research in Personality*, 41(5), 1107–17.

Musek, J. (2007). A general factor of personality: Evidence for the Big One in the five-factor model. *Journal of Research in Personality*, 41(6), 1213–33.

Nielsen, R. (2010). A new look at humility: Exploring the humility concept and its role in socialized charismatic leadership. *Journal of Leadership & Organizational Studies*, 17(1), 33–43.

Ponterotto, J. (2010). Multicultural personality: An evolving theory of optimal functioning in culturally heterogeneous societies. *The Counseling Psychologist*, 20(10), 1–45.

Riemann, R., Angleitner, A. & Strelau, J. (2006). Genetic and environmental influences on personality: A study of twins reared together using the Self- and Peer Report NEO-FFI scales. *Journal of Personality*, 65(3), 449–75.

Rotter, J. (1966). Generalized expectancies for internal versus external control of reinforcement. *Psychological Monographs*, 80(1), 1–28.

Ruhe, J., & Lee, M. (2008). Teaching ethics in international business courses: The impacts of religions. *Journal of Teaching in International Business*, 19(4), 362–88.

Saks, A., Mudrack, P. & Ashforth, B. (2009). The relationship between the work ethic, job attitudes, intentions to quit, and turnover for temporary service employees. *Canadian Journal of Administrative Sciences/Revue Canadienne des Sciences de l'Administration*, 13(3), 226–36.

Schulman, P., Keith, D. & Seligman, M. (1993). Is optimism heritable? A study of twins. *Behaviour Research and Therapy*, 31(6), 569–74.

Semadar, A., Robins, G. & Ferris, G. (2006). Comparing the validity of multiple social effectiveness constructs in the prediction of managerial job performance. *Journal of Organizational Behavior*, 27(4), 443–61.

Sikula, A. F. (1996). *Applied management ethics*. Chicago: Irwin.

Somech, A., & Drach-Zahavy, A. (2000). Understanding extra-role behavior in schools: The relationships between job satisfaction, sense of efficacy, and teachers' extra-role behaviour. *Teaching and Teacher Education*, 16(5–6), 649–59.

Torgersen, S. (2010). The nature (and nurture) of personality disorders. *Scandinavian Journal of Psychology*, 50(6), 624–32.

Wilson, F., Kickul, J. & Marlino, D. (2007). Gender, entrepreneurial self-efficacy, and entrepreneurial career intentions: Implications for entrepreneurship education. *Entrepreneurship Theory and Practice*, 31(3), 387–406.

PRACTITIONER INSIGHT

LEANNE KLAHSEN

SENIOR CONSULTANT (CULTURE)
HUMAN RESOURCES DIVISION,
DEAKIN UNIVERSITY

I commenced my career in Human Resources while still completing my Bachelor of Commerce degree (ironically) at Deakin University, starting with a fixed-term human resource (HR) project-officer role within a large state government department.

Career opportunities were many in the department and I was provided with an excellent grounding across all operational aspects of HR, including WorkCover and Occupational Health and Safety and Critical Incident Stress Management. My work then evolved over time to have more of a focus on more strategic initiatives.

I commenced with Deakin University in July 2007 and have furthered my skills and experience working with colleagues in the areas of culture and behaviour change, performance management, strategy and leadership development to name a few.

I look forward to my future in HR, I have a strong commitment to the work I do and the value it provides to the organisation.

INTERVIEW

What was your first job?

It was a three-month contract role as a Human Resource Project Officer in a state government department when I was in my last semester at University. It was a big decision to commence full-time employment and delay finishing my degree, however it proved to be an excellent opportunity leading to employment with the organisation for over eight years, giving me an excellent grounding in human resource management roles from the operational to the strategic.

What has been your career highlight so far?

It's difficult to narrow down one career highlight given I have had the opportunity to work on a range of exciting and significant initiatives.

One would be working with people affected by the 2002 Bali Bombings through the co-facilitation of a support group. The group included people who had themselves survived the bomb blasts, family and friends of people who were killed and people who directly helped victims in the aftermath. The group ran for over a year and was traumatic, heart-wrenching and inspiring all at the same time. While its main function was to provide psychological support, there was also a lot of work done around group dynamics and organisational behaviour (as it related to individuals workplaces).

In your current role, what does a typical day involve?

(I have responded to this question from the basis of the role I held prior to commencing maternity leave.) Variety! Undertaking regular catch-up meetings with staff, meeting with leaders regarding the organisational performance and culture of their areas, writing briefing papers and reports and analysing organisational needs and developing appropriate supports.

What's the best part of your job?

Working with engaged people who are passionate about what they do; and working with individuals and groups to achieve their best in an environment they want to be a part of and come to everyday.

What is the hardest aspect of your role?

Managing the competing demands and expectations of others, however this can be overcome with clear communication and the development of strong professional relationships.

What are the current challenges facing you, in your role?

Ensuring we continue to provide contemporary HR services which support the 'business' to achieve its objectives in an environment which is going through significant change – but that's also what makes it so exciting.

Do you regularly apply the principles or theories you learnt (when studying organisational behaviour) into your everyday work? In what way?

Yes, however this is mostly now done unconsciously as my experience has grown over the years. When working through planning processes, learning and development activities and cultural change initiatives, understanding organisational behaviour assists greatly.

How important is an understanding of 'organisational behaviour' in today's workplace?

Understanding organisational behaviour contributes to better working relationships and overall organisational performance. For those who are responsible for managing others, it provides great insight and understanding as to how to manage those people most effectively to achieve outcomes.

Is a work–life balance a reasonable expectation in a modern workplace?

Yes it should be.

What strategies do you implement in your workplace to help employees achieve an appropriate work–life balance?

Our organisation has quite an extensive range of flexible work arrangements including flexible start and finish times, part-time and job-share options, generous maternity leave and return-to-work provisions, and 48/52 leave options. Workloads are also negotiated and set-out through both the formal performance review cycle as well as regular review and monitoring.

Has technology impacted on work–life balance? Is it harder to achieve with constant access to the 'office', for example?

Technology can be said to have both positively and negatively impacted work-life balance. It provides greater flexibility to work at home for example and around 'outside' commitments (where the nature of the work allows), however it can also create a perceived pressure of therefore having to always respond to work demands regardless of the time of day or day of the week for example.

Are there greater expectations (on you or your workplace) to help motivate and engage employees in their work than ever before?

Working with our workforce to ensure they are engaged in the organisation's mission, core commitments and strategic objectives is currently a strategic plan goal, however that is not the only reason for undertaking work in this area. A motivated and engaged workforce which has a clear understanding of the flow-through contribution—from an individual to the group to the organisation—is extremely powerful in its impact on performance, employee well-being and motivation.

Motivation and Job Satisfaction

INTRODUCTION

The environment of organisations is globalised, diverse, interconnected and changing. Managers and staff need intelligence, emotional sensitivity and learning ability to be able to adapt and still be productive. Organisational measures such as productivity, absenteeism and staff turnover are indicative of how satisfied and motivated staff may be. The problem is that people are all very different from one another and the things that satisfy or motivate them can vary widely. In addition, it is not always clear that keeping people satisfied is motivating, but then, how can dissatisfied workers be motivated to perform better? There is a lot of conflicting information and a very lucrative consulting industry in the field of workplace motivation. This chapter provides a succinct overview of the theories of **motivation** that have been most widely researched and applied in organisations and proposes new ways of thinking about satisfaction, leadership, learning and **empowerment** as key concepts relevant to improving people management.

■

Motivation
The energy and the processes that provide individuals and groups with direction and perseverance towards their goals.

■

Empowerment
Providing staff with the power to show initiative.

LEARNING OBJECTIVES

Understanding this chapter will help you to
- define motivation
- describe and explain the main content theories of motivation
- describe and explain the main process theories of motivation
- define empowerment
- explain how relational factors can affect motivation
- discuss how theories of leadership and learning connect with motivation theories.

OVERVIEW

Learning Objective
Motivation defined

Chapter 1 raised the question of why people are motivated to work at all and Chapters 2 and 3 emphasised learning and individual difference factors as contributors to attitudes, values and behaviours in relation to work. What exactly is *motivation*? It is the energy and the processes that provide individuals and groups with direction and perseverance towards their goals. From this foundation we are able to survey the theories and concepts that comprise the field of motivation. Humans have fundamental needs as well as processes of thinking and feeling. Theories of

■

Content theory
A motivation theory that describes the contents of human needs.

motivation are traditionally grouped according to the contents of needs (**content theories**) or the processes that are observed in people's minds and emotions (process theories). In the light of new understanding about the complex neural network of organisational life and the continuous dialogue that must take place if learning is to occur appropriately, some combinations of content and process theories appear to be relevant in any given example of a motivated worker.

DOES SATISFACTION LIMIT MOTIVATION?

One thing should be kept clear: the thought of becoming satisfied may be motivating, whereas the event of satisfaction could, at least temporarily, remove the motivation to work any further. This is the essential paradox of the management of motivation in the workplace (Audia et al., 2000). Further, while a sense of satisfaction can come from some of the tasks a person completes at work, the very fact that it is called 'work' and not 'play' refers to the social compulsion that underlies people's jobs (Gorgievskia et al., 2010). When someone is required to do something there is a certain external tension applied. The promise of a reward or a feeling of relief at the conclusion of the required task can contribute to an internal drive towards the objective. When the internal drive leads an individual to successfully achieve the external task, there is a cancelling out of both forces. The individual becomes fleetingly inert (lacking motivation), although feeling satisfied.

The lucky few who genuinely view their work as a kind of play may not experience the same uncomfortable tension that drives workers on towards their goals of satisfaction or relief. However, this may be a semantic difference only. Play is also an activity that demands energy and pushes for the completion of certain goals and objectives. Human activity of any kind is a blend of external and internal forces expressed in various tensions and only when they come into perfect alignment after a period of activity does a feeling of satisfaction emerge.

Thought pathway

The saying 'No pain, no gain' was mentioned in Chapter 2 in relation to resistance to change. Think about the motivational reasons why pain can lead to gain. Are there instances when this would not be the case?

The challenge for managers is to identify the right blend of external factors, such as job design, rewards and other tangible aspects of work with the diverse internal features and aspirations of their staff. Some useful theories and models exist in the motivation literature that can help managers become aware of the right balance of individual human needs and processes of thinking and feeling about work and satisfaction.

NEEDS-BASED MOTIVATION: THE CONTENT THEORISTS

From a range of early psychological research, managers were quick to recognise the usefulness of key observations of the basic needs of humans. The spark that first ignites the internal drive to do something must come from somewhere. There are a number of theories from the 20th century that famously describe the contents of human needs.

Maslow and the needs hierarchy

Learning Objective
The main content theories of motivation

Abraham Maslow started with the fact that humans have to fight for survival. Life is not easy and we have to work at it even to stay alive. For Maslow the survival instinct underpins all others and has to be satisfied before other kinds of needs can progressively become motivating. He conceived of a hierarchy of human needs (Maslow, 1954). Once the physical needs are fulfilled, then we have safety and security needs that drive us most strongly until we are satisfied. The next level in the hierarchy is belonging needs and once they are satisfied we move on to self-esteem or ego needs. Finally we progress to the need for self-actualisation or being the best we can be. Maslow's hierarchy (see Figure 4.1) appears to suggest that one level of needs must be satisfied before the next level begins to dominate motivation behaviour (Maslow, 1962). This has been a criticism of the model. Some have noted that while one might be very hungry, for instance, there can be events linked to higher needs that are perceived by the individual to be more motivating than just the desire to find and eat food (for example feeling shame, or having the chance to win a big prize).

Contrary to the structure of the model, needs on a higher level of the hierarchy may be the dominant motivator at any given moment despite lower needs remaining unfulfilled. Another fact that has added to the critique of Maslow's model is that more than one need exists in people at any moment. The hierarchy implies that only one felt need at a time should occur and this is simply not the practical reality.

Figure 4.1   Maslow's hierarchy of needs

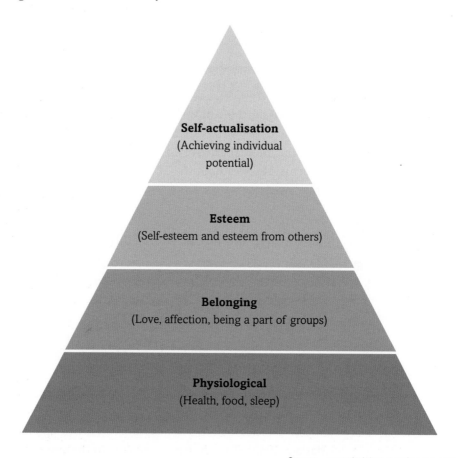

Source: <www.timlebon.com/maslow.htm>

Despite the hierarchical structure of the model being challenged by some research, Maslow's needs are widely accepted as fundamental. Humans of most varieties appear to be moved by the needs he identifies, although the intensity of feeling about the needs, especially the higher ones, can be influenced by cultural, physiological, demographic and other factors of diversity (Kesebir et al., 2010). Theorists coming after Maslow tend to acknowledge this and adapt their models around similar kinds of needs.

WINDOW ON COMMUNICATION

Consequences of interrupted tasks

May 20, 2010

Research from Curtin University of Technology in Perth, Western Australia published in the *Journal of Clinical Nursing* found that three-quarters of nurses working in both the private and public sectors had experienced violence at work, but only one in six incidents were officially reported.

Lead author Dr Rose Chapman said:

'Many of the nurses who took part in the research said that they did not report incidents because they felt that workplace violence was just part of the job.'

The study was based on 113 nurses, the majority of whom were female, in their early 40s and with an average service of about 18 years (ranging from six months to 40 years). Nearly two-thirds worked part-time. Respondents reported 2354 incidents of which 92 per cent involved verbal abuse, 69 per cent physical threats and 52 per cent physical assault. Nurses faced an average of two to 46 incidents a year.

Researchers found that the number and type of incidents varied depending on the health care setting involved: 25 per cent experienced incidents on a weekly basis, 27 per cent about once a month, 25 per cent about once every six months, and the remaining 23 per cent had not experienced violence in the course of their work.

The majority of incidents were reported by nurses working in the emergency department (an average of 46 each in the last 12 months) and mental health (an average of 40 each). The fewest incidents were encountered by those working in midwifery (an average of two each) and in surgery or paediatrics (an average of four each).

Incidents involving a weapon were reported by 40 per cent of respondents including hospital equipment (32 per cent), guns (6 per cent) and knives (3 per cent). Again, the most common settings were emergency (weekly) and mental health (monthly) with 3 per cent of respondents reporting a weekly incident involving violence.

The greater experience of violence was not reflected in official reporting figures. Nurses working in the emergency department were much less likely to report incidents (42 per cent) compared to colleagues working in other specialities (76 per cent).

Overall, only 16 per cent of incidents were reported. About half of those responding had reported incidents verbally to line managers (29 per cent) other senior nurses (14.5 per cent) and/or to friends or colleagues (6 per cent). Half said that senior managers had failed to take effective action when they had reported an incident, 30 per cent did not report because they regarded such events as an inevitable part of their job.

Nearly three-quarters (70 per cent) said they would report an incident that involved injury, the possibility of charges against the perpetrator or a claim for compensation.

Rose Chapman said:

'The nurses in our study were reluctant to report episodes of workplace violence unless they considered the event to be serious. This finding was supported by a retrospective audit of the hospital's formal incident reports, which showed that 96 per cent of the reporting nurses had received one or more injuries as the result of a violent incident in the workplace.

'Understanding why nurses do or do not report incidents is very important as it can help educators and administrators to develop programmes that help to reduce workplace violence. Further research on how individuals adapt to violence in the workplace is also warranted.'

Roger Watson, editor of the *Journal of Clinical Nursing* commented:

'Workplace violence is never acceptable and it is a very sad indictment of society today that so many of the nurses in this study saw these incidents as part of their job. Many of the studies published by the nursing media have focused on public facilities, but this study shows that violence is also an issue when patients are receiving private health care. It is vital that workplace violence is tackled to ensure that healthcare systems are able to retain good quality, trained staff. Any studies that provide an insight into how staff cope with violence, and what influences their decision to report incidents, are to be welcomed.'

PREVIOUS STUDY

Almost one-third of nurses who took part in a large-scale Tasmanian study reported that they had been subjected to both physical and verbal abuse in the previous four working weeks and a quarter had considered resigning as a result, according to research published in the September 2006 issue of the UK-based *Journal of Advanced Nursing*.

The survey was conducted by researchers from the University of Tasmania and was supported by the Australian Nursing Federation. Questionnaires were sent to the 6326 nurses registered with the Nursing Board of Tasmania in late 2002. Some 38 per cent completed the survey, but when this was adjusted for the number of registered nurses actually working during this period, the figure was nearer 55 per cent.

Some form of abuse in the previous four working weeks was reported by two-thirds of the 2407 nurses who took part. This ranged from being sworn at, slapped and spat upon to being bitten, choked and stabbed.

The abused nurses described an average of four verbal incidents and between two and three physical incidents during the period covered.

Of nurses who had been physically abused, 69 per cent had been struck with a hand, fist or elbow and 34 per cent had been bitten. A further 49 per cent said they had been pushed or shoved, 48 per cent had been scratched and 38 per cent spat at. In addition, 6 per cent reported that they had been choked and just less than 1 per cent stabbed.

Verbal abuse was most likely to take the form of rudeness, shouting, sarcasm and swearing. However, 2 per cent said that their home or family had also been threatened. Patients and visitors were the most likely people to abuse nurses, but 4 per cent who reported physical abuse said that it was carried out by another nurse and 3 per cent by a doctor. Of those reporting verbal abuse, 29 per cent said that the perpetrator was a nurse colleague and 27 per cent a doctor.

Lead author Professor Gerald Farrell, now based at La Trobe University School of Nursing and Midwifery in Victoria, Australia, said:

'The present findings point to a work environment that is both distressing and dangerous for staff. Eleven per cent of nurses told us that they had left a post because of aggression and 2 per cent had left nursing completely. Two-thirds of those who experienced aggression said that it affected their productivity or led to errors in their work. Ten per cent said it was the most distressing aspect of their work, after the 51 per cent who cited workload as the biggest problem.

'Another key finding of this research was that although verbal and physical [abuse] spreads across every branch of healthcare from paediatrics to psychiatry and community services to critical care few staff made their complaints official.'

The researchers believe that the restricted time frame of the study and the fact that aggression was carefully defined, with clear distinctions between verbal and physical abuse, may have captured a greater range of incidents than previous studies. The study concludes that workplace aggression is a world-wide problem and further research is needed to discover why levels are so high in modern healthcare settings.

Gerald Farrell continued:

'Our research shows that many nurses are working in environments in which they cannot provide the care that they think is best for patients. At the same time they have to contend with high levels of verbal and physical abuse. It's not surprising that some nurses have left the profession altogether and many more are thinking about it.

'We live in an era when employers are constantly being told that they have a duty of care for employees. It's a sad reality that nurses who spend their lives caring for others and providing such a valuable service continue to feel so vulnerable in the workplace.'

*Source: <www.hrmguide.net/australia/general/
nurses-abuse.htm>*

This Window on Communication reveals the challenges managers can encounter even in the most modern, post-industrial workplaces. Even though safety is identified as a basic human need by Maslow (1954), the taboo about reporting work violence is evident to this day. Some process theories later in this chapter may serve as part of the explanation.

Alderfer and ERG

ERG
Short for Existence-
Relatedness-Growth: the
three levels of human needs
identified by Alderfer.

Clayton Alderfer's theory reduces Maslow's five needs to three: existence, relatedness and growth (ERG) (Alderfer, 1972). **ERG** theory retains a hierarchical approach in that E needs have priority over R needs, which have priority over G needs, though the order of the needs can vary for different people. Here are some other points of note:

- Alderfer suggests there may be an addictive quality to the satisfaction of some needs, that is, when a person starts satisfying higher needs, these can become more intense for the next time.

- In contrast to Maslow, Alderfer's ERG theory allows for different levels of needs to be pursued simultaneously.

- Alderfer identifies a **frustration-regression principle** whereby if a higher-level need remains unfulfilled, the person may revert to trying to satisfy lower-level needs that appear easier to address.

Frustration-regression principle
If a higher-level need remains unfulfilled, the person may revert to trying to satisfy lower-level needs that appear easier to address.

The frustration-regression principle serves as a warning to managers who happen to limit staff or deny them rewards, which may prevent the attainment of higher-order needs. Organisational objectives are normally better served by workers who are fulfilling their relatedness and growth needs rather than regressing to behaviours directed towards fulfilment of lower-order needs. By noting the addictive quality of need satisfaction, Alderfer helps explain why some managers do aspire very strongly to repeatedly perform well. The phenomenon of never being satisfied despite apparently achieving highly could be observed and utilised by astute managers.

Herzberg's two-factor theory

Two-factor theory
Herzberg's theory that two separate categories of human needs create motivator and hygiene effects. The two factors are based on the observation that the opposite of job satisfaction is actually no satisfaction and, on an entirely separate continuum, the opposite of dissatisfaction is no dissatisfaction.

Frederick Herzberg makes an original observation about job satisfaction by pointing out that its opposite is actually no satisfaction. On an entirely separate continuum, dissatisfaction has its opposite of no dissatisfaction. This forms the basis of Herzberg's **two-factor theory** of motivation (Herzberg, 1959). He effectively categorises the higher-order needs of the hierarchy on the satisfaction/no satisfaction continuum and refers to the fulfilment of needs in this context as motivators. So, for example, the worker with needs to do with self-esteem may receive praise from a supervisor for a job well done and this would have a motivating effect. The lower-order needs Herzberg places on the dissatisfaction/no dissatisfaction continuum and refers to need fulfilment there serving a function of maintenance or hygiene. So, for example, the worker with needs to do with physical warmth in the office may be given a new heater and this would maintain the worker's disposition to continue to work but would not necessarily be motivating for them to strive for continuous improvement.

Figure 4.2 Comparison of satisfiers and dissatisfiers

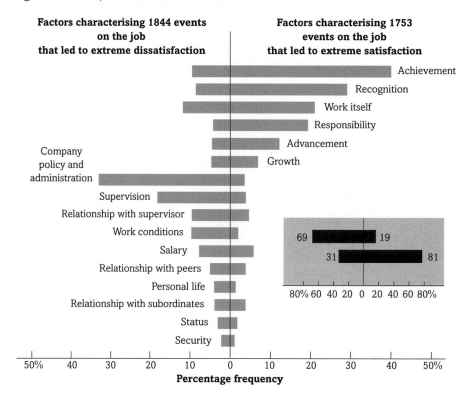

Source: Harvard Business Review, reproduced by permission. "Comparison of Satisfiers and Dissatisfiers" An exhibit from One More Time: How Do You Motivate Employees? By Frederick Herzberg, Jan 2003. Copyright © 2003.

The implications of Herzberg's study resonate at a practical level for managers (Lundberg et al., 2009). He identified sets of management actions that could be classified as either motivators or maintenance (hygiene) factors. Motivational actions include providing for staff a range of opportunities for:

- responsibility
- recognition
- promotion
- achievement.

Hygiene actions remain important but should be recognised for not being motivating in and of themselves. Hygiene actions mean paying good attention to:

- supervision
- salary
- work environment
- organisational policies
- staff relational factors.

The model raises serious debate about contemporary issues, such as the level of salary for senior managers. Consider that Herzberg identified salary as a hygiene factor rather than a motivator and you will begin to understand why, beyond the level at which salary is sufficient to take care of the lower-order physiological and safety needs, additional money does not necessarily motivate someone to work harder or better.

WINDOW ON ETHICS

Workplace bullying case 'worst ever seen'

BEN SCHNEIDERS

Dean Hutchinson's claims of workplace bullying are disturbing.

When Dean Hutchinson looked up from his tools, a piece of wood about 30 centimetres long smacked into his temple.

The strongly built labourer fell to the ground and the laughter of his workmates washed over him. Mr Hutchinson, 21, felt dazed from the incident, which happened last month, and could not see straight, but pretended to keep working. Later, he vomited.

The claims by Mr Hutchinson of workplace bullying at a Sunbury company that makes building frames have been described by a senior union leader as the most serious he has seen.

In interviews with *The Age* Mr Hutchinson has alleged:

- A supervisor regularly fired a nail gun at staff and pretended to fire a nail gun at close range, without saying it was empty.
- Mr Hutchinson had his thumb broken and a wrist broken in two places in a machine, two weeks after warning his boss that it was dangerous.
- He had his pay docked after taking to hospital a colleague who had shot himself in the leg with a nail gun.
- The supervisor would throw wood or hard cardboard at staff nearly every day.
- No fans were provided in summer and staff were banned from bringing their own fans as it would use electricity.
- No safety gear or glasses were provided. Mr Hutchinson's tools were covered in sap by a supervisor and would be stolen and hidden.
- Staff were forced to pay inflated rates for safety equipment from the boss, Danny Schneider, including as much as $8 for a pencil.
- Pay was regularly docked for taking too long on a task, or cleaning tools, and Mr Hutchinson and other staff were regularly abused.
- Staff were warned not to join a union.

Sources have confirmed key parts of the account, but Mr Schneider, the co-owner of Sunbury Wall Frames & Trusses, said he completely rejected all the allegations.

There are also claims that letters sent to the homes of at least four workers by the Australian Electoral Commission were ripped open or tampered with. They included ballot papers on whether to have an enterprise agreement at the workplace.

On April 6, the day after nine staff signed a ballot asking for a union agreement, six of the same people signed another petition rejecting an agreement. The second petition was signed by Rob Guthrie, the Macedon Ranges mayor, who wrote that there was no coercion from the boss. He did not disclose that he was also an employee of the firm but defended this later, saying he wanted to give it as much credibility as he could by signing as a councillor.

The company this week won that ballot six votes to three with four employees not voting.

Mr Schneider, who is being represented by the Victorian Employers Chamber of Commerce and Industry, said that Gisborne police had told him they had no record of an alleged assault at his factory.

But *The Age* has confirmed that police had been notified of the allegations by Mr Hutchinson and it is believed police referred them to the furnishing products division of the Construction, Forestry, Mining and Energy Union.

The union is to launch an 'adverse action' against the employer for breach of workplace rights. WorkSafe is investigating the bullying claims.

Mr Hutchinson, who is on WorkCover, started work at the company in mid-2008 and said the factory was a revolving door, with staff hired on the spot. He said he helped train more than 30 people but most left quickly with fewer than a dozen workers in his part of the business.

Speaking with his father next to him, he said he stayed in the job because he 'always wanted to be a builder' and he wanted to make the 'best of what I've got'. He said nothing ever came of promises from Mr Schneider for him to be trained.

The bullying had a serious emotional effect on him, he said; abuse from Mr Schneider started in his first week.

CFMEU furnishing products secretary Leo Skourdoumbis described it as the worst bullying case he had seen in his 20 years as a union official and accused the employer of exploiting a workforce.

Mr Schneider said his was a 'small, regional, family-run business who looks after its employees'. He said he would welcome a WorkSafe investigation and said sworn statements by employees used in a hearing at Fair Work Australia last week had rejected Mr Hutchinson's earlier claims.

Source: <www.theage.com.au/small-business/managing/workplace-bullying-case-worst-ever-seen-20100428-tshs.html>

This Window on Ethics is a sad indictment of the supervisor. Herzberg (2003) includes good supervision as a hygiene factor and one can imagine that if this supervisor simply stopped inflicting physical violence on the labourer this would help maintain his desire to return to the job, but would by no means create an environment that would really motivate the labourer to higher and better overall performance at work. A far more motivating scenario would be to have a supervisor prepared to give the labourer a sense of responsibility, positively recognise his good work, and offer opportunities for promotion and training, as well as other avenues for continued achievement.

McClelland and acquired needs

David McClelland makes the assertion that specific needs are acquired over time and are shaped by a person's early life experiences (McClelland, 1955). He goes straight to the acquired higher-order needs as the primary sources of work motivation. He acknowledges the higher-order ego and categorises this as the need for achievement (n-ach). Social needs identified by Maslow and others are also relevant to McClelland, who categorises this as the need for affiliation (n-aff). Then he adds the need for power (n-pow) into the mix (McClelland, 1975).

Thought pathway

Some people appear to shun responsibility and dislike the idea that they should have any kind of power over other people. If McClelland is right and having a sense of power is a motivating human need, consider what could be the reasons why some people avoid responsibility.

Not many motivation theories are so explicit about the human need for power or authority over others, but this aspect of McClelland's work tends to be borne out by the findings of sociologist Stanley Milgram in the Milgram experiments and psychologist Philip Zimbardo in the Stanford Prison experiments, which acknowledge the prevalence of power and control in social situations and warn of how easy it is to slip into abusing acquired power. Chapter 9 covers the organisational behaviour issues associated with power, control and authority.

SITUATION-BASED MOTIVATION: THE PROCESS THEORISTS

■

Learning Objective
The main process
theories of motivation

While human needs are fairly consistent, there is still some cross-cultural variation and the models do not always explain why people choose to behave in some ways when alternatives for need satisfaction may be available. It was realised that the situation itself can affect motivation behaviour and that the process of thinking about one's work situation can be studied for a clearer understanding of why certain actions are chosen. There are three widely researched and applied process theories of motivation that deserve the attention of people managers: goal-setting theory, expectancy theory and equity theory.

Locke: Goal-setting theory

Edwin Locke identifies that specific and challenging goals lead to higher performance than easy or no goals (Locke, 1964). A lack of clarity and challenge tends to leave the individual or the group adrift. Goals, rather self-evidently, help us to focus efforts in a specific direction. It is a clear example of how our very own thought processes impact heavily on the level of motivation that we have. If we are not thinking clearly and purposefully about our jobs, we will be unable to follow through and achieve what the organisation requires. This theory helps to explain why strategic planning is so important for organisations. It also acts as the underpinning for the leadership approach of Management by Objectives (MBO). In addition, performance appraisal systems are predicated on the idea that goals need to be established and monitored in line with the mission and objectives cascading from the top of the organisation. If performance appraisal is organised effectively (which unfortunately it rarely is) it will capitalise on the premise of goal-setting theory and have a motivating effect on staff.

WINDOW ON DECISION-MAKING

Media room—media releases

RADIO AUSTRALIA
April 30, 1997

The Chairman of the ABC Board, Donald McDonald, today said that the Board welcomed the Government's decision to contribute to the maintenance of a core service for Radio Australia.

The Government has indicated that it is prepared to fund English language and Tok Pisin Radio Australia services delivered by satellite and short-wave.

It has also indicated that this money would be given to the ABC in addition to its base appropriation.

Mr McDonald said that the Board had decided it would build on this funding, extending the minimalist service beyond English and Tok Pisin to include Bahasa Indonesian, Mandarin, Khmer and Vietnamese.

'This service, which will continue to reach a broad population base, maintains a strategic focus for the ABC's international broadcasting. 'The total programming cost would be around $6 million—less than half the current cost of existing services,' Mr McDonald said. 'We regret that we have not been able to maintain the current level of programming to all of our regional audiences, as we also regret the inevitable impact on committed long-serving Radio Australia staff.

'The widespread concern about Radio Australia's future reflects the valued place of the service within the region.

'Nevertheless, this decision will ensure that the ABC maintains a significant broadcasting presence in the Asia Pacific region.

'There is potential to enhance the future role of Radio Australia through, for instance, collaboration with the education sector in delivering services internationally.

'Today's decision by the Board will allow us to explore such possibilities.'

Mr McDonald said the Board could not make a decision on domestic services until it had received firm advice from Government about its base appropriation.

'These decisions will be made at a special Board meeting on 15 May after the Federal Budget is handed down,' he said.

'Clearly, the Board still has real concerns that the ABC's base funding will fall short of the minimum $500 million which the ABC requires to maintain existing domestic services. 'Cuts to these services would be fiercely resisted by our audiences.'

At its Melbourne meeting today, the Board also expressed its deep concern about industrial action undertaken by the Community Public Sector Union and the Media Entertainment and Arts Alliance.

'The ABC must always put its audiences first,' Mr McDonald said.

'While the Board understands the anxieties of staff about the changes which the ABC is facing, disruption of programs cannot be supported.'

Mr McDonald said that the Board was committed to the restructuring directions which had been jointly developed with ABC management.

'We will continue to drive the implementation of changes which will place the ABC in the strongest position possible, within its funding constraints, to meet the challenges of the new media age,' Mr McDonald said.

'ABC management will continue to honour the process of consultation with staff and unions in the implementation of the changes.'

Source: <www.abc.net.au/corp/pubs/media/ s508552.htm>

This Window indicates how decision-making has a cascading effect on organisational goals at the strategic level and right down to the individuals who have to work with the effects of decisions at the customer interface. Motivated action is pre-empted by decision-making and goal-setting. The performance of people at work rests on utilising key performance indicators as benchmarks.

Expectancy theory
The theory that people approach their work with expectancies about individual performance, organisational rewards and personal goals; and the nature of the effort–performance relationship, performance–reward relationship and the rewards–personal goals relationship that help determine the level of individual motivation.

Vroom: Expectancy theory

Extending the understanding of how goals are achieved, Victor Vroom (1964) observes that people approach their work with certain expectations about how they will do it and what the outcomes will be. These expectations develop at key stages during the process of determining whether a job is worth pursuing. Vroom refers to the four factors of individual effort, individual performance, organisational rewards and personal goals. The relationships between these factors are important and identified as the effort–performance relationship, performance–reward relationship and the rewards–personal goals relationship. Figure 4.2 illustrates the factors and relationships in **expectancy theory**.

Figure 4.3 Expectancy theory

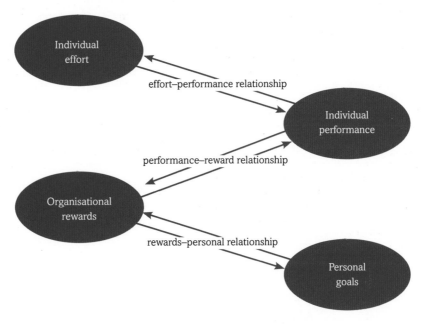

Expectation (E)
A factor in expectancy
theory that measures
a person's expectation
about whether individual
effort will lead to
successful performance of
the task.

Instrumentality (I)
A factor in expectancy
theory that measures
how confident a person
is that performance of
a task will lead to an
appropriate reward from
the organisation.

Valence (V)
A factor in expectancy
theory that measures
the expectation that
organisational rewards
are aligned with the
personal goals a person
has in mind.

At each stage the individual develops types of **expectation**. First, there is an expectation about whether individual effort will lead to successful performance of the task. The more a person believes their effort will lead to performance, the more motivated they will be to engage. The next stage asks how confident the person is that performance of the task will lead to a reward from the organisation; if such expectation is high, so will be motivation. This is referred to as **instrumentality**. Next is the expectation that organisational rewards are aligned with the personal goals a person has in mind; this reward–personal goals relationship is called **valence** by Vroom. Expectancy theory says that if an individual's expectations are high at each stage, motivation will be maximised but, of course, there is every chance that one or more of the relationships between expectancy factors will fall short, and this is the explanation for any diminishment of motivation. For example, a new young worker at the supermarket checkout may have a high effort–performance expectation, and also feel comfortable with their promised first pay slip (a high performance–reward relationship) because it matches with what their friends earn in the same industry. However, they may find the reward–personal goals relationship is below expectation, especially if they do some shopping around on the new sports car they want to buy. There are many other possible combinations of expectancies. For instance, sometimes people do not feel they have the requisite skills to complete tasks they have been given, or, sometimes completing a difficult task does not lead to the reward an individual was hoping for. This theory can be presented as a probability equation. The effort–performance relationship is the primary expectancy (E), the performance–reward relationship is instrumentality (I) and the rewards–personal goals relationship is valence (V), therefore:

Motivation = E x I x V

Expressing the multiplier effect in this way reveals the significant positive or negative motivation effects that can occur in each stage of the cognitive process.

Thought pathway

Consider the extent to which your work aligns at all with your personal goals. If you can truly say your life is aligned with your work, think about the positive and negative implications.

To maximise workforce motivation, expectancy theory says managers have to be sure all three relationships in the model are functioning at the highest number of factors possible (Vancouver, 2008).

Adams: Equity theory

The question arises about where our expectations about work come from? John Stacey Adams (1965) draws attention to the ways that people compare their situations with each other. Four comparison (referent) situations are possible:

- self inside
- self outside
- other inside
- other outside.

This simply means that a person working in a particular organisation constantly checks up on others doing similar work within the same organisation as well as those in similar positions in other organisations. This is in addition to the individual comparing their own current work to other jobs they could be doing in their organisation, as well as similar jobs in other organisations.

Equity theory
A process theory that identifies not only the comparisons individuals make about their jobs inside and outside their organisation but also the options for behavioural responses to those comparisons.

The trouble with all of this self-reflection and comparison with others is that people can often feel inequity as a result. It is common for there to be differentials in workloads, pay and alternative reward outcomes within and between organisations. Even where the real differences may be small, sometimes misperceptions can occur and make the differences seem large. When people feel they are currently doing better in terms of workload and reward than if they were in another position, this is positive inequity and it is very motivating. Alternatively, when people feel they are worse off than others, this is negative inequity and it can be quite demoralising. **Equity theory**, therefore, identifies not only comparisons individuals make inside and outside their organisation but also the options for behavioural responses to those comparisons. A sense of inequity moves an individual to action. Six behavioural options emerge when inequity is perceived:

- reduce effort
- work harder to increase conditional reward (e.g. piece rate pay)
- change perceptions about self (I used to think I was a hard worker, now I know I slack off a bit compared with them)
- change perceptions about others (e.g. her job is not as good as I thought it was)
- compare with someone else
- quit the job.

Managers need to be aware of these thoughts and behaviours, which may be occurring more often than many people think. Awareness of the comparative pay and workload of positions within the organisations and in the industry as a whole helps managers make informed decisions about rewards given for particular jobs. Where misperceptions about job comparisons are part of the picture, the manager can educate staff further about the reality of the situation.

Thought pathway

Think about how regularly you compare the things you do at work with others.

■

Organisational justice
The overall perception of what is equitable in the workplace.

The concept of **organisational justice** intersects with equity theory (Greenberg, 1987; Goncalo & Kim, 2010). People need to feel that rewards are distributed fairly, that procedures are followed with balance, and that interactions with supervisors and peers occur with respect, trust and dignity (Fincham & Rhodes, 2005). As equity theory suggests, there are many individual permutations for how this feeling of justice may manifest. The overall perception of what is equitable in the workplace contributes to organisational justice.

CASE STUDY

Avoiding staff turnover in boring jobs

Vicki Green's resignation didn't really surprise Harold. He knew she was bored and typically he only managed to keep these girls in the job for about a year or two. The job was mundane and he usually wound up recruiting girls who had no formal qualifications and no real career aspirations. A few years' work was all he really expected before they moved on to something else—usually at a similar level in a different company or off to get married.

'Here we go again,' he thought, 'a string of people from Centrelink, another week wasted sorting them out and trying to find someone who will put up with the monotony of entering purchase requisitions into the ordering system.'

Harold Simpson has been Procurement Manager for Thompson Components for over 20 years. The Company sourced electronic components for the automotive industry so relied on speed and reliability of supply to keep customers.

He was aware these clerks found there was no challenge in the job but he couldn't understand why they didn't just stick it out for a bit longer, learn the business and then maybe he could promote them to the position of Procurement Officer. That's how he made it to the top. 'They don't make them like they used to,' he was always fond of saying.

He always warned the new employee that it was boring so they wouldn't get any surprises and be disappointed. They seemed to accept this and tell him they would be happy to take it on. 'Maybe they say that just to get the job,' he pondered, 'after all we do pay fairly well and it is a very nice office to work in.' Harold had been a key player in the move to the new Head Office and the fitting out. He even made sure it had a good coffee machine. Having spent many years in the old offices, which were fairly antiquated, he couldn't understand how people could leave this place.

The job was mainly receiving orders from the branches by email and entering them into an ordering system that was then used to place orders with suppliers. It was an important task because the orders had to be correct. If there were mistakes it could cause delays in their customers' manufacturing operations and potentially cost significant amounts. A few mistakes with the same customer could cause them to change suppliers and Thompson would lose business. However, he also knew it was repetitive work. He tried to give them a bit of variety by having them do a few odd jobs around the office such as filing or reconciling some end-of-year accounts with suppliers. But if they were good enough to be reliable and accurate they were soon looking for something else and were gone.

He had thought for a while that the re-entering of information from emails into the system manually was not very efficient but things were so hectic he had no time to stop and change the process. He realised that it would not be that difficult to develop a procedure where branches could directly input orders. This would save time in Head Office, probably be even more efficient at branches and remove a step that was prone to errors. However, he considered none of the people who had been in the position in the past would be capable of doing the job and changing the system as well.

Now he was under pressure from his Manager because of staff turnover. Someone had calculated how much it really cost to lose someone, recruit and then retrain. He was told he had to 'change his management style'. 'After all these years, now they tell me!' he thought.

CASE STUDY QUESTIONS

1 Using Vroom's Expectancy Theory, describe how Vicki Green's thought processes may have progressed from when she applied for the job until she resigned.

2 Referring to Maslow and Herzberg's theories and others, how would you have managed Vicki and the previous employees to have them stay, and perform, in the job.

3 If your view of managing people is different from Harold's, describe how it differs. If it is the same, describe how you think things are going wrong for him.

4 If Harold is going to change his management style, as requested by his Manager, how would you help him do this? Which three sections from the chapter do you think he would find most useful and enlightening? Why?

5 Now he has a vacancy to fill, how can Harold take the opportunity to make some changes? If he read the section on empowerment, how might he use this?

EMPOWERMENT

Learning Objective
Empowerment

Chapter 3 identifies the personality trait of self-efficacy as a feeling of control that arrives by having experiences of situations where one is able to direct and achieve things (Wilson et al., 2007). It is a combination of predispositions and work environment inputs that determines how empowered one feels. Managers are faced with a dilemma when it comes to allocating work tasks to staff. Needs theories suggest that empowering people to do certain tasks can be motivating; however, a process perspective such as equity theory explains how a worker's comparison with others, internally and externally, may affect their willingness do more. The fact that motivation itself derives from a blend of internal feelings (intrinsic factors), external stimulus (extrinsic factors) and cognitive processes makes for a level of uncertainty about relying on any one initiative to try to motivate an entire workforce (Moynihan, 2010). Providing staff with the power to show initiative can certainly satisfy some higher-order needs but sometimes situational factors such as perceptions of equity, expectations about workload and work–family balance, and relationship issues in the workplace can dampen the effects.

WINDOW ON CONFLICT AND NEGOTIATION

In the middle of DJ's disgrace

ALAN KOHLER

Every corporate middle manager should read Kristy Fraser-Kirk's statement of claim against David Jones as a guide to how not to react when you're caught between your boss's rampant libido and a staff member.

In some ways the shocking punitive damages claimed by Fraser-Kirk and her lawyer, Harmer's, for 5 per cent of DJ's profits while Mark McInnes was CEO ($35 million) and another 5 per cent of McInnes' salary ($2 million) are a distraction from the substance of this case.

That substance is not only about the behaviour of McInnes, but also that of the managers standing between him and his target.

Those three people are also the victims in this affair because they don't appear to have had clear guidelines on how they should react. They were the board's front-line troops in this affair and they let the company down, but if they hadn't been told what to do when the boss gropes a staff member then they have been let down as well.

According to Fraser-Kirk's statement of claim, the problems began on May 23 this year when, at a lunch, and in full view of everyone else, McInnes suggested she try a dessert because it's 'like a f★★★ in the mouth', then put his hand under her clothes, invited her to his apartment in Bondi and gave her a hug while repeating the invitation.

According to the statement, her immediate supervisor Tahli Koch, and the PR General Manager, Anne-Maree Kelly, both saw what happened, and when Fraser-Kirk made an official report to them, they confirmed that.

It's alleged Kelly told Fraser-Kirk: 'next time that happens, just say no to Mark and he'll back off'.

Fraser-Kirk alleges that over the next four days McInnes sent her a series of emails, repeating the invitation to Bondi.

On June 7, Fraser-Kirk had to go to another function where Mark McInnes was present. He took up where he left off, according to the statement, inviting her to Bondi, trying to kiss her and then once again putting his hand under her clothes.

The next day he rang her up and allegedly said: 'I could have had guaranteed sex with that brunette last night but I wanted you', and then followed up with a text message.

The day after that, Fraser-Kirk reported the matter to her boss, Anne-Maree Kelly, who, according to the statement, said other employees had been harassed by McInnes in the past, and said she would speak to her boss, Damian Eales, group general manager—financial services and marketing.

According to the statement, Fraser-Kirk then met with Eales and Kelly and they told her to go home. There was talk of a meeting with McInnes, which suggests that Eales had spoken to the CEO. That night Fraser-Kirk got a text message from McInnes saying 'I want you to have a fantastic career at David Jones'.

The next day she went to Harmers and then she and DJs began communicating through lawyers. On June 11, DJs lawyers told her lawyers that McInnes [had] been instructed to make no further contact with Fraser-Kirk, but on June 14 there were two voicemails and five text messages, starting at 8.08am and finishing at 8.30pm.

Four days after that McInnes was gone—and was paid a settlement of $1.5 million.

Clearly, McInnes deserved the sack and probably shouldn't have got any money at all. Whether the directors also behaved badly in the situation depends on what they knew and when they knew it; it is possible that none of them knew McInnes was not apparently fully in control of his libido, if I can put it that way, but it doesn't sound likely.

More interesting, in my view, were the alleged actions of Damian Eales, Anne-Maree Kelly and Tahli Koch, and the board's responsibility to protect them, not just Kristy Fraser-Kirk.

It seems that they had an out-of-control CEO who, according to the statement of claim, has a history of bullying, and they have a staffer complaining about harassment. What to do?

The answer is: it must go straight to the person's superior, whoever it is—in this case the chairman. To protect [the] middle manager caught in the middle this must be clearly set out as company policy, so there is no choice in the matter: every sexual harassment complaint must be elevated immediately to the alleged harasser's superior.

That is not to pre-judge the matter, but to protect the manager to whom the complaint has been made. Clearly, Eales should have gone to Bob Savage on June 10, not McInnes, and there should have been a company policy in place that instructed him to do that.

Earlier than that, Anne-Maree Kelly should have told Eales about it on May 24, and it should have been elevated to Savage then.

Whether Kristy Fraser-Kirk's nominated charity gets a big lump of money from David Jones or not, this case should set the standard for a board's responsibility to provide clear guidance for middle managers.

Source: <www.businessspectator.com.au/bs.nsf/ Article/David-Jones-DJS-McInnes-Kirsty-Fraser-Kirk- sexual--pd20100803-7XT5X?opendocument&src=rss>

This Window on a conflict situation illustrates the delicate balance that exists in manager–subordinate relationships in the workplace. It can become very difficult to separate the responsibilities and obligations of the different people in such circumstances. From a motivation perspective, actions in the case are variously driven by a blend of needs and process factors. The case is one where the CEO felt empowered to act a certain way and the staff member felt powerless in response. Senior executives may also have allowed the complex relationships in the case to affect their motivation to behave in ways that may have delivered different outcomes.

WORK–FAMILY BALANCE AND RELATIONAL FACTORS AT WORK

Learning Objective
How relational factors can affect motivation

The social and relational needs of people exist within the workplace and beyond it. Most of the content and process theories of motivation acknowledge the role of good relationships. There is a kind of halo effect when something especially motivating happens at work; you may find yourself going home and spreading your general happiness and drive with your friends or family. Inversely, when your relationships at home are firing you up and keeping you motivated, your energies in the workplace can also be noticeably higher (Bianchi & Milkie, 2010; Burke, 2010).

The adoption in recent decades of networked mobile communication and information-processing technology has made people readily accessible across the boundaries of work and family (Wajcman et al., 2010). Knowing exactly where the line should be drawn or how to cut off when work demands your attention at home (or when family demands your attention at work) is increasingly difficult. Understanding that motivation can be affected by events in either the work or family realms does not make the manager's task easier, but it can highlight possible sources of issues when motivation problems are not responding to actions in individual cases.

Learning and reinforcement through leadership

Learning Objective
How theories of leadership and learning connect with motivation theories

Process theory
A motivation theory that describes the processes that are observed in people's minds and emotions.

The complex interactions that occur in the modern workplace demand a sophisticated approach to management for improved worker motivation. Any one needs-based theory, or **process theory**, will be insufficient on its own to explain why some workers are motivated and other are not. There is much that is unknown and much that can be learned in a continuous fashion by leaders to improve professional practice. Chapter 2 introduces learning and reinforcement as tools through which behaviour can be modified. Motivation is expressed by individuals and groups through socialised behaviour and this makes learning an essential component of the experience. Leaders and immediate supervisors play a critical role in providing the kinds of immediate feedback that serve to reinforce the behaviours an organisation wants to see.

Thought pathway

Think about those times where a leader has made a decision that really motivated you. Also reflect on the time when a leader's decision frustrated you and made you lose motivation for a job or task.

The ideal of the learning organisation is elusive unless leaders create the vision and the impetus to bring the vision to reality. Chapter 6 covers leadership theory and serves to explain the link between leaders, their styles and behaviours, and overall workplace motivation.

CASE STUDY

Two different kinds of motivation

Milford Construction is a large construction business that usually has several projects under way at one time. These could be major buildings, roads, bridges or tunnels. The Head Office has over 200 employees and each project recruits contractors or takes established Milford employees according to the needs of the project.

Greg Osborne is the Financial Controller in HO and has recently filled two vacancies for accountants. He managed to find two excellent people but he senses they are quite different and isn't sure how to manage them.

Margaret Knight is 26. She graduated at 21 in business, did some overseas travel and then worked for one of the big four accounting firms. When Greg was recruiting her she asked a lot of questions about the career prospects and the practice Milford has of moving staff among the projects. She seemed particularly interested in obtaining exposure to different aspects of the Company, learning as much as she could about the industry and advancing her career. She volunteered to Greg that she was single, had enjoyed her travel and was very flexible about where she worked. She is living with her parents and is enjoying a good social life.

Greg found her technical abilities very good and decided she could slot in to most parts of the business over time and so would be a very valuable long-term asset.

Greg's other star recruit was Michael Sanchez. He had emigrated from the Philippines when he was only 20, studied business and accounting and had worked for the same major manufacturing business for over ten years. He had worked in various parts of the business and gained some excellent skills and experience. Unfortunately he was in a part of the business at a time when it suffered a major setback and was closed down. There were no other opportunities within the business and he was made redundant.

While he had some savings at the time, it was a shock for him as he was married and had a young child. He had also recently bought a house and had quite a large mortgage. He was very proud of his achievements as he had come from a very disadvantaged background in the Philippines.

Greg had Michael and Margaret working with him in Head Office and was very pleased with both of them. In fact he was so pleased he worried about losing them. He paid them as close to the top end of the salary grade as he could and made sure they were told of all the training that was available—both technical and management.

Margaret grabbed every training opportunity there was and actively interacted with people in all parts of the business. She regularly asked Michael how the key projects were progressing from an accounting perspective and seemed to pick up a lot of the technical information on them from people she interacted with.

In addition to her work commitments, she is also a regular at the gym and has undertaken a photography course.

Michael was different. He was technically excellent and worked hard. He took on training that directly related to his accounting duties and introduced several improvements in his area of responsibility. While he was very pleasant to all he came into contact with he did not necessarily go out of his way to socialise with others at work.

When Greg had his performance management sessions with them he thought he would like to get an understanding of what they were after in their careers as he wanted to make sure he was managing them appropriately. He was also aware that he would be sitting down with the rest of the senior management in a few weeks to do succession planning and he wanted to make sure he could put the right information into the department's plans.

When asked how he saw the next few years at Milford for his career, Michael replied, 'I just want to really get on top of my current area and implement the very best systems so we can be productive and keep costs down.' He added that 'I'm very happy with the way things are progressing. How do you think I'm going?' He seemed

very relieved when Greg told him he was very happy with his performance and was really looking at what his next move might be. 'Ah no,' Michael said, 'don't worry about that, I'm very happy where I am.'

Margaret had a different response to Greg's questions. 'I'd like to get onto one of the projects if it was possible,' she said. Greg was worried that he might lose her and have to recruit again. 'There's really no guarantee what job you would get when the project finishes,' he pointed out. 'That's OK,' she responded quickly, 'I'll take my chances. I just think that if I get a few projects under my belt I may be of more use in Head Office and be able to progress faster.' 'It's all very well to aim high,' thought Greg, 'but I think you need to keep your feet on the ground. Some of those engineers will have you strung up if you make mistakes out there.'

Greg locked himself in his office for the afternoon to write up his notes on the performance management sessions and prepare for the succession planning meeting.

They were both good accountants and he didn't want to lose them from the business. He didn't want to have Michael get bored by keeping him in the same job and he didn't want to lose Margaret by not letting her gain the experiences she wanted or having her join a project and then possibly leave the business if that didn't work out well. If only he could be really sure of what they wanted.

CASE STUDY QUESTIONS

1 With reference to the section on 'Needs-based motivation: The content theorists', explain where you think Michael and Margaret differ in their needs.

2 If you think there are differences in Michael and Margaret's needs, explain how you think these arose. If you think there are no fundamental differences, explain why their responses to Greg's questions were different.

3 With reference to the section on 'Situation-based motivation: The process theorists', explain how you think Greg may go about motivating Michael to take on a more ambitious career path.

4 How do you think Greg can maintain Margaret's motivation but shield her from trying to go too far, too fast, and coming unstuck. Is he being too protective and should she just learn from any mistakes she makes?

5 At the succession planning meeting, when he is asked what the potential is for Margaret and Michael, how do you think he should respond?

CONCLUSION

Motivation theories have been categorised as needs-based or process-based. The fundamental human needs outlined by Maslow and redefined by Alderfer, Herzberg, McClelland and many others are useful for managers but they do not offer a full explanation of the key indicators of motivation: productivity, absenteeism and staff turnover. The cognitive processes of goal-setting, establishing expectations and then comparing work situations and outcomes with others are also powerful drivers or inhibitors of workplace behaviour. In the contemporary environment, process theories such as equity theory and expectancy theory are more widely supported by research findings; however, needs-based understanding of workers continues to be relevant and helpful for managers seeking to understand the drivers of motivation. Ultimately, the factors of motivation and job satisfaction are closely related to overall job design and workflow planning. The next few chapters turn to issues of group and team dynamics, leadership, and power, control and influence. These are all relational factors in the workplace which, if handled well, lead to a much greater likelihood that human needs and cognitive processes are satisfied to the extent that staff motivation will be sufficient and sustainable.

KEY POINTS

This chapter has

- defined motivation
- described and explained the main content theories of motivation
- described and explained the main process theories of motivation
- defined empowerment
- explained how relational factors can affect motivation
- discussed how theories of leadership and learning connect with motivation theories.

KEY TERMS

CONTENT THEORY
A motivation theory that describes the contents of human needs.

EMPOWERMENT
Providing staff with the power to show initiative.

EQUITY THEORY
A process theory that identifies not only the comparisons individuals make about their jobs inside and outside their organisation but also the options for behavioural responses to those comparisons.

**STUDY AND
REVISION
QUESTIONS**

ERG
Short for Existence-Relatedness-Growth: the three levels of human needs identified by Alderfer.

EXPECTANCY THEORY
The theory that people approach their work with expectancies about individual performance, organisational rewards and personal goals; and the nature of the effort–performance relationship, performance–reward relationship and the rewards–personal goals relationship that help determine the level of individual motivation.

EXPECTATION (E)
A factor in expectancy theory that measures a person's expectation about whether individual effort will lead to successful performance of the task.

FRUSTRATION-REGRESSION PRINCIPLE
Alderfer identifies the frustration-regression principle whereby if a higher-level need remains unfulfilled, the person may revert to trying to satisfy lower-level needs that appear easier to address.

INSTRUMENTALITY (I)
A factor in expectancy theory that measures how confident a person is that performance of a task will lead to an appropriate reward from the organisation.

ORGANISATIONAL JUSTICE
The overall perception of what is equitable in the workplace.

PROCESS THEORY
A motivation theory that describes the processes that are observed in people's minds and emotions.

TWO-FACTOR THEORY
Herzberg's theory that two separate categories of human needs create motivator and hygiene effects. The two factors are based on the observation that the opposite of job satisfaction is actually no satisfaction and, on an entirely separate continuum, the opposite of dissatisfaction is no dissatisfaction.

VALENCE (V)
A factor in expectancy theory that measures the expectation that organisational rewards are aligned with the personal goals a person has in mind.

Q *'The phenomenon of never being satisfied despite apparently achieving highly could be observed and utilised by astute managers.' What does this observation mean? Discuss the implications with reference to theory.*

Q *Explain why performance appraisal systems should, according to theory, be quite motivating for staff at all levels in the organisation.*

Q *Think of a line supervisor working in a car manufacturing facility who has just learned that the same position in a facility owned by a competitor attracts a salary that is $5000 higher and has a better superannuation contribution. Write scenarios for each of the possible actions this person could take for the six behavioural options suggested by equity theory:*
- *Reduce effort*
- *Work harder to increase conditional reward*

- *Change perceptions about self*
- *Change perceptions about others*
- *Compare with someone else*
- *Quit the job.*

Which one of your scenarios would you choose and why?

Q *Discuss whether as a leader you can realistically choose one of the motivation theories and apply this as your catch-all tool for improving worker satisfaction and performance.*

REFERENCES

Adams, J. S. (1965). Inequity in social exchange. In L. Berkowitz (ed.), *Advances in experimental social psychology*, vol. 2. New York: Academic Press, pp. 267–99

Alderfer, C. P. (1972). *Existence, relatedness, and growth: Human needs in organizational settings.* New York: The Free Press.

Audia, P., Locke, E. & Smith, R. (2000). The paradox of success: An archival and a laboratory study of strategic persistence following radical environmental change. *Academy of Management Journal*, 43(5), 837–53.

Bianchi, S., & Milkie, M. (2010). Work and family research in the first decade of the 21st century. *Journal of Marriage and Family*, 72(6), 705–25.

Burke, R. (2010). Do managerial men benefit from organizational values supporting work–personal life balance? *Gender in Management: An International Journal*, 25(2), 91–9.

Fincham, R., & Rhodes, P. S. (2005). *Principles of organizational behaviour.* Oxford: Oxford University Press.

Goncalo, J. & Kim, S. (2010). Distributive justice beliefs and group idea generation: Does a belief in equity facilitate productivity? *Journal of Experimental Social Psychology*, 46(5), 836–40.

Gorgievskia, M., Bakker, A. & Schaufeli, W. (2010). Work engagement and workaholism: Comparing the self-employed and salaried employees. *Journal of Positive Psychology*, 5(1), 83–96.

Greenberg, J. (1987). A taxonomy of organizational justice theories. *Academy of Management Review*, 12(1) 9–22.

Herzberg, F. (1959). *The motivation to work.* New York: Wiley.

Kesebir, S., Graham, J. & Oishi, S. (2010). A theory of human needs should be human-centered, not animal-centered. *Perspectives on Psychological Science*, 5(3), 315–19.

Locke, E. A. (1964). The relationship of intentions to motivation and affect. PhD thesis, Cornell University.

Lundberg, C., Gudmundson, A. & Andersson, T. (2009). Herzberg's Two-Factor Theory of work motivation tested empirically on seasonal workers in hospitality and tourism. *Tourism Management*, 30(6), 890–9.

Maslow, A. H. (1954). *Motivation and personality.* New York: Harper.

Maslow, A. H. (1962). *Toward a psychology of being.* Princeton, NJ: Van Nostrand.

McClelland, D. C. (1955). *Studies in motivation.* New York: Appleton-Century-Crofts.

McClelland, D. C. (1975). *Power: The inner experience.* New York: Irvington.

Moynihan, D. (2010). A workforce of cynics? The effects of contemporary reforms on public service motivation. *International Public Management Journal*, 13(1), 24–34.

Vancouver, J. (2008). Integrating self-regulation theories of work motivation into a dynamic process theory. *Human Resource Management Review*, 18(1), 1–18.

Vroom, V. H. (1964). *Work and motivation.* New York: Wiley.

Wajcman, J., Rose, E., Brown, J. & Bittman, M. (2010). Enacting virtual connections between work and home. Journal of Sociology, published online 18 May 2010: <http://jos.sagepub.com/content/early/2010/05/17/1440783310365583.full.pdf>

Wilson, F., Kickul, J. & Marlino, D. (2007). Gender, entrepreneurial self-efficacy, and entrepreneurial career intentions: Implications for entrepreneurship education. *Entrepreneurship Theory and Practice*, 31(3), 387–406.

PRACTITIONER INSIGHT

LOUISE JENSEN

DIRECTOR, HR (GRANT THORNTON AUSTRALIA LIMITED)

An experienced human resources practitioner with a strong line management and consulting background.

After spending six years operating in a corporate environment within a large manufacturing company, Louise moved into a consulting role with Towers Perrin. Since that time she has worked in a range of consulting roles culminating in her move to Hewitt Associates, where, together with two work peers from KPMG, she opened the Melbourne office for Hewitt Associates in early 1997.

Moving back into an in-house Human Resources line management role in 2000 with William Buck, Louise is currently Director, Human Resources for Grant Thornton Australia Limited, Melbourne, following the merger of William Buck Melbourne with Grant Thornton in 2008.

Louise holds a Bachelor of Business (Business Administration) Degree. She has wide ranging human resources experience, having consulted to both public and private organisations in a variety of industry sectors prior to, and during, her employment with Grant Thornton. In addition, while working in the consulting space, Louise took on a number of Casual Lecturer postings with Deakin University, tutoring both undergraduates and post-graduates in the areas of General Management and Compensation and Benefits.

Louise has considerable experience in the assessment and definition of organisational structures and roles, aligning them to the strategic goals, people requirements and competitive pressures of the businesses concerned. In addition, she has worked extensively on the design, development and implementation of effective compensation, performance management and employee communication strategies.

An accredited Myers-Brigg Type Indicator facilitator in early 2008, Louise was invited to act as a specialist HR Advisor and member of the HR Committee of a not for profit organisation.

INTERVIEW

What was your first job?

My first role was a graduate role. My title was Salary and Administration Officer. I was part of the national 'personnel' team and was located in Head Office.

What has been your career highlight so far?

A difficult question to answer as each role has had its own highlights. Perhaps, in terms of personal positive affirmation, when I moved from a role with a business consulting firm to work under my own banner for a while, my key clients at the time followed me. A practice-related highlight would be working through the Award Modernisation process with legal advisors and stakeholders in competitor firms to ensure continued exclusion of professional accounting staff from a new general award.

In your current role, what does a typical day involve?

There is no 'typical' day. Working with people as your client base means that your work environment is not static and matters continually arise outside the framework of projects currently being undertaken. In broad terms, an average day would involve:

- covering off emails
- liaising with my boss and other Directors
- project management (there is usually more than one project on the go at once, so time would be spent keeping these running within timeframes and deadlines)
- catching up with my staff/encouraging them and seeing if and where they need backup
- liaising with the national People and Capital team as necessary.

What's the best part of your job?

Being part of the senior management team, ensuring that Human Resources initiatives, processes and policies are aligned with the strategic plan and contribute to the firm achieving its business outcomes.

What are the current challenges facing you, in your role?

Our firm has recently gone through a merger and the move from a federated model to a national corporate model. While this occurred 'on paper' a couple of years ago, it is an enormous process to bring together financial and operating systems onto one national platform. Similarly, the move to a national structure is one which takes time and negotiation. This has been a phased project and a current key focus is to bring together national competency frameworks, balanced scorecards and remuneration models. This process requires involvement of key stakeholders, communication and change management elements.

Do you regularly apply the principles or theories you learnt (when studying organisational behaviour) into your everyday work? In what way?

Always. Understanding how organisations work is key to enabling you to function within a workplace. Organisational structure and management mechanisms or frameworks must be understood and worked with to achieve desired outcomes. Respect and understanding of these behavioural parameters and their evolution is essential for success.

How important is an understanding of 'organisational behaviour' in today's workplace?

It is an imperative. Equally vital is the understanding that what works behaviourally in one workplace may not work in another. Cultural dynamics impact the behaviour of an organisation and, therefore, no two workplaces will be absolutely identical. Senior executive and leadership groups drive the culture of an organisation, therefore senior executive changes can alter an organisation's behaviour. Similarly, as an organisation grows and potentially becomes more rigid in structure, there may be a resultant impact on the cultural dynamic and organisational behaviour. Economic conditions can affect the behaviour of an organisation. In other words, no organisation is static, so an effective human resources practitioner must have a good understanding of the dynamics of organisational behaviour.

Is a work–life balance a reasonable expectation in a modern workplace?

Yes. There are many options available to individuals to work flexible hours to achieve a good work/life balance. Technology allows people in some employment situations to work remotely for part of their working week. Generally, organisations are increasingly able to accommodate flexible work options for their staff.

What strategies do you implement in your workplace to help employees achieve an appropriate work–life balance?

We have many part-time employees, across all levels of the organisation. Some employees (both part and full time) work remotely for a portion of their standard weekly hours. For example a .60 FTE staff member, may work 2 days in the office, and the third day from home.

In addition, all staff are able to apply for a variety of Flexible Work Options. These options include:

- moving to .80 FTE or .90 FTE
- applying to purchase up to an additional 3 weeks of leave
- taking a semester of unpaid leave to study.

Has technology impacted on work–life balance? Is it harder to achieve with constant access to the 'office', for example?

As mentioned previously, remote access has real benefits in terms of allowing staff to increase their work/life balance by working from home either regularly, or on an as needs basis. However, the 'flip side' of this is that staff with this access can feel it is harder to get away from the office.

This means that there is an increasing onus of responsibility on affected individuals to physically and mentally divide their time between work and home.

Are there greater expectations (on you or your workplace) to help motivate and engage employees in their work than ever before?

Definitely. Talent attraction, engagement and retention are key issues for all successful organisations. While this has always been the case, social networking ensures that employees are much more connected with the market and, therefore, internal retention and engagement strategies are more critical.

Do your people manage themselves or are you called upon frequently to deal with relational issues?

In general my staff manage themselves. We have weekly meetings to 'touch base' and ensure that everyone is tracking well, and to establish whether tasks and/or resourcing need to be reallocated to meet deadlines. My staff would usually seek my advice where there was a relational issue. Following discussion, I would give the staff member the opportunity to deal with the issue on their own in the first instance, but would always be available to step in where they felt assistance was needed.

03

Relational
Factors

5 Groups and Teams 125

6 The Leadership Function 153

7 Power, Control and Influence 179

Groups and Teams

INTRODUCTION

All you read in the opening chapters can now be applied in thinking about how to better manage groups and teams. The architecture and atmosphere of an organisation is integrally aligned with that of the groups and teams within it. Individuals make up groups and teams but there is a unique expression from each collective that challenges managers to capitalise on the advantages and minimise the disadvantages. Motivation and learning can lead to high performance from groups and teams, but problems of task complexity, communication, power and conflict can equally lead to underperformance. This chapter establishes the theoretical underpinnings of group and team theory and then outlines key processes, characteristics and approaches that can be taken by managers and team members to make the most of organisational team experiences.

LEARNING
OBJECTIVES

Understanding this chapter will help you to
- define groups and teams
- describe the team development sequence
- explain some of the main reasons for punctuated equilibrium in team performance
- discuss the implications for team performance of groupthink, synergy and social loafing

- describe team decision-making approaches
- define high-performance work teams
- discuss team roles, cohesiveness and leadership as key aspects of team management.

OVERVIEW

Why work together at all? Why not just work individually on tasks and then trade goods or services whenever we need something that we have not already got? The answers are derived from the delicate balance that humans must find between competition and cooperation (Burton-Chellewa et al., 2010). Some tasks are simply too big for one person alone to achieve. Many objectives can only be achieved by people working together in organisations, pooling resources and sharing the workload. Paradoxically, organisational objectives are often in competition with other organisations; thus a certain team spirit, tribalism or cohesion can grow around the need to prevent other groups or organisations from succeeding at diverting the available finite resources. As the tools of computing and robotics have proliferated, so has the overall complexity of organisational strategy and operations (Orlikowski, 2009). Today, it is expected that groups and teams will form the basis of most tasks in the workplace in all but the smallest of enterprises. The global landscape is one of many groups and teams working in increasingly complex and changeable environments requiring proactive leadership and collaborative skills. This is against the general backdrop of intensified local and global competition. The imperative, therefore, has become to 'collaborate in order to compete'. This chapter defines groups and teams and then surveys the predominant theories and concepts that can indicate ways to effectively manage in such a contradictory environment.

GROUPS VERSUS TEAMS

■
Learning Objective
Groups and teams
defined

■
Group
A collection of individuals
working on achieving
similar goals.

■
Team
A collection of individuals
working interdependently
with shared vision and
cohesion on achieving
jointly agreed goals.

You learned in Chapter 4 that the content motivation theories identify social interaction as one of the basic human needs. It will therefore be no surprise that working in groups can be at once motivating as well as fulfilling the competitive impetus identified above. Many people find that belonging to a **group** or a **team** can be highly motivating. Others find the complexity of interactions, the potential abuses of leadership and control, and the delicate balancing of relationships that seems to have to happen in groups to be quite demanding (Maner & Mead, 2010). To improve our understanding of the dynamics, it is important to have a clear distinction between groups and teams. A group is a collection of individuals working at achieving similar goals. A classroom of students is a group; so is a stadium full of football supporters, as is a gathering of staff to hear a new CEO address them. When interdependency develops between the individuals in a group and a shared vision emerges to encourage cohesion to grow, then a team has formed. A small number of students working on a collaborative class project or an interdepartmental project committee are more likely to be called a team, although this still does depend on their levels of cohesion. This means that a team is always classified as a particular kind of group, but a group is not classified as a team unless key conditions are met.

Figure 5.1 A team is a special type of group

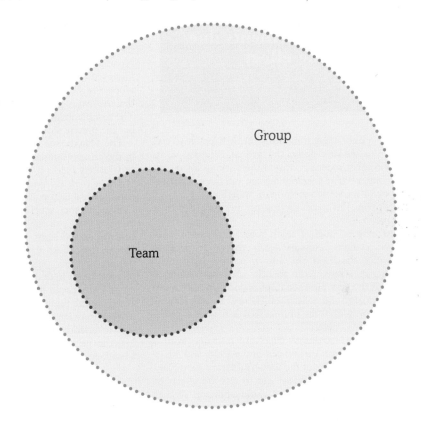

Figure 5.1 portrays the more integrated team as one part of the broader definition of a group. Group theory has emerged from many studies in the sociology and psychology disciplines. From these bases, a specialised field of team theory has gradually been developed in organisational behaviour. Effectively managing teams is a crucial aspect of good people management. The Hawthorne studies are famous for revealing the effect that can occur when a supervisor is seen to be paying attention to workers in a work team (Mayo, 1931). Subsequent studies have tended to confirm the importance of human relations and the dynamics of groups in developing and sustaining workplaces (Hodgetts & Hegar, 2008; Stone, 2010). One modern culmination is the emergence of workplace wellness programs, which have the dual productivity purposes of tapping the Hawthorne effect among work groups and keeping workers generally healthier and more able to complete their tasks (Lee et al., 2010).

WINDOW ON ETHICS

Posture improvements due to Hawthorne effect

ASHLEY KARR

More than once a day something funny happens to me. Maybe I'm walking down the hall in Lehman, or to Starbucks, or wandering around the parking lot trying to remember where I parked my car, and out the corner of my eye, I see someone stand up straighter.

'Hi, Ashley. I'm remembering my posture, see?' they say to me.

I just have to laugh. I teach Yoga and Pilates classes here on campus, assistant teach the undergraduate ergonomics class, and am known in my department for sitting in a 'knee chair' to help with my posture. It seems that my very presence inspires good posture in my friends, students, and colleagues. There is a name for this phenomenon within the human factors field. It is called the Hawthorne effect.

The famous Hawthorne effect got its name from a series of experiments carried out in the 1920s and 30s at the Hawthorne Works of the Western Electric Company. The researchers originally set out to test the effects of rest pauses, shorter hours, and illumination on worker productivity and fatigue. What they found was something quite different from their original intentions. In one manipulation, the researchers dimmed the lighting and recorded the effects on production. Then, they increased the lighting and recorded the effects on production. No matter what the manipulation of the lights, output increased. The researchers drew the conclusion that whenever the lighting changed, the workers remembered that they were part of an experiment and worked harder. The specific manipulation did not affect worker behavior, but the presence of researchers did.

The Hawthorne effect has earned an important place in the areas of human factors, organizational psychology, and related fields. It drew researchers' attention to the fact that personal and social factors play a greater role than physical factors in determining worker productivity. Human factors specialists carry this importance with them as they evaluate or create industrial and technical systems and designs. Even if we don't consider the Hawthorne effect, it will consider us, as in the case of posture and my presence around campus. Although a physical factor in design, such as an ergonomically correct office chair, could help someone maintain good posture and therefore prevent back pain, having your ergonomics or Yoga instructor walk by seems a much more effective way to encourage you to take care of your spine. The Hawthorne effect. Know it. Love it. Use it to your advantage.

Source: <http://ashleywellnesscoaching.com/home/2010/2/5/posture-improvements-due-to-hawthorne-effect.html>

The point made in this Window is that a balance between personal, social and physical factors is important at work. The issue of work–life balance is once again central to considerations of how to best manage people in the workplace. While balance can appear costly up front, it is ethically and motivationally important for people to have a healthy workplace, and the longer term gains for organisations are quite obvious. You might also consider the ethical stance of the company that runs wellness programs for its staff. Is this motivated by human concern or done only for the purpose of improved productivity? The next sections describe some of the important group concepts in the context of organisations and discussion follows in each section to provide insights about team theory.

Group types and the team development sequence

■
Learning Objective
The team development
sequence

A variety of groups and teams are commonly found in the workplace. The architecture of organisations expressed through organisational charts naturally puts people into groups for the purpose of completing the tasks and objectives that are strategically important. So a division, a department, a business unit or office locations are all possible ways of putting people into groups. Some formal groups are more fluid in their membership but still quite clearly functional, such as committees, task forces, quality circles, project teams and even virtual teams.

Thought pathway

Referring to the definition of a team, identify all the different kinds of work teams in an organisation with which you are familiar.

Just how cohesive a group becomes and whether the group can be clearly called a team depends on the dynamics of the group formation process. One influential study (Tuckman, 1965) identified a distinctive sequence of group development. This was especially in the context of people forming groups for the purpose of human relations training. It was found that when groups of people first come together, the many instances of interpersonal orientation, testing and dependence can be collectively viewed as group-*forming* events. The next stage of conflict and polarisation over interpersonal factors can be seen as a *storming* period where differences are ironed out. When the storm dies down and people in the group reach a level of understanding about their different roles and some cohesiveness has developed, this is a demonstration of *norming*. Next the group roles can become flexible and functional and the stage of *performing* the group's intended purpose is on display. Another study (Tuckman & Jensen, 1977) added a final stage to the process, *adjourning*, which accounts for the closing down or finishing up behaviours when a team's task has been completed. Figure 5.2 portrays Tuckman's general group development sequence. If you have had a number of group and team formation experiences, you will probably agree with the general flow of the development process. However, there are sure to be variations to the sequence depending on the type of task and the numbers of people involved.

Figure 5.2 Tuckman's group development sequence

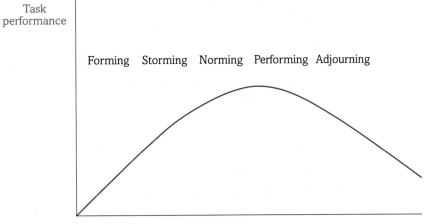

Group development over time

Some studies of groups in organisations suggest there are size limits beyond which group or team functioning is not necessarily optimal (Ogungbamila et al., 2010; Xiao & Jin, 2010). Most of these studies acknowledge that the type of task, the mix of personalities in the team and the timing and nature of the overall team objectives make it quite difficult to set a hard-and-fast rule about optimal team size. A general principle seems to be that the larger the group, the more unwieldy it becomes to coordinate things consistently well. However, there are many industrial examples where quite large teams are able to do very well. The best rule of thumb for a team manager would be to think of the tasks to be performed and start with the minimum number of people estimated as necessary, but to be prepared to monitor progress regularly through the group development stages and ensure new people can be easily brought in if their expertise is needed.

You may get the sense at this stage that there is a 'messy' but 'good' aspect of team work. Figure 5.2 displays a smooth symmetry that probably overstates the reality of team functioning. Observations of all kinds of natural phenomena suggest that the more likely state of teamwork is one of relative equilibrium of activity occasionally interrupted by bursts of energy and activity (Gould, 1989; Gersick, 1991). Successful team functioning depends on a lot of different variables, so the mapping of progress might be expected to be asymmetrical.

Punctuated equilibrium in team performance

Drawing from evolutionary theory (Gould, 1989), the punctuated equilibrium concept was adapted by Gersick (1991) to form an intuitive, organic view of how teams actually perform. Figure 5.3 maps the asymmetrical reality of team performance over time.

Figure 5.3 Punctuated equilibrium: The realities of teamwork when deadlines loom

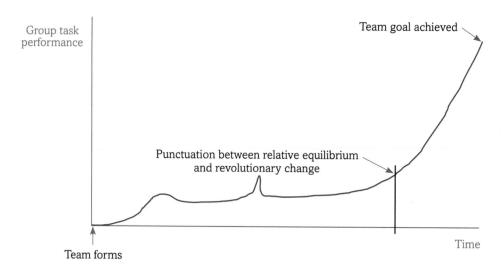

The organisational reality is that a series of peaks and troughs of activity would occur between when a team forms and when the major punctuation occurs between relative equilibrium and revolutionary change. You will know from your own experience that when a group or team first forms, there might be a rush of activity but then it often drops away. There might be one or a few more spikes of activity as certain mini-deadlines or milestone-reporting requirements occur. But the main activity normally happens a bit later when someone realises that the completion deadline is drawing near, or some key enabling aspect of the project, such as the budget, finally comes into place.

Thought pathway

Reflect back on a team project you may have been involved with where there was a frenetic culmination of activity quite close to the key deadlines.

Additional explanations for the uneven nature of teamwork can be found in studies of particular group dynamics phenomena, such as groupthink, synergy, social loafing, and general group decision processes.

Groupthink

Learning Objective
Implications of groupthink for team performance

Groupthink
When the views of the more dominant members of a group become accepted as the consensus.

Sometimes the views of the more dominant members of a group, for convenience or lack of desire to usurp established power relationships, or simply a mistaken belief that everyone is in agreement, are accepted as the standard views. This sort of uncritical adoption by individuals of a certain point of view is known as **groupthink** (Janis, 1972; Millward et al., 2010). If you have ever served on a committee or been in a meeting where time is limited, or where a persuasive person is leading the discussion, you will have an idea of the way groupthink works. Sometimes it is just too easy to vote in favour of something you might otherwise disagree with to save time, avoid confrontation, or cover for the fact you do not know very much about the issue being discussed.

WINDOW ON COMMUNICATION

ABC chair criticises climate change coverage

BRENDAN TREMBATH
March 10, 2010

ABC chairman Maurice Newman has attacked the media for being too willing to accept the conventional wisdom on climate change. In a speech to senior ABC staff on Wednesday morning, Mr Newman said climate change was an example of 'group think'.

He says contrary views on climate change have not been tolerated and those who express them have been labelled and mocked.

'It's really been the question of what is wisdom and consensus rather than listening perhaps to other points of view that may be sceptical,' he said.

But he believes the ABC has been more balanced than other media organisations when it comes to reporting on climate change.

'I think that we've listened to the words of sceptics as well as those who are scientists in the field,' he said.

'Climate change is at the moment an emotional issue.

'But it really is the fundamental issue about the need to bring voices that have authority and are relevant to the particular issue to the attention of our audiences, so that they themselves can make decisions.'

Mr Newman has doubts about climate change himself and says he is waiting for proof either way.

'My view on any of these topics is to keep an open mind, and I still have an open mind on climate change,' he said.

'Many of the people who have a different point of view on the climate science are respectable and credentialed scientists themselves.

'So as I said, I'm not a scientist and I'm like anybody else in the public, I have to listen to all points of view and then make judgments when we're asked to vote on particular policies.'

*Source: <www.abc.net.au/news/
stories/2010/03/10/2842322.htm>*

Synergy
High levels of effectiveness and efficiency that sometimes cannot be explained by just breaking down the aspects of the processes that created the event. Synergy is when the whole becomes greater than the sum of its parts.

This Window highlights an important point about the integral connection of group consensus with emotional responses. Groupthink would not happen at all unless people were motivated either by positive or negative emotion to actively promote or benignly accept the principle under discussion. There are facts and then there are motivating forces within individuals driven by the various factors discussed in Chapters 2, 3 and 4. We are all brought up differently and have diverse views to put forward. Sometimes we are simply too tired to think critically and want to be carried along by the support systems of the group. This is not to say group consensus is always negative. The very reason for using groups to arrive at understanding is that a wider scope of knowledge and experience can lead to more robust understanding. The positive aspects of groups are clearly articulated through the concept of **synergy**.

Synergy

Learning Objective
Implications of synergy for team performance

Parts working together sometimes produce inexplicably high levels of innovation, quality or productivity. It is informative that Forbes et al. (1953) reduced a human cadaver down to its chemical components and found it consisted of approximately 55% water, 19% protein, 18% ether extract, 5% carbon (ash), 2% calcium and 1% phosphorus. This is certainly not romantic but it is a great illustration of the old adage 'the whole is greater than the sum of its parts'. The essence of synergy is the realisation that when you bring things together, whether chemicals to be infused with the spirit of a person, or people into groups for organisational purposes, the result is phenomena that can be far more agreeable and useful than merely looking at the components that went into the process. Managers and leaders long for those moments when a smoothly functioning group delivers an outcome that is exceptional. Many great organisational achievements seem to come from teams producing high levels of effectiveness and efficiency that sometimes cannot be explained by just breaking down the aspects of the processes that created the event. As a people manager you can think of synergy on the level within a single team (intragroup) or at the level of different teams working together in the larger organisation (intergroup). When a small team achieves productivity gains against the odds, intragroup synergy may have contributed to the success. Landing a person on the moon in the 1960s is an example of a synergistic intergroup outcome from a set of resources that are lean by today's standards. Small and large synergies emerge in workplaces around Australia and the world every day, and when they do the people involved are able to witness innovations, gains, improvements and all kinds of positive rewards (Stahl et al., 2010). Synergy can be elusive but well worth the effort to bring it about.

Thought pathway

Reflect on a moment of success you have experienced as part of a group or team. Consider how much you feel synergy was at work in that success. Some people refer to luck or serendipity when successful moments occur. Perhaps you can think about the differences, if any, between luck and synergy.

The field of organisational behaviour is replete with concepts and theories that would make the workplace very nice if they were all properly implemented. Of course, imperfection and exception are far too common. Synergy is just as elusive as the learning organisation, the fully motivated workforce, and the non-discriminatory manager. It does not mean managers should not keep trying to achieve best practice but there does need to be moderation of expectation at times.

Learning Objective
Implications of social loafing for team performance

Social loafing
Also known as the Ringelmann effect; when a person relies on the hard work of others to carry them through.

Social loafing

Sometimes groups deliver the opposite of synergy, that is, their total performance is less than the sum of the parts. One explanation of this negative synergy may be found in the phenomenon of **social loafing** (Kidwell, 2010). Loafing describes what happens when a person relies on the hard work of others to carry them through. Social loafing refers specifically to group dynamics and the phenomenon of individuals sitting back and letting others in the group do the bulk of the work required to achieve the group objective. Social loafing is sometimes referred to as

■
Ringelmann effect
Also known as social
loafing; when a person
relies on the hard work
of others to carry them
through.

the **Ringelmann effect** because of the rope-pulling experiments conducted by the German industrial psychologist Max Ringelmann (Moede, 1927; Ingham et al., 1974). Ringelmann found that, despite the reasonable expectation that the addition of people to a team pulling on ropes should lead to linear increases in total pulling power, the actual result came to less than what was possible. Some people simply did not seem to put in the extra effort that was promised. Many possible reasons have been given for the phenomenon, such as lift versus drag and slippage effects when rope-pulling, unclear expectations of participants about the intention of the experiment, unbalanced pulling techniques, or collisions while pulling. Regardless, there is plenty of anecdotal workplace evidence of teams of people being able to identify those members who do not 'pull their weight' on various work tasks.

Even before Ringelmann's observations, Frederick Taylor, the founder of scientific management, coined the term 'soldiering' to describe workers who gave the impression of working hard but were actually letting others carry the bulk of the work (Taylor, 1911). Whichever way it is labelled, social loafing is very close to human nature and sits at the nexus between people's desire to be cooperative and their need for self-preservation. In other words, the loafer may be physically or psychologically burnt out and needs others in the team to help them along for a while. This is not easily understood since the people carrying the extra load may also be tired. One of the common tasks of people managers seems to be to quell the interpersonal conflict that can emerge when someone is accused of social loafing, normally after an important team objective has not been attained. The situation is likely to be more complex than it first appears and some sensitivity is needed to get to the bottom of the issue.

WINDOW ON CONFLICT AND NEGOTIATION

Team building: A waste of time and money

JAMES ADONIS
April 23, 2010

I've been saying it publicly for years, and now research has just been released backing what many have suspected: team-building activities don't build teams. For a long time employees have endured the banality of mindless and childish games for the sake of team solidarity, but finally, reluctantly, it's game over.

The study, conducted by British universities Chester and Liverpool Hope, explored the impact on team cohesion among athletes when they engage in initiation practices. It found no positive relationship between the two. None. Even simple team-building activities, like grabbing a bite to eat together, resulted in breadcrumbs of team unity.

There's a great advertisement by American Airlines that perfectly encapsulates what it's like to be a worker at an off-putting off-site. Stuck at an employer's team-building event, an executive secretly tries to catch an earlier flight as a way of getting out of there. The ad ends with the tagline, 'Making your escape. Sooner.' Anyone who's ever had to suffer one of these experiences will understand what it's like to desperately want to flee these excruciating retreats.

High morale and productivity have always been the ultimate aims of the enthusiastic team-building organiser. It's difficult to comprehend how forcing people to play games they hate in locations they deplore and at times they find inconvenient will cause them to bond. Instead, the smart ones abscond.

When there's conflict between workers, hiring a facilitator to run blindfolded role-plays won't solve the issue. When lack of trust is prevalent, inflicting pain with skirmish paintball isn't going to change it. And when a team isn't working well together, a three-legged race will still leave them tied down and tangled up on a stumbling track of poor performance.

Often competitive in nature, team-building days achieve the opposite of what was intended. You don't build tight teams by getting the individuals within it to fight each other in a contest. Creating losers isn't exactly good for morale.

A team's problems aren't cured by superficially dealing with the symptoms. The fix only comes when you deal with the root causes of the angst. It might be minimal opportunities for employees to share among the group their ideas and suggestions. It could be they're unaware of each other's communication styles, learning methods, and work preferences. It may be they haven't got access to the team's goals, strategy, and statistics. It's not a contrived team-building event that's required. Rather, just some vital information.

The bigger question is whether a team is needed…at all. In many cases, the answer will be 'yes'. But there'll be plenty of occasions where it'll be clear upon reflection that creating a team might be counterproductive. It's not unusual to discover that people working on their own are sometimes more likely to produce a better outcome than if they were to work in tandem with others. You can see this unfold in what is the biggest waste of space known to humankind—the committee—which tends to attract volunteers that need to be committed.

Those who embrace the archaic 'together everyone achieves more' maxim will disagree. Collectively, yes, a team's progress can be accelerated, but the productivity of the individuals within that team decreases the larger the group becomes. Max Ringelmann, an engineering professor, proved this in a study. He got people to pull a big rope on their own while he measured the strength of each individual's pull. He then asked all the participants to pull the rope together at the same time, and was astonished to find the total strength of the entire group's pull was less than the sum of the individuals.

So, will this change anything? Probably not. Companies will still spend money and squander time sending workers to team-building days that don't make a difference. But then again, as many of us know, it's not always about making a difference, but about being seen to be doing something. Anything.

Source: <http://blogs.smh.com.au/small-business/ workinprogress/2010/04/23/teambuildinga.html>

This Window is a useful example of critical thinking. Teamwork involves regular conflict and negotiation over responsibilities and expectations. The organisation's aspiration is to achieve synergy from a team through high morale and motivation. The realistic goal is to minimise loafing and bickering over the compulsion to work with others. The art of good people management is to keep the positive aspiration partly visible and responsively and thoroughly attend to the negative interpersonal issues that inevitably arise each day.

Capitalising on group energy: Getting to a decision

Learning Objective
Approaches to team decision-making

The advantages of groups as a source of diverse inputs and brainstorming for innovation and creativity are compelling (Baer et al., 2010), but the disadvantages, such as interpersonal and political conflicts, are a genuine challenge. Making a decision on your own is often difficult enough. Gathering the full amount of necessary data, settling on a process of making sense of the data to turn it into strategic knowledge, and following through with the right approach to evaluation of the decision outcome can be onerous. Now add to that the complex interpersonal dynamics of a group. Making an important organisational decision while catering to the different opinions and agenda of diverse team members, many of whom have unique political alliances, puts group decision-making into context. This problem has not gone unnoticed and there are a range of group decision-making tools that have been used with various degrees of success (Kuhn, 2010). Group decision methods with a democratic basis include the **Delphi Method**, the **Nominal Group Technique** and the common committee-based approaches that prevail in larger organisations. As decision deadlines loom, so these group methods often converge with less democratic decision tools and techniques deployed by managers, such as **judgment heuristics** and **bounded rationality**.

The Delphi Method (Dalkey & Helmer, 1963) is a way of building consensus on a course of action by using a series of questionnaires to collect data from a panel of selected experts on the matter at issue. Selected Delphi participants give their views but also have the opportunity to reassess their initial judgments about the information provided in previous questionnaires. It is more than a single loop system. Since the questionnaires are mailed or emailed rather than conducted face to face, there is some flexibility and the method can provide anonymity to respondents and a controlled feedback process, and the data can be subject to statistical analysis techniques if needed (Hsu & Sandford, 2007). It can also be usefully applied in virtual teams. The drawback is that it can be time-consuming to get multiple cycles of feedback. Decisions with tight deadlines may not always be possible with this method.

Unlike the Delphi Method, the Nominal Group Technique occurs face to face and aims to balance participation, apply different processes for different phases of creative problem-solving, and reduce possible errors in aggregating individual judgments into group decisions (Islam, 2010). The general process is:

- The group silently generates ideas in writing.
- A facilitator aggregates ideas on a chart through group discussion.
- A preliminary silent, independent vote is sought on priorities.
- Facilitated discussion of the preliminary vote occurs.
- A final silent, independent vote is sought on priorities.
- The facilitator lists and obtains consensus agreement on prioritised items.

Participants tend to notice the inclusive nature of the Nominal Group Technique and the feeling that normally emerges that everyone's ideas have at least had a chance to be tabled.

Committee decisions are a time-honoured way in which large organisations attend to all kinds of routine and complex decisions. Some committees may choose to use the Delphi Method or Nominal Group Technique for some decisions, but it is usual for committees to follow the well-established procedures for establishing agenda items, generating general discussion, moving and seconding motions, calling for votes, and minuting all that goes on. It is common in organisations for committee members to bemoan the tedious and repetitive nature of committee meetings, especially where

Delphi Method
A way of building consensus on a course of action by repeatedly applying a series of questionnaires to collect data from a panel of selected experts on the issue.

Nominal Group Technique
A face-to-face method to balance participation, apply different processes for different phases of creative problem solving, and reduce possible errors in aggregating individual judgments into group decisions.

Judgment heuristics
Judgment patterns formed from previous decision outcomes which can act as guides for future decisions.

Bounded rationality
The fact that incomplete (bounded) information is applied in making any decision.

meetings are prone to the views of dominant personalities. Groupthink and social loafing are each well represented at standard committee meetings in Australia and around the world.

Individuals and groups can find it useful to refer to previous decision outcomes which can act as judgment patterns (or heuristics). The more precise and transferable the factors of one decision are to another, the more likely a heuristic will be helpful. Routine decisions can sometimes be mapped into software or templates that can prompt the team to arrive at the best outcomes. Even complex decisions can sometimes display standard characteristics that can be translated into a heuristic pattern, thus giving the team a consistent approach (Åstebro & Elhedhli, 2006). It is through application and experience that the past can best inform the decisions of the future. Researchers have observed how experienced managers and teams can successfully apply what Simon (1991) refers to as bounded rationality. Since the necessary information about any single decision is potentially infinite, we must somehow draw a line or a boundary in the data and make a decision. The decision is by definition based on incomplete information. This is one reason why experienced teams, committees and managers are sometimes able to deliver good results quickly, but can also run a risk of making a wrong decision. The combined background experience enables swift processing of large amounts of data which will improve the chances of success, but the inherent bounded rationality remains. Those with less experience are working with less background knowledge of the decision variables.

WINDOW ON DECISION-MAKING

Garrett left out of Rudd's 'gang' on ETS backflip

PETER VAN ONSELEN, CONTRIBUTING EDITOR
FROM: THE AUSTRALIAN
June 5, 2010.

Environment minister Peter Garrett has admitted he was not consulted about the government's decision to ditch its proposed emissions trading scheme and that he knew nothing about it until he read it in the newspapers.

Mr Garrett said the decision was taken by Kevin Rudd's inner Cabinet as part of the budget process and he had taken no part in the discussions. He said it was disappointing that the decision had been leaked and revealed that the first he knew about it was when he read a story in a newspaper report on April 27.

'That was an announcement and a decision that was leaked and I found out about it when it was leaked,' Mr Garrett told Sky News' *Saturday Agenda.*

Mr Garrett's admission is confirmation that the ETS decision was not discussed by the full cabinet and that the discussion was restricted to the so-called gang of four: Prime Minster Mr Rudd, his deputy Julia Gillard, Treasurer Wayne Swan and Finance Minister Lindsay Tanner.

It also confirms that the ETS proposal was abandoned as part of the Budget process. Factoring in the ETS costs would have made it harder for the government to meet its accelerated target for eliminating the budget deficit.

Reports today have suggested Mr Tanner was a voice of dissent when discussing the idea, but the other three senior figures carried the day.

When questioned about his exclusion from the decision making process, Mr Garrett said it was disappointing that the decision had been leaked before the government had completed its internal discussions.

'It's always disappointing when you get information that makes its way through into a newspaper and that the processes of discussion that otherwise would happen aren't able to happen, but it's a decision that was taken.

'And I guess my response to that is that the special budget committee is the one that makes these decisions. I don't sit on that budget committee. And at the end of the day, the government had determined that this was the way it wanted to approach the CPRS, and it had a very good reason for doing so.

'The thing about it is that the decision was made and this is what you respond to when decisions are made. You understand the reason for the decision and you get on with doing your job. And obviously if you get an opportunity to participate strongly in discussions, and those opportunities obviously arise in a range of areas, you take them.

'But at the end of the day the responsibility for taking that decision lay with that group.

'We do have exhaustive discussions in the Cabinet and I get every opportunity to participate as is appropriate.'

Mr Garrett blamed opposition in the Senate for the decision to postpone further consideration of an emissions trading scheme until 2013 at the earliest.

'The fact that we didn't have any bipartisan consensus on moving forward on this issue means that to take the legislative actions that underlie the CPRS, you're at that sort of end game point.

'The conviction that the party, including Kevin, has about climate change, is an enduring conviction.'

Mr Garrett's admission is further evidence that major decisions in the Rudd government are made by the so-called 'gang of four' and are not considered or reviewed by a wider circle of ministers before they are announced.

Opposition leader Tony Abbott jumped on the revelation, saying it shows the government is being run by the 'gang of four'.

'It shows the decisions are taken by a "gang of four" without any real consultation with anyone,' he told reporters in Sydney today.

Small business minister Craig Emerson told ABC *Lateline* on May 13 that he did not know the government was proposing to introduce a resource rent tax on mining until the news was broken by *The Weekend Australian* in April.

Mr Abbott said the Rudd government was looking as chaotic as its NSW Labor counterpart, which yesterday suffered two ministerial resignations in one day.

Responding to a new poll in Queensland showing the federal coalition with a lead over Labor in the state, on a two party preferred basis, Mr Abbott said he maintained it would still be difficult to beat a first term government.

He dodged questions about whether, as the latest polls seem to indicate, voters leaving federal Labor are adding support to the Greens, saying simply that Mr Rudd had suffered a major fall in support.

Source: <www.theaustralian.com.au/national-affairs/climate/garrett-left-out-of-rudds-gang-on-ets-backflip/story-e6frg6xf-1225875832909>

This Window reveals the problems that can emerge from group decision-making processes. Consensus is difficult to achieve and in some cases it can never be. Dominant team members, by perceived necessity, may try to push through their views, maybe in quite Machiavellian ways. The democratic ideal that the majority should rule inevitably leaves some individuals isolated. Once again, the artful manager has to find a way to draw effective decision data from the diverse members of the team, but cannot always delay important decisions even in the face of team conflicts.

CASE STUDY

Staff leave in spite of excellent team performance

John Rossi founded Rossi Fine Foods five years ago and he is the CEO and Sales and Marketing Director. Rossi Fine Foods imports, and sources locally, Italian and other European foods and ingredients which are sold to small retailers and restaurants throughout Australia. The Company employs 50 people and, of these, 20 are sales representatives who spend most of their time on the road visiting customers.

John Rossi has built the business through not only being an astute business person with a deep understanding of fine food, but by being a gregarious personality who is excellent at developing relationships with suppliers, customers and staff.

John is very proud of his sales team and works hard on ideas to help them to be more productive.

While there are distribution facilities in each state, the sales reps usually operate from their homes. The Company has set each sales rep up with computers and mobile phones and they are encouraged to plan their days effectively by setting appointments from home and then spending as much time as possible on the road.

There is an excellent incentive program in place where high performers can earn good financial rewards. The performance of the team and each individual is tracked on a weekly basis and the results are posted on the sales team's website, which can be viewed by all employees.

John is a great believer in competition: between businesses and between people. He feels that this brings out the best in everyone so he arranges the performance of the sales reps in a league table. He personally either visits or calls those whose performance is at the lower end of the table to coach and encourage them. In the past he has terminated people whose performance has not been up to his standard.

Each year, in January, all the sales team meet for a three-day conference on the Gold Coast. They celebrate successes, make awards to high performers and undertake team exercises to build their teamwork skills. Company marketing people give sessions on the new products being introduced and often a trainer runs programs on selling skills. John always gives very inspiring team speeches and he often has visiting motivational speakers to give the team a boost before they head off to start another sales year.

Recently there has been an increase in resignations from the sales team. Being an optimist and always putting a positive spin on things, John has said of the leavers, 'good, they weren't performing very well anyway. We're better off without them.' In many cases this was true but there were always some of the better performers leaving as well.

The CFO, Sergio Verdi, noticed a disturbing trend in the costs of the staff turnover in the sales team and tackled John about it. 'Are we recruiting the wrong people or driving good people away?' he asked. 'Whatever it is, it is costing us a lot and it is increasing each year.'

'Neither,' responded John, a bit agitated, 'we want really good team players and if they can't hack it we should be happy they move on.'

CASE STUDY QUESTIONS

1 Referring to the section 'The architecture and atmosphere of high-performance teams', describe how the sales team rates against these criteria.

2 Using the section 'Group types and the team development sequence', and looking at the different types of teams that are possible, describe what type of team Rossi Fine Foods sales team is.

3 What type of team or group would best suit the needs of the Company?

4 What should John Rossi do to build this type of team or group?

5 Is John Rossi the best type of leader for the circumstances? Describe the qualities he brings to the job and also any areas where his attributes may be a negative.

THE ARCHITECTURE AND ATMOSPHERE OF HIGH-PERFORMANCE TEAMS

Learning Objective
High-performance work teams

There are teams and then there are teams. For example, the team at the bottom of a competition ladder is clearly still a team with shared vision, interdependency and cohesion, but it differs markedly from the team at the very top of the ladder. High-performance teams are studied closely for this reason (Creed et al., 2008; Oldham & Hackman, 2010). What is it that makes some teams so good at achieving objectives compared with others? Katzenbach and Smith (1993) suggest that a high-performance work team exhibits clear communication across all levels of organisation, balance of skills (technical and interpersonal), clear and accepted rules of behaviour modelled by the leader, and recognition of successes. Marquardt et al. (2010, p. 244) list eight characteristics of high-performing teams:

1. clear and meaningful goals
2. explicit positive norms
3. strong interpersonal and communication skills
4. competence and commitment around solving problems and performing tasks
5. trust, openness and group cohesiveness
6. ability to manage conflict
7. shared leadership and accountability
8. continuous learning and improvement.

Thought pathway

Consider whether you fully agree with Marquardt, Seng and Goodson's eight characteristics of high-performing teams. Does your experience suggest any other characteristics should be included?

Team characteristics are one thing, but each team is also composed of individuals. It is informative to consider what kinds of people make up the best kinds of teams.

Belbin's team roles

UK scholar and consultant Meredith Belbin is among those who study the functions and skills of people within high-performing teams (Belbin, 1981; Belbin Associates, 2010). The difference is that his contribution is to identify and describe styles of behaviour and cognition in individuals that condition them for one or more specific team roles. The following Belbin team roles are quite widely applied in personality tests (Fincham & Rhodes, 2005) and the general literature on teamwork: Plant, Resource Investigator, Co-ordinator, Shaper, Monitor Evaluator, Teamworker, Implementer, Completer Finisher and Specialist.

Managers are advised to critically apply this kind of trait approach. People tend towards rigid attitudes about their own and others' characteristics once they are identified in a particular category, whereas practice suggests people can and perhaps should stretch their roles beyond current classifications. Managers can limit the career possibilities of some people by adhering too closely to categorisation in these kinds of models. Just as personality testing has been criticised for stereotyping some people, so team role classification has to be realistically assessed for current validity.

Thought pathway

Can you place your own personality predominantly within one of Belbin's team roles? Think about whether you should be permanently categorised as this kind of team contributor.

Individuality is an important feature of intragroup dynamics. It is one of the determinants of team cohesion, which is a crucial characteristic of high performance.

Cohesiveness and team spirit

The team that sticks together well during hard as well as less challenging times is demonstrating cohesiveness. *Esprit de corps* is a descriptive term for the spirit that binds a team together (Andersen, 2010). Mateship and camaraderie are other descriptors for this elusive and yet important team characteristic. High-performance teams need to have good employee involvement, high levels of engagement, and individuals who exhibit motivation to achieve their work in the team. There appears to be a correlation between all of these features and a team that is highly cohesive.

There is a dark side to team spirit and cohesion because people will also stick tightly together to achieve purposes that run counter to what the organisation may wish. Subversion and rebellion rely on cohesive teams as much as do productivity and other measures of overall organisational success. Another consideration is the special challenge to cohesion that occurs in virtual teams. The disconnection from physical space that characterises virtual or online teams means that an entirely distinct approach is needed to ensure socialisation can happen at the levels of intensity necessary to build sufficient cohesion (Chutnik & Grzesik, 2010).

At the beginning of this chapter it was identified that the highly competitive global environment accentuates the sentiment that we should *collaborate in order to compete*. This strange paradox of competition versus collaboration is a recurring issue for group and team management. If there is a purpose or objective worth pursuing, then a team may be the best way to go after it. The high-performing team is focused and cohesive, and each individual is capable of assuming responsibility for tasks that must be done along the way. If someone in the team does not fully participate in the tasks, intragroup conflict can emerge. Team success, of course, means ultimately that some other individual or group has missed out on obtaining the same rewards or resources. This immediately puts the team in line for intergroup conflict as a natural part of competition. This delicate balance makes team spirit essential and yet elusive and brings the issue of team leadership to the fore.

Team leadership and control

There is an argument that says cohesiveness and successful group decisions require strong leadership (Ashkanasy, 2002). It is suggested that the role of the leader in a team is pivotal for improving overall team spirit, generating a respectful and trusting team atmosphere, and helping to create the high-performance work culture that organisations want to have in place. There is an observable tendency for individuals to delegate a leadership role to the dominant person in the group. There is a social expectation that the buck has to stop somewhere and we are normally willing to assent to someone with certain skills of directing, persuading and influencing people to become responsible for the team. However, there is another line of reasoning that acknowledges the benefits that flow when teams become self-managing (Morgeson et al., 2010). A self-managing team disperses the leadership function among all the team members. A **self-managing team** does not require a controlling leader, and the members may in fact bristle at the idea that one person tries to dominate. Such a team draws on the skills and experience of each member and delivers high-quality outputs by a collaborative synchronisation that is quite different from the idea that one leader has to push hard and is solely responsible for the team's successes or failures. Chapter 6 explores in more detail the nature and function of leadership and the extent to which different styles and expectations deliver positive results for organisations.

When you have worked in a team, you may have been lucky to experience the expression of synergy and enjoy the camaraderie that can come. But perhaps you have also felt the frustration of someone on the team loafing, or a leader being too bossy, or you may have been individually blamed by others in the team for the whole team's poor performance. The issue of interpersonal relationships in a team relates strongly to the power balance between team members. Self-managing teams may have the professional maturity and blend of personalities, perhaps the ideal mix of Belbin's team roles, to fulfil team objectives without too much fuss. But lots of teams in organisations tell stories that indicate a less ideal situation. The team leader may feel they have to cajole and push team members to perform, and members may feel manipulated, underrewarded and generally dissatisfied. A team leader can bear the brunt of blame when team performance is lower than expected, or they can be promoted as champions when the whole team performs very well. There are inequities and half-truths in either of these situations. Once again the motivation theories in Chapter 4 become relevant, and Chapter 6 on leadership builds further knowledge in this area. Remember, a leader needs to be able to lead, but the followers have to want to follow.

CASE STUDY

Tom's team resist meetings as a waste of time: A team or a group?

Tom Osborne is the Accounting Manager at Southern Doors Limited, a manufacturer and distributor of doors to the building industry and retailers. He reports to the Finance Director. Tom has eight people reporting directly to him and they cover the areas of Wages Payroll, Salaries Payroll, Accounts Receivable, Accounts Payable, General Ledger, Credit Control and Purchasing.

Tom has been in his job 15 years and most of his staff are also fairly long-term employees. He is quite happy with the way things are run and there are very rarely any hiccups.

When the global financial crisis struck, Southern Doors had a tough year. One of the key shareholders wanted a thorough review of the financial situation.

Consultants were appointed to do this and, among other things, they found that there were probably efficiencies to be made in Tom's department. The Finance Director wanted Tom to look at what could be improved. He suggested Tom had a team meeting to generate some ideas and make some recommendations. In addition to this, the Head Office was moving into a new building and the CEO thought it would be a good idea for each department to be able to choose their new colour scheme, the layout and office furniture and partitions from a list provided by the supplier.

Tom never really thought of his people as a team. They all did their jobs well but there was not a lot of need for interaction. Tom took some pride in this. He thought if the systems were effective and everyone did as they were supposed to, it should all come together without lots of time-wasting meetings. In fact, Tom was fairly sure there were a few people who didn't get on with each other so they probably avoided communication as much as possible.

As far as finding the efficiencies that were required, Tom thought he knew what could be done and had been asking for computer and software upgrades to achieve this. If he was allowed to purchase these he wouldn't have to go through endless meetings to get to the same answer.

However, to appease his Director, Tom thought he had better hold a 'team meeting' and get it over with.

Tom announced to his people by email that they were going to have a meeting to discuss possible improvements in the department and also the new office.

'What's all this about then?' demanded Janice Moore, who was the Payroll Officer and had a problem with anything changing, even if it meant a new office.

'Look, it's just something we have to do to keep our Director happy,' responded Tom with a shrug of his shoulders.

He had a few other approaches from staff over the next few days with the same amount of enthusiasm. He was not looking forward to running the meeting.

It didn't start well. Tom ran through the agenda: improvements to the way the department operated followed by their ideas on the new office. Without exception they all said that they did their jobs as well as could be expected and they could see no room for improvement.

'We've all been here for years Tom,' protested Cecil Johnson, the Accounts Payable Officer, 'I'm sure if there is a better way of doing things we would have found it by now. Just get some faster computers and that should speed things up.'

Tom wrote the suggestion on the whiteboard.

Suggestions for the colour scheme for the new office and the type of furniture didn't go much better. Everybody seemed to have different ideas. Mary O'Brien, the Accounts Receivable Officer, thought it would be wonderful to have a 'theme' to link the different ideas and started coming up with all sorts of suggestions.

Roger Nguyen from Purchasing said he had found some websites with office planning templates and he had also found some free software that would help with the layout. On top of all this Meena Kumar, the Credit Controller, was trying to take over the meeting by writing up everyone's ideas and organizing who would do what.

Tom thought the whole thing was a mess and realised he would have to make the decisions regarding the office move.

When he had his weekly meeting with the Finance Director he was asked how the meeting went with the staff and what recommendations he had for improvements and the office move.

'It really comes down to new computers and upgraded software,' he said. They've all been doing their jobs for years, they know what they're doing. And as for the move, well, I'll give you a list of our requirements. If I left it up to them to agree on something, we'd never move!'

The Finance Director looked Tom in the eye and took on a serious tone. 'So you've got a bunch of people with no ideas?'

'That's about right, but they do a good job,' Tom responded.

He left the meeting feeling that his boss wasn't very happy but couldn't understand why. After all his department delivered all they were supposed to.

CASE STUDY QUESTIONS

1 Does Tom have a group or a team? Use the definitions provided to discuss this.

2 Does Tom need a team in this department? What would the advantages be in the normal day-to-day operations?

3 If Tom had an effective team, how might they have gone about finding improvements in their operations other than new computers and upgraded software?

4 How could Tom have used a team approach to working on the office move?

5 If you think Tom should start to build a more effective team, what actions do you think he should take? If you think this is not the direction he should take, can you suggest other improvements he could make in managing his people?

CONCLUSION

This chapter has brought together ideas of individual differences, learning and motivation from the earlier chapters to focus on the practical nature of group development and teamwork. Knowing that a team is a focused version of a group and that some teams perform better than others, you now have a selection of concepts and knowledge to help manage through a variety of team decisions, actions and outcomes. The synergy of good teamwork that promises so much for the achievement of organisational objectives can sometimes be elusive. Smooth team development is not as common as punctuated equilibrium. The inherent aspects of human nature, such as a tendency for social loafing and a preoccupation with power and control, often lead to conflicts within and between teams. There are well-documented features of high-performing teams and clarity of individual roles in best practice teams which can help managers improve the chances of success. Ultimately, there is no way to avoid the step up in complexity that occurs when moving from individual work to teamwork. The decision variables become so much more convoluted. There are models available for trying to reach consensus and harmony in team activities, but team leaders must always be alert to the issues that can emerge. Chapter 6 focuses specifically on leadership and augments many of the ideas covered in this chapter.

KEY POINTS

This chapter has

- defined groups and teams
- described the team development sequence
- explained some of the main reasons for punctuated equilibrium in team performance
- discussed the implications for team performance of groupthink, synergy and social loafing
- described team decision-making approaches
- defined high-performance work teams
- discussed team roles, cohesiveness and leadership as key aspects of team management.

KEY TERMS

BOUNDED RATIONALITY
The fact that incomplete (bounded) information is applied in making any decision.

DELPHI METHOD
A way of building consensus on a course of action by repeatedly applying a series of questionnaires to collect data from a panel of selected experts on the issue.

GROUP
A collection of individuals working on achieving similar goals.

GROUPTHINK
When the views of the more dominant members of a group become accepted as the consensus.

JUDGMENT HEURISTICS

Judgment patterns formed from previous decision outcomes which can act as guides for future decisions.

NOMINAL GROUP TECHNIQUE

A face-to-face method to balance participation, apply different processes for different phases of creative problem solving, and reduce possible errors in aggregating individual judgments into group decisions.

RINGELMANN EFFECT

Also known as social loafing; when a person relies on the hard work of others to carry them through.

SELF-MANAGING TEAM

A team that draws on the skills and experience of each member and delivers high quality outputs by a collaborative synchronisation without needing a single defined leader.

SOCIAL LOAFING

Also known as the Ringelmann effect; when a person relies on the hard work of others to carry them through.

SYNERGY

High levels of effectiveness and efficiency that sometimes cannot be explained by just breaking down the aspects of the processes that created the event. Synergy is when the whole becomes greater than the sum of its parts.

TEAM

A collection of individuals working interdependently with shared vision and cohesion on achieving jointly agreed goals.

STUDY AND REVISION QUESTIONS

Q *Team leaders have to work hard to ensure a cohesive team so that appropriate motivation and coordination occur between members and team objectives are achieved. Under what circumstances might cohesion in a team be problematic for the team leader or the organisation?*

Q *Compare and contrast Nominal Group Technique with the standard committee-based approach to making group decisions.*

Q *Belbin's team roles could be applied every time a new team is established. What would be the positive and negative outcomes if this were to be the case?*

Q *Discuss the idea at the beginning of this chapter that we must 'collaborate in order to compete'.*

REFERENCES

Andersen, M. (2010). Creating esprit de corps in times of crisis: Employee identification with values in a Danish windmill company. *Corporate Communications: An International Journal*, 15(1), 102–23.

Ashkanasy, N. M. (2002). Leadership in the Asian century: Lessons from GLOBE. *International Journal of Organisational Behaviour*, 5(3), 150–63.

Åstebro, T., & Elhedhli, S. (2006). The effectiveness of simple decision heuristics: Forecasting commercial success for early-stage ventures. *Management Science*, 52(3), 395–409.

Baer, M., Leenders, R., Oldham, G. & Vadera, A. (2010). Win or lose the battle for creativity: The power and perils of intergroup competition. *Academy of Management Journal*, 53(4), 827–45.

Belbin, R. M. (1981). *Management teams: Why they succeed or fail*. Oxford: Butterworth-Heinemann.

Belbin Associates (2010). Home to Belbin team roles. Belbin Associates. <www.belbin.com>

Burton-Chellew, M., Ross-Gillespie, A. & West, S. (2010). Cooperation in humans: Competition between groups and proximate emotions. *Evolution and Human Behavior*, 31(2), 104–8.

Chutnik, M., & Grzesik, K. (2010). Performance through relationships: Towards a cohesive virtual intercultural team. *Journal of Intercultural Management*, 2(1), 49–56.

Creed, A., Zutshi, A. & Swanson, D. (2008). Power and passion: Remoulded teamwork in a plastics factory. *Team Performance Management*, 14(5/6), 196–213.

Dalkey, N. C., & Helmer, O. (1963). An experimental application of the Delphi method to the use of experts. *Management Science*, 9(3), 458–67.

Fincham, R., & Rhodes, P. S. (2005). *Principles of organizational behaviour*. Oxford: Oxford University Press.

Forbes, R., Cooper, A. & Mitchell, H. (1953). The composition of the adult human body as determined by chemical analysis. *Journal of Biological Chemistry*, 203(1), 359–66.

Gersick, C. (1991). Revolutionary change theories: A multi-level exploration of the punctuated equilibrium paradigm. *Academy of Management Review*, 16(1), 10–36.

Gould, S. J. (1989). Punctuated equilibrium in fact and theory. *Journal of Social Biological Structure*, 12(2–3), 117–36.

Hodgetts, R. M., & Hegar, K. W. (2008). *Modern human relations at work*. Thomas Southwestern, Ohio.

Hsu, C., & Sandford, B. (2007). The Delphi technique: Making sense of consensus. *Practical Assessment, Research & Evaluation*, 12(10), 1–8.

Ingham, A., Levinger, G., Graves, J. & Peckham, V. (1974). The Ringelmann effect: Studies of group size and group performance. *Journal of Experimental Social Psychology*, 10(4), 371–84.

Islam, R. (2010). Group decision making through nominal group technique: An empirical study. *Journal for International Business and Entrepreneurship Development*, 5(2), 134–53.

Janis, I. L. (1972). *Victims of Groupthink*. Boston: Houghton Mifflin.

Katzenbach, J., & Smith, D. (1993). The discipline of teams. *Harvard Business Review*, 71(2), 111–20.

Kidwell, R. (2010). Loafing in the 21st century: Enhanced opportunities—and remedies—for withholding job effort in the new workplace. *Business Horizons*, 53(6), 543–52.

Kuhn, K. (2010). Can managers be trained to make better decisions? *Industrial and Organizational Psychology*, 3(4), 434–37.

Lee, S., Blake, H. & Lloyd, S. (2010). The price is right: Making workplace wellness financially sustainable. *International Journal of Workplace Health Management*, 3(1), 58–69.

Maner, J., & Mead, N. (2010). The essential tension between leadership and power: When leaders sacrifice group goals for the sake of self-interest. *Journal of Personality and Social Psychology*, 99(3), 482–97.

Marquardt, M., Seng, N. & Goodson, H. (2010). Team development via action learning. *Advances in Developing Human Resources*, 12(2), 241–59.

Mayo, E. (1931). *Industrial research at the Western Electric Co., Inc.* (U.S.A.). Geneva: International Management Institute.

Millward, L., Banks, A. & Riga, K. (2010). Effective self-regulating teams: A generative psychological approach. *Team Performance Management*, 16(1/2), 50–73.

Moede, W. (1927). Die richtlinien der leistungs-psychologie. *Industrielle Psychotechnik*, 4(1), 193–207.

Morgeson, F., DeRue, D. S. & Karam, E. (2010). Leadership in teams: A functional approach to understanding leadership. *Journal of Management*, 36(1), 5–39.

Ogungbamila, B., Ogungbamila, A. & Adetula, G. (2010). Effects of team size and work team perception on workplace commitment: Evidence from 23 production teams. *Small Group Research*, 20(10), 1–21.

Oldham, G., & Hackman, J. (2010). Not what it was and not what it will be: The future of job design research. *Journal of Organizational Behavior*, 31(1), 463–79.

Orlikowski, W. (2009). The sociomateriality of organisational life: Considering technology in management research. *Cambridge Journal of Economics*, 34(6), 125–41.

REFERENCES

Simon, H. (1991). Bounded rationality and organizational learning. *Organization Science*, 2(1), 125–34.

Stahl, G., Makela, K., Zanderd, L. & Maznevski, M. (2010). A look at the bright side of multicultural team diversity. *Scandinavian Journal of Management*, 26(4), 439–47.

Stone, K. (2010). Kaizen teams: Integrated HRD practices for successful team building. *Advances in Developing Human Resources*, 12(1), 61–77.

Taylor, F. W. (1911). *The principles of scientific management*. New York: Harper Bros.

Tuckman, B. W. (1965). Developmental sequence in small groups. *Psychological Bulletin*, 63(6), 384–99.

Tuckman, B. W., & Jensen, M. A. (1977). Stages of small-group development revisited. *Group & Organization Management*, 2(4), 419–27.

Xiao, Y., & Jin, Y. (2010). The hierarchical linear modelling of shared mental model on virtual team effectiveness. *Kybernetes*, 39(8), 1322–9.

PRACTITIONER INSIGHT

REBECCA WOODWARD

HUMAN RESOURCES
MANAGER, MADGWICKS

Rebecca is HR Manager for Melbourne-based business law firm, Madgwicks. Prior to taking up this role in 2007 upon her arrival in Australia, Rebecca worked for a UK charity and has held HR roles for a UK water provider and government agency. Rebecca holds a Bachelor of Arts Degree and a Postgraduate Diploma in HR, accredited by the Chartered Institute of Personnel and Development (CIPD), which is the UK equivalent of AHRI. Rebecca is a member of the Australian Human Resources Institute and the CIPD.

INTERVIEW

What was your first job?
My first job was working in Sainsburys (UK equivalent of Coles) on a Saturday whilst at school.

What has been your career highlight so far?
I would have to say it was when I worked for Sue Ryder Care (a UK Charity). It was really rewarding working for a charity and feeling that even in a small way, by making sure the nurses were engaged and motivated, I was doing my bit to help.

What's the best part of your job?
The best part of my role is the variety of work and tasks I am exposed to and the fact that I don't know what will be next. I also enjoy the strategic elements such as forward planning new initiatives that help to motivate, retain and reward our staff.

What is the hardest aspect of your role?
When there are people involved there are inevitably tough times when I have to introduce initiatives or sanctions that are unpopular. It can be a loveless and thankless job and I don't think you will be successful in HR if you want to be liked and be everybody's friend. Sometimes you have to make the tough calls.

Anything involving dismissals or retrenchments is always difficult.

What are the current challenges facing you, in your role?
Time is always a challenge—not enough of it! We have just finalised our strategic plan for the next three years so the challenge will be rolling that out and coming up with new initiatives that are different and will help us engage and retain staff.

Do you regularly apply the principles or theories you learnt (when studying organisational behaviour) into your everyday work? In what way?
I do, but I think it is more subconsciously than consciously. By that I mean, I don't think or speak to my Partners using HR language of theories or principles that I have studied, but I practice what I have learnt and apply that into my everyday working situations.

For example, when thinking about initiating change into the workplace I will consider a large number of the principles and theories learnt through my studies such as, the people involved, the culture of the firm and the particular team, how it might impact upon the firm's values, how it impacts or supports the overall vision of the firm, how it might be received by staff, what approach we will take in communicating the new initiatives to staff.

How important is an understanding of 'organisational behaviour' in today's workplace?

I think it's really important to have a broad understanding of organisational behaviour within the workplace. Particularly if you want to evolve the workplace, retain staff, cultivate a positive culture and initiate change.

I also find that candidates in interviews these days, more than ever before, want to know about the organisational behaviour of our firm and I will often be asked to describe the culture, values and vision of the firm. Some of the Partners have also been asked to describe their management style and how they supervise staff.

Is a work–life balance a reasonable expectation in a modern workplace?

I think it can be achieved if you have a supportive boss and workplace that actively encourages and recognises the need for it. I think there is the need for staff and workplaces alike to recognise that a work–life balance is a give and take exercise. I think it is best to work in an environment where the expectation by all parties is that you do your job and that there is flexibility from both sides about how you do that. Working harder is not always about how many hours you spend in the office. It is about producing quality not quantity and about ensuring that there is give and take.

What strategies do you implement in your workplace to help employees achieve an appropriate work–life balance?

We offer part-time working arrangements and we have the option for staff to vary their start and end times (in consultation with their manager). We try to offer flexibility, which takes into consideration the needs of the employee and the employer. This could mean that people leave early on particular days, take extended lunch hours or arrive later on occasions.

Our Partners lead by example too meaning they don't tend to unnecessarily work really long hours, which can sometimes be associated with the reputation of law firms. Our staff work hard and there are occasions when they have to put in the long hours, but this is only expected when it is necessary to complete a job rather than as a matter of course.

We also have a Mind and Body @ Madgwicks programme which offers amongst other things corporate gym membership rates, lunch time sessions on nutrition and other lifestyle matters. We have a lawn bowls team, we have run weekly corporate personal training sessions and we've held yoga classes in the Boardroom at lunch time.

Has technology impacted on work–life balance? Is it harder to achieve with constant access to the 'office', for example?

Definitely. I think technology has impacted on work–life balance in both a positive and negative way. The accessibility to the office through advances such as BlackBerrys means that you do not have to necessarily be in the office to work. You can leave early to enjoy outside pursuits or pick up children and you can still be in touch with what's going on. The downside though is you have to be disciplined or you can find yourself checking emails late at night and on holiday because you can.

Also, if people know that you have a Blackberry then they know that you will have received the email they have sent you. If you do not manage the expectations of clients and your boss, you may find your holiday is filled with the need to respond to work emails.

What do you believe makes a good manager or decision maker? How would you describe your own management style?

There are quite a few qualities that I believe make a good manager or decision maker and have listed them here (in no particular order):

- Good communication skills—you have to be able to communicate clearly to staff about your expectations, any concerns or issues, updates on the business, future plans and so forth.
- Good listening skills—you should really listen to your staff and seek input from them about how they too think things can be improved or any suggestions they may have.
- Decisiveness—you need to be able to make a decision at the end of the day. It's good to seek input, but you have to be prepared to make the hard, and sometimes unpopular decisions.
- Vision and leadership—you have to be able to inspire and lead your team. They need to have confidence in you and your abilities.
- Fairness—you need to be fair in your treatment of staff and transparent in your decisions. Another cliché, but you should treat people the way you would like to be treated. When making a tough call I will always tell my managers to put themselves in the other person's shoes. As long as they can sleep at night knowing that they acted fairly and did everything that they could to prevent a particular outcome then their decision is the right one. It's important to remember that staff will look to see how you handled a particular situation or issue and use this as an indicator of how they would be treated in a similar situation. They will then use that gauge to judge whether they perceive you as a fair employer or not.

6

The Leadership Function

INTRODUCTION

Each leader is a little bit different, which makes the task of finding a unified theory of leadership difficult indeed. Each organisation, group or team needs the leadership function fulfilled, whether by one or a number of circulating leaders. History is replete with examples of great leaders, but the present and the future are filled with uncertain situations, some that have never before been confronted by any leader. This chapter surveys the prominent categories of leadership theory and distils this into a contemporary view. The thinking about leadership has come almost full circle over thousands of years. If you are a leader or plan to be one in these momentous days, it is well worth your while spending good critical thinking time in this chapter.

LEARNING OBJECTIVES	Understanding this chapter will help you to	describe some universal characteristics of leadership

LEARNING OBJECTIVES

Understanding this chapter will help you to
- discuss the historical and current perspective on leadership theories
- define leadership theories according to trait, behavioural, situational or contemporary categories

- describe some universal characteristics of leadership
- debate the role and function of leaders in the context of the modern organisational environment.

OVERVIEW

■

Learning Objective
The historical and
current perspective on
leadership theories

Two of the most pressing current issues for individuals and organisations, rapid change and the threat to environmental sustainability, require resolute leadership if effective responses are to be implemented. The hyperconnected neural network bringing people, teams and organisations together globally has a melting pot effect that risks a loss of clarity about how to act. This comes at a time when we must act more definitively than before if organisations through their constituent groups and teams are to be a part of the solution to the problem of diminished and degraded resources. This chapter explores the role of leadership and identifies the categories of theories that traditionally emerge in the field. Leadership traits, styles and situational theories, and an overview of the current best thinking about leadership, drawing on factors such as charisma and emotional or social intelligence, are all part of the mix. When wondering whether leaders are necessary at all, it is often suggested that the leadership role is crucial even if the person fulfilling it may change. If you find yourself in a leadership position at this momentous point in organisational history, the ideas and theories presented in this chapter can help you to understand your role and draw on lessons from the past to help improve your future effectiveness.

LEADERSHIP TRAITS

When the early generations of managers after the Industrial Revolution began to think about the importance of leadership in the new organisational climate, they began to focus on the examples of highly successful leaders. It was a natural first step to observe the characteristics or traits of famous military, business and political leaders. Fincham and Rhodes (2005) refer to the implicit theory of leadership that most of us apply by admiring great leaders, noticing their traits, and concluding that such characteristics probably form the foundation of how we can train future leaders. **Trait theory** is, therefore, a group of theories any of which aim to identify and define key traits that leaders exhibit, ideally but not always universally. Some examples of observed traits in various leaders from history include courage, intelligence, honesty, persuasiveness and decisiveness. There are many more examples.

■

Trait theory
A group of theories any
of which aim to identify
and define key traits that
leaders exhibit, ideally but
not always universally.

Thought pathway

Think of at least one influential military, political, religious, sporting or business leader of today or days gone by and list for each person the traits by which you would describe them.

There is a clear logic to trait theory because success at leadership must be based on something about the leader. To begin searching their characteristics is a reasonable starting point. There is, of course, a potential fallacy in this approach because every individual leader and their circumstances are quite distinctive. If it were said, for example, that Winston Churchill was courageous and therefore all leaders should learn to be similarly courageous, this would be overlooking another highly successful leader, not in a war situation, who did not rely on courage but, say, strategic thinking, to achieve their major success. If we were to look at every characteristic of every great leader and then say to the next generation of leaders that they should express all of these traits to be successful, we would be asking for a superhuman effort. There is also an implied inherited aspect of many of the traits. This is the suggestion that leaders are born and not made. Chapter 3 covers the debate about nature versus nurture and the fact that we cannot rely so much on genetics as we can upon education and socialisation in the formation of personality. So this is the main limitation of trait theory. It shows us glimpses of what a good leader should be but does not fully explain the learning processes and situations that help leaders develop their personalities, functional behaviours and practical overall style in various situations.

Are there universal traits?

Despite the limitations, trait theories do promise to yield a few generic characteristics that help to frame a universal perspective on leadership. World religions each encourage people to express certain characteristics that if widely followed would promote harmonious social relations. The ancient Greek philosopher Aristotle referred to a set of virtues that people, not least leaders, would be well advised to try to express. Some of these virtues include courage, temperance, friendship and justice (Jones, 1970). It is noted that some of the virtues are bound by their context; for example, what was virtuous in ancient Greece may not be culturally quite as important today (Hume et al., 1991). While people are bound to either shortage or excess of some virtues, if they would try to exhibit what Aristotle called the 'golden mean' or moderate behaviour in relation to the virtues, then social experiences of all kinds would probably be far more civilised. He went as far as establishing a 'golden rule' which is that *one should treat others as one would like others to treat oneself.* This ancient window on thinking about character traits influenced Renaissance philosophers and theologians and thus has translated through literature into modern theories of psychology, theology and sociology.

In organisational behaviour, one trait theory that is a useful starting point in the leadership literature is Theory X and Theory Y (McGregor, 1960). From a motivation perspective, McGregor's research takes a two-factor approach to Maslow's needs hierarchy and identifies that workers with prevailing lower-order needs are more likely to appear lazy and will avoid working on organisational goals in favour of attaining their own ends; he calls them Theory X workers. The other factor is linked to workers with higher-order needs who are more likely to be ambitious and self-motivated and exercise self-control; he calls them Theory Y workers. While this does not provide much practical information about how to motivate workers, there is another level to McGregor's approach that focuses on features of work group leaders. The Theory X leader perceives that workers try to avoid responsibility and that it is the manager's job to keep team workers focused on the job. Theory X leaders think the job itself should be motivating and there is no need to be especially courteous, generous or empathetic to people, except in order to achieve the work task. By contrast, the Theory Y leader thinks of workers as equals, shows concern for people's feelings, builds a climate of trust and expects that people are self-motivated and able to be responsible for their own work as long as social support is available. Thus it is in the perceptions of leaders about their workers that McGregor's research tends to have the most pragmatic value.

Thought pathway

Think of leaders you know in organisations, or generally, who you might be able to categorise as either Theory X or Theory Y leaders. Decide which kind of leader you would prefer to work under. Does that say anything about you as either a Theory X or Y worker?

The five-factor model of personality discussed in Chapter 3 includes the trait of conscientiousness, which research has indicated is the most widely cited positive trait in all kinds of workers. In addition, high levels of conscientiousness are noted to contribute to higher levels of job knowledge and organisational citizenship behaviour, which is well aligned with the function of effective leadership (Musek, 2007). Think about the definition of conscientiousness; it is linked with having a conscience and means to be dutiful, attentive to tasks, and considerate of the needs of everybody within the moment. Wouldn't you like those leading you to have such qualities? Can you be that kind of leader if the occasion calls?

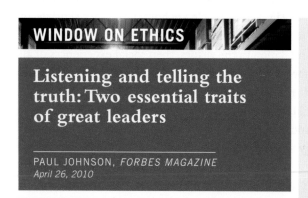

WINDOW ON ETHICS

Listening and telling the truth: Two essential traits of great leaders

PAUL JOHNSON, *FORBES MAGAZINE*
April 26, 2010

Any leader aspiring to greatness must do two things, and he must do them not just at supreme moments or occasionally but all the time. Of course, there are many other things a leader must do, but these are the two that matter most: to listen and to tell the truth.

How has Mr Obama scored? Half and half. At the last moment, as his historic health care measure hung in the balance, the President decided to listen to a group of antiabortion Democrats and act on what he heard. That was decisive. But Mr Obama has yet to tell the nation the full truth about what his health care project is going to cost. Perhaps he's not even told himself or dared to find out and so does not know.

But a leader must know the truth, however awful, even if—in wartime, for instance—he cannot divulge it. Winston Churchill blamed himself for not knowing—because he did not take the necessary steps to find out—the extent of Singapore's military weakness. The ignominious fall of that military base to the Japanese in 1942 came as one of the biggest shocks in the history of the British Empire.

Not knowing is often the result of not listening to those who do know. If Mr Obama were to listen harder, not just occasionally but as a matter of ingrained habit, he'd have no illusions about what his health care plan is going to cost or the ramifications of those costs for individuals and the economy.

Listening carefully and telling the truth are each rare traits to be found in politicians, and rarer still in combination. But it does happen. George Washington listened all his life because he loved to learn and because he had no overwhelming desire to speak, unlike most of those in public life. One passion a leader should forgo, if possible, is a love affair with his own voice (and here even Winston Churchill fell below the mark). Washington, happily, liked the sound of his own silence. He also told the truth, even if at times he followed Edmund Burke's advice and was economical with it. When I was writing my book *George Washington*, I failed to come across any occasion when he had deliberately concealed the truth from anyone who had a right to know it.

One President who admirably combined taciturnity and veracity was Calvin Coolidge, that unobtrusive and so underrated man. He was aptly called 'Silent Cal.' He listened courteously to all his visitors but would not be drawn out. He said: 'Nine-tenths of a President's callers at the White House want something they ought not to have. If you keep dead still they will run down in three or four minutes.'

So Coolidge would remain mute. Slight twitches of his facial muscles spoke for him. He was described as 'an eloquent listener.' When he did speak, however, it was the truth. He told his countrymen that the business of America is business but that 'it rests squarely on the law of service.' And that, in turn, had its 'main reliance [on] truth and faith and justice.'

Every American, each in his or her role, has to save the others—by telling the truth, keeping faith and applying strict justice. That is a message worth giving and hearing but not one we hear much nowadays.

WHO WILL SET THE EXAMPLE?

If we turn to Abraham Lincoln we find a marked combination of listening and truth-telling. Lincoln listened hard, no easy matter in the deafening cacophony of voices just before and during the Civil War.

Considering all he had to do and say, Lincoln spoke amazingly little. As he put it (on Aug. 6, 1862), 'I am very little inclined on any occasion to say anything unless I hope to produce some good by it.' His Gettysburg Address is a classic instance—there is none better in history—of using as few words as possible (261, to be precise) while conveying a powerful message.

Lincoln always endeavored to tell the truth and to ensure that all heard it by clothing it in arresting language. He never won a vote or scored a political advantage by even the most minute sacrifice of factual accuracy. He believed rightly that people would rise to a challenge, however daunting, provided they were convinced the leadership was being honest.

Ronald Reagan, another notable President, also showed himself ready to listen, even though he didn't always hear. And he carefully studied a speaker's body language. Reagan believed that national leaders were too eager to avoid trouble and therefore toned down the truth. He rated his best speeches as those in which he spoke the unvarnished truth—notably his 'Evil Empire' discourse. He personally strengthened its truth element just before delivery.

The world always needs the twin capacities of listening and truth-speaking. The signs point to our being on the eve of high drama in the Middle East, where few listen and most lie. Who involved will set the example of listening with care, then distilling and delivering the truth of what he hears?

Source: <www.forbes.com/forbes/2010/0426/ opinions-paul-johnson-obama-health-care-current-events. html>

This Window illustrates the ease with which we can relate to trait theory. Descriptions of great leaders can inspire us to want to be like they are. The risk is that the particularities of such distinctive historical figures cannot easily be emulated by most people in leadership positions today, and it is also valid to wonder if trying to copy the characteristics of past leaders is of any lasting benefit.

LEADERSHIP STYLES (BEHAVIOURAL THEORIES)

Behavioural theory
Any of the leadership theories that focus upon observations of leadership styles which can be changed by the leader, autonomously or by training.

In the early 20th century, the limitations of trait theories looking at great leaders and the recognition of more universal traits such as conscientiousness and Theory X and Theory Y, factored into leadership research, began to shift attention to leadership styles and behaviours. It was realised that leaders may have dominant behavioural characteristics but that they could also change their overall style at different times and under different circumstances. Behaviours can often be learned and unlearned, whereas other kinds of traits are often hard to change. Behavioural theories, therefore, focus on observations of leadership styles that can be changed by the leader autonomously or by training along the way.

The Michigan and Ohio State studies

As an antecedent of the underlying tenets of the leadership aspects of Theory X and Theory Y, a detailed questionnaire study of leadership styles at Ohio State University in the 1940s delivered some often quoted results (Stodgill, 1963; Szilagyi & Keller, 1976). Two main leadership dimensions were identified as initiating structure and consideration. Initiating structure is the way that a leader establishes order and organises the work team for the completion of tasks, which is very similar to the emphasis of a Theory X leader. Consideration refers to a leader's concern for the welfare of the members of the group, which equates somewhat to the approach of a Theory Y leader.

Another study at University of Michigan came to similar conclusions with slightly different terminology (Bowers, 1973). Characterising a leadership style spectrum ranging from democratic through to autocratic, the Michigan studies found that leaders could be classified as either employee-centred or job-centred. Employee-centred leaders show a high degree of concern for the needs and wishes of staff, again similar to a Theory Y leader. Job-centred leaders focus most directly on the tasks that have to be achieved, which is aligned with a Theory X leader.

The managerial grid

Continuing with research that identifies the two underlying directions of leadership style, Blake and Mouton (1964) proposed a grid of different leadership styles mapped on the concern for people versus the concern for production axes. Figure 6.1 is a representation of the leadership grid showing concern for people on the y-axis and concern for production on the x-axis with the various style blends described within.

Figure 6.1 Blake & Mouton's managerial grid

Source: adapted from Blake and Mouton (1964). The Managerial Grid:
key orientations for achieving production through people.

One critique of behavioural theories of leadership is to suggest they may be just an extension of trait theory. If we say, for example, that a leader is more production-oriented than people-oriented and we label them on Blake and Mouton's grid as a 'produce or perish' manager, there is no consideration up to that point of the circumstances by which the leader was constrained. In other words, the situational variables are not fully considered under the behavioural theories.

WINDOW ON CONFLICT AND NEGOTIATION

Facebook sackings

LEON GETTLER
November 17, 2010

Facebook and other social networking sites are becoming flashpoints for workplace claims. People are now being sacked for comments they have posted. These sites are forcing us to redefine our expectations around privacy.

As reported here, there have been at least five cases before Fair Work Australia where employees have been sacked after something they wrote or did was recorded on Facebook. That's likely to be the tip of the iceberg. There would be many more dismissals that would never have been challenged, let alone reach the tribunal.

Similar sorts of stories are happening overseas. There was one famous case in England last year where a woman came home after a hard day at the office and decided to vent her spleen on Facebook. 'My boss is a total pervy wanker always making me do s— stuff.'

That was mistake number one. Her second was forgetting that her boss was a Facebook friend. He responded: 'That "s— stuff" is called your "job", you know, what I pay you to do?…Don't bother coming in tomorrow. I'll pop your P45 (pink slip) in the post, and you can come in whenever you like to pick up any stuff you've left here. And, yes, I'm serious.'

Or then there is the case of the Connecticut woman who was fired for slagging off at her boss on Facebook. That's what you get when you call your boss a 'dick' and a 'scumbag' on Facebook.

You would have to ask why these people are doing it. Why are they criticising their employers, or writing abusive stuff when they know it's not a private space? Don't they think? Then again, they might see it as a bit of idle chat. As far as they would be concerned, their comments were made in what they felt was a private space.

The interesting part about that case is that a US federal agency, the National Relations Board, has taken up the case and has argued that the company illegally sacked Dawnmarie Souza and that the criticism of her boss on Facebook was generally 'a protected concerted activity'.

And that is why we might need to redefine privacy, particularly when it comes to workplace tribunals. Or alternatively, we need to set down some appropriate rules for what can and can't be said.

These sorts of cases raise a number of important questions. Is Facebook a private space? How do you classify interaction among a closed Facebook circle of friends? Is that a private conversation, or does dissing your job or boss on Facebook become the equivalent of making a public statement that defames and destroys reputations?

Does it matter how many people are in that network?

How many actually have to contribute to your post with their own comments to make it a 'concerted' activity? And are the remarks put up to elicit a response or to tell the world how awful the boss is? Or are the comments being made because someone is just feeling unhappy? What's the intent? And for that matter, if the intent is to vent, are you venting it as part of a private conversation? Or is it the equivalent of scribbling graffiti on a wall or writing a letter?

We don't yet know the answers. But these are the sorts of questions lawyers will be raising in courts around the world.

In the meantime, no doubt, there will be lots of advice, like the kind of stuff offered up by CNN, telling people to think before they post anything and to be careful who they friend on Facebook. In other words, don't be stupid.

But then, is it right to advise people to suppress their private feelings as a career strategy? The reality is that employees will always complain about jobs and bosses. They always have, always will. All technology does is enhance something that's always been there.

Source: <www.theage.com.au/executive-style/ management/blogs/management-line/facebook- sackings/20101113-17rny.html>

This Window demonstrates that leaders can adopt styles of behaviour that are not always widely accepted by followers. You may like to assess the Facebook sacking approach according to Blake and Mouton's managerial grid. Notice that there are unique situational variables in this example. Leadership theory evolved to begin to cater for the contingencies that emerge in certain circumstances.

SITUATIONAL LEADERSHIP THEORIES

■
Learning Objective
Leadership categories: situational theories

■
Situational theory
Situational theories factor in the situations such as relationships between leaders and followers, preferred leader styles, and other situational variables to try to explain successes and failures in achieving organisational objectives.

Research projects to more readily align situational variables with behavioural approaches have contributed to a rich theoretical body in the field of situational leadership. The latter half of the 20th century saw a variety of theories emerge to give a broader view of leadership in the increasingly complex global environment. **Situational theories** factor in the situations such as relationships between leaders and followers, preferred leader styles, and other situational variables to try to explain successes and failures in achieving organisational objectives.

Path–goal theory

House (1971) contributes to the situational leadership literature with path–goal theory, which builds on expectancy theory from the motivation field. He posits that an important leadership function is to compensate for any gaps between the effort–performance relationships of staff. The personal goals of staff are also recognised as relevant motivators. The situational factors that House identifies as most relevant are employee attributes and work-setting attributes. He suggests four main leadership behaviours that can help employees navigate towards their goals at work: leaders can be directive (giving particular advice), supportive (friendly and needs-focused), achievement-oriented (setting high goals, asking for high quality) or participative (consultative and communicative). Depending on the combination of leadership behaviours with the situational variables, employee outcomes can be achieved ranging from job satisfaction, to acceptance of the leader, and motivational behaviour.

Thought pathway

Consider which of the four main leader behaviours in path–goal theory you would feel most comfortable applying as a leader in various situations at work.

The path–goal links to expectancy and goal-setting theories give a solid grounding for this situational approach to leadership. Other theorists have contributed additional useful views in the field.

Fred Fiedler

In a wide-ranging review of what actually happens between leaders and followers, Graen and Uhl-Bien (1995) find that many managerial processes in organisations occur on a dyadic, or person-to-person, basis with managers developing different relationships in line with professional direct reports. This supports the earlier work done by Fiedler (1967) to effectively establish the situational leadership field with the view that situational control levels determine leader effectiveness. Where situational control is high, leaders are more able to predict the likely success of a directive (Fiedler & Chemers, 1984). The measures of control are achieved on multiple levels: leader–member relations, task structure and position power. It was found that leader–member relations are the most significant impact factors on control levels (Fiedler, 1967; Graen & Uhl-Bien, 1995); task structure and position power are the next most important. The measure of leadership style is achieved through the least preferred co-worker (LPC) scale, which is another representation of the task versus relationship dichotomy. High LPC equates with relationship orientation in leadership style; low LPC equates with task orientation. Figure 6.2 is adapted from Fiedler (1967) and shows how different blends of the three key situational variables—leader-group relations, task structure, and position power—merge with LPC scores and lead to eight different degrees of favourability for overall leadership performance.

Figure 6.2   Situational favourability and the LPC score

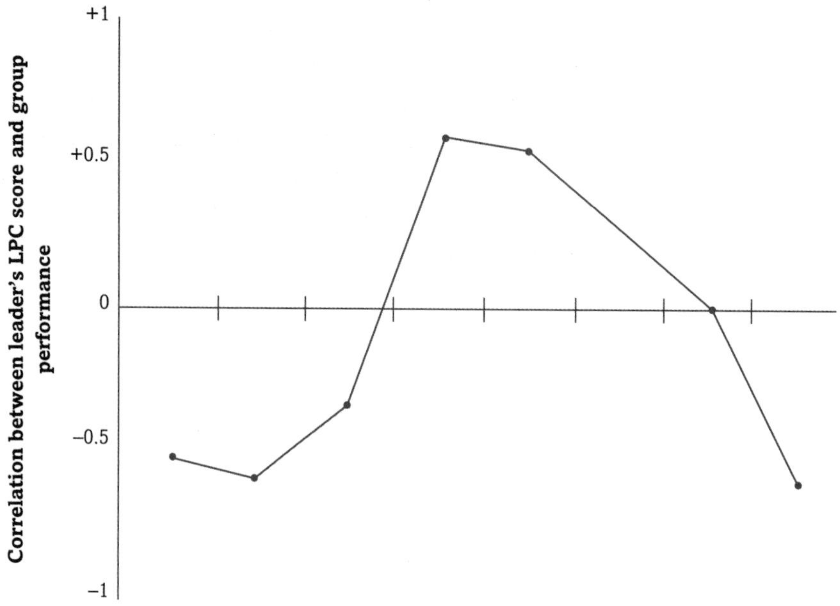

Octant	Situational favourability							
	1	2	3	4	5	6	7	8
Leader-group relations	Good	Good	Good	Good	Poor	Poor	Poor	Poor
Task structure	High	High	Low	Low	High	High	Low	Low
Position power	High	Low	High	Low	High	Low	High	Low

Source: Principles of Organizational Behaviour, *Fourth Edition by Robin Fincham and Peter Rhodes (2005) by permission of Oxford University Press UK.*

While it is relatively simple to identify the most favourable and least favourable circumstances from this chart, there is an inherent complexity in the model. The interdependency between the LPC ratings and the gearings of the three situational variables can be quite subtle. Some critics have also questioned why there should not be more than three main situational variables, which would make the model even more complex. In addition, the LPC rating could easily fluctuate and affect predictability (Smith & Peterson, 1988). These issues are more to do with the practicality of referring to the model in dynamic, evolving leadership situations. The opportunities for further research and refinement of this situational theory remain.

Hersey & Blanchard

Two writers who help simplify and intensify the interest in situational leadership are Hersey and Blanchard (1988), who focus on the degrees of readiness of followers as key situational variables. There are four follower readiness states: able and willing or confident; able but unwilling or insecure; unable but willing or confident; and unable and unwilling or insecure. Four key leadership styles are offered for selection depending on the state of readiness of followers: delegating, participating, selling or telling. Figure 6.3 is a representation of the Hersey and Blanchard situational leadership model.

Figure 6.3 Hersey & Blanchard's situational leadership

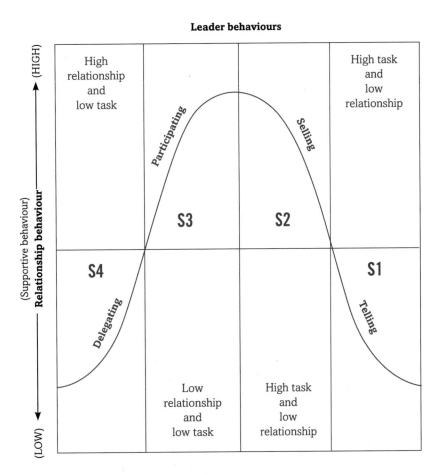

Source: Principles of Organizational Behaviour, *Fourth Edition by Robin Fincham and Peter Rhodes (2005) by permission of Oxford University Press UK.*

This model is simple for a leader to apply: make an assessment of the readiness level of the followers for a particular task, and then use the appropriate leadership style for that situation. Of course, the hidden issues are about how to accurately diagnose follower readiness, whether this can be done independent of any political and interpersonal biases, and whether the leaders can effectively adopt styles or changes readily from one style to the next.

Overall, the situational leadership theories are comparatively sophisticated but not as widely adopted as they could be in management practice. It takes quite a lot of time, energy and money to do a full situational analysis. This is a daunting prospect in fast-changing global environments when quick decisions are often required for competitive advantages to be grasped or protected.

WINDOW ON DECISION-MAKING

Meet the CEO, David Thodey

NARELLE HOOPER
October 19, 2010

David Thodey has been in the top job at Telstra since May 2009, following on from high-profile Sol Trujillo. These are challenging times for Telstra and Thodey is committed to making tough decisions, transforming the company from within and keeping investors happy. He says one of the key challenges is that Telstra is seen as public property—often politicised and constantly analysed by the media to the point where it's the most talked about Australian company. 'It's like Days of our Lives,' he says. Nonetheless, the future looks positive. Demand for Telstra products is high and traffic on Telstra's mobile network doubles every 12 months.

Most of Thodey's efforts for the next two years will be focused on transforming the company from inside the ranks. The aim is for Telstra to move from being an engineering-focused company to one focused on customer service. But like many large companies, he says the challenge is to create a transparent culture 'where it's OK to tell the truth'—including inconvenient truths so management can implement improvements. Thodey says he looked at other models of improved customer service and now Telstra staff have up to 40% of their incentives tied to customer satisfaction. He says: 'I dislike the term "cultural change"—it's a misnomer.'

Thodey says the key to implementing change as a leader is to be resolute in your execution, believe in what you're doing and demand results. 'Results' is a word Thodey keeps coming back to—he admits to having a poor work–life balance himself but measures staff on what they achieve not the amount of hours they work. How will he know when Telstra has reached its goal of change? 'Our customers will tell us.'

Thodey is a leader committed to gender equality. He recently won a US based Catalyst award for his efforts to champion gender diversity. This is something Thodey is working on—Telstra does set gender equity targets but he says ultimately it's about the best person for the job, not filling quotas.

Australia has the highest penetration rate of Iphones in the world. As the country's premier telco carrier, Telstra wants to be a leader in innovation. Thodey regularly travels to Silicon Valley and Israel to see the latest technology and he writes an internal and external company blog about innovation. Thodey says the current challenge is to marry Telstra's new and innovative IT systems to the company's 60-year-old copper foundations. The goal is to simplify: 'Complexity tends to rise up everywhere,' he says.

On the National Broadband Network, Thodey says Telstra is working hard and is 'in the position where you just get on with life'. Alternate plans are in place if the National Broadband Network falls through but Thodey hopes the legislation will get through Parliament. He says the NBN is an incredibly complex project that requires re-writing of several acts of Parliament, dealing with regulators and committing to a 30-year contract.

To round off the evening, a question from an alumn[us] on what will Telstra's business model look like in five years time: 'About 20 billion of our 25 billion dollars comes from Australia…but we have to build new businesses. We are strong in Asia…we're very cautious but quite determined about our Asia presence. We will continue to be strong in media and content. Probably in five years time 20%–30% of our business will be from new revenue sources.'

Source: <www.asb.unsw.edu.au/newsevents/ mediaroom/media/2010/october/Pages/davidthodey.aspx>

'Results' and being 'resolute' are admirable leadership aspirations but they do not fit easily into the sort of complex, unpredictable environment with which Thodey is confronted. This Window demonstrates what has happened in leadership thinking in recent times. Business reality makes leaders seek to express certainty for their followers. In this way, particular traits or styles have reappeared in contemporary leadership literature. A clear, observable trait is easier to demonstrate by a leader in full flight than a full situational analysis of hundreds of possible response permutations. The next section brings us almost full circle to the earliest thinking about what makes a great leader.

CONTEMPORARY LEADERSHIP

Learning Objective
Leadership categories:
Contemporary theories

The practical gaps in trait and behavioural theories and the general complexity of factoring in all relevant issues in situational leadership theories have encouraged researchers to continue in more concise fields. Leadership theory today draws from its rich past but in a pragmatic twist has turned back again to key leadership traits to help navigate through the hypernetworked and complex global situation. Some things about leadership do appear to be universal and this 'back-to-the-future' view has some differences from the earliest trait theories. The contemporary focus is on things that can be learned rather than believing leadership might be largely inheritable by lineage or by inborn characteristics. Being attentive to both tasks and relationships are surely things modern leaders can learn to do. Emotional or social sensitivity, ethics, and charisma in times of transformation are the essential items emerging in leadership today.

CASE STUDY

Problems with the new immigrants in Shirley's dispatch team

The dispatch team in the warehouse at Toy Deals on Line comprised mainly new immigrants to Australia who had come from a variety of backgrounds. Their time in Australia ranged from nine months to five years and there were eight women and five men. They all spoke English but with mixed abilities and a wonderful array of accents. Shirley Bond, the new Supervisor, thought the range of cultures represented was fascinating and looked forward to her new job working with the team and finding out more about where they came from and their stories.

Shirley had come from another distribution company and felt she was well qualified to take on the role at Toy Deals on Line as she had managed teams before.

Unfortunately for Shirley, her first Management meeting with the logistics team nearly shattered her confidence in being able to build the sort of team she wanted. The Warehouse Manager reported that stock was going missing and strongly suspected some of Shirley's team, although there seemed no particular reason for this and there could have been other explanations, including inaccurate stocktaking. The Customer Service Manager reported that orders were not being picked correctly and were often late. The Purchasing Manager helpfully pointed out that his people had trouble understanding their accents and they always seemed to be in the lunch room cooking up something that smelled strange. The Transport Manager volunteered that when Shirley was not around, they spent a lot of time talking among themselves and tended to bunch up according to their home countries: India, Sri Lanka, the Philippines and China. He also pointed out that they were always the last in to work and the first out.

Shirley's boss, Roy Gupta, the Logistics Manager and an immigrant himself, took her aside after the meeting. 'You'll need to get tough with that bunch. If they can't get orders out on time and accurately, we may as well close down. People order our products on line because they want the right price and fast delivery. They definitely want the right products. They are probably responding to what their kids want so we cannot afford to get it wrong. We have grown because of word of mouth; we can collapse just as easily. Get it fixed!'

Shirley knew that riding her team by checking everything they did was just not practical. There weren't enough hours in the day. Pulling them up and giving warnings each time they made a mistake was a possibility but that was also going to take time. Then there would be recruiting replacements if they were dismissed or resigned. The location and salary level meant that applicants were going to be from a similar demographic. She didn't want to go through all that if it was going to turn into an ongoing process of just turning over staff.

'No,' she decided, 'there has to be some other way of having them do a good job. I know they can do the job, I've seen them do it properly, it's not that hard,' she thought, 'and I know they would be distraught to lose their jobs! They are so proud of the lives they have built in Australia.'

Shirley went home for the weekend determined to come back on Monday with a plan that would turn things around.

CASE STUDY QUESTIONS

1 With reference to McGregor's Theory X and Theory Y, describe how the management team might view Shirley's team and why they might have this view.

2 If the management team's perceptions are correct, why might the dispatch team be behaving in this way? You may refer to sections in Chapter 4 on motivation as well as the sections in this chapter.

3 How would you describe Roy Gupta's leadership style and why he might have this approach?

4 Could Roy have used an alternative approach with Shirley and would this have made a difference?

5 What are Shirley's options if she wants to maintain her own credibility and have her team perform?

Emotional (social) intelligence

Emotional intelligence
The ability to sense and respond appropriately to emotional or social cues in our relationships with other people.

Good leadership, good teamwork and good negotiation all rely on a highly refined sense of how people around us are feeling and responding to the things we do and say. Since so much about organisational strategy and activity depends on people and relationships, a high emotional quotient (EQ) is increasingly crucial if one is going to be a competent leader (Cherniss, 2010). **Emotional intelligence** is the feeling-based counterpart of the Intelligence Quotient (IQ). It is the ability to sense and respond appropriately to emotional or social cues in our relationships with other people (Goleman, 2006; Badea & Pana, 2010). A good leader is both smart and sensitive. This is essentially about leaders being good at relationships so that a level of trust can build about expected responses. If a worker can go to their leader and confidently expect a fair hearing, socially responsive feedback and a reasonable level of empathy about any emerging problems, then a supportive and trusting relationship is formed and most kinds of issues can be surmounted (Harms & Crede, 2010).

WINDOW ON COMMUNICATION

How do I help build trust within my team?

POLLYANNA LENKIC
July 29, 2010

I lead a team of highly talented and very individual people. However, a recent team survey has highlighted a lack of trust and confidence within my team. How do I help build the trust?

Trust is the foundation of all successful relationships. In teams and organisations business processes are conducted via relationships and trust is the foundation of healthy and productive relationships. Building trust within your team will be a key ingredient to your team's long-term success, the retention of team members, motivation of individuals and productivity.

Trust cannot be demanded of others. If you command the loyalty of others and expect them to follow you, the best you can hope for is a following based on fear.

Trust is experienced based and built up through repeated experiences. If a person proves themselves to be trustworthy, people will trust them. If they show themselves to be the contrary, people will respond appropriately.

Trust is about reliability and doing the right thing. Distrust increases tension and negative behaviour, which can damage the spirit of the team, negatively impacting collaboration, and ultimately affect productivity.

As the leader some steps you can take to help build trust in your team are:

Create a safe environment where you (or an external person) can facilitate an open and honest discussion about the results of the survey and hear the thoughts and responses from your team members. Set firm ground rules/agreements prior to the discussion taking place.

Once your team members have opened up be sure to listen with an open mind and avoid any defensive behaviour. As their leader, model the behaviour you want to see.

Focus on the issues presented and solutions going forward, avoiding and not tolerating any personal attacks.

Clearly define unacceptable behaviours.

Clearly communicate accountabilities and consequences if team members are engaging in unacceptable behaviours.

Establish the underlying reasons for the lack of trust within the team.

Have a discussion about trust and what actions you can all take to increase trust levels.

Discuss the types of behaviours and actions that would promote trust within the team. You may wish to develop an agreed Code of Conduct going forward that clearly communicates acceptable and unacceptable behaviours and actions.

Identify the positive outcomes for each team member and the team as a whole by investing in this process. In order for them to act they will need to understand what's in it for them. Find a compelling reason in which you are all aligned.

Take a moment to reflect on how you feel about your team (as a team and also the individuals within the team). Do you trust them? Do your behaviours demonstrate this?

Be courageous in your leadership and ask the 'hard questions' in service of building and protecting the integrity of the team and the organisation.

Do your team members perceive you as trustworthy? Below are some tips for ensuring that you continue to model and help build a trusting environment:

Ensure that you always resolve issues with direct communication to the relevant person/parties, avoiding discussing issues with other team members.

Ensure that you acknowledge individuals'/the team's contributions both personally and publicly, avoiding taking credit for team/individual achievements yourself.

Only make promises that you know you can honour; if you can't, be honest about it.

Be clear and direct in your communication at all times.

Schedule regular meetings with team members to discuss ongoing issues/concerns and successes.

Avoid behaviours that erode trust, for example: shaming, belittling, criticising, manipulating, breaking promises, teasing and withdrawing.

Engage in behaviour that promotes trust: honesty, congruency, consistency, being authentic, supportive and loyalty.

Source: <www.smartcompany.com.au/second-time-around/20100729-how-do-i-help-build-trust-within-my-team.html>

This Window promotes openness and sensitivity in a leader as one of the ways of helping to build trust. When a leader is abrupt and insensitive, the team culture can become guarded and overall productivity is likely to suffer. Implied with the expectation of trust comes the sentiment of respect for each individual. To be able to show respect requires a developed ability to understand people and their needs. Finding a proper ethical balance in leaders also overlaps with broader concepts of accountability and business sustainability (Svensson & Wood, 2009; Svensson, 2010), and this has encouraged some contemporary theorists to continue to explore the notion of ethics in leadership as something of a possible panacea (Piccolo et al., 2010). Some of the research perspectives in this field are quite encouraging, especially in the context of emerging global, social and geopolitical changes (Magala, 2010).

Ethical leadership

Learning Objective
Some universal characteristics of leadership

What does it mean to say that a leader is ethical? Are they authentic (Avolio & Gardner, 2005)? Are they awakened (Marques, 2010)? Do they care about the organisation, the community, or the condition of the planet? Much of the central idea of ethics relates to the perspective of self versus others. If you are acting to please yourself alone, then you are more likely to be perceived as unethical. If you can suitably accommodate the needs of others in your daily actions and communications, you are more likely to be perceived as ethical. The balance is crucial. It is probably in getting the balance right between the needs of others and catering to self-interest that the leadership of work–life balance in the workplace, for example, becomes exemplified.

With implications for the expression of ethics, the environment of frenetic and constant change is increasingly unavoidable. Leaders need to take stock of the changing nature of the global environment and its impacts on organisational structure and strategy. A cursory approach to change management opens leaders to accusations of unethical leadership. Transformational leadership theory suggests it is a central requirement that leaders possess the skills to successfully navigate people through turbulent times (Bass & Aviolo, 1990), and this is essentially because to get it wrong is a fatal mistake for leaders. Transformational leaders should be able to give their followers individualised consideration, intellectual stimulation, inspirational motivation and idealised influence (Aviolo et al., 1991). To some extent, this aligns with the concept of being a conscientious leader (Musek, 2007), which is one of the Big 5 personality attributes. The flow-through from the individual to group to leader factors is evident when flux and transformation are prevalent and ethics is being considered.

Thought pathway

The global financial crisis and the collapse of large corporations lead many business commentators to suggest that ethical leadership is no longer optional but essential. In what ways do you think an ethical leadership approach would do anything more for the financial success of a company than simply taking a strategic approach to maximising profit?

Being ethical is not the only thing that matters for leaders. Followers can sometimes take a negative view of a leader not perceived as 'strong' and prepared to make tough decisions. Leadership in times of change especially requires attention on what it is that persuades followers to follow leaders.

Charisma and the leadership of change

Learning Objective
The role and function of leaders in the modern organisational environment

Emotional intelligence and an ethical disposition are among the characteristics that might be attributed to a charismatic leader (Ashkanasy & Tse, 2000), but there is an implication of more general persuasion and influence involved (Conger & Kanungo, 1988), especially in highly changeable times. Transformational leadership applies to the set of qualities that seem to enable leaders to succeed in the midst of environmental turbulence. Transformational leadership is best expressed by a charismatic communication style, the communication of a clear vision, the effective implementation of the vision, and directly relating to followers as individuals. There is a real art involved with this kind of ability. John F. Kennedy, Bill Clinton, Martin Luther King, Mohandas Gandhi and Nelson Mandela are among famous leaders credited with having charisma and transformational capabilities.

Thought pathway

Can you identify precisely what it is that makes each of the abovementioned charismatic? Can you think of business leaders that you would be prepared to label charismatic?

Change leadership theory, as well as catering for the big picture transformations, also acknowledges the more detailed, incremental changes that take place. Transactional leadership builds upon the situational views of House (1971) and Fiedler (1967), especially the link with leader–member relations. The transactional leader is hands on every day, working side by side with staff, regularly using the reward system for motivation. You can probably think of examples that support these two kinds of change leadership. There are transformational leaders who use their charisma, make their vision clear, communicate the vision really well and seem to have popular appeal at a broad personal level for their followers, but manage to delegate most of the hard work in the process. Then there are transactional leaders who have a more approachable kind of charisma demonstrated by rolling up their sleeves and working alongside staff, who have a detailed knowledge of the intricacies of the job and are very responsive to successes and ensuring rewards are distributed fairly for successes achieved. Maybe you can even think of leaders who are able to apply their charismatic qualities in both transformative and transactional ways according to the need of the day.

CASE STUDY

When the main customer disappears, more of the same won't do

David Barclay was very pleased with the initial meetings he had with his managers. They seemed personable, committed to the Company and enthusiastic about their jobs. They had all been there for quite some time, from eight to 15 years, and he was looking forward to working with them.

David had just joined Victorian Furniture Designs Ltd (VFD) as CEO. His predecessor had been there for 12 years and was popular with all the staff. The company, which designed period furniture and manufactured overseas and locally, was performing quite well and had been left in good shape. Or so David thought until he looked more closely at the past sales and the forward orders. It looked as if the fortunes of VFD were due to significant sales to one major chain of stores, George's Home Furnishings, over the years. This business had recently been bought by a Malaysian company and their future orders had since reduced drastically.

'What's happened to George's?' David asked Sam Pilbury, the Sales Manager. 'They've started bringing in lots of cheap Chinese stuff,' said Sam.

'Well, they were 30% of our business, how do we replace that?' Sam just shrugged and mumbled, 'it should come right as the economy gets back on its feet.' David started to worry. 'I don't think they've been through tough times,' he thought.

He spent his weekend going through the accounts to see how he could stay in the black while they worked on finding more business to fill the hole left by George's.

At the managers' meeting on Monday morning he announced that there would have to be some belt-tightening to get through the next year while they looked for more sales. David was surprised that they seemed to take this news without flinching. 'I'm not sure you realise how serious this is,' he said. 'This may mean cuts in staff, and it certainly means we are going to have to come up with some new ideas and work hard at keeping costs down.'

David took a particular interest in watching his managers over the next few days while he kept examining the accounts and looking for savings. They did not appear to be worried and life seemed to go on as usual.

The next week he arranged meetings with each of his direct reports to listen to their cost-saving ideas. He wanted a new sales and marketing strategy from Sam and he also arranged tours of the local manufacturing plants.

He knew as soon as he walked into the first plant that it was not well managed. Housekeeping was sloppy, with raw materials stacked in a haphazard way all around the assembly areas. Excessive wastage was evident from the bins lined up in the dispatch area and the staff did not seem to move with much purpose. The receptionist was reading a magazine at the front desk and there seemed to be lots of small groups standing around laughing and joking. While David thought people should enjoy their work and their relationships he could just tell this situation he had inherited was way beyond that.

His attendance at the monthly sales meeting didn't lift his spirits either. When the sales reps were reporting on their sales the figures all seemed to be flat or down and they didn't seem to worry about this. Their plans seemed to be to keep on doing more of the same. They even used poor figures produced by the Accounts Department as an excuse, which just indicated to David that he probably had a problem in that area as well.

At his next managers' meeting he laid it on the line. He spelled out clearly that the current performance was not sustainable and he wanted new targets from all areas that would either increase sales or cut costs. He wanted these by next week at his individual meetings with the managers.

After his individual meetings he began to have doubts about his communications abilities. They didn't seem to understand. Their new targets were either similar to their old ones with just minor modifications

or, in the case of Neil Reid, the Manufacturing Manager, nonexistent. Neil stressed that his plants were 'best practice' and there was no room for improvement. He had been praised by the previous CEO for his performance in the past and felt he did a great job.

David spent his weekend redoing the numbers for the rest of the year and wrote plans for his managers that had key performance indicators he knew would shock them. He intended to do just that and to follow up on a weekly basis to make sure they were met.

Two months later David assessed the situation. Out of six direct reports, one had met his targets, two had resigned and three were on their second warnings.

He was going to have to explain this situation to the board and tell them how he was going to address it. He knew he was going to be busy recruiting for a few months and he wanted to make sure he hired the right sort of people.

CASE STUDY QUESTIONS

1 What sort of leader do you think David's predecessor was? What sort of traits do you think he may have possessed?

2 Where do you think David's actions fit into the situational leadership model?

3 What do you think David could have done differently? Use any of the models described in the chapter to support your ideas.

4 What should David do now with the people he has remaining?

5 When David recruits his new management team, how do you think he should go about integrating them into the Company and obtaining the best performance possible?

LEADERSHIP IN THE NEURAL NETWORK

Network theory identifies hubs as crucial connection points that sustain the network (Mukherjee, 2009). Like a major road intersection, some type of switching and coordination mechanism is essential in network hubs so as to avoid major disruption. You understand what happens when a crucial transformer goes down in a power network, or when a software glitch happens in a major hub in the internet. Leadership in organisations can be equated with network hubs (Sawhney & Nambisan, 2010). The more connected and functional the main leadership centres are, the more resilient the whole organisation will be. Leadership plays a crucial role in determining when and where resources can flow. Chapter 5 considers the self-managing team as a potential substitute for a single leader and one can see how this applies in network theory. A group can be a hub as much as an individual. It is the function of coordination and control that is most important rather than exactly who is assigned the task. There is a maturity required of all of the members of a self-managing team to be able to effectively circulate the leadership role. In addition, automation and computerisation can and do replace leaders in certain decision centres. It is relevant for every leader to consider the extent of their expendability and the fact it is the function rather than the possession of the role that is most important.

CONCLUSION

The motivation of groups and teams, the realisation of organisational vision and the charting of achievement through dynamic organisational environments are the primary goals of the leadership function. This chapter identified trait, behaviour, situational and contemporary categories of leadership theories. There is not one best approach; however, elements of each of the categories remain relevant today. Of special note is the consistency of the research showing two general styles of leadership: production, task or structure versus people, relationships and concern for others. There is general agreement that leaders can be trained and can learn to be better. There is current emphasis on the need for ethical and emotional sensitivity of leaders, which is heightened by sustainability and accountability issues in the increasingly volatile global organisational environment. Leaders today have to help organisations navigate change and this requires an artful blend of charisma, knowledge, emotional intelligence and an ethical disposition. Leadership is like a hub in the organisational network metaphor. Some of what a leader does can be shared, automated and transferred, but the leadership function still has to be fulfilled effectively if people are collectively going to be prepared to follow along.

KEY POINTS

This chapter has

- discussed the historical and current perspective on leadership theories
- defined leadership theories according to trait, behavioural, situational or contemporary categories
- described some universal characteristics of leadership
- debated the role and function of leaders in the context of the modern organisational environment.

KEY TERMS

BEHAVIOURAL THEORY

Any of the leadership theories that focus upon observations of leadership styles which can be changed by the leader, autonomously or by training.

EMOTIONAL INTELLIGENCE

Also referred to as Emotional Quotient (EQ), the feeling-based counterpart of the Intelligence Quotient (IQ). Emotional intelligence is the ability to sense and respond appropriately to emotional or social cues in our relationships with other people.

SITUATIONAL THEORY

Situational theories factor in the situations such as relationships between leaders and followers, preferred leader styles, and other situational variables to try to explain successes and failures in achieving organisational objectives.

SOCIAL LOAFING

Also known as the Ringelmann effect; when a person relies on the hard work of others to carry them through.

SYNERGY

High levels of effectiveness and efficiency that sometimes cannot be explained by just breaking down the aspects of the processes that created the event. Synergy is when the whole becomes greater than the sum of its parts.

TEAM

A collection of individuals working interdependently with shared vision and cohesion on achieving jointly agreed goals.

TRAIT THEORY

A group of theories any of which aim to identify and define key traits that leaders exhibit, ideally but not always universally.

STUDY AND REVISION QUESTIONS

Q *What are the main examples in the Window on Ethics that have relevance for the section of this chapter that deals with ethical leadership?*

Q *Explain why the work of Hersey and Blanchard is categorised as a situational theory of leadership.*

Q *Discuss this comment: 'Contemporary leadership theories are nothing more than trait theory brought back again.'*

Q *In the Window on Decision-making, Telstra CEO David Thodey says, 'the key to implementing change as a leader is to be resolute in your execution, believe in what you're doing and demand results.' Do you agree? And to which category of leadership theories would you relate this approach?*

REFERENCES

Ashkanasy, N. M., & Tse, B. (2000). Transformational leadership as management of emotion: A conceptual review. In: N. Ashkanasy, C. Hartel & W. Zerbe (eds), *Emotions in the Workplace: Research, Theory and Practice*. Westport, CN: Quorom Books, pp. 221–35.

Avolio, B., & Gardner, W. (2005). Authentic leadership development: Getting to the root of positive forms of leadership. *Leadership Quarterly*, 16(1), 315–18.

Aviolo, B., Waldman, D. & Yammarino, F. (1991). Leading in the 1990's: The four I's of transformational leadership. *Journal of European Industrial Training*, 15(4), 9–16.

Badea, L., & Pana, N. (2010). The role of empathy in developing the leader's emotional intelligence. *Theoretical and Applied Economics*, 17(2), 69–78.

Blake, R. R., & Mouton, J. S. (1964). *The managerial grid: Key orientations for achieving production through people*. Houston: Gulf Publishing Company.

Bowers, D. (1973). OD techniques and their results in 23 organizations: The Michigan ICL study. *Journal of Applied Behavioral Science*, 9(1), 21–43.

Cherniss, C. (2010). Emotional intelligence: Toward clarification of a concept. *Industrial and Organizational Psychology*, 3(2), 110–26.

Conger, J., & Kanungo, R. (1988). *Charismatic leadership, the elusive factor in organisational effectiveness*. San Francisco: Jossey Bass.

Fiedler, F. E. (1967). *A theory of leadership effectiveness*. McGraw-Hill series in management. New York: McGraw-Hill.

Fiedler, F., & Chemers, M. (1984). *The leader match concept*, 2nd edn. New York: John Wiley & Sons.

Fincham, R., & Rhodes, P. S. (2005). *Principles of organizational behaviour*. Oxford: Oxford University Press.

Goleman, D. (2006). The socially intelligent leader. *Educational Leadership*, 64(1), 76–81.

Graen, G. B., & Uhl-Bien, M. (1995). Relationship-based approach to leadership: Development of leader–member exchange (LMX) theory of leadership over 25 years: Applying a multi-level multi-domain perspective. *Leadership Quarterly*, 6 (2), 219–47.

Harms, P., & Crede, M. (2010). Emotional intelligence and transformational and transactional leadership: A meta-analysis. *Journal of Leadership & Organizational Studies*, 17(1), 5–17.

Hersey, P., & Blanchard, K. (1988). *Management of organizational behaviour*. Englewood Cliffs, NJ: Prentice Hall.

House, R. (1971). A path goal theory of leader effectiveness. *Administrative Science Quarterly*, 16(3), 321–39.

Hume, D., Selby-Bigge, L. A., Nidditch, P. H., & Sayre-McCord, G. (1991). *Enquiries concerning human understanding & concerning the principles of morals [with] A treatise of human nature*. Oxford: Oxford University Press.

Jones, W. (1970). *A history of Western philosophy*, 2nd edn. New York: Harcourt, Brace, Jovanovich.

Magala, S. (2010). Ethical control and cultural change (in cultural dreams begin organizational responsibilities). *Journal of Public Affairs*, 10(3), 139–51.

Marques, J. (2010). Awakened leaders: Who are they and why do we need them? *Development and Learning in Organizations*, 24(2), 7–10.

McGregor, D. (1960). *The human side of enterprise*. Toronto: McGraw-Hill.

Mukherjee, A. (2009). Leading the networked organization. *Leader to Leader*, 2009(52), 23–9.

Musek, J. (2007). A general factor of personality: Evidence for the Big One in the five-factor model. *Journal of Research in Personality*, 41(6), 1213–33.

Piccolo, R., Greenbaum, R., den Hartog, D. & Folger, R. (2010). The relationship between ethical leadership and core job characteristics. *Journal of Organizational Behavior*, 31(2–3), 259–78.

Sawhney, M., & Nambisan, S. (2010). *The global brain: Your roadmap for innovating faster and smarter in a networked world*. Upper Saddle River, NJ: Wharton School.

Smith, P. B., & Peterson, M. F. (1988). *Leadership, organizations and culture: An event management model*. London: Sage.

Stogdill, R. M. (1963). *Manual for the leader behavior description questionnaire—Form XII*. Columbus, OH: Bureau of Business Research, Ohio State University.

Svensson, G., & Wood, G. W. (2009). *Business ethics: Through time and across contexts*. Lund: Studentlitteratur.

Szilagyi, A., & Keller, R. (1976). A comparative investigation of the supervisory behavior description questionnaire (SBDQ) and the revised leader behavior description questionnaire (LBDQ-form XII). *Academy of Management Journal*, 19(4), 642–9.

Wagner, B., & Svensson, G. (2010). Sustainable supply chain practices: Research propositions for the future. *International Journal of Logistics Economics and Globalisation*, 2(2), 176–86.

PRACTITIONER INSIGHT

RITA
D'ARCY

Rita is a well-seasoned Human Resources professional with over 18 years in her chosen field. With formal qualifications in Strategic Human Resources Management and Industrial Relations Law, and a Fellow member of the Australian Human Resources Institute, Rita has held key HR leadership roles within local and global organisations. Rita has also consulted to businesses on people strategies in a number of sectors including retail, IT, infrastructure, professional services and not-for-profit. This background has enabled her to be a results-oriented business partner, offering organisations expertise in effective people management and engagement strategies.

Rita has a great interest in enabling organisations to achieve their vision and business goals through great people—people who are contributing, inspired, engaged and ultimately, true ambassadors of their organisation's brand and culture.

An important theme constantly on Rita's agenda as she engages with business is leadership development. Most HR professionals would agree that at the core of employee engagement and performance is strong, respected, supportive and inspirational leaders. Therefore, Rita believes that the strengthening leadership skills in organisations is absolutely pivotal to business growth and success.

Rita is married with a young daughter. She lives in Sydney and is currently pursuing her Masters in Organisational Development through distant education. She also holds a Diploma in Company Directors Course and Certification IV in Training and Assessment. In her spare time, she enjoys writing articles for professional publications, charity work, the company of family and friends over a home-cooked dining extravaganza, theatre and ballroom dancing.

INTERVIEW

What was your first job?
Casual Sales Assistant at Coles Fosseys Thursday nights and Saturday morning.

What has been your career highlight so far?
Heading up the HR function for IKEA Australia. This was my first appointment as a true transformational leader. Working again within a global company, with a strong brand presence and culture, learning about 'Swedishness' and being unleashed and empowered to truly make a difference during a period of intense organisational transition in the Australian market

In your current role, what does a typical day involve?
At a high level, coaching and supporting a team of HR professionals; understanding the business strategy and drivers; meeting and engaging with employees; collaborating with senior management; ensuring the people strategy lines up

with and is supporting the business direction and; ensuring strategy transforms effectively from planning stage to delivery and results.

What is the hardest aspect of your role?
• Letting good people go from your business
• Maintaining strength and courage during a crisis
• Managing transformational change.

What are the current challenges facing you, in your role?
• Developing female leaders into senior positions
• Having a pipeline of the next generation leaders and business critical specialists
• Convincing senior management of innovative people strategies and programs
• Having a good mix in the HR team of 'transactors' and 'business partners'.

Do you regularly apply the principles or theories you learnt (when studying organisational behaviour) into your everyday work? In what way?

Most definitely. I can think of numerous examples:

- Managing transformational change in the organisation and identifying the people impacts upfront
- Designing in-house leadership programs
- Developing a performance management system and taking values and behaviours into consideration
- Mapping out a recruitment strategy with diversity in mind.

How important is an understanding of 'organisational behaviour' in today's workplace?

I believe this is a critical requirement of leaders in today's workplace. There are many drivers for this including: our transition to a service economy over the years; globalisation; immigration; advanced technologies; more educated workforce; aging population; increasing mental illness; Government policy, etc, etc. No matter which way you slice it up, organisations achieve through people. So, to get the right business result requires a better understanding of human behaviour and how it responds to business stimuli each and every day. That is, if I make x business decision, what is the y people response, which gives me z result.

Is a work–life balance a reasonable expectation in a modern workplace?

Yes it is, within reason. People have many balls up in the air, juggling these on a daily basis. It is unreasonable to expect that the belief of our previous generation that you 'leave your personal matters at the front door of work' is applicable in today's society. It probably wasn't applicable back then either but we are now wise about the importance of engaging employees in the workplace in a more holistic and innovative way. Naturally, there needs to be clear rules and boundaries to ensure a sustainable workplace. It is about 'give and take'. My experience shows that workplaces who allow for that balance win in the end through a highly committed, loyal and hard-working workforce.

What strategies do you implement in your workplace to help employees achieve an appropriate work–life balance?

- Flexible working hours/days
- Paid parental leave
- Study leave
- Extended leave without pay
- Remote/mobile office with supporting technology
- Trial retirements
- Breastfeeding facilities
- Purchase of extra annual leave.

Are there greater expectations (on you or your workplace) to help motivate and engage employees in their work than ever before?

I don't know if the expectations are actually greater now than before. I believe it is more a case of managing a workforce who articulate their expectations more confidently and clearly. If the employer fails to then motivate or engage the individual, they will simply shun the loyalties reflected by past generations and move to a new employer who can satisfy their needs at work. Diversity plays a role in this. It means that HR professionals cannot design their policies as a 'one size fits all'. They need to understand the motivational triggers by individual and group these up into more customised policies and practices. Then, they have to partner with business leaders to help them implement these policies and practices in order to better satisfy employees.

How do you communicate company strategy with staff at all levels?

You can have all of this outlined in the most snazzy documentation and place it in an email or on your company intranet site but unless you are spending time explaining this to people all year through, giving context and communicating as things develop or have been achieved along the way, people will not understand, let alone come on the journey with you. Some initiatives I have used include:

- Regular phone links – once per fortnight with direct reports and the alternate fortnight with the whole HR team
- Group meetings
- Office communicator
- Dedicated HR team site on the company intranet with strategy posted and regular monthly updates on how we are tracking
- My scorecard is based on the strategy and plan and this cascades through into the team's scorecard and objective-setting process
- Work progress meetings or annual appraisals
- Development plan and career discussions
- Travelling to different worksites and being accessible during those visits to all employees (and not just the ones I have a meeting with)
- Induction presentations
- Brown paperbag lunches
- Annual kick off meetings
- Cross-sectional project groups.

Power, Control and Influence

INTRODUCTION

Social and anthropological studies often revolve around the power dynamics of groups and social structures. The field of organisational behaviour also depends on a better understanding of the ways that power is gained, exercised or lost. The need for power is part of being human. Individuals and groups are constantly dancing around their objectives, some of which align but many of which conflict. The understanding, and balanced exercise, of power is an essential management art in the context of organisations.

LEARNING OBJECTIVES	Understanding this chapter will help you to

Understanding this chapter will help you to
- define power
- explain the sources of power
- describe the difference between potential and actualised power
- identify some techniques for applying power for influence
- explain how to apply power in ethical ways.

OVERVIEW

Learning Objective
Power defined

People's feelings of competence and motivation depend on the empowerment they experience from within as well as the power made available to them by their environment. Chapter 4 explains the combination of individual predispositions and work environment inputs that contribute to the sensation of empowerment. Chapter 3 identifies the personality trait of self-efficacy as a feeling of competence that arrives by having experiences of situations where one is able to direct and achieve things (Wilson et al., 2007). To feel in control is also important for the leadership function, as identified in Chapter 6. Understanding that power derives from external as well as internal factors helps organisations and individuals plan effectively to maximise motivation, productivity and other key performance criteria. It can be helpful to think of power as energy.

THE SOURCES OF POWER

Learning Objective
The sources of power

There are some basic principles of energy from the field of physics which are helpful guides for how patterns of power can manifest at work:

- Energy can never be created or destroyed, but it can be transformed from one form into another (Atkins, 2010).

- Energy can either attract or repel (or be neutral) depending on its polarity (Thornton, 1927).

- Every time energy is transformed from one state to another, there is a reduction (entropy) in the amount of energy available to perform useful work in the future (Atkins, 2010).

- To every action there is always an equal and opposite reaction (Newton, 1687).

- Energy is either potential (at rest) or kinetic (active) (Penrose, 1989).

    The relationships between people at work can normally be aligned with such principles; for example, a leader who expends energy making staff do jobs they don't want to do can certainly expect a backlash, which is the equal and opposite reaction feature. Or the fact that people admire and sometimes cherish the role of powerful leadership is a feature of the fact that energy attracts. Another instance could be when a leader delegates an important task down the chain of command and a staff member is not fully motivated to complete the task in a thorough fashion, which is the entropy feature of energy transformation. Energy (power) is everywhere and good management is a matter of finding how best to exercise it. The wrong use of energy is destructive. The correct use of energy is constructive and represents the prime objective of individuals and organisations who wish to make a positive impact on the world.

Potential power

Potential power
The latent power that is capable of affecting the ways that others think, feel and behave once it is actualised.

Simply being manifest as a human being with an identity gives the potential for power. Every individual is a participant in social interactions and therefore capable of affecting the ways that others think, feel and behave (Smeed et al., 2009). We have some degree of choice about the extent of kinetic impact we make upon others. Much of our physical, mental and emotional power rests latent until we elect to exercise it. However, we can also inadvertently or unconsciously bring about the actualisation of our power. Being aware of both **potential** and **actualised power** is important so that strategic as well as ethical actions can be properly planned.

Thought pathway

People sometimes comment about the death of someone with whom they were acquainted but did not know very well, noting that since the person died they really miss them and now understand how important they were. Consider the extent to which this phenomenon might be attributed to the now passed person's power potential.

Actualised power
Potential power made active. Power is actualised when influence is enacted.

Knowing that every person has potential power sets the foundation for respectful behaviour at work. It is smart management to realise that the person who is currently reporting to you could quite easily become your own boss; after the passing of time and certain events nothing is impossible.

Actualised power

Learning Objective
The difference between potential and actualised power

It is only when previously latent power is made active that the process of influencing others is put into place. Power is actualised when influence is enacted. Being an effective leader (or a good worker in general) is mostly a process of properly applying one's power. Sometimes people comment about their fear of responsibility and actively try to avoid leadership positions (Weeks et al., 2010). This comes from an innate understanding that every action creates an equal and opposite reaction (Newton, 1687). In other words, there are consequences every time power is exercised. Leaders are responsible and accountable for the decisions they make and some people do not like the idea of being put in that position. Of course, whether one is a leader or part of the rank and file, there is no way to completely avoid actualising one's power, so it is best to learn this fact and train oneself in the art of better management of oneself and available resources.

Thought pathway

When we say that a person has the power to hire or fire, do you think we refer more directly to potential or actualised power?

The secret behind good management of power is that constructive actions must be made in order to qualify for rewarding consequences. It is in the proper understanding of actualised power and its consequences that ethical behaviour makes sense. To abuse others is to abuse yourself. To be considerate of others is to be respectful of your own place in the organisation.

Individual versus organisational power: The basis of industrial relations

There are some powerful individuals. You may be able to immediately identify people you know who you would say are powerful. Perhaps you are among them. There are surely other individuals you do not pay much attention to and they effectively lack power in your mind. At the organisational level there are groups, divisions, departments and committees that also express different degrees of power. The distinction between potential and actualised power is important in this context because a lot of strategising goes on in relation to power in the workplace. Individuals and groups may need to plan and act with foresight about where and when to exercise their power. Sometimes it is best to act immediately, sometimes to wait until just the right moment. Individual workers often find themselves in power differentials with collectives. For example, a company is its own legal entity and operates for its own objectives. The workers are hired for their propensity to help the organisation achieve its objectives; however, individuals also have their own goals that may sometimes diverge from the company's preferred direction. Sometimes workers even collaborate to promote their objectives as a group, such as in a labour union.

WINDOW ON CONFLICT AND NEGOTIATION

Union playing safety card for industrial reasons—Joyce

November 29, 2010

Alan Joyce has defended the sacking of a Jetstar pilot.

Qantas CEO Alan Joyce has accused AIPA (the Australian and International Pilots Association) of playing the 'safety card' when it is instead waging an industrial dispute over Jetstar's sacking of first officer Joe Eakins for a recent newspaper article, noting that Eakins had breached Jetstar's code of conduct.

'When something is related to industrial relations issues and it's a breach of the code of conduct we're going to act in that way,' Joyce told ABC TV's *Inside Business* program in an interview which aired on November 28. 'And again, for the union to use this as an example and use this to say it's all about safety is them using the safety card for industrial relations. It's purely that yet again. It is outrageous that they keep doing this.'

Said Joyce of Eakins' actions, 'He was given opportunities to come in and talk about why he was doing it and to correct the action. He refused to come in and talk to the management and the management were left with no other action but to actually terminate his employment.'

Joyce also defended Jetstar's decision to base pilots in Singapore on Singaporean wages and conditions, Eakins' key point of contention in his newspaper article.

'What the pilots in Singapore are actually employed to fly for [is] Jetstar Asia which is a Singapore entity, flying and competing against all of the carriers in the region and the pilots are paid quite well,' Joyce said.

'They're paid in the top few per cent of the population in that country.'

Meanwhile, AIPA has launched a petition protesting the sacking, which will be sent to Jetstar Australia and NZ CEO David Hall, and a support fund to raise money for Eakins.

'You can be sure that this event is a turning point for Australian aviation. Pilots' jobs and the safety regime they fly by is under attack by airlines, particularly aggressive

low cost carriers such as Jetstar that pretend to welcome feedback but sack people when that feedback is too clear and too compelling to hear,' AIPA posted on the pprune. org website.

'You can also be sure that AIPA will devote whatever is required to assist Joe Eakins return to his career as a pilot.'

Source: <http://australianaviation.com. au/2010/11/union-playing-safety-card-for-industrial-reasons-%E2%80%93-joyce>

Where objectives diverge, a battle can easily emerge. Industrial disputes with unions or court cases with individuals versus the company can become expensive and very consuming for all involved. It is therefore crucial for managers and staff to develop reasonable understanding and expectations about the function and outcomes of power, with good perspective on past experience, present applications and the strategic future.

HOW TO GET POWER

To understand power in the context of organisational behaviour, one needs to know the fundamentals. The sources of power are from either personal factors or organisational position characteristics. A blend of both is the usual basis on which people develop potential or actualised power.

Personal power

Learning Objective
The sources of power

The most immediate and pervasive power base comes from our own individual characteristics and skills. We are each born with a personality and an ability to learn. Who you are right now has a certain influence over various people in your lives. The things people learn and the skills they can develop are also able to ultimately influence others. In this **personal** realm of **power** there are two broad contributors, referent power and expert power.

Personal power
Power that comes from one's own individual characteristics and skills. The two broad factors that contribute to personal power are referent and expert.

REFERENT FACTORS

As socially primed organisms, humans are generally willing to look to others as a reference point. Those we respect, with charisma or a degree of fame or acquired status, are candidates for our referent attention. Our referees hold power since they can influence our opinions and affect the opinion of others about us. Referent power derives increased strength from emotional or social responsiveness (Levine, 2010). One variety of referent power is deference to a charismatic leader, as in cults or dictatorships, but also in pep rallies in some commercial organisations (Israelite, 2010). The power of referent power can sometimes transcend logic.

EXPERT FACTORS

The acquisition of intellectual and skills-based knowledge is a valued human trait. We are prepared to assign additional responsibility and control to those we perceive as experts in a field. This is among the reasons why a very skilled computer technician, for example, may find they are a sought-after friend of many people in an organisation. Key leadership positions are often filled by people with very specific technical or knowledge-based skills (Jayasingam et al., 2010). Adept leaders ensure they have a handle on key technical issues to provide an overall impression of being expert.

Thought pathway

During the Queensland, New South Wales and Victorian flood crisis of 2011 the State Emergency Service, fire brigade, police and some political leaders were frequently interviewed by national media and consulted by local authorities. Consider the mix of personal power sources that contributed to these leaders becoming prominent during the flood crisis.

Whether personal power stems from referent or expert factors, one positive thing to remember is that this type of power can be directed in all directions in any organisation. You do not need to be in a leadership position to become influential based on personal power. However, once you become a formal leader, your personal power is a useful augmentation to the position you occupy.

Position power

Learning Objective
Techniques for applying power for influence

Despite the fact that personal power is most pervasive, the architecture of organisations indicates that there are key positions with formal lines of authority and accountability. Anyone who occupies a formal position in an organisation therefore holds **position power**, which derives its strength from control of rewards and perceptions of legitimacy.

Position power comes from occupying key positions with formal lines of authority and accountability. It derives its strength from control of rewards and perceptions of legitimacy.

REWARD FACTORS

Reward power is the knowledge that people have of the formal manager's ability to sign off on benefits linked with work performance. Immediate supervisors often hold reward power. Performance appraisals or regular performance-monitoring systems are among the mechanisms that put supervisors in positions of power. The higher up one is in the hierarchy, the more reward power is usually evident. The financial influence of certain senior managers is another indication of position power based on the capacity to reward. Have you noticed the deference a CEO or CFO can get from managers and staff when approval for spending on certain projects or initiatives is being sought? The ability to dish out rewards, or potentially hold them back, influences the motivation and behaviour of staff.

LEGITIMACY FACTORS

Authority, respect and coercion are phenomena linked variously with legitimate position power. When a manager is appointed to a position, it is implied that the formal lines of communication and authority feed through this position. In order for the social structure of the organisation to function, subordinates need to respect the manager's legitimacy and/or agree to submit to their authority. Such submission is obviously best when there is shared understanding about the leader–follower role. Chapter 6 highlighted Fielder's situational leadership theory with its emphasis on leader–follower relations as a key contingency for success. It is useful to understand that leaders are only as powerful as their followers allow them to be. Legitimacy is assigned by one's position but verified only by one's relationships. Sometimes the perceptions that followers have of their leaders are not what those leaders would wish.

WINDOW ON COMMUNICATION

Medvedev 'playing Robin to Putin's Batman'

November 29, 2010

Diplomats have used colourful and less than flattering language to describe some of the world's most powerful leaders, according to classified US cables exposed by WikiLeaks.

European leaders fared the worst among the cables written by various diplomats, but other key US allies did not escape harsh criticisms either.

The US's Moscow embassy referred to Russian prime minister Vladimir Putin as an 'alpha-dog', while president Dmitry Medvedev—officially the more powerful of the pair—is 'pale and hesitant' and 'plays Robin to Putin's Batman'.

US diplomats in Rome also raised concerns about the relationship between Mr Putin and Italian president Silvio Berlusconi, mentioning lavish gifts, energy contracts and a 'shadowy' Russian-speaking Italian go-between.

The diplomats wrote that Mr Berlusconi 'appears increasingly to be the mouthpiece of Putin' in Europe.

The Italian leader was also described as 'feckless, vain and ineffective as a modern European leader' by US charge d'affaires in Rome, Elizabeth Dibble.

In another instance he was called 'physically and politically weak' and his 'frequent late nights and penchant for partying hard mean he does not get sufficient rest'.

According to one dispatch, German chancellor Angela Merkel 'avoids risk and is rarely creative', while the US embassy in Paris called French president Nicolas Sarkozy 'an emperor with no clothes' who governs with a 'thin-skinned and authoritarian personal style'.

'Serious political criticisms' were raised about UK prime minister David Cameron and there are also claims of inappropriate behaviour while overseas by a yet unnamed member of the British Royal Family.

The leaks apparently reveal US president Barack Obama's disdain for Europe, saying he has 'no feelings for Europe' and would 'look East rather than West'.

North Korean dictator Kim Jong-il was called a 'flabby old chap' who, as a result of his stroke, had suffered 'physical and psychological trauma', according to diplomats who were quoting sources.

Iran's president, Mahmoud Ahmadinejad, was compared to Hitler by US officials, while Zimbabwean president Robert Mugabe was labelled 'the crazy old man' by South Africa's international relations and co-operation minister.

Libyan leader Colonel Moamar Gaddafi is 'just strange', wrote an adviser to the Sultan of Oman, and he is apparently accompanied everywhere by a 'voluptuous blonde' Ukrainian nurse, according to a Ukrainian political officer.

Afghanistan's president, Hamid Karzai, was called 'an extremely weak man who did not listen to facts but was instead easily swayed by anyone who came to report even the most bizarre stories or plots against him', by US diplomats in Kabul.

Israel's prime minister, Benjamin Netanyahu, fared slightly better on a personal level; being described as 'elegant and charming', but never keeps his promises, according to a cable from Cairo.

Source: <www.abc.net.au/news/stories/2010/11/29/3079151.htm>

There is humour in this Window, especially for those who are not currently in legitimate positions of power, but the seriousness of having legitimacy undermined would not be lost on the leaders mentioned in the article. Such loss of respect for authority is not ideal for the leadership role.

Another variant of power that stems from legitimate positions held by people is coercion. There is a fine balance between the proper and improper wielding of legitimate power (Drew, 2010). The person with legitimate power can delegate work, but to what extent can they force or coerce people to follow orders? It may be a question of style but also of law. For anyone in a position of power, it is generally illegal to intimidate, bully, threaten or demean people, but it is quite legal to issue orders and requests. There is a difference between being assertive (direct, clear and concise) or aggressive (rough, threatening and angry). Legitimately powerful people are more likely to hold on to their power in the long term through assertive rather than aggressive behaviours. This view is supported by the growing body of legislation in Australasia and globally that removes legitimacy from coercive actions such as bullying and other kinds of discrimination (Hutchinson & Eveline, 2010).

It is evident that sources of power can develop gradually through personal development and positional changes, or appear relatively quickly as a result of situational changes. Once power is attained in an organisational setting it becomes the responsibility of the bearer to use their influence legally, ethically and only for the purposes the followers and the organisation intend.

THE EXERCISE OF POWER

The actualisation of power generates influence, persuasion and sometimes compulsion, which drive those subjected to the power towards the objectives that initiated the action. This can be a good thing. Many organisations have positive, constructive objectives. The reality is that resources used to achieve one organisation's objectives are often consumed at the expense of individuals and other organisations. Prioritisation and achievement of one organisational objective take resources away from objectives with lower priority. So even some very noble achievements can result in harm being delivered (often unwittingly) to others. Add to this delicate situation some individuals who are not what you would call 'ethical' and the organisational arena can become a battleground as the exercise of power delivers hurts to some and successes to others.

One of the key organisational objectives in the exercise of power is to transfer a sense of empowerment (motivation) to workers. Chapter 4 identified the needs, expectations and behaviours associated with an empowered workforce. One problem stems from the principle mentioned at the start of this chapter that energy can attract more and more energy. In other words there can be a magnification of the effects of actualised power. This has serious implications, especially where negative effects are being felt from bad decisions. Empowerment is positive where positive effects are occurring, but it is negative and increasingly so where unethical, disrespectful and harmful actions are implemented.

Ethics and evil in organisations

Learning Objective
How to apply power in ethical ways

When people do bad things, it can be because of illness or a lack of consideration or a lack of accountability, each reason being logical but not completely satisfactory for those getting hurt. One political commentator, Hannah Arendt, refers to the 'banality of evil' as the result of studying the characteristics of war criminal Adolph Eichmann, who was a very effective organisational leader and a key figure in the forced transportation and tragic killing of millions of Jews (Arendt, 1963). Arendt concludes that there was no particular personality disorder, no obvious malice, in Eichmann's relationships with anyone, including those being killed by his actions, and he was aware of his position of responsibility. He was simply good at his job, which was, unfortunately a job that created unfathomable pain and despair.

Building the knowledge of how power is magnified and abused, Milgram (1974) and Zimbardo (2007) identify one troublesome human trait, the willingness to transfer accountability to someone else, which seems to contribute to decisions and actions that can appear quite evil. Like Arendt, Milgram aims at finding how a wartime organisation was able to institutionalise the objective of genocide. Using a sociological experiment that had people believing they were following instructions and administering increasingly severe electric shocks to people (subjects who were simply pretending to be electrocuted), it was found about two-thirds of people were prepared to follow right through and administer lethal levels of electricity. This was especially so when an authority figure encouraged them to complete the experiment. The conclusion was that many of the people directly engaged with the logistical tasks of processing people towards their deaths in the Second World War may have also been justifying their work by believing that 'Officer XYZ' was responsible, and so on, up the chain of command. In other words, the removal of personal accountability helped people to justify evil actions. The Stanford Prison Experiment is also famous for showing how a role-play activity can quickly get out of hand (Zimbardo, 2007). A similar observation was made in that the guards in particular (but oddly also the prisoners) felt that the organising Professor was in charge of the experiment and wanted them to carry through the role-play to its logical (abusive to the prisoners) conclusion. The experiment had to be cancelled early because the darker side of human nature was coming forth quicker than the Professor had anticipated. The role-play was encouraging the actualisation of real bullying despite everyone being conscious that was just an experiment. This has sobering implications for those of us going to work each day fulfilling our roles in different kinds of organisations: are we thinking deeply enough about whether our daily actions are hurting anyone?

Bruno Bettelheim, a psychologist and prison camp survivor, makes biting observations about the structure of large organisations and the subtle, soul-destroying nature of the power and control relationships that seem to emerge within them (Bettelheim, 1960). His point is that prisoner situations are gross examples of power wrongly applied and magnified and wonders whether, in fact, the more benign organisations that many of us work for in times of peace are more subtle and therefore better positioned to destroy the souls of anyone who is unable to resist their inherent power. The very consuming and stress-giving nature of organisational politics would appear to lend support to Bettelheim's views (Giacalone & Promislo, 2010). Many chapters of this book have referred to the growing dialogue about the difficulty of achieving balance between work and life, which can often be traced to politics and power imbalances between home and work. There are many subtle ways that organisations are able to suck the energy out of us. Leavitt (2007) adds the observation that most organisations are unhealthy places to work. Obedience to authority is an inbuilt aspect of a large hierarchy and constant subservience tends to diminish the resilience of people. This situation makes the role of ethical relationships all the more important. Leaders and followers alike need to understand relational roles and obligations in order to sustain an appropriately ethical work climate.

Ethics is a field beset with divisions, one of which is between recommending that people should pay most attention to the needs of others and recommending attention to the needs of self or the organisation. This paradoxical continuum is illustrated in Figure 7.1.

Figure 7.1 A continuum of ethics: Self and others

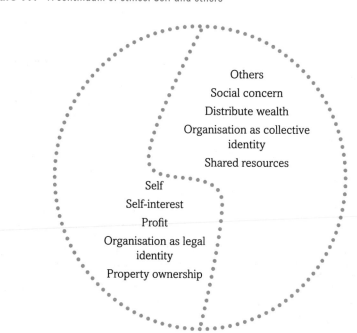

Others
Social concern
Distribute wealth
Organisation as collective
identity
Shared resources

Self
Self-interest
Profit
Organisation as legal
identity
Property ownership

■
Machiavellian
Said of someone given to
self-interested political
actions.

Machiavellianism and self-interested political actions are commonly observed in the workplace, but so are the other-centred expressions of magnanimity, collegiality and teamwork. The modern workplace is a melting pot of mixed ethical views. This is exacerbated by the fact that there are different kinds of organisations with different overall objectives. Commercial organisations are naturally more competitive, self-interested and prone to adopt utilitarian views that favour the sustainability of the organisation itself. Government and not-for-profit organisations are established primarily for social rather than commercial purposes and so their activities are generally directed towards social justice and rights-based approaches to ethical behaviour. Regardless of the type of organisation, the types of people within them also contribute to the ethical climate. A government department or a car manufacturer, for example, could each be filled with Machiavellians, or just as easily with philanthropists. Organisational politics (and ultimately organisational culture), being centred in human relations, seems to be able to transcend situations and typologies.

WINDOW ON ETHICS

Pfeffer book explains acquiring and maintaining power

RICK NOBLES

Through three decades of teaching and writing about power, Jeffrey Pfeffer has emphasized a pithy but potent concept: Politics often trumps performance.

Pfeffer, the Thomas D. Dee II Professor of Organizational Behavior at the Graduate School of Business, can tell countless stories of networkers and self-promoters who shot to the top while others went nowhere or lost positions despite laudable achievements. Many of those stories punctuate his new book, *Power: Why Some People Have It—and Others Don't*.

'It's a book about surviving and succeeding in organizations,' says Pfeffer, who has taught these lessons to students since creating a course called Power and Politics in Organizations (now renamed The Paths to Power) at the business school in 1979. Now he's spreading the message to a wider audience.

'I wrote the book for three audiences,' Pfeffer said.

'First of all, people who work in organizations and want to be more successful than they currently are need to understand the rules of the game, which are not necessarily the rules they are told.

'Number two, I wrote it for people who've already become powerful and want to maintain their power.

They need to understand the potential problems of having power, and why and how people lose it.

'Third, the book is for people who are just interested in understanding the games that go on inside of companies so that they can become more astute observers of the organizations they deal with on a daily basis.'

Pfeffer starts his guide to power by explaining why people should want it: Power can improve your health and increase your wealth, and it's necessary to get things done.

Once motivated to pursue power, he says, people need to overcome the obstacles to getting it. Atop the list is the belief that good work is the key to success. Competence is overrated, Pfeffer says, as the titans of the financial industry have shown in recent years. 'Great job performance by itself is insufficient and may not even be necessary for getting and holding positions of power.'

Another obstacle is relying on the ubiquitous leadership literature written by people who tout their own careers as models but 'gloss over the power plays they actually used to get to the top'. These leaders' ability to promote themselves as noble and good is the reason they reached high levels in the first place, Pfeffer says. Their advice could be accurate, 'but more likely it is just self-serving'.

Finally, people handicap themselves by choosing not to risk failure. People want to feel good about themselves, Pfeffer says, and 'any experience of failure puts their self-esteem at risk'. But, he emphasizes, the only way to master the power game is to practice.

Pfeffer's students get plenty of that. Through the years, he has added exercises, projects, and lots of coaching to teach them how to get noticed, earn the favor of their bosses, build social networks and reputations, and act and speak with power. The work doesn't come naturally to most of them.

'This class is like cod liver oil,' Pfeffer says. 'They understand that it's good for them. But they are uncomfortable—many of them, not all—with the ideas. They believe the world is a just and fair place, and if they work hard and do a good job they will be successful.'

Pfeffer says that older, more experienced students swallow his medicine more readily than younger ones and that each generation of students finds it more bitter than the previous one.

'In general, the current students are harder to teach this material to. And that is because the current generation of students...has been raised in a much less competitive environment,' he says, citing the example of swim meets in which every swimmer gets a ribbon.

'We live in a world in which people believe, because of social media and because of a bunch of other stuff, that hierarchy is dead and that everybody's cooperating with each other,' Pfeffer says. 'And what I would point out to people is that it is still the case that there's only one CEO, it is still the case there is only one president, there's only one school superintendent, there's only one congressperson from each district, there's only one dean of Stanford business school.'

Despite the challenges, Pfeffer has changed the outlook of many starry-eyed millennials. 'In some instances there's a true transformation during the course of the class,' he says. After implementing his advice through exercises and projects, students often find that they like doing it, they are good at it, and 'it's not as hard as they thought'.

Jenny Parker, MBA '07, validated his point. She was skeptical when Pfeffer told her that asking someone for a favor could give her power. But when she tried it, she says, 'they immediately asked for something in return.'

'I have fulfilled the prophecy that he preached,' she said. 'I came back eyes wide open.'

People who have taken his class will find plenty of new information in the book, says Pfeffer, who has written two other books about power. 'The class has changed a tremendous amount over the past 30 years.'

The book includes case studies Pfeffer has added to modernize the class. In the beginning, the cases were heavy with public figures such as former President Lyndon Johnson and Robert Moses, the New York parks commissioner who fashioned much of the city and surrounding area's infrastructure. Pfeffer now uses more examples of regular people, such as marketing maven Keith Ferrazzi and former software executive Zia Yusuf, who reflect the cultural diversity of today's MBA classes.

Many of the new examples are 'stories that my former students have told me about how they use the material.

It is relevant, I hope, to a wider range of people who can look at this book and say these are people like me. This isn't some unusual politician who was probably born with some gift that I will never have.'

As an educator, Pfeffer chooses cases for their instructive value and is careful not to judge what people do with power. When Oliver North pulled his Marine uniform out of mothballs and stared down members of Congress during the Iran-Contra hearings while admitting—under immunity—that he had shredded documents, Pfeffer saw an example of someone speaking and acting with power, and used him in his book. 'I'm not teaching business ethics,' he says.

He is similarly agnostic when he tells leaders not to fret about putting their careers ahead of their organizations, 'because there is lots of data to suggest that organizations don't care very much about you'.

But anyone who follows Pfeffer's blogs, magazine essays, or his books on human resource management knows he's comfortable lecturing corporate leaders for acting against the long-term interests of shareholders, employees, or customers. 'We all put on different hats,' he says, acknowledging the distinction in how he writes about different subjects. 'If you eat a meal, you don't eat all steak or eggplant or whatever your favorite food is. Most people will eat a buffet.'

So what would Pfeffer like to see people do with power?

'I would certainly like to have our leaders in corporations make decisions based on the facts as opposed to ideology, belief, what everybody else is doing, what some consultant has sold them,' he says. 'I've said that if doctors practiced medicine like managers practice management, most of them would be in jail. You would not tolerate the kind of sloppy thinking that I see on a regular basis inside business organizations.'

The problem, Pfeffer says, is that corporate leaders don't believe that management is a science and prefer to use their intuition. The solution may be for people who agree with Pfeffer to pursue power for themselves.

They must begin that process by looking within, he says. 'Stop waiting for things to get better or for other people to acquire power and use it in a benevolent fashion to improve the situation...It's up to you to build your own path to power.'

Source: <http://gsb.stanford.edu/news/ bmag/sbsm1008/feature-pfeffer.html?utm_ source=newsletter&utm_medium=email&utm_ campaign=october>

Taking your own initiative is definitely important and the exercise of one's power almost immediately presents ethical questions: Do the things you do with your power potentially or actually harm others? If so, what should you do to mitigate the consequences? On the other hand, to what extent should you become preoccupied with power and its effects rather than focusing on the actual performance of tasks and the achievement of organisational objectives?

Various other power tactics also emerge. For instance, the application of strategic embarrassment (naming and shaming) is one way that people can be coerced into behaving in ways that suit the directives of the organisation and its leaders (Cavicchia, 2010). The difficulty is that public humiliation can lead to guilt and embarrassment, which blocks learning and makes people defensive. This defensiveness creates a barrier for future learning and development in an organisation (Ladyshewsky, 2007). Harassment, bullying and discrimination are other prevalent barriers to individual and organisational performance that derive from the imbalanced application of power. As the exercise of power so quickly leads to awareness of social differences, it rapidly becomes a political balancing act.

CASE STUDY

The manager learns from an unlikely worker

The Distribution Centre at Delta Select Chemicals Ltd has a team of ten people all of whom have between five and ten years' experience and are managed by Barry Evans, who has been at the Company for 18 years. Their newest recruit is George Yeoman, who is well qualified and has extensive experience in logistics across a number of industries. Barry wasn't keen on hiring George because he was older than the rest of the team and he thought he was more experienced than he required. He told Amy Prescott, the HR Manager, that George wouldn't fit in with the rest of the team. Amy pointed out to Barry the benefits of having more experience on the team and also took the opportunity to enlighten him about the Equal Employment Opportunity legislation, which meant he could not discriminate on age.

Barry had other problems. The warehouse needed expanding and also needed a special section to be sealed off because of a particular new range of chemicals they needed to stock. He wasn't making any progress with his boss Theo Petrides, the Operations Director, who was reluctant to spend money when sales were flat and costs rising. He didn't seem to understand the difficulties of working with the current set-up or the regulations that applied to the new range of chemicals.

'You'll just have to manage with what you have,' he was told.

Barry noticed that the rest of his team, while polite to George, didn't really allow him to be part of the team. 'Maybe they'll work it out over time,' he hoped. 'Meanwhile I've got bigger problems trying to cope with lack of space and complying with the law.'

George caught Barry in the lunch room one day going over the layout of the warehouse and asked him what he was working on. Barry ended up telling him his problems. 'Probably caught me at a vulnerable time,' he thought later when he was wondering why he wound up telling him so much.

George dropped in on Barry a few days later with a floor plan and some brochures from a racking supplier. 'I've been in this bind before,' he explained, 'and there may be some options if we lay out the back end of the warehouse a bit differently and install some new racking that will save some space and allow us to build an internal partition for sealing off an area. Barry heard him out but thought there wouldn't be much chance of getting this solution approved even though it was cheaper than extending the building.

'Why don't you run it past Theo?' George suggested. 'I've done a bit of homework and I think I know where we can sell the old racking for a good price. I also know the supplier of the new stuff we need. They are having a tough time so we may get a good price there. Here,

I've noted down a few estimates. Have a think about it.'

Barry was surprised the next week when Theo dropped in on him. 'I ran into your new chap George the other day at the football,' he announced. 'He said you had a few different ideas about getting around this storage space issue. Show me what you have.'

Barry couldn't believe it. Theo stayed for 20 minutes looking at the sketches George had made and flicking through the brochures. He then said, 'if we can get this all done at the right price I reckon it's the answer to our problems.'

Barry spent the rest of the week finalising the plans and working with George to get the pricing agreed.

He had the final proposal to Theo on the following Monday and the next day it was approved.

'I think I owe you a few beers, George,' he said when he spotted George that afternoon. 'What's all that about?' he heard one of the team ask George as he moved off towards his office. 'Maybe they'll learn something from him,' he thought. 'I know I have.'

CASE STUDY QUESTIONS

1 Referring to the different types of power described in the chapter, describe Barry Evans' power and influence and if you think this is useful to the business. Could he develop this further? How?

2 When George Yeoman joined the business, what power did he possess?

3 How did George go about using his power and influence to bring about the change that was necessary to the warehouse.

4 How would Barry see the involvement of George in the warehouse planning project in terms of their relative power and influence?

5 How would Theo Petrides have seen the sharing of power between Barry and George?

Organisational power and politics

Political behaviours fall into two broad categories: self-interest and consensus-seeking. The self-interest approach has gained much attention since Machiavelli's writings (Machiavelli et al., 1905), especially in the context of leadership (Frank & Moore, 2010). It is, unfortunately, quite common for self-serving decisions and behaviours to take precedence over more consensus-based approaches. Recent research has even highlighted the apparent high levels of psychopathy within senior management positions (Boddy et al., 2010); this is the extreme expression of self-interest. Consensus-based actions, of course, are more aligned with helping others along the way (Stahl, 2010), but there is some debate about the role of individual self-interest motives within consensus-based decision models (Sauermann & Kaiser, 2010).

Thought pathway

Think about your own preferences for making decisions that affect a whole group, say, your family, or a sport team, or a work group. Identify whether you are comfortable making the decision on behalf of the group with little or no consultation, or would you prefer to seek everyone's opinions first before deciding?

Impression management
The conscious planning and control of the balance between real and perceived outcomes, in relation to oneself as well as others.

Political actions are sometimes less about making good things actually happen and more about ensuring that people's perceptions of what is going on are positive. The conscious planning and control of the balance between real and perceived outcomes, in relation to oneself as well as others, is known as **impression management**. The concept of 'saving face' stems from the idea that power depends a lot on the image a person projects (Miles, 2010). Would you follow the directions of someone who appears weak? You would surely rather follow a proven leader and someone who you think will be able to deliver what they say they can do—someone who is authentic (Drew, 2010). This is what most people want: a leader who provides a balance of real and perceived results.

Thought pathway

Identify a prominent leader who has influence over you. Think realistically about this person's self-interest and consider what it is that helps them to factor your interests into decisions they make that directly affect you.

Much about the politics of organisational leadership depends on satisfying the needs and expectations of followers. Since there is a prevalence of bad motives and behaviours in the workplace, people can be relieved and become quite loyal when their leaders show authentic delivery of ethical outcomes (Walumbwa et al., 2011). Leadership that demonstrates good governance ensures that a consensus-based approach is applied to cater for the needs of diverse stakeholders. Some situations make good governance easier to apply than others. The reality is that impression management is also part of the political game even where governance issues are concerned. This is because self-interest and consensus are often intertwined.

Fiji Water closes operations in Fiji

November 30, 2010

Fiji Water on Monday closed its operations in the South Pacific country that gives the popular bottled drink its name, saying it was being singled out by the military-appointed government for a massive tax increase.

A company statement announcing the decision did not say whether the company was shutting down permanently in Fiji, where an aquifer deep underground has been the source of one of the world's most popular bottled water brands.

The company, owned by California entrepreneurs Lynda and Stewart Resnick, said it was closing its facility in Fiji, cancelling orders from suppliers and putting on hold several construction contracts in the country.

But the company wanted to keep operating in Fiji and was willing to hold discussions with the government about that, said the statement, issued from the company's headquarters in Los Angeles.

In the statement, Fiji Water president John Cochran said Fiji's government announced last week that it was imposing a new tax rate of 15 cents per litre on companies extracting more than 3.5 million litres of water a month—up from the current one-third of 1 per cent rate. Fiji Water is the only company extracting that much water.

'This new tax is untenable and as a consequence, Fiji Water is left with no choice but to close our facility in Fiji,' the company, which sells its bottled water in more than 40 countries, said.

The tax rise comes amid a deep downturn in Fiji's economy that is blamed on political instability following a coup in 2006 by armed forces chief Commodore Frank Bainimarama—Fiji's fourth coup since 1987. Key trading partners have imposed various sanctions on the government, including European Union restrictions on the vital sugar industry.

Bainimarama's government has also taken a hard line with foreign companies. Rupert Murdoch's News Ltd in September sold its controlling stake in Fiji's main daily newspaper after the government imposed strict new foreign ownership limits on media companies.

Bainimarama did not immediately comment on Fiji Water's statement.

Cochran said Fiji Water was the only company that would be affected by the tax increase.

The government's action 'sends a clear and unmistakable message to businesses operating in Fiji or looking to invest there: the country is increasingly unstable, and is becoming a very risky place in which to invest,' Cochran's statement said.

He said Fiji Water remained 'willing to work through this issue with the Fiji Government, as it would be our preference to keep operating in Fiji.'

Fiji Water is a well known brand of bottled water, sold in several dozen countries including the United States where it is one of the top 10 bottled waters.

The Resnick's Roll International Corp bought Fiji Water in 2004 for an undisclosed sum from Canadian billionaire David Gilmour, a resort owner who founded the water company in 1996. The company has sought to stay clear of Fiji's volatile politics, but recently became embroiled in a dispute between Bainimarama and his deputy.

Earlier this month, Fiji Water executive David Roth was deported from Fiji to the United States for what the government said was acting 'in a manner prejudicial to good governance and public order'.

The deportation caused Acting Prime Minister Ratu Epeli Ganilau, who was also Minister for Defence, Immigration and National Security, to resign. Ganilau, a highly regarded official and traditional chief, had refused to issue the removal order against Roth.

Bainimarama issued the deportation order from China, saying it was based on reliable information verified and confirmed by relevant authorities.

'It is unfortunate that David Roth saw fit to engage in activities outside of his work permit conditions,' Bainimarama said in a statement at the time, without giving details.

Bainimarama said the decision to deport Roth would not affect the government's positive attitude toward overseas investors but that Fiji would not tolerate foreigners interfering in its domestic affairs.

Fiji Water's Director of Operations Anna Morris said at the time the company had no comment on the deportation.

Fiji Water trades on its product's purity. The company says its water comes from an artesian spring deep underground in Fiji and that the water never comes into contact with the air before it is bottled, making it clear of pollutants.

The water comes from the remote Yaqara Valley on Fiji's main island of Viti Levu, where the company also has its bottling plant.

Cochran said Fiji Water currently pays millions of dollars in duties and income tax, as well as substantial royalties and trust fund payments to Fijian villages near the company's facility. He said hundreds of Fijians would lose their jobs because of Monday's decision.

Source: <http://money.ninemsn.com.au/article.aspx?id=8172768>

This Window on Decision-making depicts a complex mix of stakeholders engaged in an essentially political situation trying to balance consensus with individual needs and to separate real from perceived outcomes. Many workplaces are fraught with complexity, and the challenges that arise from the exercise of power and control can be difficult to navigate. The conscious knowledge of sources of power establishes a foundation for tactical planning.

Techniques of influence

The section 'How to get power' introduced the potential sources of energy derived from personal and position factors. The process of actualising these energy sources generates influence on the various situations in an organisation. Table 7.1 summarises the various power sources and relates them to some techniques that are known to increase influence.

Table 7.1 How to increase influence under each power source

SOURCE OF POWER	HOW TO INCREASE INFLUENCE
Personal:	
referent	Become more visible in your work; attend all meetings, volunteer for key roles, etc. Maximise personal attractiveness; good manners, good dress, good grooming all help. Demonstrate ethical behaviour; work hard, help others and be balanced in your views. Develop emotional sensitivity and responsiveness to the emotional and social cues in the workplace.
expert	Ensure key information flows first through your office. Engage in lifelong learning and train for each new skill that becomes important to the organisation. Develop decisiveness in key technical issues.
Position:	
reward	Ensure a good budget for the material reward of high-performing staff and follow through with appropriate reward dissemination. Develop abilities in providing appropriate non-material rewards for staff such as personal praise, awards, and other supportive interactions.
legitimate	Delegate routine activities and become central in the creative tasks of new projects. Develop extensive and strong networks of colleagues in different levels of the organisation in key positions.

Some of the techniques in Table 7.1 require styles of behaviour that may or may not be a natural fit with your personality or align with your underlying values and attitudes. This is not a summary of things that have to be done at work. The actualisation of power and the generation of influence are serious things tailored somewhat to each individual. The earlier discussion about ethics and evil must always be considered when you are called upon to make a decision using your power sources. The consequences always matter. When influence is used for purposes properly aligned with organisational objectives, as well as what is a right fit for individuals working authentically within the organisation, then the best outcomes emerge.

CASE STUDY

Can too much power steamroll ethics?

RLG Tools Ltd is a subsidiary of RLG Tools Inc., whose Head Office is in New York. The Australian subsidiary employs 250 people with 120 in the Melbourne Head Office and the rest in the distribution and sales functions in each of the capital cities.

Ted Hopkins is the Australian Managing Director and has been with the Company for nearly 20 years. He knows the tool supply industry very well and has built a profitable business for RLG Tools. In the ten years since he became MD he has doubled the size of the business. The Australian business is one of the strongest in the Company and the US Head Office usually leaves Ted alone to run it the way he wants as long as the monthly numbers look in line with the plan.

Ted knew how to keep Head Office happy. Each year, about February, to escape the New York winter Ted thought, the Vice President, International, and a team of executives would visit Australia. Ted would have his direct reports make presentations on the state of the business and their forecasts, give the visitors a tour of some of the facilities and then wine and dine them in true Melbourne style.

This was a regular annual event and worked well. Ted's team knew what they had to do: have the visitors tick the 'Australia' box so that incentives would be paid and they would be left alone for the rest of the year.

Fiona Parker had recently joined the company as HR Director and was concerned about the way the senior management team was functioning. Ted was both revered by his team for the performance of the Company over the years and their credibility in the eyes of Head Office, but they also feared being on the wrong side of him.

Fiona experienced some of what they had been telling her when she was preparing her presentation for the US visitors. Ted queried her headcount numbers saying, 'these are too high, way above last year. I've told New York we would achieve our growth without an increase in headcount.'

'These were the extra people you authorised for the new distribution system project team,' responded Fiona, 'plus the four people you have added to the Internal Sales team, 15 in total.'

'OK, we'll call the project team contractors and can we make the admin jobs casuals so we don't have to show them on our headcount?'

'We can't really do that' said Fiona cautiously. 'The project people were employed as established staff because Harold wanted them to stay on in IT for future projects. He says he has plenty of work to keep them occupied over the next five years as he replaces some of our old systems. You authorised that last year after Harold presented his five-year strategy. And those admin people were employed as established staff because you wanted to build the Internal Sales team and try and cut down on our field sales people. We haven't been able to do that due to the growth in our customer base. The new customers want reps to visit them rather than dealing with a call centre.

'Well, you're not showing them those numbers,' snapped Ted, 'I won't allow it!'

Fiona returned to her office to reflect on the situation. Harold Dent, the IT Director, had needed to offer the project people permanent positions in order to recruit them. He had obtained Ted's authorisation as the distribution system was going to improve customer service and cut costs. The increase in the internal sales team was going to do the same but now he didn't want the down side—an increase in head count.

Fiona talked to Harold and some of the other directors about the situation. 'It happens all the time,' said Harold. 'You had better only present what he wants or you'll be looking for your next job.'

'You mean I have to lie?' she asked incredulously.

'I wouldn't say lie,' said Harold, 'more like leave out the truth. Alex used to be our Operations Director; he's been off on stress leave for 18 months now. He used to get on well with the Americans and wound up telling them more than Ted wanted them to know. When Ted found out he made Alex's life misery. Ted's fine when everything goes his way. Don't get on the wrong side of him or he will make things very difficult.' Fiona was shocked at this information and even more disturbed when she spoke to others at the senior management level who corroborated Harold's views.

'What are my options?' she thought. 'I'm not going to lie about the headcount and as HR Director I have a responsibility to change the culture here. However, I'm not much good to anybody without a job.'

CASE STUDY QUESTIONS

1 Referring to the different types of power described in the chapter, describe what power, if any, Ted Hopkins has.
2 How would the VP, International, describe Ted's power or ability to influence from what he sees of him each year?
3 Using the various types of power and influence outlined in the chapter, describe how Harold and other direct reports might define the good points of Ted's style and the weak points.
4 How did the management team respond to Ted's use of power and was this of benefit to the business?
5 What power does Fiona have and how can she use it for her own benefit and for that of the business?

CONCLUSION

This chapter explained the central position of power in organisational behaviour. Principles of energy exist at the heart of power and politics. The constant human endeavour to gain and hold on to power drives many actions and decisions at work. While power can be latent or potential, it can also be kinetic or actualised. Many positive things can come from the appropriate exercise of power and influence; however, negative, painful and evil outcomes are also possible. Strategic and ethical application of power is called for, perhaps, even more so in the complex, global and interconnected organisational environment. The consequences of wrongly applied power can reach very far and wide, therefore positive and appropriate exercise of power can also achieve very significant results. The techniques for exercising power derive from the personal and position-based sources that are unique to each individual. We can now move forward with conscious knowledge of power and the ways that positive influence can be turned to achievement of aligned organisational and individual objectives. It is time to consider in the next chapter how power and leadership can affect groups and individuals and flavour the very atmosphere of an organisation through its culminating expression of culture.

KEY POINTS

This chapter has

- defined power
- explained the sources of power
- described the difference between potential and actualised power
- identified some techniques for applying power for influence
- explained how to apply power in ethical ways.

KEY TERMS

ACTUALISED POWER
Potential power made active. Power is actualised when influence is enacted.

IMPRESSION MANAGEMENT
The conscious planning and control of the balance between real and perceived outcomes, in relation to oneself as well as others.

MACHIAVELLIAN
Said of someone given to self-interested political actions.

PERSONAL POWER
The power that comes from one's own individual characteristics and skills. The two broad factors that contribute to personal power are referent and expert.

POSITION POWER
The power that comes from occupying key positions with formal lines of authority and accountability. It derives its strength from control of rewards and perceptions of legitimacy.

POTENTIAL POWER
The latent power that is capable of affecting the ways that others think, feel and behave once it is actualised.

STUDY AND REVISION QUESTIONS

Q   *Why do some people not wish to take on leadership positions in an organisation?*

Q   *Why is the finding that most people have a willingness to transfer accountability to someone else significant?*

Q   *From your own experience in a work, sport or family situation, describe some examples of where each of the factors of personal power, i.e. referent and expert, made a difference. Also describe examples where each of the factors of position power, i.e. reward and legitimacy, played a role.*

Q   *Referring to Table 7.1, develop a plan to increase your levels of influence at work in the coming months. Establish a reasonable time-frame and plot a number of specific actions you can follow as part of the plan. Commence the plan with a statement of objectives and conclude it with an acknowledgment of consequences and observation of specific legal and ethical responsibilities that will come from your increased influence.*

REFERENCES

Arendt, H. (1963). *Eichmann in Jerusalem: A report on the banality of evil.* New York: Viking Press.

Atkins, P. W. (2010). *The laws of thermodynamics.* Oxford: Oxford University Press.

Bettelheim, B. (1960). *The informed heart: Autonomy in a mass age.* Glencoe, IL: Free Press.

Boddy, C., Ladyshewsky, R. & Galvin, P. (2010). Leaders without ethics in global business: Corporate psychopaths. *Journal of Public Affairs*, 10(1), 121–38.

Cavicchia, S. (2010). Shame in the coaching relationship: Reflections on organisational vulnerability. *Journal of Management Development*, 29(10), 877–90.

Drew, G. (2010). Enabling or 'real' power and influence in leadership. *Journal of Leadership Studies*, 4(1), 47–58.

Frank, S., & Moore, S. (2010). Reading, study, and discussion of the 'great texts' of literature, philosophy, and politics as a complement to contemporary leadership education literature. *Journal of Leadership Studies*, 3(4), 71–80.

Giacalone, R., & Promislo, M. (2010). Unethical and unwell: Decrements in well-being and unethical activity at work. *Journal of Business Ethics*, 91(1), 275–97.

Hutchinson, J., & Eveline, J. (2010). Workplace bullying policy in the Australian public sector: Why has gender been ignored? *Australian Journal of Public Administration*, 69(1), 47–60.

Israelite, L. (2010). Talent management is the new buzzword. *T + D*, 64(2), 14–14.

Jayasingam, S., Ansari, M. & Jantam, M. (2010). Influencing knowledge workers: The power of top management. *Industrial Management & Data Systems*, 110(1), 134–51.

Ladyshewsky, R. (2007). A strategic approach for integrating theory to practice in leadership development. *Leadership & Organization Development Journal*, 28(5), 426–43.

Leavitt, H. (2007). Big organizations are unhealthy environments for human beings. *Academy of Management Learning & Education*, 62(2), 253–63.

Levine, E. (2010). Emotion and power (as social influence): Their impact on organizational citizenship and counterproductive individual and organizational behaviour. *Human Resource Management Review*, 20(1), 4–17.

Machiavelli, N., Whitehorne, P., Dacres, E., Bedingfield, T., Cust, H. J. C. & Liberty Fund. (1905). *Machiavelli.* London: D. Nutt.

Miles, E. (2010). The role of face in the decision not to negotiate. *International Journal of Conflict Management*, 21(4), 400–14.

Milgram, S. (1974). *Obedience to authority: An experimental view.* New York: Harper & Row.

Newton, I. (1687). *Philosophiae naturalis principia mathematica: Autore Js. Newton, Trin. Coll. Cantab. Soc. Matheseos Professore Lucasiano, & Societatis Regalis Sodali.* Imprimatur S. Pepys, Reg. Soc. Praeses. Julii 5. 1686. Londini: Jussu Societatis Regiae ac typis Josephi Streater. Prostat apud plures bibliopolas.

Penrose, R. (1989). *The emperor's new mind: Concerning computers, minds, and the laws of physics.* Melbourne: Oxford University Press.

Sauermann, J., & Kaiser, A. (2010). Taking others into account: Self-Interest and fairness in majority decision making. *American Journal of Political Science*, 54(3), 667–85.

Smeed, J. L., Kimber, M., Millwater, J. & Ehrich, L. C. (2009). Power over, with and through: Another look at micropolitics. *Leading & Managing*, 15(1), 26–41.

Stahl, R. (2010). Executive S&OP: Managing to achieve consensus. *Foresight*, Fall, 34–8.

Thornton, W. (1926). What is electricity? *Journal of the Institution of Electrical Engineers*, 65(367), 674–80.

Walumbwa, F., Luthans, F., Avey, J. & Oke, A. (2011). Authentically leading groups: The mediating role of collective psychological capital and trust. *Journal of Organizational Behavior*, 32(1), 4–24.

Weeks, J., Jakatdar, T. & Heimberg, R. (2009). Comparing and contrasting fears of positive and negative evaluation as facets of social anxiety. *Journal of Social and Clinical Psychology*, 29(1), 68–94.

Wilson, F., Kickul, J. & Marlino, D. (2007). Gender, entrepreneurial self-efficacy, and entrepreneurial career intentions: Implications for entrepreneurship education. *Entrepreneurship Theory and Practice*, 31(3), 387–406.

Zimbardo, P. G. (2007). *The Lucifer effect: Understanding how good people turn evil.* New York: Random House.

PRACTITIONER INSIGHT

TOM
HUTCHINSON

PRINCIPAL CONSULTANT,
HASSETT PEOPLE SOLUTIONS

Tom works with bespoke recruitment firm HASSETT People Solutions in Melbourne, who specialise in Accounting and Finance, Sales and Marketing, and General Management roles. Tom holds a Bachelor of Commerce degree from the University of Melbourne, in addition to a Graduate Diploma of Business (Human Resource Management) from Swinburne University. He is a Certified Professional of the Australian Human Resources Institute, and joined HASSETT in February 2010 from leading mid-tier chartered accounting firm Grant Thornton where he held the position of Human Resources Manager.

INTERVIEW

What was your first job?

Human Resources Assistant with Grant Thornton, an international accounting & consulting firm.

What has been your career highlight so far?

Joining Hassett People Solutions in March 2010 – we are a bespoke Executive recruitment business, and I have thoroughly enjoyed the career change.

In your current role, what does a typical day involve?

As an Executive recruiter, my standard day would include: interviews with prospective candidates, phone calls and face to face meetings with our clients and general networking to create business development leads for the future.

What's the best part of your job?

Meeting the people that I do; my job is incredibly diverse, and I have an opportunity to shape someone's career by providing them with a work opportunity that they may not have otherwise known about. There is a great deal of satisfaction when I place a job seeker into a role and the client provides positive feedback about how well that person is performing in their organisation.

What is the hardest aspect of your role?

Constantly managing the demands of executing hands-on recruitment tasks with the need to continually focus on business development and generate future business. It is a balancing act, and something that I am improving with more experience in the industry.

What are the current challenges facing you, in your role?

2011 looms as an incredibly tough year to find high quality accounting & finance staff within Australia. We are nearing full employment, and a tight employment market means that attracting top performing staff for our clients will be difficult, but achievable with the right networks.

How important is an understanding of 'organisational behaviour' in today's workplace?

Organisational behaviour shapes any organisation; increasingly, people and subsequently intellectual property are recognised as the key drivers to the success of many businesses. Workplaces have to nurture talent and understand how to influence the behaviour of their staff to keep them engaged and extract that discretionary effort from them.

Is a work–life balance a reasonable expectation in a modern workplace?

Yes, I think it is; empirically, Australia has relatively low work–life balance compared with many other developed nations. We need a change of mindset within business that focuses on results and not 'face time' in the office. As technology continues to evolve, the structure of family units changes and urban sprawl continues, the traditional 9–5 day will become less common. I think business is embracing this slowly, but signs are positive.

What strategies do you implement in your workplace to help employees achieve an appropriate work–life balance?

Recruitment is a flexible career–outside of interviews, networking opportunities and face to face meetings with clients, a lot of work can be done remotely. Our staff are provided with laptops, phones and remote broadband which allows a flexible office to be created at will; flexible working hours can also accommodate personal or family commitments.

Has technology impacted on work–life balance? Is it harder to achieve with constant access to the 'office', for example?

Technology has created a virtual office anywhere in the world for us–this has been a positive. I make an active decision not to link work emails to my iPhone, as I think respite from work after hours is a good thing for me.

Are there greater expectations (on you or your workplace) to help motivate and engage employees in their work than ever before?

With an Australian economy that continues to perform strongly, and a highly competitive labour market, there is no shortage of alternative jobs out there for our staff. We are continually reviewing our remuneration and reward strategies, but most importantly engaging staff in the direction and future of our business to drive their motivation.

What do you believe makes a good manager or decision maker? How would you describe your own management style?

A good manager elicits the best out of their team; they are decisive and are terrific communicators, which includes the ability to empathise and listen to those around them; they delegate effectively and empower others to reach their personal and business goals. I am constantly working towards these ideals and enjoy learning by watching other managers in action.

How do you communicate company strategy with staff at all levels?

As a bespoke business, we meet regularly and discuss strategy. It is important to take time out of working in the business to actually work on the business.

What do you believe is the best way for a manager to avoid conflict in the workplace? And is this an easy approach to take?

Good communication throughout a business is central to avoiding conflict, as is setting clear expectations about the work performance of your staff. Managers need to keep lines of communication open with all staff, and constantly reinforce expected standards of behaviour and where appropriate, recognise and reward exceptional efforts.

Have the implications of globalisation presented new challenges for your workplace (for example global companies with global workforces, employees seeking international work, the changing nature of workplaces (larger, more diverse)...)?

Globalisation has created a more mobile workforce; Australian workplaces are more diverse now than they have ever been, and business is now embracing diversity. Our staff are well rounded, often with international recruitment experience, which gives them more credibility when dealing with our multinational clients.

There is an old adage that power corrupts. Does your experience suggest the decision of who to give certain powers in an organisation is, therefore, very important?

Recruitment and selection decisions are scrutinised like never before; in the old days, one interview and a crisp suit might have got you the corner office! Today, there are myriad of other tools used to determine suitability for a position of power such as psychometric testing, personality profiling, skip interviews, background and reference checking. This gives organisations far more objective data at their disposal to make sure that the right people are appointed to these positions in the first place.

Do you think the workplace environment really is changing faster than ever before? Or are people always prone to feeling anxious when the inevitable changes occur?

We are creatures of habit, and resist change because change is hard and it takes time and patience to implement. We have seen cosmic change in the workplace over the last 10 years, and I think this will continue to evolve in the future. People must be resilient and adaptable, or else risk being left behind.

Are you able to find much time to think about the strategic design of work in your organisation?

It is too easy to work to established practices and maintain the status quo. Businesses do not evolve and maintain relevance without constantly reviewing and assessing work practices. This is something that we are always thinking about and continue to work at on a daily basis.

04

Organisational Factors

8 Culture 205

9 Equitable Design and Negotiation
of Work Arrangements 231

10 Stability and Change 257

Culture

INTRODUCTION

Individuals, teams, leadership styles and power dynamics culminate in a unique culture for an organisation. Culture is one of the key components of overall organisational atmosphere. It is the net expression of all of the physical, mental and emotional contributions of individuals, groups and resources in the organisation. When you walk into an organisation for the very first time, some essence of culture will be immediately evident. Signs are present in colour schemes, office layout, manner of staff and leaders, timeliness of responses, sounds, smells and design of work and space. This chapter provides detail about the main elements of culture and the particular challenges of ethics, work–life balance and leadership in times of change.

LEARNING OBJECTIVES	Understanding this chapter will help you to	• discuss the interplay between culture, leadership, ethics, and work–life balance.
	• define culture	
	• explain the implicit and explicit factors of culture	• describe the challenge of culture change in context with individual and organisational learning.
	• distinguish between subculture, organisational culture, national culture and global culture	

OVERVIEW

■

Learning Objective
Culture defined

■

Culture
One of the key components of overall organisational atmosphere. It is the net expression of all of the physical, mental and emotional contributions of individuals, groups and resources in the organisation.

All the previous chapters have been leading up to this one. Organisational culture is the total atmosphere of the workplace; it makes up the climate (Ashkanasy & Wilderom, 2010). **Culture** is the result of a recipe of ingredients: the dispositions of individuals and groups, the ways they work together, the kinds of leadership, and the ways that power, control and politics together manifest each mix in a complex operating environment to create the unique flavour of culture. There are powerful unseen forces that contribute to culture through the shared values and attitudes of the people who work together. There are also very visible expressions of culture through spoken language, behavioural norms, stories, rituals and various other tangible symbols of design and decoration. This chapter describes each of the main elements of culture and explains how overall organisational culture has a reciprocal relationship with current issues such as globalisation, ethics, work–life balance and learning. The chapter concludes with a discussion of the difficulty of culture change and considers the next challenges managers confront trying to ensure that a positive organisational culture contributes to appropriate outcomes.

IMPLICIT CULTURAL FACTORS: SHARED VALUES AND ATTITUDES

■

Learning Objective
The implicit factors of culture

■

Implicit cultural factors
The largely invisible values and attitudes of the people working in the organisation making the most of its architecture and processes.

Visible components of organisational culture, those things you see, feel, smell and hear when you walk into the workplace, are merely the tip of an iceberg. Most of what goes into creating culture is invisible (Frontiera, 2010). At the very heart of the matter are the **implicit aspects**: the values and attitudes of the people working in the organisation making the most of its architecture and processes (Yang, 2010). In fact, values are the most difficult to discern, whereas attitudes are, to some extent, the behavioural expression of values, although still difficult to trace fully to their source. Chapter 3 explains the way that values and attitudes combine with physical traits to establish the foundation of individual personality and diversity. The very same foundations lie at the core of the broader group and organisational culture. In organisational behaviour we are most interested in staff being able to develop attitudes related to job satisfaction, job involvement and organisational commitment (Aletraris, 2010). This is not something easy to do with a universal solution, as our journey through motivation and leadership theories has shown. Improving overall job satisfaction, involvement and commitment starts with recruitment, selection, induction and training to ensure the people with the right dispositions are retained, and continues with appropriate work design and reward systems to keep people interested in staying the distance. The rest is up to what happens when diverse people mix together in the workplace and power and influence play out to generate the overall organisational atmosphere. Managers and leaders can prompt and guide but can rarely completely control the nature and direction of organisational culture. The current of implicit values and attitudes runs far too deep for that (van Vuuren & Cooren, 2010).

The obscure nature of values gives rise to debate about which ones are present or even important in various organisations. Jaakson (2010) builds on the work of Strickland and Vaughan (2008) in highlighting some generic organisational values that derive from Maslow's hierarchy of needs and include financial competence, accountability, reciprocity, respect, integrity and self-actualisation of the organisation. It seems appropriate to search for such universal values but, of course, the diversity of organisations means the conclusion is still undecided.

Thought pathway

Given the diverse origins of organisations around the world, consider the extent to which the organisational values of financial competence, accountability, reciprocity, respect, integrity and self-actualisation of the organisation are likely to be universal.

Managers are confronted with the predetermined facets of values and attitudes along with the challenge of trying to ensure the culture evolves in positive directions. Even though values and attitudes are hard to change, there are many occasions that require managers to try to steer the organisation in particular directions.

WINDOW ON COMMUNICATION

Innovation in the Australian Public Service

Innovation is at the heart of good public administration. A high-performing public service is relentless in its commitment to continuous improvement. It never assumes that the current policies, processes and services are the best or only solution.

The opportunity for innovation attracts many to the public service. These Australians want to help make changes that benefit the wider community, and empower citizens to help themselves.

Without innovation, the public sector is destined to disappoint—both those it serves and those it employs. An effective public sector must be one that recognises, rewards and nurtures innovation.

The Australian Public Service (APS) has been the source and incubator of many significant innovations. These initiatives cross the spectrum of APS activities and have ranged in scale from the development of the Higher Education Contribution Scheme to improvements in the breeding of detector dogs. But the need for innovation is increasing.

As the pace of economic and social change quickens, governments must be more responsive than ever. Complex policy challenges are arising that require swift but surefooted responses. The APS must ensure it provides Ministers with the evidence and options to make informed decisions.

At the same time, new technologies are creating opportunities for government to improve the services it offers to citizens. The private sector is utilising these tools to deliver increasingly tailored services to consumers, amplifying demand for public sector providers to follow suit. Without a culture of innovation underpinning the public sector's activities it will struggle to deliver what is required within the resources available.

To this end, there is a very real need for the Australian Public Service to start making changes, both to how it thinks and how it operates. Barriers to innovation must be identified and overcome at all levels. The red tape and siloed thinking of the past have no place in the high performing APS our citizens expect and deserve.

Many of the necessary steps are being taken. In June 2009, the Australian Government commissioned the Government 2.0 Taskforce to identify how the public sector can better use the tools available for online innovation. The Taskforce report, *Engage: Getting on with Government 2.0*, was delivered in December 2009. Public sector innovation is similarly a central theme in *Ahead of the Game: Blueprint for the Reform of Australian Government Administration*. The Blueprint, released by the Prime Minister in March this year, outlines a new vision and agenda for the APS.

It seeks to equip staff and leaders with the skills to develop innovative, high calibre policy advice and services, tailored to the needs of citizens.

These reports, and the respective Government responses, will better position the APS to respond to the shifting requirements and expectations facing it.

They will build on the success of initiatives already underway within APS agencies.

The Australian National Audit Office, for example, recently developed a better practice guide for public sector innovation which will help those conducting innovative projects navigate many of the considerations involved.

Work undertaken to date highlights the significance of the present report.

The Management Advisory Committee (MAC) recognised that tailored solutions are needed in order to foster the innovative spirit of the APS. The process of innovation is rarely an easy one. This report investigates the barriers faced in innovating in the public sector and considers how those barriers may be addressed or managed.

It outlines what agencies can do to further encourage innovation in what they do. It looks at what individual public servants can do to promote innovation. It suggests options for how the APS can better enable agencies to develop, implement, deliver and disseminate innovative solutions.

This report is part of a broader agenda for rejuvenating the APS.

The MAC Executive believes strongly that embedding a culture of innovation within the APS is a vital component of that rejuvenation. This dedicated review of innovation will help to create a solid foundation for tackling not only the challenges of today, but those that are yet to arise. The report's recommendations will be addressed by agencies as part of their operations or, where appropriate, as part of the ongoing reform work.

The MAC Executive commends this report to the agencies and to the individual public servants who form the APS. And while this report specifically addresses the APS, it is increasingly clear that all levels of public administration, both in Australia and overseas, face similar challenges and a similar need to innovate in an ongoing and systematic fashion. In the spirit of the collaboration and knowledge sharing which this report recommends, the MAC Executive commends the report to all our colleagues throughout the public sector.

Terry Moran AO
Chair of the Management Advisory Committee

Source: Empowering Change: Fostering Innovation In The Australian Public Service - report by the Management Advisory Committee, Australian Public Service Commission, 2010, piii. At: <www.apsc.gov.au/mac/empoweringchange.pdf>

This Window reveals a value sentiment expressed at the top of the organisational hierarchy. Whether the desire to be innovative permeates as fully as the vision espouses will require alignment of the implicit values with the explicit expressions of organisational culture.

EXPLICIT CULTURAL FACTORS: OBSERVABLE CULTURE

Learning Objective
The explicit factors of culture

Explicit cultural factors
The things a worker or any observer encounters as they engage or enter the space occupied by a particular organisation. Explicit culture is a blend of language and stories, behavioural norms and rituals, and designs (involving patterns of colour, sound and smells).

By the time the unseen factors work themselves out into expression as observable culture, only small remnants are visible. These **explicit cultural factors** are, nonetheless, very potent and recognisable. The things a worker or any observer encounters as they engage or enter the space occupied by a particular organisation take the form of some blend of language and stories, behavioural norms and rituals, and designs (involving patterns of colour, sound and smells).

Language and stories

Just as a single nation has a history and a set of descriptions and stories that help to define what it means to be from that country, so an organisation is flavoured by the words that were applied at the time of its foundation, and by the events that the founders experienced, and the retelling of those events over the years. This unique language and catalogue of stories makes each organisation quite different from the next (Thompson & Flynn, 2009). As an organisation evolves it develops a vocabulary to cater for the particular processes and events that define its operations. People strive for ways of describing the things they experience. If you have ever changed jobs, going from one organisation to the other you will have noticed that the acronyms change too. There may also be different titles for the same kinds of jobs. For some organisations different metrics may be used to define success, thus making that terminology more prominent. The language is an immediately visible component of culture.

Thought pathway

Think about an organisation with which you are very familiar. Do you know the story of its foundation? Consider the earliest story you can find about how the organisation was set up or run. Identify influential leaders during its history. What remnants of the operation today appear to be linked back to the values, attitudes and actions of the people from the early days of that organisation?

It is from the memorable events that stories are told and retold in ways that build uniqueness in an organisation. Even patterns of behaviour at work can be said to be set and refined by things from the past.

Norms and rituals

There are a range of behavioural norms that contribute to overall cultural atmosphere or climate (Ashkanasy & Wilderom, 2010). The research suggests some continua along which assessment of cultural climate might be made on the basis of behavioural norms and rituals. The factors to observe are the extent of innovation, the attention to detail, the emphasis on task completion, the level of aggressiveness and the rate of organisational growth. There are opposites for each of these. When you enter a workplace it is possible to begin to audit the norms and rituals on these continua.

INNOVATION—CONSERVATISM

Can you see innovation being celebrated or rewarded in the organisation? Perhaps slow and steady strategic planning is more the norm. This scale is about the level of risk-taking people are prepared to engage with. The contents of planning documents and discussions, and the structure and timing of meeting rituals will indicate which end of the spectrum the organisation rests on. The Window on Communication earlier provided an example of one end of this spectrum in the Australian Public Service.

PRECISION—IMPRECISION

Is there a high level of attention to detail apparent in the policies and systems of the organisation? Perhaps there are detailed and frequent report forms being submitted, or meeting rituals may require specific kinds of feedback. Work quality may also be emphasised as something that gets close attention. Some organisations may show the opposite sentiments; that is, ad hoc or very casual reporting requirements, little concern for continuous quality procedures, and a tolerance for error or unexpected changes to strategy and tactics.

WINDOW ON DECISION-MAKING

The employment interview—a dreadful predictor of job performance

ROBIN MCKAY

I've sat in on a few interviews over the last 40 years—both as interviewer and interviewee. Couple this up with what science has taught me about the interview process and I think I can speak with some authority on the subject of employment interviews.

From my experience, I see two main types of interview. The first one is the 'meet and greet'. Here, the hiring manager arranges to meet the prospective candidate for a general chit-chat. It's a free-wheeling conversation where decisions, from both parties, will be based on emotion—do we like each other?

This type of interview provides very little information to enable sound decision making. In fact, because they are usually conducted very early in the process, they are darn right dangerous.

As humans we are programmed to make quick decisions. In psychology we call this the 'fight or flight' syndrome. We just don't have the luxury of time to research all our decision making, so we tend to 'satisfice'—we look for the first sufficiently satisfactory solution—we take mental short-cuts.

With the 'meet and greet' interview, the first five minutes is critical—particularly for the candidate. If they make a good impression, dress well, talk well, this possessiveness will put them in the driver's seat to get the position. And from the hiring manager's perspective, just because a candidate talks and presents well is no indication that they can do the job well!

The second form of interview is usually the 'sell and tell'. Here, the hiring manager does all of [the] talking upfront. Usually the contents are based on how wonderful the company is to work for, opportunities to progress, what the company requires in their people.

After this stellar selling job, the manager then asks the candidate some questions. Bright candidates only need to 'parrot' back answers based on information given first up to win the heart and mind of the manager. This type of interview is very common.

It is a scientific fact that the unstructured interview is absolutely useless in predicting job success. In fact thousands of psychological experiments tell us that the predictability is between .05 and .15. This means, at the very best, you have a one-in-six chance of getting it right. Pretty poor odds if you're gambling with a $50,000 annual salary!

OK you say, what's the panacea? Well for a start, let's structure the interview. All candidates get the same questions based on the performance criteria for the job. Each question seeks concrete examples of past experience—past behaviour reflects future behaviour. Finally there needs to be two plus interviewers who 'rate' replies to each question.

The structured interview will improve your odds. Science tells us our predictability will rise to .50. That's still the toss of a coin, 50% of the time you'll get it right.

One of the biggest impacts on interview outcomes is 'candidate schooling'. I Googled 'How to ace a job interview' and got 646,000 hits—lots of videos too. When I did the same on Amazon, I got 40 books. Even with a structured, behaviourally based interview, candidates can still give you 'book' answers.

Despite the fact that we are seeking actual workplace examples, most interviewees will try and give you opinions and, as we all know, it is very easy to give an opinion on just about anything.

Most of the managers I speak to think the interview is the least expensive part of the selection process. Reality tells us interviews are the most expensive when weighed up against the cost of management time versus the results—and very, very expensive due to the risk of making a poor hiring decision. Given the abysmal predictability and expense of interviews, it's amazing how they are the most used and most relied upon tool for hiring.

This confirms my suspicions; there are a tremendous number of managers out there who think they can read minds. These managers and Sales Managers are the biggest culprits; think they can 'pick 'em when they see 'em'. If this is the case, how come their organizations are not bursting at the seams with star performers and turnover is zero? These managers would make more money doing tarot card readings!

Yes, you do need the interview, but structure it and do it at the back of the selection process. Prior to this, use unbiased tools to filter out the 'turkeys' so only the 'eagles' make the final interview hurdle.

We suggest, a structured application form; forget CVs, these will only tell you how good a writer they are, or somebody else is, and contain only the information the candidate wants you to know. After selecting out those that don't have the knowledge, skill and experience to do the job, put the remainder through a brief (4 questions) telephone interview, followed by reference/background checking.

Those that made the 'CAN they do the job' cut-off can now be put through a validated employee profiling assessment. Here, we recommend PeopleCLUES or Prevue. This will highlight the REAL person—'HOW will they do the job' before you waste management time on expensive and risky interviews. Lessen this risk by ensuring the main interview is structure[d], with behavioural based questions and two or more interviewers.

Most managers will hire on the CAN, but will always have problems, or terminations based on the HOWs and WHYs.

Source: <www.articlesbase.com/human-resources-articles/the-employment-interview-a-dreadful-predictor-of-job-performance-1999248.html>

This Window alludes to the differences in attention to detail that can emerge in managerial decision-making. The desire to be thorough cannot always be actualised because of time and resource constraints. Sometimes people revert to professional judgment or bounded rationality (Simon, 1991; and see Chapter 5). The extent to which due processes are adhered to in organisations can give some indicators of underlying cultural values in relation to precision.

RELATIONSHIP ORIENTATION—TASK ORIENTATION

Chapter 2 points out that two key tensions in the organisational behaviour field are to manage for task performance or to manage for maintaining and developing relationships. Chapter 6 reiterates this fact for the issue of leadership, especially noting the Theory X (task-focused) leader versus the Theory Y (relationship-focused) leader (McGregor, 1960). Throughout the ranks within the organisation culture you might see close attention being paid to making workers feel loyal and committed, and a general embracing of teamwork and collegial approaches to work relationships. At the other extreme, people in the organisation may be mostly goal-driven and concerned with achieving key performance indicators rather than worrying about what the people around them may be thinking or feeling.

Thought pathway

Think about your own preferences for organisational culture. Do you feel you operate more effectively when co-workers and leaders are interested in relational issues of teamwork, collegiality and sharing? Or are you better off working where everyone stays to themselves and just focuses on getting tasks completed?

■

High-context culture One where lots of communication between people occurs beyond verbal discussion, that is, implicit things like body language, facial expressions and other unspoken behaviours, including the broader context of power relationships, are applied and interpreted in the course of normal interactions.

■

Low-context culture One where explicit written or spoken words are relied on to convey meanings to each other.

A related perspective is the research into high- and low-context cultures (Mujtaba et al., 2010). A **high-context culture** is one in which lots of communication between people occurs beyond verbal discussion, that is, implicit things like body language, facial expressions and other unspoken behaviours, including the broader context of power relationships, are applied and interpreted in the course of normal interactions. A **low-context culture** is one where explicit written or spoken words are relied on to convey meanings to each other (Hall & Hall, 1987). By definition, a relationship orientation is more closely tied to high-context culture since a high degree of emotional and social sensitivity is needed to communicate effectively non-verbally. A task orientation is more closely linked with a low-context culture because the people need their contracts clarified as explicitly as possible in the absence of underlying understanding about people's intentions.

AGGRESSION—CALMNESS

Some organisations seem to run at a frenetic pace. People can appear driven and competitive as they focus on achieving their targets. Leaders may encourage this type of culture by rewarding aggressive achievement behaviours and not rewarding staff displaying meeker approaches (O'Neill & O'Reilly, 2010). At the opposite extreme the organisation may be filled with people who are quiet and calm and seem to go about their work without much fuss. There may be a nurturing kind of environment where people share their workloads and accept the view that group rather than individual achievement is most worthwhile. Leaders may encourage this by rewarding only team or organisation-wide endeavours.

GROWTH—STABILITY

How important does the status quo appear to be? Are people engaged in planning and careful management to ensure a slow and steady situation, or is there a fast-paced, high-growth emphasis in their actions? By positioning the culture on this continuum a manager can better understand the disposition that is confronted when changes are being proposed. There is an art to the management of change which is covered in the final chapter of this book.

Design

From the type of logo that an organisation chooses, to the colours of any uniforms and the symbols used in marketing, plus the decoration of offices, machinery and other resources, to the particular sounds that emerge while work is under way, design makes a pervasive impact on culture. Much of this can be intentionally designed and implemented but some of it happens serendipitously. The unique way that some printed material smells in an office, or the unusual sound that is made when a certain manufacturing process happens, are among the emergent things that imprint themselves on people's memories, and when discussion about organisational culture occurs, many will recall feelings associated with these design factors. When you are thinking about the way to arrange work space to be beneficial to overall organisational culture the patterns of colour, sound and smell are all part of the mix.

CASE STUDY

Culture and the manager's style

Gordon Lau's Sales Department was exciting and dynamic. Everybody said so. They had weekly sales meetings where account managers made presentations on their targets for key customers and sales reps would present their latest figures and ideas on how they would increase them the next month. Product specialists would be brought in from Marketing to explain new products being developed. Sometimes Gordon would invite motivational speakers in to speak to the team.

'The carpet business is an exciting mix of technology, fashion and lifestyle,' Gordon would say, 'so everyone is a prospect for Sheepsback Carpets. We have potential not only to increase our market share with better products and service but to grow the whole industry by making carpets a fashion item that people will change more often.'

Gordon was a numbers man and as Sales Manager he made sure each Account Manager and Sales Rep had specific targets for each month and progress was tracked on a weekly basis. There were charts on the wall of the office so everyone could see everybody else's performance. 'No one would watch football if they didn't keep score,' he was fond of saying. High performers were presented with awards at the weekly meetings and those lagging behind were asked to present on the changes they were going to make to catch up and 'not let the team down'.

The result of Gordon's management style meant that sales targets for the Department were met and often exceeded but staff turnover was quite high. While high performers received accolades and financial incentives, those that struggled were left to their own devices and usually resigned. Gordon believed he would attract the right people if he paid a lower than average base salary with higher than average incentives. If people didn't perform there were no pay increases and no incentives. 'They won't be able to afford to stay if they don't perform,' he said when he explained his rationale and refusal to take part in the Company's normal performance management system.

When the turnover issue was raised with Gordon by the HR Director, Trevor Fleming, he responded that 'it's a dog eat dog world out there'. And another one of his favourite sayings: 'We can't afford to carry passengers.'

While Gordon certainly achieved his sales targets, Trevor had done some analysis on the overall costs of the Department and reviewed the succession plans for the business. Once the costs of recruiting new staff and training were taken into account, the additional profit achieved by the increased sales was lost. He had also heard from the Marketing Director that there had been some rumours in the industry that Sheepsback might lose some key accounts due to a breakdown in relationships. He was also concerned about the development of people for the future. While Sheepsback Carpets always needed sales people, he felt the successful ones that Gordon kept were not really management material. He also looked back a few years and looked at individual performances. He was surprised when he did some modelling to find that if there were a full team of mid-range performers, in total the team would achieve the same sales, probably without the staff turnover and consequent costs.

When Trevor raised his findings with the CEO he was interrupted. 'He's the most dynamic Sales Manager we've ever had. Sales are through the roof. If you think costs are too high we'll just have to make some cuts somewhere else.'

CASE STUDY QUESTIONS

1 Referring to the 'Norms and rituals' section, how would you describe the way the Sales Department operates?

2 In terms of 'Relationship orientation—Task orientation', where do you think the current sales team is and what are the positives and negatives of this? Where do you think it should be and could Gordon move it there?

3 Could a sales department in a competitive industry have a high relationship orientation and be successful? What else would they need apart from this?

4 What sort of qualities do you think Trevor might be looking for in managers and how might their experience in Gordon's Sales Department help or hinder them developing those qualities?

5 How do you think the remuneration and recognition practices in the Sales Department influence the culture? If you wished to change the culture, how would you alter these two factors or would you leave them alone?

GLOBAL CULTURE

Learning Objective
Culture at subculture,
organisation, nation
and global levels

There is an interplay between culture at the organisational, national and international levels. This is logical since the workers in an organisation also live in the country where they work and, increasingly, interact with workers from a variety of national backgrounds. Each identifiable culture can also be divided into sets of subcultures. Like any labelling exercise, it becomes necessary to identify valuable reasons for giving a name to a subculture, such as if it is significant in its size and influence. But taking a finer view, subcultures are composed of diverse individuals. If you think about it, each person is a cultural expression of the physical and social elements that compose them; each subculture is a cultural expression of the group of personalities that compose it; each organisational culture is a broad expression of the identities of the collection of groups and individuals that compose it; and each national culture is the collection of impressions from organisations, groups and individuals within a geographic boundary. This connection between cultural levels, represented in Figure 8.1, is a helpful way to ensure that the commonality of culture is recognised.

Figure 8.1 People, groups and culture have common heritage

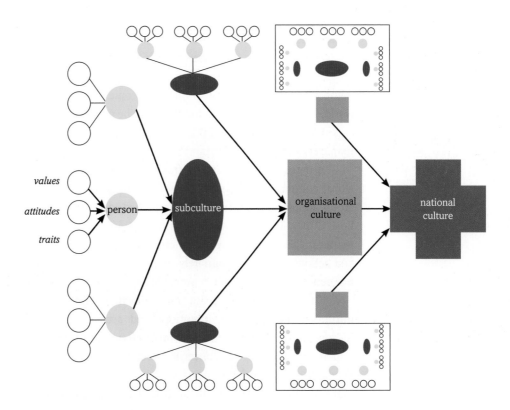

values
attitudes
traits

person — subculture — organisational culture — national culture

People come together to form subcultures, which coalesce to create organisational culture, and combinations of organisations and individuals make up national culture. It is like a complex neural network. Despite the connections between the cultural levels, the differences between cultural groups remain relevant and present challenges for managers whose focus is on maximising efficiency and effectiveness at the organisational culture level. Briefly covered in Chapter 3, Geert Hofstede's often quoted study of organisational culture focuses on one organisation (IBM) operating in many different countries (Hofstede, 1980). This gives a useful perspective on the ways that national culture impacts on organisational culture and flows into the globalisation issues. The scales on which his research into the cultural expressions at the different office locations was drawn include:

Power distance
One of Hofstede's dimensions of international organisational culture which measures the extent to which the less powerful members of organisations and institutions accept and expect that power is distributed unequally.

- **Power distance**: the extent to which the less powerful members of organisations and institutions accept and expect that power is distributed unequally

- Individualism versus collectivism: the degree to which individuals are integrated into groups

- Masculinity versus femininity: the distribution of roles between the genders

- **Uncertainty avoidance**: the extent to which a culture programs its members to feel either uncomfortable or comfortable in unstructured situations

- Long- versus short-term orientation: the extent to which a culture programs its members to deal with virtue regardless of truth.

Uncertainty avoidance
One of Hofstede's dimensions which measures the extent to which a culture programs its members to feel either uncomfortable or comfortable in unstructured situations.

Hofstede's ongoing research leads to classifications of various national cultures according to the above dimensions. At the organisational level this can be useful to a point, certainly when trying to manage people in different office locations around the world. Like any form of labelling there can be problems with stereotyping of individuals and nations (McSweeny, 2002), but the variables do provide a starting point for managers seeking to understand more about the complexity of work culture.

A natural question arising from this line of thinking is whether there is truly a global culture? It seems safe to say that humanity probably does express a particular group atmosphere. Some studies have tried to identity global values (Rapaille, 2006; Erez, 2010). The most practical thing to think of, however, is your current role as a manager and the people who are currently affected by or are affecting your decisions and actions. To act appropriately in the local cultural context without forgetting the inherent diversity of people is probably the best outcome for any people manager.

The reality of diversity in relation to international culture is frequent misunderstanding of the intentions and actions of individuals and organisations (Segon, 2010). This can take the form of embarrassment or expressions of apparent impoliteness, through to concerns about bullying or other locally illegal behaviours. When it comes to determining whether corruption or bribery is taking place, for example, there needs to be detailed understanding of cultural differences in context with prevailing local, national and international norms and expectations (Zutshi et al., 2010).

WINDOW ON CONFLICT AND NEGOTIATION

Cultural nuances imperative to conducting business with China

ERIN BROWN

Tapping into China's burgeoning economy has become a key component of the business strategy for many progressive Western companies. Although commercial negotiations with Chinese enterprises have become an integral part of Western business ventures, the Chinese market is not as open to foreign negotiation as it was in the 1990s and early 2000s. The government's focus seems to have shifted, with the maturity of its business sectors, to cultivate national industry through policies that favour local companies. In this climate, it is critical when entering into commercial negotiations with Chinese enterprises to have an appreciation of the cultural nuances, business etiquette and expectations that permeate business dealings, to maximise the benefit of an arranged meeting and establish successful business relations with China.

KEY CONCEPTS: GUANXI, RESPECT, STATUS AND FACE

These four interrelated concepts underlie Chinese culture and dictate the rules of relationships, both business and personal.

Guanxi can be simply translated as 'relationship', and describes the emphasis placed in Chinese culture on the development of trust and rapport. Business is not undertaken in an impersonal, purely contractual basis in China. In the absence of a legal system that provides transparent independent legal remedies, it is imperative that you have a deeper understanding of your potential business partner's position. Gaining an introduction through a third party contact or referral can be instrumental in developing guanxi.

Respect is a vital part of Chinese culture, and showing respect is central to all relationships. Chinese people have a strong generational hierarchy, which also transpires into a strong respect for commercial and organisational hierarchy. Great respect and honour is shown to those who have reached advanced age. Respect is also gained through achieving success and gaining status.

Status is another key consideration as it influences the way in which Chinese people interact with others. It is important for Chinese business people to understand your status or seniority. This should always be clearly

enunciated. In addressing or introducing acquaintances, it is appropriate to refer to the individual's title, such as chairman or director, and begin introductions with reference to the most senior or highly ranked person first.

Familiarity with the concept of 'face' will assist greatly in comprehending Chinese behaviours. 'Face' is a multifaceted word, generally referring to one's reputation, honour and the impression one's actions give others. Preservation of face is of primary importance and accounts for many aspects of relational interaction. Face is lost, among other ways, through the exposure of poor conduct or inadequacy and through being shown disrespect. Face is gained through the receipt of respect and compliments from others directly or via a third party.

DEMEANOUR

Displays of emotion are not common in Chinese culture. Chinese people pride themselves on decorum and maintenance of composure. It is expected that interactions will be formal and to do so shows respect. It is not appropriate to be prematurely informal, and attempts at jocularity and humour may not be appreciated. Similarly, one should respect personal space and refrain from engaging in physical contact. Introductions should be acknowledged with a light handshake or nod of the head. Overly firm or vigorous handshakes can be construed as aggressive.

EXCHANGE OF BUSINESS CARDS

The exchange of business cards is very important in Chinese culture, as it is a way of demonstrating status. Business cards should have your position or title clearly stated and it is a good idea to have the reverse side of the card translated into Chinese. Business cards should be proffered with both hands and with the Chinese translation facing upwards. Others' business cards should also be received with both hands, and should be carefully perused on receipt. Placing business cards away immediately without reading them is a sign of disrespect. It is best to put them into a card case rather than directly into your pocket.

MEETINGS

Punctuality is a key sign of respect and is highly valued. Endeavour to always be early for meetings as they will generally start promptly. It is very important to wait for your host to welcome you. His welcome speech may be long and it is very rude to interrupt. Your host will generally signal when he is finished and ideally, you will then respond in a complimentary way to your host's remarks.

Business dealings in China often continue over a meal. Taking part in culinary rituals is another way of building the trust and rapport that is essential to successful business relations. The pace is unhurried and negotiations begin after a period of small talk. In making small talk it is essential that certain taboo topics are avoided. Steer clear of political discussion, particularly current government policies and leadership. Negotiations often take place simultaneously with the food being served and eaten. During meals, it is impolite to begin eating or drinking until your host has done so. You should try everything that is offered to you but eat modest quantities.

Seating arrangements for a Chinese business meal are predetermined in accordance with personal importance, reflecting the focus on status and seniority. The most important guest will occupy the seat of honour, facing the entrance or the most easterly position, and others will be seated according to seniority beginning with the seat to the left of the place of honour and then the right and so on, until the least important guests meet in the middle on the opposite side, nearest the entrance. This is a very important aspect of a formal meal and can be used to demonstrate respect for the other party by offering a favourable seating position.

NEGOTIATION STYLE

Chinese business people are renowned for being shrewd and tenacious negotiators whilst being unfailingly polite. It can be quite difficult to adjust to their negotiation style. Ensure you enter a negotiation with a clear strategy and knowledge of what you are willing to concede. It is becoming increasingly common for negotiations to take place in Mandarin, and therefore, it is essential that you engage a translator with the relevant technical knowledge to eliminate the risk of misinterpretation. Negotiation can take considerable time and be punctuated by significant pauses. Be patient and resist the urge to speak to fill gaps in the conversation. Displays of frustration and impatience give a poor impression and are considered unprofessional. Successful negotiation requires a delicate balance of determination and diplomacy.

IN SHORT

Diligent research into the strengths, weaknesses and unique characteristics of a potential business associate should be routine when entering any negotiation. As Chinese cultural nuances are so intrinsically linked to business behaviour and expectations, gaining an appreciation of them should be a routine part of the due diligence process. The scope of the features that distinguish Chinese business culture and etiquette from our own may seem daunting. However, mastering just a few of the examples of Chinese business protocols mentioned above will go a long way towards minimising cross cultural challenges and optimising your potential when doing business with China.

Source: <www.lawyersweekly.com.au/blogs/ opinion/archive/2010/08/04/cultural-nuances-imperative- to-conducting-business-with-china.aspx>

Relational ethics
An ethical field that focuses on the relationships between people with factors such as processes of communication, the methods for finding rapport with others, and techniques for being respectful at work.

Some recent research focuses on the relationships between people at work as among the best hopes for finding a universal way to manage across cultures. If we pay attention, for example, to the processes of communication, the methods for finding rapport with others and techniques for being respectful, then it matters far less if someone looks or talks a bit differently. The **relational ethics** approach may be one step closer to a more universal cross-cultural management solution (Creed et al., 2009). The discussion about power and ethics in Chapter 7 may be recalled at this point because these factors are very influential in establishing, sustaining and, ultimately, understanding the cultural atmosphere of an organisation.

CULTURE AND ETHICS: COMPETITION AND COLLABORATION

Drawing from a variety of cultural research, an organisation's culture can be perceived on a continuum from very aggressive and competitive through to highly collaborative and nurturing (Hofstede, 1980; Cordes et al., 2010). The extremes illustrated in Figure 8.2 are stereotypical but do indicate traits that are recognisable in some ways as you walk into any organisation. It is possible to approximate organisations in a position on the continuum which can pre-empt a more thorough assessment of ethical standards in the wider culture.

Figure 8.2 One cultural continuum: Compete or collaborate?

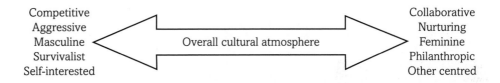

Competitive		Collaborative
Aggressive		Nurturing
Masculine	Overall cultural atmosphere	Feminine
Survivalist		Philanthropic
Self-interested		Other centred

Younger, go-getter, motivational, profit-driven commercial organisations may align more readily on the left of the continuum. Well-established, networked, human-centred, values-driven organisations may find a place towards the right of the continuum. All kinds of variations are possible in between.

Among the measures of an organisation's ethical climate are the presence and content of codes of ethics or statements of governance. Helin and Sandström (2010) note the cyclical nature of attention being paid to formal codes of ethics, often as a response to a corporate collapse. One could contend that such scandals are often precipitated by following the self-interest motive in Figure 8.2. Of course, not showing enough attention to gaining and retaining profitability is also a possible source of financial trouble (Svensson et al., 2009). A question quickly emerges when trying to balance the needs of others against the needs of self or the objectives of an organisation. How does one find a balance between work and the rest of life? Codes of ethics may suggest one course of action, but people's own values and attitudes, or the overall culture of the workplace may suggest another, and various other combinations of these variables.

WORK–LIFE BALANCE

Learning Objective
The interplay between culture and work–life balance

■ There is growing recognition of the blurred line between work and private space. Information and communication technologies make lots of jobs and workers accessible outside traditional times and places (Wajcman et al., 2008). The culture of the workplace sets expectations about the level of flexibility workers can have between work and home responsibilities (Craig et al., 2010; Hannif et al., 2010). There are some organisations that require workers to stick to set hours and work from specific locations. Others are more concerned with key performance indicators (KPIs) and do not have rigid time and place requirements as long as KPIs are achieved. This cultural tone of rigidity or flexibility evolves over time and is reinforced by leadership at any given moment.

WINDOW ON ETHICS

Flexible schedules could benefit employees, business owners

AMERICAN Express is proud of the leadership position it has taken to support staff who wish to work flexibly. There have been various business benefits to American Express since developing a policy of encouraging flexible working arrangements, including improved employee retention, increased staff productivity and higher job satisfaction levels.

Although it might seem tricky to put in place a policy that encourages flexible working in a small business, it's not impossible as long as thought and consideration goes into designing a system that works for both the business and its staff.

'Supporting flexible working arrangements means striking the right balance between what staff need and what the business needs,' said Jason Fryer, Head of Small Business Services Australia, American Express.

'The idea is to think about how flexibility might work in the business and how the team could operate so that there's enough staff on deck when the business experiences heavy workflow, and not too many staff working when there's a lull in business activity,' Mr Fryer said.

'A key to making flexible working a success is to ensure staff rostered on at the same time have complementary skill sets, rather than ending up in a situation where skills are doubled up.'

For example, in a retail business it could be tricky to offer staff the flexibility to take weekends off regularly, but it might be much more possible to be able to offer flexible working arrangements on weekdays when business is quieter.

American Express offers a diverse range of flexible working options, including compressed work weeks, working from home options and part-time work.

'We try to offer staff a variety of working styles and hours,' Mr Fryer explained.

'One of our popular flexible working options is the compressed work week, which is a system small business owners could also use.

'Staff who successfully apply to work a compressed week work 37.5 hours over four days, so they get a day off every four days.

'Staff who work like this still have a full-time workload,' he says.

This works well for American Express because as a global business, many staff need to communicate with offices in the UK, Europe and the US.

Having a longer working day enables them to do this easily.

Small businesses that also have a global footprint might also be able to consider offering something similar.

'Many staff also work from home a certain number of days each week.

'When they come into the office they might log into a non-dedicated workstation, or they might have a dedicated workstation in the office and work from home from time to time.

'We work this out on an individual basis,' Mr Fryer said.

According to Mr Fryer, the benefits of supporting an environment that encourages flexible working are enormous.

'American Express benefits from better staff retention rates, less sick leave and a healthy work/life balance for staff, which increases their goodwill toward the business. It's really a win-win for all,' he added.

If you're thinking about enabling a flexible working culture in your business the idea is to think strategically about how this system could work without damaging the business and its ability to run smoothly.

Then, talk to staff about the flexible working arrangements they would be interested in participating in and develop a system that works both for the business and for employees.

'Although you might think it's harder to do this in small business, in a lot of ways it can be very easy to manage in a smaller firm that has fewer staff,' Mr Fryer said.

'The idea is to try it out, see what works and make changes to the system incrementally to ensure staff are working the way they want to, but the business is also operating to its full potential.'

Source: <www.news.com.au/business/business-owner/introducing-flexible-work-practices-in-small-business/story-fn5ybm8e-1225929845107>

This Window on Ethics reveals a best-case scenario. To have read this far in the book, you must know enough about motivation and leadership theory, as well as the ideas of empowerment and ethics, to understand how the flexible schedule offered by American Express would appeal to staff and help the organisation change direction when it needs to. But there are underlying questions about how the flexibility of workplaces such as this impacts on the personal lives of the workers. Globalisation and a broad range of socio-technological factors are changing the nature of work and a renegotiation of the boundaries is under way. There is frequent discussion in Australian and international workplaces about the spillover of work into home life and vice versa (Brown et al., 2009; Naithani, 2010). Those organisations that are best able to adjust to the discourse are tending to attract the best staff and are finding a balance that enables productivity, satisfaction, staff retention and general levels of motivation to be maximised. The challenge comes from the fact that the balance is just so delicate. A wrong word from a supervisor, a phone call from a supervisor to a worker at home, a poorly planned new policy, or a slight change to an organisation's strategic plan can potentially plunge people into negativity about their sense of balance. The fear of change is among those things that make the management of culture so awkward.

LEADERSHIP OF CULTURAL LEARNING AND CHANGE

Learning Objective
The interplay between culture and leadership

With all the complexity and subtlety of culture there is a final dimension to be considered: strong versus weak cultures. Sometimes people have very strong values and attitudes and these may be accentuated in cohesive team situations. A resilient team spirit can form and ensure that any proposed change to the culture is very difficult to achieve (Liedtka, 1989; Casali & Day, 2010). At the other extreme are organisations with weak cultures. There may be a loose gathering of individualistic people who don't team up very much or relate especially strongly to a shared vision. It can sometimes be easier to generate change where the culture is inherently less cohesive. Of course, caution is advised because even individualistic people can dislike the idea of change, so careful assessment is needed of the strength of a culture and of the dispositions of everyone whose support you need before initiating change programs.

A strong organisational culture takes a long time to establish itself and rests mostly on the implicit, unseen values and attitudes of the organisational founders and current leaders and staff. It is fundamentally difficult, though not impossible, to change people's attitudes and values. As discussed in Chapter 2, learning is not only possible but pivotal to the ongoing sustainability of organisations. The task of creating an atmosphere conducive to cultural change, therefore, is not one to be taken lightly. Time and plenty of energy are needed to manage cultural change through engagement with learning processes.

It was noted at the outset the powerful effect that original founders and subsequent leaders can have on the cultural atmosphere of an organisation. For any kind of culture change, large or small, within a strong or a weak cultural context, the support of leadership must be displayed before, during and after every change (Majeed et al., 2010). The last chapter of this book expands considerably on the theories of change management and culminates this consideration of the pervasive nature of culture.

CASE STUDY

In practice: Managing culture during change

On her first day in the job Erin knew she had some challenges. She suspected that the receptionist who greeted her with a tired look would really rather be reading her *'Gloss and Glam'* magazine than having to call the MD to announce Erin's arrival.

Erin Gilbert was the new HR manager at Piper Insurance Company Limited, which was a subsidiary of GTA Insurance Inc in the USA. Her appointment was noteworthy as she was the first Australian on the management team. When GTA took over Piper five years ago they fairly quickly replaced the local management team with expatriates. This was initially because they

wanted to change some of the practices the Company had perpetuated and because this was seen as a good training ground for up-and-coming international executives. They generally stayed two years and then returned to the USA or moved into larger branches overseas.

As Erin met key people at Piper she began to realise the staff were not highly regarded by management. 'They just don't seem to have any drive,' said Phil Young, the MD from Chicago, who had now been in Australia for six months. 'Maybe you Aussies have such a good life here in the sun and on your beaches you have just learned to take it easy.'

Erin protested mildly that not all Aussies were like that and maybe there was something else causing this perception.

Unfortunately, meeting more of the people and observing body language and work habits seemed to support Phil's views. People did tend to cluster around the coffee machines, walk slowly, arrive right on the official start time of 8.30am, or slightly after, and be gone by five. 'Not good signs,' thought Erin as she started to analyse the staff records to try and get an understanding of the type of people she was working with.

Erin found most of the staff had been with the Company over ten years and could have jumped to the conclusion that this was an indication of a stable workforce. On closer analysis of turnover, performance and qualifications, however, she found that those who would have been able to find other employment in the industry had left and those whose performance was mediocre and who were less qualified had stayed. There had been very few promotions since the takeover. When there was a vacancy, people were brought in from outside. There was no succession plan. Generally, the only training that had been provided was industry-based compliance courses that were almost a necessity for some people. On reviewing the salary system she found that salary increases were awarded, with very few exceptions, using a blanket approach. Everyone seemed to get the same increase, which was generally similar to the CPI.

When she queried the salary issue with Phil she was met with a puzzled look. 'You Aussies have something called awards?' he said. 'I was told that pay increases are normally done that way to avoid any problems. It does seem strange to me though.'

Erin spoke to a few people and a few groups over her first month and found there was very little taste for building a career within Piper or even trying to do anything other than just get on with their jobs and stay out of trouble. 'They don't seem interested in any new ideas', 'They just keep to themselves and only speak to Chicago' were fairly common comments. The 'they' particularly concerned Erin. She was used to people saying 'we' when referring to the company they worked for.

After her first month she set up a meeting with Phil and the other senior managers, all of whom were American or European.

'I find the calibre of our employees fairly mediocre,' she started off. 'They are not motivated and do not feel engaged. They are here because it is a job and many of them do not have the confidence to find another one. We seem to have a culture of survival rather than growing and we, as the management team, need to take responsibility for it. Yes, I'm told, the Company is profitable, so we don't have to worry. However, I believe we are financially successful because of some decisions made many years ago to get into specific markets. We have done well in these markets but, I also understand, the industry is changing and new players are entering Australia. We will have to change if we are going to compete. We will not be able to change with our current people performing the way they do.'

'Fine,' said Phil, 'what do we do, fire them and start all over again? You are the HR Manager; you had better come up with a plan because I think you are right.'

CASE STUDY QUESTIONS

1 How do you think a typical employee at Piper might describe their work, the environment and the management? Refer to the section 'Global culture' and discuss if employees are likely to blame some of the issues on an 'American' versus an 'Australian' approach to management.

2 What factors do you think have led to the current culture at Piper?

3 If you were Erin, what would be your top three issues to address in preparing Piper for a changing environment, and why?

4 How would you go about addressing those top three issues?

5 How would you describe the sort of culture you would want to introduce to Piper and, referring to the section 'Implicit cultural factors: Shared values and attitudes', describe what employees may find appealing about working in the organisation after you have made the changes.

CONCLUSION

Organisational culture depends on the input of individuals but develops its own atmosphere or climate according to the inter- and intra-group relationships that occur. The national culture also intermingles with organisational culture. There are powerful invisible forces that contribute to culture through shared values and attitudes. There are also very visible expressions of culture through spoken language, behavioural norms, stories, rituals and various other tangible items of design and decoration. Leadership, power and politics are prevalent aspects of human relationships in the workplace and contribute significantly to the cultural tone. There are a range of characteristics that can help to determine the kind of culture within an organisation: overall self-interest, competitiveness, power distance, collectivism, uncertainty avoidance, time orientation, financial competence, accountability, reciprocity, respect, integrity, and self-actualisation of the organisation. Many of these factors require immediate ethical consideration as part of the analysis of culture. The networked complexity of the cultural mix is an indicator of the challenge managers confront when trying to change the organisational culture. It is through learning that change can occur, but the embedded nature of the implicit aspects of culture in particular can be very strong. The next chapter discusses the ways that work can be designed to facilitate continuously improving work outcomes, and the final chapter debates the merits of retaining the status quo versus engaging with a proactive change process.

KEY POINTS

This chapter has

- defined culture
- explained the implicit and explicit factors of culture
- distinguished between subculture, organisational culture, national culture and global culture
- discussed the interplay between culture, leadership, ethics, and work–life balance.
- described the challenge of culture change in context with individual and organisational learning.

KEY TERMS

CULTURE
One of the key components of overall organisational atmosphere. It is the net expression of all of the physical, mental and emotional contributions of individuals, groups and resources in the organisation.

IMPLICIT CULTURAL FACTORS
The largely invisible values and attitudes of the people working in the organisation making the most of its architecture and processes.

EXPLICIT CULTURAL FACTORS

The things a worker or any observer encounters as they engage or enter the space occupied by a particular organisation. Explicit culture is a blend of language and stories, behavioural norms and rituals, and designs (involving patterns of colour, sound and smells).

HIGH-CONTEXT CULTURE

A culture in which lots of communication between people occurs beyond verbal discussion, that is, implicit things like body language, facial expressions and other unspoken behaviours, including the broader context of power relationships, are applied and interpreted in the course of normal interactions.

LOW-CONTEXT CULTURE

A culture in which explicit written or spoken words are relied on to convey meanings to each other.

POWER DISTANCE

One of Hofstede's dimensions of international organisational culture which measures the extent to which the less powerful members of organisations and institutions accept and expect that power is distributed unequally.

RELATIONAL ETHICS

An ethical field that focuses on the relationships between people with factors such as processes of communication, the methods for finding rapport with others, and techniques for being respectful at work.

UNCERTAINTY AVOIDANCE

One of Hofstede's dimensions of international organisational culture which measures the extent to which a culture programs its members to feel either uncomfortable or comfortable in unstructured situations.

STUDY AND REVISION QUESTIONS

Q *The Window on Communication displays a preface to a report by the Management Advisory Committee of the Australian Public Service Commission which encourages a more innovative culture to emerge in the Australian Public Service. It is noted that such a change will require alignment of the implicit values with the explicit expressions of organisational culture. What are some of the things that may have to happen in the average Public Service workplace to create this alignment?*

Q *Why is the redesign of a work space an insufficient approach on its own for creating cultural change?*

Q *Referring to the Window on Ethics, look back over this and earlier chapters in the book and draw from motivation, plus leadership theory and ideas of empowerment and ethics, to explain how the flexible schedule offered by American Express might appeal to staff but also threaten to change people's work–life balance.*

Q *'Culture change is easy to manage.' Explain your opinion about this statement.*

REFERENCES

Aletraris, L. (2010). How satisfied are they and why? A study of job satisfaction, job rewards, gender and temporary agency workers in Australia. *Human Relations*, 63(8), 1129–55.

Ashkanasy, N. M., & Wilderom, C. P. M. (2010). *Handbook of organizational culture and climate*. Thousand Oaks, CA: Sage.

Brown, K., Ling, S., Bradley, L., Lingard, H. & Townsend, K. (2009). What about me? Avoiding fatigue and gaining personal time in the work to leisure transition in work–life balance initiatives. In: *23rd Annual Australia and New Zealand Academy of Management Conference (ANZAM 2009)*, 1–4 December 2009, Southbank, Melbourne.

Casali, G., & Day, G. (2010). Treating an unhealthy organisational culture: The implications of the Bundaberg Hospital Inquiry for managerial ethical decision making. *Australian Health Review*, 34(1), 73–9.

Cordes, C., Richerson, P. & Schwesinger, G. (2010). How corporate cultures coevolve with the business environment: The case of firm growth crises and industry evolution. *Journal of Economic Behavior & Organization*, 76(1), 465–80.

Craig, L., Mullan, K. & Blaxland, M. (2010). Parenthood, policy and work–family time in Australia 1992–2006. *Work, Employment and Society*, 24(1), 27–45.

Creed, A., Zutshi, A. & Ross, J. (2009). Relational ethics in global commerce. *Journal of Electronic Commerce in Organizations*, 7(1), 35–49.

Erez, M. (2010). Culture and job design. *Journal of Organizational Behavior*, 31(1), 389–400.

Frontiera, J. (2010). Leadership and organizational culture transformation in professional sport. *Journal of Leadership & Organizational Studies*, 17(1), 71–86.

Hall, E. T., & Hall, M. R. (1987). *Understanding cultural differences*. London: Intellectual Press, Inc.

Hannif, Z., McDonnell, A., Connell, J. & Burgess, J. (2010). Working time flexibilities: A paradox in call centres? *Australian Bulletin of Labour*, 36(2), 178–93.

Helin, S., & Sandström, J. (2010). Resisting a corporate code of ethics and the reinforcement of management control. *Organization Studies*, 31(05), 583–604.

Hofstede, G. (1980). *Culture's consequences: International differences in work-related values*. Beverly Hills, CA: Sage.

Hofstede, G. (2002). Dimensions do not exist: A reply to Brendan McSweeney. *Human Relations*, 55(11), 1355–61.

Jaakson, K. (2010). Management by values: Are some values better than others? *Journal of Management Development*, 29(9), 795–806.

Leavitt, H. (2007). Big organizations are unhealthy environments for human beings. *Academy of Management Learning & Education*, 62(2), 253–63.

Liedtka J. (1989). Value congruence: The interplay of individual and organisational values systems. *Journal of Business Ethics*, 8 (1), 805–15.

Majeed, K., Bhatti, A., Nemati, A., Rehman, I. & Rizwan, A. (2010). Can cultural change with different leadership styles enhance the organizational performance? Research *Journal of International Studies*, 17(9), 102–32.

McGregor, D. (1960). *The human side of enterprise*. Toronto: McGraw-Hill.

McSweeney, B. (2002). Hofstede's model of national cultural differences and their consequences: A triumph of faith—a failure of analysis. *Human Relations*, 55(1), 89–118.

Mujtaba, B., Khanfar, N. & Khanfar, S. (2010). Leadership tendencies of government employees in Oman: A study of task and relationship based on age and gender. *Public Organization Review*, 10(2), 173–90.

Naithani, P. (2010). Overview of work–life balance discourse and its relevance in current economic scenario. *Asian Social Science*, 6(6), 148–55.

O'Neill, O., & O'Reilly, C. (2010). Careers as tournaments: The impact of sex and gendered organizational culture preferences on MBAs' income attainment. *Journal of Organizational Behavior*, 31(1), 856–76.

Rapaille, C. (2006). *The culture code: An ingenious way to understand why people around the world buy and live as they do*. New York: Broadway Books.

Segon, M. (2010). Corruption as part of national culture: The disconnect between values, ethics and etiquette. *International Review of Business Research Papers*, 6(6), 259–75.

Simon, H. (1991). Bounded rationality and organizational learning. *Organization Science*, 2(1), 125–34.

Strickland, R. A., & Vaughan, S. K. (2008). The hierarchy of ethical values in non-profit organizations. *Public Integrity*, 10(3), 233–51.

Svensson, G., Wood, G., Singh, J. & Callaghan, M. (2009). Implementation, communication and benefits of corporate codes of ethics: An international and longitudinal approach for Australia, Canada and Sweden. *Business Ethics: A European Review*, 18(4), 389–407.

Thompson, R. M., & Flynn, C. (2009). Traps for the unwary: Reform stories of private sector managers entering public service. In: *13th International Research Society for Public Management Conference (IRSPM XIII)*, 6–8 April, Fredericksberg, Denmark.

van Vuuren, M., & Cooren, F. (2010). 'My attitude made me do it': Considering the agency of attitudes. *Human Studies*, 33(1), 85–101.

Wajcman, J., Bittman, M., Jones, P., Johnstone, L. & Brown, J. (2008). *The impact of the mobile phone on work/life balance—Final Report*, <www.amta.org.au/amta/site/amta/downloads/pdfs_2008/Work%20life%20balance%20final%20report%2026Mar08.pdf>

Yang, J. T. (2010). Antecedents and consequences of job satisfaction in the hotel industry. *International Journal of Hospitality Management*, 29 (1), 609–19.

Zutshi, A., Creed, A. & Rudolph, H. (2010). Interpretations of corruption in intercultural bargaining. *International Journal of Business Governance and Ethics*, 5(3), 196–213.

PRACTITIONER INSIGHT

VIN LUCAS

HR DIRECTOR,
SCHWEPPES AUSTRALIA

Vin Lucas is a senior HR professional with an extensive background and proven career record of success, in particular leading industrial and employee relations reform within the aggressive Australian industrial relations landscape. Vin has well-developed HR management capability with demonstrated success in leading teams through challenging business agendas and delivering core business outcomes.

As HR Director, Vin leads the human resources function for Schweppes Australia. He was an integral part of the formation of the beverage company on its separation from Cadbury Schweppes in April 2009, and has more than 20 years service with the two entities.

Vin's key philosophy is that HR works for the success of others.

INTERVIEW

What was your first job?
Bank officer.

What has been your career highlight so far?
Current role and helping to establish Schweppes Australia as a standalone business after separation from Cadbury Schweppes in 2008.

In your current role, what does a typical day involve?
Everything from strategic thinking and planning through to operational HR and people issues, such as recruiting, people development, remuneration, grievance management and industrial relations.

What's the best part of your job?
Making a positive impact on the business through employees, that is, growing employee engagement and productivity.

What is the hardest aspect of your role?
Bringing together the diverse styles, behaviours, thoughts and energies of people.

What are the current challenges facing you, in your role?
Working forward with organisational change; aligning people to the company's goals and priorities.

Do you regularly apply the principles or theories you learnt (when studying organisational behaviour) into your everyday work? In what way?
Yes, I apply theory but you always need to place it in a situational context and consider how decisions and actions will impact on both organisational and individual behaviour.

Is a work–life balance a reasonable expectation in a modern workplace?
The realities and challenges of a modern workplace mean that this is, in some ways, more difficult to achieve. Workplace balance can mean different things to people.

What strategies do you implement in your workplace to help employees achieve an appropriate work–life balance?
This is managed at an individual and team level. The key is being flexible, to ensure that both individual and business objectives can be met.

Has technology impacted on work–life balance? Is it harder to achieve with constant access to the 'office', for example?
Technology has changed people's accessibility to the office. While it means people can access messages and be connected when away from the office, it has increased the expectation

that people are available beyond the traditional office hours. In some ways, technology has blurred the boundaries between personal life and work life.

Are there greater expectations (on you or your workplace) to help motivate and engage employees in their work than ever before?

It is very important for us to keep employees motivated and engaged. We know employees who are motivated and inspired deliver greater individual performance which leads to greater organisational success. It is when your employees are engaged that they voluntarily go above and beyond the bare minimum of their role, and this is critical for organisational success.

What do you believe makes a good manager or decision maker? How would you describe your own management style?

I have a democratic and collaborative style, and empower my managers to be accountable and responsible for their team's results.

How do you communicate company strategy with staff at all levels?

We have a comprehensive internal communication and engagement programme to involve and engage employees in our strategy and ensure that they fully understand the business priorities. We are currently launching our new business strategy which will take the organisation through the next five years. Our programme includes regular workshops with our senior leaders in the business, following which they are provided with communication materials and are expected to discuss strategy and performance with their teams. We have a strong focus on face-to-face communication so that employees can ask questions and engage in dialogue to fully understand the business and individual objectives and performance against those objectives. We continually reinforce and align all of our corporate communications to our strategy.

What do you believe is the best way for a manager to avoid conflict in the workplace? And is this an easy approach to take?

It's more about ensuring that employees are 'conflict competent' rather than 'conflict incompetent'. We have a set of values that provides expectations of what is and is not acceptable behaviour in our organisation. We expect people to have the courage to challenge each other, and to do so in a constructive, value-adding way.

Have the implications of globalisation presented new challenges for your workplace?

We operate in a world that knows no boundaries, and people are able to (generally) move freely between companies and countries. We know and understand that as an Australian-based company we have some restrictions in what we can offer people in terms of international postings, so we aim to make our offer attractive in terms of the culture and development opportunities people can experience while they work for Schweppes. We often have people returning to work with us after a career or travel break, having gained more experience.

There is an old adage that power corrupts. Does your experience suggest the decision of who to give certain powers in an organisation is, therefore, very important?

I personally believe in empowering and trusting people, providing coaching and guidance along the way. Governance structures, policies and processes are important as they help to define the boundaries in which individuals can act. With these solidly in place, allowing the right people to have decision-making power can engage and empower your employees, as they can see faster turnaround, greater accountability and reward for performance.

Do you think the workplace environment really is changing faster than ever before? Or are people always prone to feeling anxious when the inevitable changes occur?

Throughout my career I've experienced constant change. Organisations are continually evolving and improving. Change is not always negative. We need to feel comfortable living with ambiguity and be ready to adapt to new opportunities, as and when they arise.

Are you able to find much time to think about the strategic design of work in your organisation?

There is always tension between finding time for long-term planning versus the need to respond to daily operational challenges. It is important to regularly schedule time to think about the long-term vision and goals and regularly review the immediate priorities to ensure we deliver against our long-term commitments.

Equitable Design and Negotiation of Work Arrangements

INTRODUCTION

If culture is a significant part of the atmosphere of an organisation, then the way that work is analysed, planned, designed and implemented is a large component of organisational architecture. In fact, it is the interplay between these factors that determines the optimal outcome for organisational behaviour. To get the design of work right is to create opportunities for higher levels of motivation, productivity, well-being and profitability. As this journey through the key theories of organisational behaviour approaches its conclusion, this chapter aims to draw together the most pragmatic ideas of job design in ways that can give the practising people manager a toolkit for daily evaluation and application.

LEARNING OBJECTIVES

Understanding this chapter will help you to

- explain why the proper design of jobs contributes to more effective people management
- describe the different approaches to job design and how they might be integrated
- explain the functions and challenges of performance appraisal
- discuss the effects of job design on the work–life balance and health of staff
- describe how job design, learning and change are relevant for performance improvement.

OVERVIEW

This penultimate chapter brings the discussion of organisational behaviour theories into practical focus. The design of work is where the factors of atmosphere and, especially, architecture in an organisation are directly tested. A range of job design options are described, including job rotation, enrichment, enlargement and the various schedules of pay and other reward distribution incentives in individual and group or team contexts. Links are drawn back to the motivation and leadership chapters and recurring themes around the importance of effective communication and negotiation strategies are highlighted in the case examples, especially as they relate to job satisfaction and work productivity. There is also an integrated design model outlined in the job characteristics theory. Implications of job design for work–life balance are developed. The roles of learning and behavioural change are also tied to work design theories and related to the need to cater for equity in increasingly diverse and complex work environments.

DESIGNING WORK

Think about this question: Have machines changed work? There is a socio-technical view to suggest that the answer is a definitive *yes* (Marx, 2010). Automation has altered the ways we think about work, the types of tasks we can achieve and the scale of expected outputs. Transportation and communication technologies have also altered the ways we think about space, time and our relationships with each other. For instance, differences have been noted in the social responses of the genders to technological changes at work (Wajcman, 2010), participants' expectations of group work over vast distances (Bygstad et al., 2010) and the response times people anticipate in their exchanges at work (Cohen, 2010). The research notes general trends such as a greater tendency among males to adopt certain kinds of engineered technological applications, new expectations about the possibilities of virtual teamwork, and a general intensification of work speeds in response to technological change. Such fundamental change leads to the need for transformation of the ways that work is perceived and conducted.

■
Learning Objective
The proper design of jobs contributes to more effective people management

In a society beset with altered expectations there is renewed importance placed on getting job design right if retention of key staff is important. The architecture of work has lasting effects on motivation, leadership, power balance, culture balance and work–life balance (Munyon et al., 2010; Oldham & Hackman, 2010). For instance, Chapter 4 discusses equity theory and the fact that worker motivation is affected in various ways by making comparisons of their situations with others. Catering for people's impressions is one of the key elements of job design.

■
Psychological contract
The agreement workers make in their minds with organisations when they accept a position. An expectation is established about what energy will be spent and which duties the worker will be comfortable carrying out. In return, the organisation has expectations about the resources and support they will provide for the worker.

The **psychological contract** is the agreement workers make in their minds with organisations when they accept a position. An expectation is established about what energy will be spent and which duties the worker will be comfortable carrying out (Chambel, 2011). In return, the organisation has expectations about the resources and support it will provide for the worker. Where expectations are broadly met, the contract is honoured and all parties tend to stick with the relationship. Where breaches of expectation occur, however, there is diminishment of trust and increased likelihood that the contract will break; workers will leave or lose motivation, and organisations will reduce levels of support (Bal et al., 2010).

WINDOW ON COMMUNICATION

Chef Neil Perry roasted for sacking pregnant employee from Rockpool

BARCLAY CRAWFORD

CELEBRITY chef Neil Perry has been severely criticised by the country's labour tribunal for the 'bizarre and unacceptable' sacking of a pregnant employee at his celebrated restaurant Rockpool.

Perry's decision to dump five-month-pregnant reservations assistant Michelle de Leon after a telephone complaint from the concierge of a five-star hotel was 'nothing short of appalling and manifestly unfair', Fair Work Australia Deputy Justice Peter Sams said in his decision.

'What makes the respondent's conduct even more incomprehensible is that it employs some 150 employees at three well-known premium restaurants in Sydney and Melbourne,' he said.

At 4.30pm on October 16, Mrs de Leon, who was earning $40,000 a year, was called into a meeting with general manager Jeremy Courmadias and administration manager Lauren Treweek. She was stunned when told the divorcee chef wanted her out immediately for being rude in a phone call three hours earlier.

The complaint had been made to Rockpool general manager Penny Watson-Green by Four Seasons Hotel concierge James Nobleza. Mr Nobleza had telephoned Rockpool at 2.30pm to ask who had designed the restaurant.

Mrs de Leon, who had been at the restaurant for six months and two days, did not know the answer. As only one of a team of three available at the time, she told the concierge to either call back later or she would get someone to call him.

'Mr Perry had felt that the applicant was guilty of misconduct and should be immediately dismissed,' Justice Sams' judgment said.

Mrs de Leon told *The Sunday Telegraph*: 'They called me in and told me Neil Perry had decided to sack me. I was asked to give an explanation, but I was confused, and I didn't know what to say. I was pregnant and very emotional so I started crying.'

Mrs de Leon, who had more than eight years' experience in five-star hospitality, said she had taken the job because of Mr Perry's reputation.

Mr Perry is one of Sydney's highest-profile chefs, praised for the quality of his food at Sydney institutions Rockpool, Rockpool Bar & Grill and Spice Temple.

The sacking left Mrs de Leon, 31, depressed and battered her self-esteem.

'I just kept asking myself, "Why? What did I do wrong?"'

Mrs de Leon's termination could not have come at a worse time. Not only was she pregnant, but her husband, Bryand, had also just been retrenched from his job.

The restaurant group said Mrs de Leon had been rude and unprofessional and had jeopardised an important customer relationship.

But Justice Sams dismissed the arguments and ruled the decision to sack Mrs de Leon was unjust, unreasonable and harsh. He ordered Mr Perry to pay Ms de Leon 12 weeks' pay, of $9230.76.

Perry, speaking from Las Vegas yesterday, maintained there were 'underlying issues' with the new mother and the phone conversation 'was the final straw'.

'But maybe we didn't go about it the right way.'

Source: <www.dailytelegraph.com.au/business/ star-chef-neil-perry-slammed-for-unjust-sacking/story- e6frez7r-1225867241747>

The design of work needs to factor in two broad concerns: one is about getting the right job done in the right way for the right customer at the right time; the other is about the skills inventory and learning capacity of the person assigned to complete the job. To think only of the task runs the risk that the person doing it will be harmed or discriminated against; to think only of the person runs the risk that the work outcomes will be inadequate. The complex reality is that machines and people coexist in the contemporary workplace and managers have the dual concern of maximising output while also avoiding the creation of harm or inequities. Careful thought about the tasks, the available people, and the methods for ongoing improvement can lead to better design of work.

CASE STUDY

Benefits officers denied the satisfaction of full responsibility

Sometimes the work was frustrating but the range of people Amanda Jackson dealt with kept her interested and there were always plenty of challenges in her role as Benefits Officer in the State Department of Welfare Services.

Amanda spent most of her time handling queries from people who had complex welfare needs and her job was to liaise between local, state and federal government agencies to ensure her clients received the best possible outcome and their legal entitlements. These clients were usually referred to her from charities and welfare organisations so she needed to deal with their needs as well. Quite often the client could not speak English so there was also a translator involved.

All this complexity made the job fascinating for Amanda and juggling the needs of the various parties and the related regulations provided plenty of challenge for her communications skills.

Much of the interaction was by phone and email but there was also enough face-to-face contact to build a worthwhile relationship with the client and many colleagues across the other departments and agencies.

The process usually involved Amanda and her colleagues taking a brief from one of the referring agencies and then liaising with all the other parties and the client to put a case together with recommendations as to what support and benefits the client should receive. The clients often had some form of disability or disadvantage. They were sometimes unemployed, new arrivals to the country, or had suffered an injury, and were often in need of financial support or medical or psychological help. They sometimes required transport or accommodation assistance and a range of other support that quite often was just not readily available.

The job has its fair share of stress but Amanda and her colleagues knew they were doing something worthwhile for people. That's what they joined for. The big disappointment for them was that after they had prepared a report on each client with a recommendation it was elevated to their Supervisor, Freya Novak, and then to her Manager, Luke Davidson, to make a final decision. This decision then triggered the action by the various departments and the job was finished as far as Amanda and her colleagues were concerned. Unless there were problems further down the line they never heard from the client again.

Several of Amanda's fellow team members had left over the last year or so and the word was that it was the stress in the job that had caused this. Amanda knew this was not the case. None of them had taken any leave related to stress and, while there was certainly stress in the job, they tended to thrive on it.

Luke Davidson was moving into another department and his replacement was to start in another month. He had already visited the Department and they had heard he was concerned about the staff turnover and the possibility of stress being a cause. There had been talk of restructuring the department and redesigning some of the jobs. Amanda and her colleagues didn't like the idea of this.

Over lunch they had discussed the topic a number of times and it seemed to Amanda that they all took great pride in their work but didn't get a great deal of satisfaction from it. They often talked about their colleagues in the smaller agencies and some charities that had less scope in some ways than a government department but seemed a lot happier in their work. 'They actually get to see a happy client at the end,' one of them said. And they all agreed.

Amanda was having her six-monthly performance review with Freya and she asked what was going to happen. 'Oh, probably a reorganisation, like every other new manager who comes in,' she said, 'then we'll have new performance indicators and new job descriptions and another six months of disruption'.

'Well, I don't think that's going to help our situation much,' replied Amanda. 'Some of us have been here for years. We're all well qualified and experienced. I think people are leaving because they are not promoted or given enough responsibility. We never get to make any decisions and yet we're the ones with the most knowledge about what's going on.'

'Well, you know what it's like here,' said Freya, 'they like to make the decisions to justify their positions and cover their backsides and with all this talk of stress, possible claims and the staff turnover, I can't see how that's going to change. When I met him, he was particularly keen on understanding what everyone did and was interested in the range of work you did. He seemed to think that narrowing that down a bit may help. You know, everybody being a bit more of a specialist in a particular area.'

Amanda left the meeting with a sense that things were not going to improve. She resolved to try and make a difference by writing down her thoughts to present to the new manager.

CASE STUDY QUESTIONS

1 Referring particularly to the 'Designing work' and 'Integrated job design' sections in the chapter, describe what you think Amanda is missing in her job satisfaction.

2 Using the terminology used in the chapter, what are the key points you think Amanda should raise when presenting to the new Manager?

3 In what areas do you think Freya Novak could improve her effectiveness as a supervisor?

4 Referring to the job characteristics theory, describe where you think there may be deficiencies in the match between Amanda and her job.

5 What do you think the new Manager should do about the issues being raised by Amanda and how should he go about it?

DIFFERENT APPROACHES TO THE DESIGN OF WORK

■

Anyone currently working for an organisation will have a sense of the continuously changing nature of the environment. Even where job descriptions don't change, the actual work and the responses demanded by the relationships occurring internally and externally are undergoing transformation. The final chapter of this book discusses the pervasive nature of change and the generic strategies that organisations and individuals can follow. For a practising people manager, the field of work planning and job design is where immediate pragmatic solutions can be implemented in response to changes wrought by environmental influences. The general job design approaches available for managers include job simplification, job enlargement, job rotation and multi-skilling.

■

Job simplification
The process of
streamlining the work
flow of a task, or removing
some aspects of a
person's job. The aim is to
maximise efficiency and
sometimes the effect is to
enhance role clarity, which
has a positive effect on
overall job satisfaction.

Job simplification is the process of streamlining the work flow of a task, or removing some aspects of a person's job. The aim is to maximise efficiency and sometimes the effect is to enhance role clarity, which has a positive effect on overall job satisfaction. Of course, a job that is oversimplified could become routine and dull, and even risk redundancy for some people. The simpler a task, however, the easier it is to automate. The premise of scientific management, for example, is that detailed job analysis enables tasks to be broken down into discrete components and then decisions can be made about which people or machines will complete the tasks most productively (Humphrey et al., 2007). Historically, the simplification of jobs into production line work was noted to contribute to boredom and increased staff turnover. The growth of automation somewhat changes the nature of production line work and creates a number of potentially interesting evaluation or supervisory roles. Managers simply need to remember that the essence of job simplification goes to the heart of connections between efficiency, work processes and available technology.

■

Job enlargement
Adding a greater variety
of tasks to the job that a
person currently does.

Job enlargement involves adding a greater variety of tasks to the job that a person currently does. As a strategy to counter the boredom linked with simplification of work, job enlargement seems reasonable; however, the reality is that it asks people to do more than they were originally doing so it potentially diminishes motivation and job satisfaction levels if the reward and reinforcement schedule is not properly established (Morgeson & Humphrey, 2008), or if equity comparisons with other workers in similar positions are not favourable.

■

Job enrichment
A strategic version of job
enlargement that aims
to give people work that
fulfils their higher-level
needs for a sense of
meaning, achievement
and belonging.

Job enrichment is best described as a strategic version of job enlargement. From the moment when Herzberg's two-factor theory of motivation (see Chapter 4) identified higher-order needs in the workplace it became possible to identify them as motivators in daily tasks and responsibilities. By adding to people's job descriptions the right mix of tasks and responsibilities that cater to the higher-order needs, the theory is that overall motivation and satisfaction can improve. Providing a sense of meaning, achievement and belonging qualifies as enrichment for various people (Duchon & Plowman, 2005).

■

Job rotation
The opportunity to try a completely different job, thus enabling the expansion of skill sets across a number of workers and allowing people to develop a more integrated understanding of the ways different jobs come together in the organisation.

The difficulty is that managers cannot directly give staff the inner feelings that count towards job enrichment. Each worker responds differently to the external stimuli that a job or a supervisor can provide, so the extent to which job enrichment is a reliable technique has sometimes been called into question (Fein, 1975).

Job rotation gives a worker the opportunity to try a completely different job, which can alleviate boredom and in some cases reduce the negative health effects of repetitive jobs (Weichel et al., 2010). It enables the expansion of skill sets across a number of workers and allows people to develop a more integrated understanding of the ways different jobs come together in the organisation. **Multi-skilling** is one objective of job rotation.

Thought pathway

How do you feel about being asked to work on things you have never done before? Consider the limits of novelty versus consistency at work. Are your thoughts about this likely to affect your views as a manager about how to apply job rotation?

■

Multi-skilling
The collection of experiences and training that enables workers to become proficient at more than one job or skill set.

Multi-skilling is the collection of experiences and training that enables workers to become proficient at more than one job or skill set. It can build feelings of self-efficacy to be competent in a range of skills, and it can also help workers to respect each others' contributions to the organisation (Fraser & Hvolby, 2010). Formal job rotation, training programs and ad hoc experiences at having to cover for workmates are among the ways that multiple skills sets develop in individuals. All of the occasions that encourage development of multi-skilling are changes to established patterns of work. Change can be very positive but it is also resisted as a normal part of human nature. Think about it; if you are comfortable in the way you currently do your work and a manager walks in and says they want you to go and retrain or try a completely new job, well, it might depend on your mood at the time but, in general, you will recognise the energy it takes to optimistically move into such a change. Managers who are redesigning work have to be realistic about the expectations and preferences of their staff.

INTEGRATED JOB DESIGN

■

Learning Objective
How different approaches to job design might be integrated

In a dynamic and unpredictable field there has been one approach to job design that quite adeptly integrates most of the key influences. **Job characteristics theory** (or JCT, and sometimes referred to as job characteristics model or JCM) identifies a range of core characteristics of most kinds of work: skill variety, task identity, task significance, autonomy, feedback (Hackman & Oldham, 1975, 1976, 1980). The theory also identifies critical psychological states: meaningful work, responsibility for outcomes and knowledge of results. Furthermore, there is recognition of the importance of individual work outcomes such as intrinsic motivation, high-quality work, high satisfaction, low absenteeism and turnover. Finally, the theory predicts there are moderators in job design that include growth needs, knowledge and skills, and context satisfaction. JCT bridges concepts from the areas of motivation, individual differences, group dynamics, power and leadership (Fincham & Rhodes, 2005; Morgeson & Humphrey, 2008). It is a useful framework for assessing many kinds of work and situational factors.

Figure 9.1 Job characteristics model

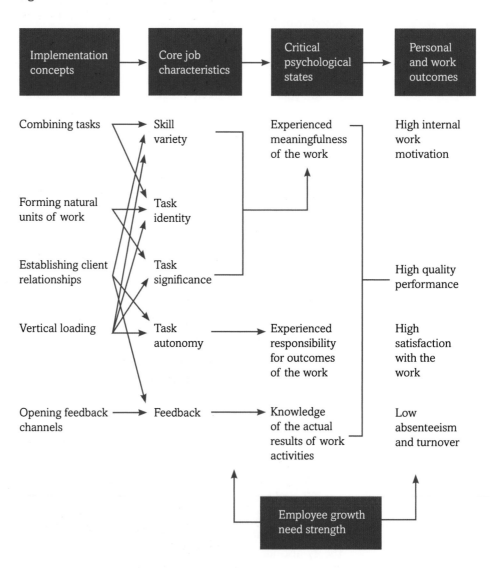

Source: Principles of Organizational Behaviour, *Fourth Edition by Robin Fincham and Peter Rhodes (2005) by permission of Oxford University Press UK.*

The definitions of the key variables can help to identify the intentions of the approach.

CORE JOB CHARACTERISTICS

- Skill variety is the range of different inputs a single job requires of a worker. Low skill variety is linked with routine work and high skill variety is a feature of more creative work.
- Task identity refers to the degree of integration of a single job. If the work results in an identifiable whole output, then task identity is high; if the work produces a partial output that contributes to some other product further along the chain, then task identity is lower.
- Task significance is the degree of importance or meaningfulness a person can see in completing the job. Meaning can be at the individual, organisational or societal level.
- Autonomy is the feeling of control and choice a worker feels in the completion of their job.
- Feedback refers to how directly the worker receives information about their outputs. Quick and direct feedback about one's work is ideal.

CRITICAL PSYCHOLOGICAL STATES

- Meaningful work is the perception drawn from task significance that the work one is completing is making a difference to self and others.
- Responsibility for outcomes is the perception drawn from autonomy at work that the results of outputs will be traced back to the source. It is a feeling of being accountable for work done.
- Knowledge of results comes from good feedback systems and contributes to the development of all the critical psychological states.

INDIVIDUAL WORK OUTCOMES

- Intrinsic motivation is the drive that emerges from within the mind and feelings of an individual.
- High-quality work is the type of output desired by organisations within the constraints of their available resources.
- High satisfaction is desired by individuals and organisations in the achievement of mutually agreeable outcomes.
- Low absenteeism and turnover means that people are happy to come to work and stay there.

MODERATORS

- Growth needs are the individual worker's intrinsic need to learn, develop and grow.

- Knowledge and skills are relevant to the job at the present time, as well as the capacity of the individual worker to learn more and improve in the future.

- Context satisfaction is the degree to which the individual worker is comfortable with the current job in the current organisation and all of the contextual variables, such as work relationships, physical space and overall work–life balance.

The theory plays out in very complex environments and the variables interact in sometimes surprising ways. In general, the job designer can try to ensure core job characteristics are present and then, when matching staff to the job, endeavour to consider critical psychological states and particular moderators of behaviour. The overall goal should be related where possible to individual work outcomes. This may be simple enough to talk about but it is not a linear formula and ongoing dialogue, negotiation and adjustment are part of the longer-term application of JCT.

Subsequent research generally supports and expands on JCT (Fried & Ferris, 1987). In a recent review of the history of JCT, Oldham and Hackman (2010, p. 464) trace the roots of the model to the expectancy theory of motivation (see Chapter 4) and comment upon their realisation that

> rather than being motivated by, say, the promise of rewards or the prospect of receiving (or avoiding) supervisory attention, people would try to perform well simply because it felt good when they did—and it felt bad when they did not. What characteristics of jobs, we wondered, might foster that state of internal work motivation?

Without diminishing the value of their integrated theory, Oldham and Hackman (2010) follow on to suggest that major changes have since occurred in workplaces, thus leading them to believe that new approaches to job design may be warranted. Current attention of managers and researchers is being drawn towards the often fluid relationships between people that render some of the applications of JCT less effective than in the past.

Good news about bad jobs

The conventional wisdom that having any job is better than having no job at all has been turned on its head by recent research.

MARTYN PEARCE

What's the worst job you've ever had? Was it one where you felt you had little job security, and that the rug could be pulled out from beneath you at any point? Perhaps it was about the sheer weight of work coming at you? Maybe it was because that job, with its overwhelming workload and fragile security, also gave you little control about how you managed that workload? It just kept on coming.

We've all had at least one of those jobs—possibly many of them. You might even be in one of those jobs now.

But at least you've got a job, right? And at least having that job means that your mental health is likely to be better than if you didn't have a job, right? Because you've at least got an income, and at least have something productive to do with your time, right?

Well, no. Not right. In what could be a vindication for anyone who has ever felt that they hated their job so much that they could barely pull themselves out of bed in the morning, ANU researchers have found that, from a mental health viewpoint, you may be better off being in no job at all than being in a bad job.

The work was undertaken by researchers from the Centre for Mental Health Research and led by Dr Liana Leach. Using data from the 20-year Personality and Total Health (PATH) Through Life Project, the team looked at the mental health effects of being in a 'bad job'—a job with low security, high stress and little control. The results, as Leach explains, were significant.

'Our research had two main findings. First, we found that those in poor quality jobs had poorer mental health than those in good quality work. People who were in a bad job were five times more likely to be categorised as depressed and twice as likely to be categorised as anxious than those in good quality work.

'Second, over time, those who moved from being unemployed into poor quality work actually experienced a greater decline in their mental health than those who remained unemployed,' she says.

The study examined the effect of several adverse work conditions on an individual's mental health, rather than looking at the effect of specific roles or occupations.

'In our study, a bad job, or poor quality job, was one where people perceived their job was insecure, perhaps because they were on a short-term contract or casual work, they had high job demands or a heavy workload, and they didn't have much control over how they managed that workload. They also felt that it would be difficult to gain another similar job, suggesting they felt trapped in their current workplace,' says Leach.

The results indicate that, for employers, one of the keys to happy and mentally healthy employees is to keep an eye on these negative factors and work with staff to find solutions.

'The study suggests it would be best for employers to be open to negotiation with employees about their work conditions—making sure employees have reasonable workloads and some control over how they manage this workload is likely to produce employees with better mental health.

'For their part, employees might like to negotiate with employers to see if they can make their workplace one that benefits their wellbeing and mental health.

'Everybody has moments in their jobs where it's difficult and you're not enjoying what you're doing, but we hope this study helps to improve people's workplace environments so that we can improve their mental health too,' says Leach.

Source: <http://news.anu.edu.au/?p=6571>

This Window on Ethics draws a link between job design and the imperative for doing the right thing for the staff that are affected physically, mentally or emotionally by the outcome of the design. Work that is repetitive and draining can have serious effects on people's well-being. The intrinsic motivation of certain people cannot be relied on in all cases to carry them through challenging work tasks. Overall job design can and should be monitored, adjusted and regularly evaluated for its effects on motivation, satisfaction, absenteeism and turnover, as well as stress and health. Good systems for monitoring work and being flexible in relation to design are, therefore, extremely important.

PERFORMANCE APPRAISAL, NEGOTIATION AND EQUITY

There is an uncomfortable relationship in many workplaces between strategic planning, monitoring of work performance and the fair negotiation of individual workloads. There is normally plenty of work to do, but the attractiveness and quality of jobs varies widely. The motivation of diverse individuals to complete the different tasks is also variable. This puts the daily negotiation of work into a volatile context (Nankervis & Stanton, 2010). There is a power differential, especially between large organisations and individual workers, and this can leave some people vulnerable in relation to negotiating individual workload (Cusack, 2010). In smaller organisations, multi-skilling is common and people can find themselves compelled by circumstances to work frenetically, often in underregulated situations. The growth of casual or sessional work in both large and small organisations is another trend that leaves workers with less power to negotiate work conditions. In each of these scenarios, the concept of equity at work is quite challenged. Those individuals with the best negotiation skills can get the easiest, less monitored, better paid jobs, leaving the rest to carry on with the more difficult, dangerous and underpaid work.

Thought pathway

How would you go about appraising the performance of someone who works for you? Also think about the style of appraisal you would prefer from someone who supervises you. Is there a difference between these two styles?

The functions and challenges of performance appraisal

Performance appraisal is the mechanism by which work progress is monitored and matched with organisational and individual career objectives. There can be a formal procedure for supervisors and staff to engage in work appraisal and load negotiation, though it is not unusual for an informal approach to be applied by supervisors. Either approach can work well, but in terms of tracking and keeping evidence of adherence to laws related to equity and anti-discrimination, a formal system is normally recommended. Research shows that the better the quality of performance appraisal systems, the more likely staff will develop job satisfaction and overall commitment to the organisation (Brown et al., 2010).

Various formal performance appraisal systems can be applied in organisations. The underlying principle ties to motivation through goal-setting theory. When a worker knows the goal they are aiming for they are more likely to achieve it. A good performance appraisal system allows for mutual recognition by the organisation and the individual of targets or key performance indicators, or KPIs. Unfortunately, there are many less than perfect appraisal systems being used and it is not unusual for abuses of power and control to occur through some of the mechanisms of formal appraisal. Once again, it is intrinsic rather than extrinsic factors that tend to make people work more effectively. To impose systems too strongly on individuals runs the risk of problems.

WINDOW ON CONFLICT AND NEGOTIATION

3 tips to manage your stupid, annual, performance review

Annual performance reviews are the equivalent of taking a shower once a year. It stinks. You cannot remove all the nasty effects of not washing for a whole year—in one fell swoop. After the shower you're thinking about the next one.

Annual performance reviews are simply put—stupid. Meaning lacking in IQ and Emotional Intelligence.

Anyone with a higher level of IQ would realize that sitting down and talking about events that are mostly forgotten, irrelevant and unlikely to result in significant improvements in competence or motivation is a waste of time and money.

Someone with a developed sense of Emotional Intelligence would be aware that:

(a) s/he is doing a stupid, ineffective thing;
(b) s/he should self-manage to give employees feedback on a regular, daily basis

(c) everyone hates and is avoiding the inevitable annual root canal;
(d) a once a year conversation is no way to develop empathy for others;
(e) s/he has betrayed her/his key leadership ethics.

But the annual stupid conversation seems to be the norm, so here are 3 tips to help manage the mess.

1   Over the year, record: (i) What I've done well; (ii) What I need to improve on (the top three); (iii) What I need from my boss or direct report within the next 90 days. Be ready to talk about these with your boss or direct report so s/he knows what you are proud of.

2   Identify areas you want to work on in your's, or your direct reports, professional development plan. Bring a list of suggestions, courses, etc. Demonstrate your willingness to improve. Be prepared to confront your direct report about needed development areas.

3   At the end of the conversation summarize actions that need to be done, and by when.

Then set up a system for giving and receiving feedback on a regular daily, weekly, monthly basis. Stop the stupidity. Put your Emotional Intelligence to work.

Dr Jim Sellner, PhD, DipC. The ONLY business mentor who delivers live, Virtual-Instructor Led Workshops—video-based, interactive business learning experiences that increase people's on-the-job performance. <http://ezinearticles.com/?3-Tips-to-Manage-Your-Stupid,-Annual,-Performance-Review&id=3927662>

There is a fine line between encouraging and forcing everyone to work towards a collective goal. It is often in leadership or supervision styles that the conflicts can emerge in organisations. Strategic plans do need to be made and organisational goals achieved; however, all the smart people generally know this, and the systems and methods used to keep everyone's activities in alignment can mean the difference between harmonious success and tumultuous failure.

CASE STUDY

Being a mother and working from home is possible

Thomas Brewer Partners is a well-established accounting firm with six partners and 32 staff. As a suburban firm they continually have difficulties in attracting good staff and have quite a high turnover as new graduates join, complete a few years and then leave. All six partners are male and it had been suggested by the last senior female who left that they should consider promoting more females. 'Not much chance of that,' snorted Simon Thomas, the senior partner, when it was raised at a partners' meeting. 'Bound to get pregnant, disappear for a year and then start pestering us for part-time work like the rest.'

Claudia Russell had recently joined as a part-time accountant. She had given birth to her first child a year ago and was grateful for a job that allowed her to work three days a week from 9am until 1pm. This fitted in well with her mother-in-law, who looked after her daughter during those hours. Claudia met other part-time mothers at work and found that they had mostly been recruited in the last two years. When she mentioned this to her Manager, Jason Fellini, she was told 'it's difficult to attract anybody else these days to do the grunt work. All these young graduates want to move on to the interesting stuff after six months. You part-time mothers are ideal for getting the rest of the work done.'

Over the next few weeks Claudia discovered many of the other part-time mothers felt they were being underused, they had never had a performance appraisal and were going to start looking for other jobs. Claudia decided to raise it with Jason as she wanted the opportunity to move on to more interesting work in the future.

'Why do we waste all this experience the part-timers bring to the firm?' she asked. 'We're all well qualified and have good experience, but we just end up doing data entry and passing on the accounts to someone else to finish off.'

'Well, because the hours you do don't allow us to get hold of you when we want to,' countered Jason. 'Also, we never know when you're going to call in and say you can't make it because your kid is sick or something else has come up. We can't afford to have a job held up because you can't finish it.'

'Maybe we are contactable though,' she shot back, 'we all have mobiles and computers at home.'

'Don't get me started on working from home. We tried that once. An absolute disaster. Never did a thing and we could never find her when we wanted her.'

'Well, don't get me wrong,' Claudia tried to settle him down, 'I just raised it because I think Thomas Brewer Partners aren't getting value from the staff we have and I think there are some of the women who can do more complex work and be more flexible by maybe doing some work at home. Also, by just sticking at the data entry level, we are limiting what we can earn.'

Jason just rolled his eyes. 'OK, thanks Claudia.'

WORK-LIFE BALANCE, HEALTH AND FLEXIBLE WORK DESIGN

Learning Objective
Effects of job design on work–life balance and health

Throughout this book there is commentary about the importance for both managers and staff of finding balance between the demands of work and the needs of private or family life. It is fashionable to talk about aiming for work–life balance, but some of the history of the debate grows out of the health effects of poor job design. There is a long record of research into occupational health and safety, mental health and overall stress in the context of work (Pfeffer, 2010). Despite this available information, the drive for profitability, productivity and a variety of power and control issues continue to result in organisational situations where good ideas may be discussed but, at best, ad hoc solutions implemented. For good people managers there are some opportunities where lip service or Machiavellianism can be replaced by genuinely helpful, flexibly negotiated work arrangements. The healthiest designs of workplaces take full account of available space and the time factors, as well as the relational arrangements of staff.

Space design

Ergonomics and health and safety fields yield a wealth of ideas about using work spaces to maximise worker health and productivity. The foundation of scientific management and the early work of Frederick Taylor were largely about the systematic mapping and rearrangement of work spaces in alignment with the capabilities of the workers. More recently, industrial relations agreements, occupational health and safety laws and a burgeoning consulting field have enabled considerable attention to be paid to issues of work spaces. Priority is placed on minimising injuries from repetitious or dangerous work. The danger may be associated with work motion or the nature of materials being handled.

Thought pathway

Some tough old workers from years gone by think modern Australian workers have become too 'soft'. Do you think so and why?

From the discipline of operations management comes an understanding of quality and productivity improvements that can be gained by better design of workspace and the interaction of workers within that space. The continued integration of technology into work routines brings its own socio-technical challenges. Managers have to consider carefully the long-term effects of worker–machine interaction in the workplace.

Time design

Where there is space there is time. In practical terms, arrangements such as flexible work hours, online work, compressed work hours, reduced work hours, job sharing and outsourced work can enable real differences to be made for individual workers (Erez, 2010).

Offering flexible work hours is a way employers can give staff a choice about how they structure their working day. A daily or weekly working quota may be noted, but staff can be given the impetus to decide for themselves how to make up the hours. This can be an empowering situation and it is increasingly common, although it does tend to suit some kinds of work more than others and can be constrained according to the costs of completing jobs at different times in a day or a week.

While online work opportunities (virtual work or telecommuting) are proliferating, it is worth noting the management challenges and natural resistances that accompany them. A unique set of skills and a special type of hard work are needed to sustain virtual working relationships. This elevates the role of professional development and ongoing training (Creed & Zutshi, 2008). Virtual space-time is different from the usual physical work space-time. Online workers often do battle with the faster response needs of electronic requests and the sheer speed of information-processing functions, which, in a paper-based, physical environment, run at a generally slower pace. Managers of online staff need to factor different work time expectations into job design.

A compressed work week arrangement is a way to negotiate a full-time job into fewer than the usual five days. This may be appropriate for staff needing certain days for family or other private commitments. It may also suit the usual production or activity cycles of the particular organisation. In some unionised industries there may be resistance to creating significant variation in the standard work week, but this may be for good reason and there is no limitation on suggesting ideas in full consultation with all the stakeholders, especially if significant benefits can be established.

A reduced work hour schedule, or voluntary reduced work time, is a formal arrangement for a worker to trade income within the salary package in order to include extra leisure time as compensation. This can be a practical way of helping some staff achieve a better work–life balance.

Job sharing is an arrangement where one full-time job is split up between two or more workers. A reasonable sharing of communication and coordination has to be negotiated, but the arrangement may suit particular situations where the workers involved need time to do other things and yet retain their positions with the organisation.

Outsourced work is an increasing global phenomenon that straddles the space and time discussion regarding job design. Certain tasks and functions can sometimes be contracted to another organisation locally or offshore. The rationale may be on the basis of cost and time savings, but it can also mean opportunities for repetitive or menial tasks to be removed and workers given the chance to retrain or take on more meaningful work. Of course, the notion of losing one's job because it is being outsourced is naturally confronting. Unions, regulators and the local community may all have a voice to be heard when outsourcing emerges as a possibility.

WINDOW ON DECISION-MAKING

Maybe baby: Juggling home, work and family life

MAUREEN FRANK

Congratulations—you are having a baby! This is going to be one of the most exciting times of your life. I don't think there is such a thing as an 'expert' on being a working mother—because all of us find it hard. And that goes in waves: sometimes it's harder than others. But I guess I could say I have some good 'qualifications' for giving you some advice as I have twin daughters, I am a single mum and I have been since I went back to work when they were nine months old. I also built a big corporate career, working full time, when my girls were small.

Did I have any idea what I was in for when I fell pregnant?

Not at all! I wish someone had clued me in a bit more; I wish that all the books I read had been about more than just baby routines and dealing with colic. I wish someone had advised me about the work part—how do you do it, what sort of decisions do I have to make, what can I do before I have the baby (or babies) that will make it easier for me for later?

Maybe this is your first baby, or maybe you've been

there before—perhaps you weren't working then, or maybe your employer didn't offer parental leave, so the whole matter of how to take your leave and then think about going back to work just wasn't an issue for you. But, if your new baby is due on or after 1st January 2011, you'll be one of the first mums to benefit from the new Government Paid Parental Leave (PPL) scheme, entitling you to a maximum of 18 weeks paid leave from work.

First of all, think about the three big issues about having a career break, having your baby and then going back to work—and how you're going to tackle them:

1 Income—how much do you need? Plan your baby budget both before the baby is born, during your leave and when you go back to work.

2 Childcare—what plans do you have, who's going to do what for and with the baby, what are your contingency tactics?

3 Career/Life plans—what do you want to do in, say, the next five years? How can you make it happen? Who are your stakeholders, your customers and cheerleaders?

Before you leave to have your baby:
• Have some honest conversations at home with your partner, around such issues as who will return to work and when? Full or part time? What are the financial implications of these decisions? Where does our relationship fit into all of this and what's our plan for the future?
• Talk to your manager about your plans and what you're hoping to do at the end of your PPL. You want other people who are colleagues, superiors and just people in the business with influence to

know BEFORE you go on leave that you are serious about your job and that you plan to come back and really focus on your career.

- Think about how you want to keep in touch with work while you're out on leave—with whom will you stay connected, how much contact do you want or need, depend[ing] on your job?
- In preparation for your parental leave—I encourage you to find another working mother in the organisation who can mentor you through your pregnancy and time away. It's going to be very comforting for you if you can talk to someone about balancing work and motherhood who has done it all before—so I encourage you to seek someone out in your workplace who you can talk to who is already a successful working Mum—and ideally someone who you know!

And some steps to take before going back to work:

- Review the goals and plans you set before leaving for parental leave. What has changed? How do you feel now?
- Think long and hard about whether you will return to work full time or part time and what each of these will mean to you and your family, financially, emotionally and physically! There are many advantages and disadvantages to both work options, but you have to work out a plan that suits you best.
- Think again about those three big issues:
  - Income—how much do you need?
  - Childcare—what plans do you have?
  - Career Life plans—what do you want to do?
- Working full time obviously puts you back into your existing position but you may have to think about your emotional state of mind and you obviously need to organise full time child care.
- Working part time or flexibly means you can counter this balance but there is a lot of juggling going on and there may still be the need for child care. You also need to think about what you will do if your child is sick.
- Ideally, two months before you go back, advise your employer of your expected return to work date. Set a time to discuss with your manager your return to work plan. Discuss with your manager what your new work arrangement will be—if it is flexible, what will be your hours and workplace arrangements?

- Discuss with your manager what your job description will look like, if your role has slightly changed to counter your flexible arrangements or reduced hours and what your new performance plan will look like. Find out what has happened within the team.

But is it worth it? In a recent emberin survey, we spoke to working mums on a popular social networking site and they told us that these are their top ten reasons for wanting to return to work, aside from the financial considerations and cash benefits of being back in the workplace. They told us:

'It's tough! There are so many balls and sometimes, yes—they get dropped! But it's worth it.'

And here's why:

1 I get to be a person in my own right rather than just somebody's wife and mother.
2 For me, my work 'defines' who I am. I like doing what I do and feel that that person is more 'me' than being a mum is. Don't get me wrong, of course I love my kids to bits but I can't just be a mum, I need to be this other person too.
3 It gives me economic independence—and a safety net in case something goes wrong in the future—we all hope it won't, but never say never.
4 I love my job and I want to progress in it—it's why I went to university and I like feeling that I can make a difference and use my brain.
5 I see the intense child rearing period of 5–7 years too big a chunk of time to not keep up to date, and too small a chunk of time to be my new full time occupation.
6 I work three days a week, which helps me to keep my skills up to date and relevant—and that means that when I am at home, I'm more patient and appreciative of the time with my kids!
7 I honestly think my daughter benefits from being at nursery—she has so much fun with the other kids and they get to do all that messy stuff with paints and sand there rather than in my house!
8 I love the fact that I can act as a role model to my children and show them that Mummies can have great jobs and earn money, as well as Daddies.
9 I get to have a cup of tea while it's still hot!

Can't argue with that!

Source: <www.abn.org.au/site/article/maybe-baby-juggling-home-work-and-family-life-maureen-frank>

This Window on Decision-making brings to light a common contemporary issue, especially given developments in paid parental leave in Australia. The decision about whether to have children is closely tied to concerns about how to balance this with the need to continue working. It is, perhaps, the most human of issues that emerges in the job design debate. Employers are compelled now to think of people not as resources like tools or finance, but as individuals with human needs. There is a significant social impact involved in properly catering for the parents of the next generation of Australians while they are contributing to organisational outcomes along the way.

Relationship design

A thoroughly constructed organisational chart reveals formal and informal relationships and lines of communication. Taking the full picture into account when designing work and job descriptions can help ensure the right people are put into a positive relational alignment for the achievement of the tasks. This realm of design also requires enough emotional or social intelligence to know who gets along with whom. Being savvy with relational issues can maximise the levels of productivity, staff satisfaction and motivation. As always, care needs to be taken that relational alignments are not made to the detriment of genuine equity. Favouritism needs to be guarded against in the quest for finding the right person to position themselves in certain relationships within an organisation.

THE LINK WITH LEARNING

Learning Objective
How job design, learning and change are relevant for performance improvement

Job design can be structured to take advantage of the kinds of theories of learning that are described in Chapter 2. For instance, there is the principle of reinforcement and the idea that repeated schedules of activity and information can encourage the locking in of new knowledge. The regularity of salary or wage payments is one obvious reinforcement schedule: if staff are able to know that they are being paid regularly they will learn to ensure key performance indicators are met so that the regularity continues. Some wages are paid on the basis of commissions or piece rates and other performance criteria. These serve to change behavioural patterns in staff to ensure organisational objectives are achieved. Remember, any kind of behavioural change is one indicator of learning and is essential to continuous improvement (Maurer & Weiss, 2010). Of course learning is more complicated at the social level than basic principles of reinforcement, thus a more sophisticated approach to the management of behavioural change is recommended in some industry sectors (Martin et al., 2010).

Learning is of course, one of the essential elements of change. If change is important, which it is if new ways for an organisation to remain competitive are proposed, then the management of change is paramount. The final chapter of this book covers change management in detail and closes the loop on organisational behaviour. The atmosphere and architecture of a truly globally competitive workplace boil down to really effective and strategic change management that capitalises on the motivation, leadership, teamwork and power of human resources.

CONCLUSION

This chapter has emphasised the available tools for managers to effectively design work within the architecture of an organisation in order to enhance the overall culture or atmosphere and to improve organisational performance. A range of practical strategies have been described along with an integrated approach that is available in job characteristics theory. There are issues emerging in the contemporary workplace that challenge managers to continuously evaluate and adjust their approaches to job design. Socio-technological changes, the need for people to balance their work and life, the ongoing imperative for worker equity, and the centrality of these factors to the management of change and continuous learning have been explained.

KEY POINTS

This chapter has

- explained why the proper design of jobs contributes to more effective people management
- described the different approaches to job design and how they might be integrated
- explained the functions and challenges of performance appraisal
- discussed the effects of job design on the work–life balance and health of staff
- described how job design, learning and change are relevant for performance improvement.

KEY TERMS

JOB CHARACTERISTICS THEORY (JCT)
An integrated theory of job design that bridges concepts from the areas of motivation, individual differences, group dynamics, power and leadership.

JOB ENLARGEMENT
Adding a greater variety of tasks to the job that a person currently does.

JOB ENRICHMENT
A strategic version of job enlargement that aims to give people work that fulfils their higher-level needs for a sense of meaning, achievement and belonging.

JOB ROTATION
The opportunity to try a completely different job, thus enabling the expansion of skill sets across a number of workers and allowing people to develop a more integrated understanding of the ways different jobs come together in the organisation.

JOB SIMPLIFICATION

The process of streamlining the work flow of a task, or removing some aspects of a person's job. The aim is to maximise efficiency and sometimes the effect is to enhance role clarity, which has a positive effect on overall job satisfaction.

MULTI-SKILLING

The collection of experiences and training that enables workers to become proficient at more than one job or skill set.

PSYCHOLOGICAL CONTRACT

The agreement workers make in their minds with organisations when they accept a position. An expectation is established about what energy will be spent and which duties the worker will be comfortable carrying out. In return, the organisation has expectations about the resources and support they will provide for the worker.

STUDY AND REVISION QUESTIONS

Q *Referring to the case described in the Window on Ethics, take a step-by-step approach through the JCT variables and make a series of suggestions for work design changes that might help improve the situation for the young lawyers concerned.*

Q *What is the main limitation of applying job enrichment as a method of job design?*

Q *The last line of the Window on Decision-making is, 'Can't argue with that!' Explain whether you agree or disagree with this conclusion regarding the ideas in the Window.*

Q *In what way is job design connected with theories of learning?*

REFERENCES

Bal, P., Chiaburu, D. & Jansen, P. (2010). Psychological contract breach and work performance: Is social exchange a buffer or an intensifier? *Journal of Managerial Psychology*, 25(3), 252–73.

Brown, M., Hyatt, D. & Benson, J. (2010). Consequences of the performance appraisal experience. *Personnel Review*, 39(3), 375–96.

Bygstad, B., Nielsen, P. & Munkvold, B. (2010). Four integration patterns: A socio-technical approach to integration in IS development projects. *Information Systems Journal*, 20(1), 53–80.

Chambel, M. (2011). The psychological contract of call-centre workers: Employment conditions, satisfaction and civic virtue behaviours. *Economic and Industrial Democracy*, 32(1), 115–34.

Cohen, R. (2010). Rethinking 'mobile work': Boundaries of space, time and social relation in the working lives of mobile hairstylists. *Work Employment & Society*, 24(1), 65–84.

Creed, A., & Zutshi, A. (2008). The wellhouse of knowledge globalization: IT and virtual communities. *Journal of Knowledge Globalization*, 1(1), 29–42.

Cusack, L. (2010). Power inequalities in the assessment of nursing competency within the workplace: Implications for nursing management. *Journal of Continuing Education in Nursing*, 41(9), 408–12.

Duchon, D., & Plowman, D. (2005). Nurturing the spirit at work: Impact on work unit performance. *Leadership Quarterly*, 16(1), 807–33.

Erez, M. (2010). Culture and job design. *Journal of Organizational Behavior*, 31(1), 389–400.

Fein, M. (1975). Job enrichment does not work. *Atlanta Economic Review*, 25(1), 50–4.

Fincham, R., & Rhodes, P. S. (2005). *Principles of organizational behaviour*. Oxford: Oxford University Press.

Fraser, K., & Hvolby, H. (2010). Effective teamworking: Can functional flexibility act as an enhancing factor? An Australian case study. *Team Performance Management*, 16(1/2), 74–94.

Fried, Y., & Ferris, G. R. (1987). The validity of the job characteristics model: A review and meta-analysis. *Personnel Psychology*, 40(1), 287–322.

Hackman, J. R., & Oldham, G. R. (1975). Development of the job diagnostic survey. *Journal of Applied Psychology*, 60(1), 159–70.

Hackman, J. R., & Oldham, G. R. (1976). Motivation through the design of work: Test of a theory. *Organizational Behavior and Human Performance*, 16(1), 250–79.

Hackman, J. R., & Oldham, G. R. (1980). *Work redesign*. Reading, MA: Addison-Wesley.

Humphrey, S., Nahrgang, J. & Morgeson, F. (2007). Integrating motivational, social, and contextual work design features: A meta-analytic summary and theoretical extension of the work design literature. *Journal of Applied Psychology*, 92(5), 1332–56.

Leavitt, H. (2007). Big organizations are unhealthy environments for human beings. *Academy of Management Learning & Education*, 62(2), 253–63.

Martin, K., Quigley, M. A., & Rogers, S. (2010). Implementing a learning management system globally: An innovative change management approach. *IBM Systems Journal*, 44(1), 125–45.

Marx, L. (2010). Technology: The emergence of a hazardous concept. *Technology and Culture*, 51(3), 561–77.

Maurer, T., & Weiss, E. (2010). Continuous learning skill demands: Associations with managerial job content, age, and experience. *Journal of Business Psychology*, 25(1), 1–13.

Morgeson, F., & Humphrey, S. (2008). Job and team design: Toward a more integrative conceptualization of work design. *Research in Personnel and Human Resources Management*, 27(1), 39–91.

Munyon, T., Summers, J., Buckley, R., Ranft, A. & Ferris, G. (2010). Executive work design: New perspectives and future directions. *Journal of Organizational Behavior*, 31(1), 432–47.

Nankervis, A., & Stanton, P. (2010). Managing employee performance in small organisations: Challenges and opportunities. *International Journal of Human Resources Development and Management*, 10(2), 136–51.

Oldham, G., & Hackman, J. (2010). Not what it was and not what it will be: The future of job design research. *Journal of Organizational Behavior*, 31(1), 463–79.

Pfeffer, J. (2010). Building sustainable organizations: The human factor. *Academy of Management Perspectives*, 24(1), 34–45.

Jiang, X. (2010). How to motivate people working in teams. International *Journal of Business and Management*, 5(10), 223–9.

Wajcman, J. (2010). Feminist theories of technology. *Cambridge Journal of Economics*, 34(1), 143–52.

Weichel, J., Stanic, S., Diaz, J. & Frieling, E. (2010). Job rotation: Implications for old and impaired assembly line workers. *Occupational Ergonomics*, 9(2), 67–74.

PRACTITIONER INSIGHT

WENDY COOPER

HR, DEAKIN

Wendy's current role is Executive Director of the Human Resources Department at Deakin University. Wendy has worked in the higher education sector for approximately 16 years, and prior to that worked in Local and Federal Government agencies.

Wendy's current role covers the full range of human resource functions, both at an operational and at a strategic level. During her time at Deakin, Wendy has led the introduction of many efficiencies in the delivery of human resources services and most particularly through the use of technology-based initiatives. There is the constant drive to shift HR service delivery from paper-based processes to online, self-managed processes.

The range of strategic human resource services offered by the Division has also grown under Wendy's leadership. Innovative and relevant leadership programs have been a core part of the strategic work of the Division, which has seen the growth of connected and skilled academic leaders in various roles throughout the University. The leadership work has grown from the development of specific cohorts and connecting them across the University to the current space where individual and locally based consultancies are used to build leadership skills and behaviours.

Annual staff survey results are also used to underpin culture change, along with the use of a range of social technologies under the broad umbrella of participatory leadership. The positive impact of this work is evidenced by changes in behaviour that are measured each year in the survey.

The challenge of attracting and retaining the best staff also remains core to the work of the Division. A number of strategic initiatives are used in assisting the University meet this challenge: workforce planning, succession planning, genuine career planning and performance discussions, a truly reflective Employee Value Proposition, and the use of remuneration and reward strategies. Staff turnover at Deakin remains below the sector median and the quality and calibre of applicants to Deakin staff vacancies continues to grow.

Deakin University is seen as an innovative, on-the-go, and flexible environment in which to work. The work of the Human Resources Division will continue to support this promise to our staff.

INTERVIEW

What was your first job?
Payroll in the Federal Public Service.

What has been your career highlight so far?
My current role. I love it.

In your current role, what does a typical day involve?
Much variety, lots of interaction with key clients, and working with my staff.

What's the best part of your job?
All of it.

What is the hardest aspect of your role?
Dealing with difficult people.

What are the current challenges facing you, in your role?
Building more capability within the HR Division, and supporting the University in meeting its current challenges of attracting and retaining outstanding staff to achieve our aspirations.

Do you regularly apply the principles or theories you learnt (when studying organisational behaviour) into your everyday work? In what way?

Only from a framework perspective. Everyday work is about the context and the environment.

How important is an understanding of 'organisational behaviour' in today's workplace?

Less important than experience and judgment.

Is a work–life balance a reasonable expectation in a modern workplace?

It is a reasonable expectation if the staff member makes a conscious decision regarding the amount of time they wish to allocate to their career.

What strategies do you implement in your workplace to help employees achieve an appropriate work–life balance?

48/52 working year, flex time, part time work, a varied range of leave provisions.

Has technology impacted on work–life balance? Is it harder to achieve with constant access to the 'office', for example?

Again, I believe this is a conscious decision that needs to be made by the staff member for their own circumstances.

What do you believe makes a good manager or decision maker? How would you describe your own management style?

Empathic, interested in my staff and their development, firm about expectations and behaviours, firm about culture and service.

Do your people manage themselves or are you called upon frequently to deal with relational issues?

My management team deal with their staff issues. I deal with my immediate management team, who require little intervention.

How do you communicate company strategy with staff at all levels?

Divisional-wide get togethers, emails, HR newsletter, through team management meetings, regular information-sharing sessions at lunchtime with staff about what is going on, both within the Division and externally to the Division, through the performance-review process for each staff member and through the Division's annual Operational Plan.

What do you believe is the best way for a manager to avoid conflict in the workplace? And is this an easy approach to take?

Be clear about expectations on behaviours and work outputs. Be transparent about them across the Division. Deal with 'issues' straight away before they become too serious and escalate. Yes, an easy approach.

There is an old adage that power corrupts. Does your experience suggest the decision of who to give certain powers in an organisation is, therefore, very important?

I do not think the issue is about power but more about empowerment and accountability. They go together for anyone.

Do you think the workplace environment really is changing faster than ever before? Or are people always prone to feeling anxious when the inevitable changes occur?

There will always be people who will feel anxious about change, and those who embrace it. It is important that change caters to all needs and is handled well and that staff are supported through the process.

Are you able to find much time to think about the strategic design of work in your organisation?

Not enough or as much time as I would like.

Stability and Change

Organisations strive for a stable internal environment in order to retain staff and increase job satisfaction, and yet change and innovation are key drivers of competitive advantage. The global environment appears to require continuous change, but managers have to balance this against the internal need for people to feel secure and have strategic, planned processes in place. This discussion leads back to the key issues raised in Chapter 1. It also accentuates the learning processes from Chapter 2 and, in the context of established change management theories, explains how feedback or evaluation loops can be used to ensure human resource management is able to harness learning and continuous improvement models in dynamic environments. We have arrived at the end and also the beginning of this book's journey through the field of organisational behaviour.

LEARNING OBJECTIVES	
Understanding this chapter will help you to	
• describe the prevailing forces that drive organisational change	• explain some of the prominent models of change management
• discuss the cyclical nature of stability, change and learning	• discuss change as innovation for competitive advantage
	• explain the impact of change management on work–life balance.

OVERVIEW

■

Cultural web
A diagrammatic view of the components of organisational culture as developed and promoted by Johnson (1988, 2008).

■

Pettigrew Model
A step-by-step view of organisational transformation developed by Pettigrew (1985) that is quite succinct and yet captures the full range of practical issues that can emerge for managers.

■

Force field analysis
An analysis developed by Lewin (1951) to diagnose and evaluate the enabling and restraining forces that have an impact on change processes.

The atmosphere and architecture of organisations emerge from and respond to the thoughts, behaviours and relationships of their people. Emergence and response are dynamic concepts realistically based on our fundamental biology. Change is normal and necessary for survival. Stasis or stability has its place but usually only fleetingly. People like to feel stable and yet survival demands change, thus the manager is faced with a paradox that is difficult to resolve to everyone's satisfaction. This chapter explains the forces for change and stability. The different types of change are discussed and then linked with concepts of learning and continuous improvement. Practical models of change management are explained, including the **cultural web**, the **Pettigrew model**, and **force field analysis**. The imperative for innovation is discussed as a way to ensure competitive advantage, and the chapter concludes with a focus on work–life balance in the midst of organisational transformation.

FORCES FOR CHANGE

■

Learning Objective
The prevailing forces that drive organisational change

Globalisation, technology, economics, politics and history each contribute to the contemporary landscape of change in which organisations find themselves. Change as a combination of these forces is almost inevitable. The status quo is a balance of prevailing forces but the rarity of such a situation is notable today (McClelland et al., 2010). Organisations continue to globalise, technology keeps proliferating, economic systems are fragile and transformative, politics is volatile in most countries, and all of these factors have been set in train by events from history, thus giving a sense of predetermination about the current need for better change management.

FORCES FOR STABILITY

Despite the wider impetus for change, there is a strong desire for stability in people and organisations. People want job security, organisations want improved profitability, and there is growing social pressure for more ethical behaviours in organisations (Taylor, 2011). Consistency is the underlying tenet in each of these.

Job security is about continuity of tenure, profitability is about repeatedly minimising costs and maximising income, and for behaviour to be ethical it must be based on a coherent and consistent framework of principles. People respond very positively to predictability.

Thought pathway

Consider your own response to having a job that does not require you to change very much. Would you be bored, or would you be relieved that you could keep getting paid without having to exert much extra effort?

The status quo is often viewed as something to be admired, aspired to and enjoyed once it is attained (Agboola & Salawu, 2011). The concept of 'making it' or being successful is sometimes portrayed as sitting back and letting the money roll in without having to do extra work. Even though the working environment is so changeable today, maybe even within the dynamics of change there can be a way to find principles or elements that mostly remain the same. In other words, the goal of working smarter, not harder, may still be achieved with a little planning.

PLANNED CHANGE

Planning for change is almost an oxymoron. A plan is concrete and clearly defined, whereas change is by definition mercurial. However, it is certainly possible to prepare for change, or to put contingencies in place in the knowledge that some kind of change is going to occur. The essence of good preparation is therefore to know the type of change one might encounter. There is a continuum of possible change from radical right through to incremental.

Radical change
A type of change that is transformative, rapid and turbulent.

Radical change is transformative, rapid and turbulent. Sometimes it is necessary for change to be radical. When a process, system, person or entire organisation becomes stuck, dull or sluggish, then radical change may be the best way to turn things around. Alternatively, a fast-changing environment may demand radical strategies to be deployed in order for the organisation to remain competitive (Hamilton, 2011).

Incremental change
A type of change that is marginal, careful and measured.

Incremental change is marginal, careful and measured. Sometimes it is best to make haste slowly. Through regular evaluation of outcomes and systematic planning based on feedback, a relatively stable organisation can continue to improve performance by taking small steps (McKendrick & Wade, 2010). It is easier to convince people to embrace incremental change because it is closer to recognised comfort zones. The psychological contract discussed in Chapter 9 is far less strained by incremental change than by radical change. Knowledge of the different types of change is a handy way to be prepared, but there are plenty of times when change emerges unexpectedly.

UNPLANNED CHANGE

Postmodernism
The understanding that objectivity may not be possible; it proposes that all we know is really a social construct and can be challenged for accuracy.

Sometimes the best-laid plans are made redundant by circumstances. Morgan (2006) draws attention to chaos theory and the emergence of **postmodernism**, in general, as indicators of the difficulties inherent in trying to plan for change. Postmodernism is the understanding that objectivity may not be possible; it proposes that all we know is really a social construct and can be challenged for accuracy (Hassard, 1994). When the truth is subjective and social construction of the things we value is the core of our reality, we must negotiate through uncertainty at all times. In a postmodern organisation, planning for the unexpected may be the best we can do. Unplanned change does seem to happen with increased frequency now that organisations and people are more interconnected and we are dealing with the systemic repercussions of establishing supply chains based on sophisticated technology (Thompson, 2010).

Thought pathway

Think of a rapid change that affected you once at work or at home. Consider the kind of information you would have needed ahead of time in order to plan for the advent of that change. Are you able to access the same kind of information for any possible future events?

Disruptive, rapid changes can emerge spontaneously from interpersonal conflicts at work, sudden actions and decisions of leaders, the activities of competing organisations, natural events (floods, fires and so on). While the essence of postmodernism is discomforting, there is at least one small comfort: we can all learn to continuously improve.

CYCLES OF CHANGE AND LEARNING

Learning Objective
The cyclical nature of stability, change and learning

It is tempting to view change as a process, but it is rarely as simple as that (Stace & Dunphy, 2001). Change is mostly an embedded phenomenon that depends on so many interconnected things. The neural network metaphor is entirely appropriate if one is trying to picture what might happen when making change in one small aspect of an organisation. The energy of change can spread, ripple, branch and generate complex emergent phenomena like a neural pulse. The sense of organic rhythm about change is something that has also been noted (Hewison et al., 2010; Furneaux et al., 2010). Change comes around semi-cyclically like fads and fashions. What once was popular becomes fresh again but under a new name. The cynics of change raise questions about the logic of revamping something that already works. But the proponents of quality management, for example, are in no doubt about the value of continuous monitoring and adjustment of behaviour (Liao et al., 2010).

The champions of change management tend to recognise that while many new ideas are based on systems tried before, there is still value in the new perspective and fresh inputs from different people when the same idea comes again (Lewis & Juravle, 2010). The cycle is really a spiral of continuous improvement. The concept of the learning organisation is the ideal representation of the benefits of embracing change (Schon, 1971; Senge, 1990). Learning leads to change, and the interdependence of thinking, relating and behaving that happens during this time contributes to the quality of the outcomes. The definition of learning in Chapter 2 includes the following diagram which neatly presents the issues for organisational behaviour.

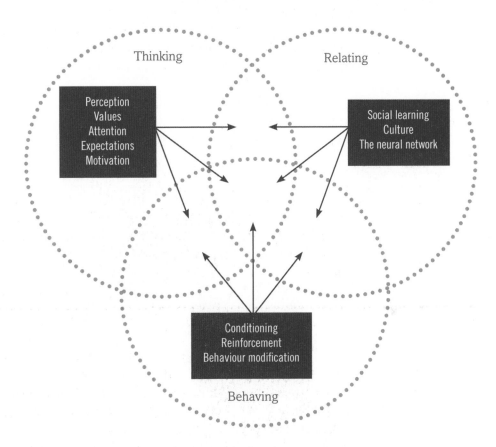

Thinking, relating and behaving are connected, moving, dynamic and changeable. The boundaries of the phenomena of change and learning within organisations can be identified in such a diagram; therefore, taking a planned view of change is possible, though only within the context of dynamism and the need for responsiveness. There are a number of change management models that are available to ensure managers take full account of the interactions of thinking, relating and behaving during change in organisations.

CHANGE MANAGEMENT MODELS

Learning Objective
Some prominent models of change management

Despite the difficulties of managing through complexity, chaos and inconsistency, there are still some helpful models of change management that can frame a people manager's view of priorities in the workplace. Among the most practical and prevalent are the cultural web, the Pettigrew model, and force field analysis.

The cultural web

The cultural web is a diagrammatic view of the components of organisational culture. Johnson (1988, 2008) describes it as a way of better understanding the organisational culture components of change. If you refer to Chapter 8, many of the elements discussed are summarised in Figure 8.1.

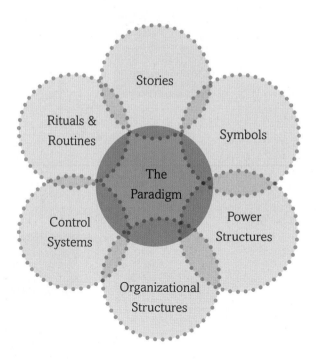

The practical nature of the model is demonstrated by Johnson (2008) when addressing the change management factors of a sample organisation and assigning each factor to the relevant sector of the cultural web diagram. Each variable in the diagram intersects with many of the others, and the hub of core beliefs (values) and assumptions connects all, which indicates the networked nature of any change situation. Managers can be made aware of the cascading effect that change in one part of the web has on most of the other parts. While predicting the type and extent of effects is always difficult, the cultural web serves as a reality check and establishes the general atmospheric parameters to consider when implementing change.

WINDOW ON COMMUNICATION

Culture club:
IT's special secret

PETER O'CONNOR

It is often said that people are a company's most important asset. In a tight employment market, this saying is truer than most and in many respects it becomes the yardstick by which successful organisations are compared.

That's why it was interesting to read recent statistics showing the job market in Australia continues to strengthen (the Australian Bureau of Statistics reported that job vacancies rose and unemployment dropped to the five per cent mark toward the end of 2010). This is great news for the workforce but from the employer side of things it means that 2011 will be a year competing for the best of the best in an already-tight talent pool.

The IT industry, however, is already well versed in a competitive labour market, so in many respects [it] can teach other industries about holding on to, and attracting, great staff.

Increasingly, the feedback being delivered about successful companies is more about a great company culture than other more tangible rewards such as salary or onsite facilities. While remuneration is important, people don't leave jobs because of their title, and often the reason they leave is not based on money. They leave because they don't feel appreciated or [because] they're not making an impact.

Corporate culture used to be one of those 'soft' management ideas washed away by the cynics as something that could be created without any real planning or hard work, or just something that happens on its own.

In reality, the opposite is true.

If companies wish to be successful in developing a high-quality culture, it requires significant work and continued review and improvement as it contributes significantly to the success of a business. It needs to be practised, implemented and monitored from the top, and accepted and reflected by every person across the organisation.

It is something that the IT industry does particularly well.

For example, if you look at the top ten best places to work in Australia as rated by the Great Place to Work Institute in 2010, it is no coincidence that half of the companies are involved in the information technology sector.

Beyond the open plan offices, bean bags and pool tables often associated with 'cool' places to work, you will find a common culture among the employees of successful companies that they strive toward growing and supporting collectively.

In our experience, we have used five fundamental principles to create our existing culture and they have had a massive and positive impact on our business. I think these principles can be readily applied to any organisation for a positive result.

1. **Attitude** Having a good attitude is not optional. Be passionate about success, bring that passion into the workplace, and nurture it in others. If you let people see it, the effect will be contagious.

2. **Candour** Encourage people to get out whatever is on their minds. Leaders don't make a business great by guessing—it's important to know what people are thinking. If people feel they can speak openly and honestly without risk, the conversations will be much more rewarding.

3. **Positivity** Too many companies focus on how others have failed. If there's a problem and you can tell me how to fix it, then let's talk. Otherwise, create a positive culture based on saying 'Thank you'. Catch someone doing something right and congratulate him or her for it publicly. Once you begin this positive culture, others in the company will start to emulate it.

4. **Leadership** Fear and intimidation don't make people perform well and go the extra distance. True leadership inspires people to extraordinary performances because nobody wants to let down a great leader.

5. **Embrace change** As a company you need to continually innovate, improve, and embrace change. Nothing is ever static, and if you are, you will be left behind. Actively think about change and how it is accomplished. If every person in your organisation begins to think this way, change will come naturally.

Culture begins with a set of common values, but these need to be developed, worked on, and practised from the top down. People want to be part of a good corporate culture. With a great culture, people are willing to sacrifice for the good of the organisation, and that's when your company will really stand apart from the crowd.

Source: <www.abc.net.au/technology/ articles/2011/02/23/3146392.htm>

This Window on Communication reveals how the culture of an organisation, in addition to being essential to the way the place runs, also transmits an image to prospective employees. The variables of the cultural web manifest in different ways for different organisations. The relativity of this form of analysis is one of its limitations. There are other models that give the manager a more universal perspective on managing change.

The Pettigrew model

The Pettigrew model is a step-by-step view of organisational transformation (Pettigrew, 1985). It is succinct and still captures the full range of practical issues that can emerge for managers. The Pettigrew model includes management issues that can be immediately seen to align with systems and events. Fincham & Rhodes (2005) summarise the steps as the development of concern, acknowledgment of the problem, planning and acting, and stabilising the changes. The issues at each step are presented in Table 10.1.

Table 10.1 Pettigrew's model of organisational change

1	THE DEVELOPMENT OF CONCERN Concern amongst a group of people that existing organizational structures and procedures are no longer compatible with the operating environment.
2	ACKNOWLEDGEMENT OF THE PROBLEM More widespread acknowledgement and understanding of the critical problem the organization now faces, analysis of its causes, and alternative ways of tackling it.
3	PLANNING AND ACTING To create specific changes in the light of the above diagnostic and objective-setting work.
4	STABILIZING THE CHANGES How the organization's reward, information, and power systems reinforce the intended direction of change.

Source: Principles of Organizational Behaviour, *Fourth Edition by Robin Fincham and Peter Rhodes (2005) by permission of Oxford University Press UK.*

This model simulates a staged approach to change, thus giving the manager opportunities for tangible measures of progress. It is also less concerned with relationships between complex variables and more with a pragmatic way to progress from each stage to the next. For these reasons, the Pettigrew model has enjoyed a good deal of application in a wide range of change programs. A weakness is that the model does not fully explain why a change succeeds or falters. More complex models, such as force field analysis, are better able to account for underlying causes.

Force field analysis

FORCE FIELD ANALYSIS An analysis developed by Lewin (1951) to diagnose and evaluate the enabling and restraining forces that have an impact on change processes.

Force field analysis is the diagnosis and evaluation of enabling and restraining forces that have an impact on the change process (Grundy, 1994). Lewin (1951) was among the first to take a wide view of the context variables of organisations. He proposed a range of enabling and constraining forces culminating in a force field that determines the progression or suppression of change initiatives. The enabling forces have to be greater than the constraining forces in order for change to succeed. A graphic view of prevailing forces as originally identified by Lewin is helpful (see Figure 10.1). The vertical, arrowed lines suggest the relative strength of each individual force for change. The length of each line is in proportion to the relative strength of the identified force.

Figure 10.1   Diverging forces of change

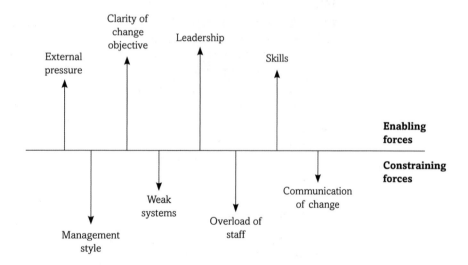

Enablers support the change process and allow it to move ahead. Restraining forces are those organisational elements that tend to block or impede any attempts at change. In the case of the force field analysis represented in Figure 10.1, on balance, the enabling forces along the top appear stronger than the constraining forces below; therefore, the change initiative (not described) is more likely to progress.

Thought pathway

Consider whether the greater balance of enabling forces in Figure 10.1 guarantees that the proposed change is going to succeed in the organisation.

Ultimately, the pragmatic view of how to move forward with a change in a field of various forces must also be considered. Lewin (1951) envisaged a three-phase approach to implementing change: unfreeze, change and refreeze.

CASE STUDY

Genuine interpersonal conflict or simply resistance to change?

'So, that's settled then. Greener Parks will start on July 1st and follow the schedule we've agreed and meet the KPIs we've listed. You'll take over our existing staff from that date. I'll get the contract finalised and send it through to you.' Tony Burton stood up and shook hands with Serge Fideli who, smiling, said 'thank you, see you later' and left. Tony is the Operations Manager of Henderson Shire Council and had just agreed to outsource the parks and gardens maintenance to Serge's family business Greener Parks Pty Ltd.

Tony had convinced the Council that all the staff would transfer across and that there would be an overall reduction in costs and no reduction in standards because Serge was able to spread his costs across several operations and get more productivity from the same number of people—something his Council supervisors were not able to do because of some entrenched work practices that were not very efficient.

'Yes I knew it was on the cards,' shouted Shaun Patterson, the union organiser, 'but I thought you'd be talking to us first about it. Last time I looked, slavery was illegal. You can't just sell off workers to another boss like that. It's not going to happen.'

'Shaun, we're not selling off anybody,' Tony tried to calm him down. 'We'll transfer them across on the same conditions. They will have more opportunities working for Greener Parks because they have operations all around the area: other councils, golf clubs, and corporate clients. They have a great range of equipment and tools. They will be able to learn new skills and have better career paths rather than just being stuck here working for a small department.

'Most of them are quite happy here,' snapped Shaun. 'You just want to offload them and cut costs. I'm not happy and nor are they. If you try and force this through I'll be talking to the rest of our members here at the Council. They will not be happy knowing they might be the next to be sold into slavery!'

Tony knew any change was going to be difficult. He had sounded out Shaun early on when the Council had told him they needed to cut costs and suggested he look at how this may be done. He wanted this to work because he had other ideas about outsourcing and also some internal efficiency measures he wanted to try. If this soured his relationship with staff it would be very difficult to make the changes he wanted.

Tony was surprised to receive a phone call from Serge Fideli who had just received the contract. 'Some of our guys know some of your guys,' he said in a worried tone. 'I'm not sure this is going to work. They've heard that your guys are going to make this whole transfer unpleasant. It may be more trouble than it's worth for us to take this on. Unless they can convince me they are willing to make a go of this I'm not sure I want to go ahead.' Tony was devastated. He needed this to work. He didn't want to go through the whole tendering process again to find another supplier.

'I'll have a talk to them and get it ironed out. I'll get back to you next week.'

CASE STUDY
QUESTIONS

1 What do you think the main concerns of the Shire employees are likely to be?

2 Referring to the section 'The cultural web', will dealing with a union make it easier or harder for Tony to communicate with employees about their concerns?

3 What are the key factors behind this change? Provide a view of how the Shire might see them and how employees might see them.

4 Identify the 'enabling' factors as described in Lewin's force field analysis model and describe how Tony might use these to communicate with the employees.

5 If the employees transfer to Greener Parks and they are unhappy, how might this affect the remaining employees at Henderson Shire Council?

Unfreezing, changing, refreezing

The first stage of unfreezing assumes that the status quo is comfortable. People naturally learn patterns of thinking, behaving and relating and then like to stick with them. It is a positive thing for a good situation or process to be frozen, or resistant to change, but this resistance has the potential to become a constraining factor, according to Lewin (1951), and then change becomes necessary. There is a need to unfreeze the status quo before a change program can proceed. The people involved must develop a felt need for change and this may happen through social pressures, declining organisational performance, competitive pressures, and ongoing communication and education about the genuine benefits of making the change. An inherent resistance to change is expected from people who are aiming to protect established patterns of work that they believe are good. But when the thing being protected is not as good as the new change proposed, sometimes it is hard to convince those with vested interests in maintaining the status quo (Erwin & Garman, 2010).

Only when the need for change is accepted can the next stage of implementing the change occur. Managers have to take the initiative and adopt appropriate systems and leadership styles for the type, scale and timing of the change. People's readiness to change combines with the available resources, technology, organisational structure and culture to manifest the change. This is the art of organisational behaviour exemplified. The change will emerge from the unique context in which it is embedded.

The third stage is refreezing, which happens after a change has been implemented and involves reinforcing, adjusting and justifying the change. If the fresh change is not locked into place, or frozen into position, there is a very real chance that people will go back to doing things the old way. The new pattern has to be reinforced through reward, performance appraisal, corridor chatter, leadership remarks, policy documents, market feedback, competitor responses, and the full range of internal and external environmental indicators. If the signs are that the change is having good effects and is being reinforced, then it will freeze into place. If the evaluation of change is not so positive, then old work patterns start to look attractive once again.

WINDOW ON DECISION-MAKING

Navy scuppered by 'can do, make do' culture

CAMERON STEWART

Of all the criticisms that Defence Minister Stephen Smith heaped on the Royal Australian Navy this week, it was his questioning of a 'can do' culture that has set tongues wagging.

Since Gallipoli the Australian Defence Force has worn the reputed internal culture as a badge of pride. 'It is almost part of the Anzac legend about the resourcefulness and innovation which defence force personnel can summon to overcome obstacles and find inventive ways to get around problems,' the Australian Strategic Policy Institute's Mark Thomson says [...]

'But what might be a merit in military operations might not be so advantageous when it comes to the long-term repair and maintenance of military assets.'

Smith's comments to a defence conference in Canberra were made in the context of the navy's much publicised mismanagement of its three large amphibious ships, *HMAS Manoora*, *HMAS Kanimbla* and *HMAS Tobruk*.

All three ships were unavailable to help in the clean-up after Queensland's Cyclone Yasi because of chronic maintenance problems associated with age and neglect, despite the navy's promise [that] *Tobruk* would be ready if needed. The new-generation helicopter and amphibious landing ships, the first of which was launched in Spain this week, are not expected to begin entering service [until] 2014.

On Tuesday an angry Smith said the cyclone fiasco 'outlines the adverse side effects of a "can do" and a "make do" culture and a lack of sufficient adherence to verification, certification and assurance processes'.

Although Smith's comments this week were made in the context of the problems with the navy's amphibious fleet, they reflect a broader and deeper maintenance and management culture within the navy that saw two-thirds of its fleet unable to operate at full capacity at some stage during the first half of last year.

As *The Weekend Australian* reveals today, a navy review of its engineering capabilities in late 2009 concluded there was a crisis in its ranks of naval engineers who were vital to the maintenance of the fleet. It said the navy had only half the engineers it needed and navy chiefs had failed to recognise the importance of its engineering arm, leading to under-resourcing and poor policy oversight.

But how does a 'can do' culture—one in which getting results somehow outweighs all other considerations—become a problem, or even a liability, for complex

organisations such as the navy? Some answers may be found in the sorry tale of the NASA space agency, which has faced parallels to the problems confronting the Australian navy.

When the space shuttle *Columbia* disintegrated on re-entry into the earth's atmosphere in February 2003, killing its seven crew members—the second fatal shuttle crash following the loss of *Challenger* in 1986—the official investigation took aim at the downside of NASA's 'can do' culture, which had propelled man to the moon.

'The *Apollo* era created at NASA an exceptional "can do" culture marked by tenacity in the face of seemingly impossible challenges,' the US Accident Investigation Board wrote in its final report. But as time went on, NASA became an 'agency that was rooted in the glories of an earlier time' and failed to appreciate the technological, financial and managerial changes that were transforming the organisation.

'Within NASA centres as managers strove to maintain their view of the organisation, they lost their ability to accept criticism, leading them to reject the recommendations of many boards and blue-ribbon panels. External criticism and doubt, rather than spurring NASA to change for the better, instead reinforced the will to "impose the party-line vision on the environment, not to reconsider it," according to one authority on organisational behaviour.'

Investigators concluded that this group-think organisational culture within NASA 'had as much to do with [*Columbia's*] accident as foam did'. (Loss of a slab of protective foam on the shuttle led to it burning up on re-entry.)

Similarly, in the case of Australia's navy, experts say there is a vacuum of critical voices inside the system willing to speak up and debate the key decisions that have led, through many years, to the present state of the fleet.

For too long, the culture inside the navy has been to instinctively say 'we can do it' without applying a rigorous reality check as to whether 'it' is possible within a certain budget or timetable.

Alan Dupont, director for the Centre of International Security Studies at the University of Sydney, says a healthy 'can do' culture must be tempered by an ability at times to say honestly that something can't be done.

'While the military has to have a can-do culture to some degree because it is essentially a "doing" organisation, there also has to be a culture which encourages reflection about decisions on complex defence projects and where responsible criticism is accepted,' Dupont says.

'But rather than criticism being seen as a positive part of the decision-making process, it looks as if it has been seen as a negative.'

Smith is frustrated that these cultural and managerial shortcoming[s] have been obvious for many years, yet Defence has been slow to act.

Back in 2007, ASPI's Thomson wrote a report on

defence management that found a lack of 'robust internal contestability' in Defence decision-making was leading, by default, to a 'group think' mentality.

'The only real contestability comes from the various "central agencies" external to Defence, especially the Department of Finance and Administration,' Thomson wrote. 'While this is proper, it is also inadequate. No external body can hope to fully understand the issues, let alone mount compelling arguments from afar— especially with Defence tightly controlling access to information and data.'

Smith believes this lack of healthy debate partly reflects an absence of accountability across the Defence hierarchy.

'We need to instil much greater rigour and individual and institutional accountability to our consideration and management of major projects, acquisition and capabilities,' he said this week.

Yet this is easier said than done. The size of the Defence bureaucracy is such that important decisions on equipment are made by a raft of different sections and divisions, so that when something goes wrong no one appears directly accountable.

ASPI's Thomson says the mismanagement of the amphibious ships provides a good example of how difficult it is to sheet home blame within the defence system.

'There is no point banging on the table of the chief of navy about this because he does not control all the necessary levers,' Thomson tells Focus.

'The crewing of these ships will be the navy's responsibility, but the facilities from which they operate will be run by the defence support group, while the responsibility for maintenance will lie with the Defence Materiel Organisation and the decisions on their deployment will be made by the Joint Operations Command. The people in [the] navy work hard and are focused on doing the right thing, they work in a dysfunctional system of accountability.' This lack of accountability encourages defence planners to shoot for the stars, knowing that if they miss, they won't be blamed.

There is no better example of this than the government's extraordinarily ambitious defence white paper of 2009, delivered by the Rudd government, which promised the largest naval expansion since World War II with 12 new submarines, three new air warfare destroyers and a fleet of more muscular frigates.

Yet less than two years later, many analysts believe this blueprint is dead in the water because it was so divorced from the reality of what was achievable.

Far from being ready to expand, the navy cannot manage or operate its existing fleet properly. It cannot send a large percentage of its ships to sea because of maintenance, crew or operational issues. [The] navy also cannot properly staff or maintain its trouble-plagued six-submarine fleet, yet it is expected to double the size of that fleet and find crews for it.

'I think the defence white paper was misconceived and over-ambitious, particularly in regard to the navy,' says Dupont.

'It exceeds what we need and what we can produce. The perfect example of this is the proposal for 12 new submarines.

'There was no proper strategic assessment of the need for 12 submarines and no rigorous assessment of the business case for a project, which is so big that it will distort every area of defence planning. You would have to say with Smith's comments this week about the state of the navy that there are now big doubts about some of these [white paper] projects.'

Smith recognises that the navy's problems, including its organisational culture, have been decades in the making. He has acknowledged [that] the navy is making belated attempts to reform the service and improve the accountability of its managers.

An example is the setting up in 2009 of the Seaworthiness Board to independently review maritime systems.

But it is notoriously difficult to change the culture of an organisation as large as Defence. Smith is hoping that a series of reviews, including one into ship management by an independent team led by strategic reformer Paul Rizzo, will help to kickstart the process.

Strategic analyst Paul Dibb says the task will be helped if Smith stays in the portfolio long enough to complete the landmark cultural change he has embarked on. Defence has had eight ministers in the past 15 years, robbing the portfolio of the continuity it needs.

'In my time we had [Kim] Beazley for six years and [Robert] Ray for six years, and we did not have the same sorts of huge problems in that period,' Dibb says. 'More needs to be done by senior management to resolve intractable cultural and institutional barriers to effective decision-making in the defence organisation.'

Source: <www.theaustralian.com.au/news/ opinion/navy-scuppered-by-can-do-make-do-culture/story- e6frg6zo-1226008357757>

This Window on Decision-making reveals the challenges some organisations face trying to balance the need for stability and tradition with the need for change and modernisation. There is a fascinating distinction between being resourceful and able to do something versus being miserly and only making do with something. Traditional, frozen organisations at times need to be unfrozen if real and positive change is going to occur. Then once the change is implemented, there has to be investment in activities that will refreeze the new approach into place. The three-phase approach can be useful as a recipe for encouraging change and building a culture of innovation.

COMPETITIVE ADVANTAGES, INNOVATION AND CHANGE

Learning Objective
Change as innovation for competitive advantage

The real driver of change is a need to be better, different and generally competitive. Complacency is not the way to win. Some of the most successful companies in the world today have developed atmosphere and architecture that facilitate speed of market feedback and evaluation, responsiveness to needs of customers and staff, flexibility of knowledge management, and an ability to continuously learn, adjust and improve. While it is not possible to guarantee successful innovations for any organisation, the abovementioned conditions are noted to be strong indicators of likely success. It is also informative to think of organisations that have lasted for many generations. There are some commercial operations, for instance, that have run continuously for hundreds and, in some cases, thousands of years. Research into these special cases reveals a similar propensity for innovation just when it is needed (de Geus, 2002). Competitive advantage once gained is not then to be ignored. A culture of continuous improvement is required to ensure sustainability. For every long-lived organisation there are probably hundreds of failed ones that were not responsive enough to the need to change. Some recent research points to the importance of high-performance teamwork and diversity of team composition in the generation of innovative approaches (Creed et al., 2008; Fisser & Browaeys, 2010). It appears that collaboration, cooperation and the human factors are once again making an impact in the competitive landscape. The view of cooperation in context with competition is an important one for organisational behaviour theories. For instance, the tension between corporate social responsibility (CSR) as a strategy versus maximising profitability persists today in theory as well as practice (Zutshi et al., 2009).

WINDOW ON ETHICS

Australian CSR review throws up challenges

SANJAY SHARMA

The results of ACCSR's *State of CSR in Australia Annual Review 2010/11* underline that Australian organisations are—like a large number of organisations globally—still working towards a fuller understanding of what corporate social responsibility means to them and their industries.

FULL UNDERSTANDING OF CSR STILL EMERGING

The report highlights that the main obstacles to adopting successful CSR strategies include the difficulty in making a business case for CSR, difficulty in integrating CSR with organisational values and practices, and the lack of organisational buy-in and commitment to CSR.

Other obstacles reported by respondents such as the lack of time and financial resources to pursue CSR practices are directly related to the above three. When an organisation finds it hard to make a business case for CSR or link it to core organisational operations, it will be reluctant to commit and allocate resources or time to such practices.

Moreover, these obstacles also point to another set of findings in the report: respondents view CSR more…as a means to manage regulatory impacts, reduce risk, and respond to stakeholders' concerns, and to a lesser extent as a strategic source of competitive advantage.

CSR STRATEGIES FOCUSING ON PROTECTION RATHER THAN COMPETITIVE ADVANTAGE

A CSR strategy that is focused on avoiding regulatory liability and maintaining a license to operate in the current business will [lead neither] to current competitive advantage nor an imagination of future business models.

Managing regulations, risk and legitimacy (license to operate) is also reflected in the main capabilities emphasised by the respondents: ethical behaviour, social accountability and stakeholder engagement.

In order to leverage its CSR/sustainability strategy for competitive advantage, an organisation needs the advanced capabilities of organisational learning and sustainable innovation. These two capabilities are critical for building sustainable business models that will lead to future sustained competitive advantage.

AUSTRALIA FACING SAME CSR CHALLENGES AS REST OF WORLD

The findings are not unique to the Australian context but emerge globally as more organisations are at the first phase of understanding the meaning of CSR/sustainability, the environmental and social impacts of their operations, stakeholder concerns about these impacts, the impact of regulations, improving CSR/sustainability reporting and communication, and more effective stakeholder engagement.

The top priority issues listed by most industries in the report reflect this focus. In order to move the understanding and insights gained in the first phase toward changes in the core operations, organisations have to move to the second phase of developing advanced learning and innovation capabilities that will help them build integrated strategies for sustainable business models to compete for the future on their economic, social and environmental performance.

While it is heartening that the surveys for 2008, 2009 and 2010/11 reveal an increasing trend of priority for social issues such as human rights, labour relations, supply chain policies, and corruption, the top priorities for organisations are still environmental impacts rather than social impacts.

This is expected for a resource dominated economy, where the negative environmental impacts of mining, resource extraction, and energy companies can outweigh the negative social impacts. The service sectors such as banking and government, as expected emphasise social issues over environmental issues. In any case, Australia is a 'welfare state' that absorbs many of the negative social impacts via its government's policies.

GLOBAL CONTEXT MUST BE CONSIDERED FOR EFFECTIVE CSR

However, all organisations are embedded in a global context and an integrated social and environmental strategy is critical for their future competitive advantage. The Brundtland Commission report that coined the term 'sustainable development' argued that improvement of ecosystem health without the alleviation of poverty, the redistribution of economic opportunity, community self-sufficiency, and human freedom, could only lead to incremental results.

Solutions to global environmental problems such as climate change involve the development and transfer of technologies to developing countries and the facilitation of grassroots economic capacity building. For example, Australian energy companies cannot tackle climate change without tackling poverty. This is because marginalised and poor societies often survive by burning wood, cow dung, and slash and burn cultivation, all of which exacerbate climate change.

Attempts at reducing greenhouse gas emissions within Australia alone will not make a dent in the global climate change that affects the entire world including Australians.

Moreover, the spread of the Internet has allowed groups and individuals to communicate and find common cause to pressure firms to address their social and environmental impacts in an integrated manner.

DISRUPTIVE INNOVATION WITH CSR INTEGRATION TO UNDERPIN SUSTAINABLE COMPETITIVE ADVANTAGE

Coalitions of NGOs and individuals—smart mobs—have made it increasingly difficult for firms to deal separately with each social, ecological or economic issue in one country or region to the exclusion of other related issues in another country or region.

Integrated ecosystems and social sustainability requires a radical change in business practice, which needs to be based on disruptive rather than incremental innovation and patient investments rather than short-term returns.

Fortunately, there is increasing interest in the former type of approaches by some corporations that are engaged in multi-stakeholder collaboration and are learning about the close integration of economic, social, cultural, and environmental issues in the poorest societies. This is the direction in which Australian companies need to move toward to achieve global competitive advantage in the future.

Source: <www.accsr.com.au/html/stateofcsr2011_sanjaysharma.html>

As long as organisations continue to operate in a world of financial crises, technological change, socio-political transformations and relentless cultural osmosis, there will be a need for them to be perpetually innovative. Intrinsic creativity and motivation can come only from the managers and staff of an organisation. Where then is the rest, the refuge, the balance that people inevitably need when work becomes so demanding?

WORK-LIFE BALANCE IN THE MIDST OF CHANGE

Learning Objective
The impact of change management on work–life balance

It is appropriate that the last part of the final chapter of this book returns to the individual needs of the people working in organisations. People are the generators and custodians of the atmosphere and architecture of the workplace. All the great organisational designs and state-of-the-art resources amount to nothing unless they are facilitated and worked by people in appropriate ways. Understanding that the people are not machines, and the emotional, intellectual and spiritual worlds of staff are just as relevant to work as any identifiable skill or tool, means that notions of equity, work balance and even respect and humanity become central to good management. When the organisation is immersed in a dynamic environment, the need for managers to help staff strive for balance is at its most critical. The ship needs people to maintain and pilot it during rough weather. The captain needs to create an environment that makes people want to stay aboard to do the jobs that are essential. Helping people find the balance between the demands of work and those of their wider lives is a genuine part of the strategic navigation techniques for managers.

WINDOW ON CONFLICT AND NEGOTIATION

Working too hard and getting nowhere?

Do you get the feeling that you're working too hard? Or that you're under-valued or under-appreciated? It's a common complaint because it's a common problem. Many organisations struggle to reward those who produce the most work or come up with the highest quality work.

For people in that situation it can be frustrating enough to plough through mountains of work for little or no reward and that frustration can turn to despair if you see people less qualified and less competent being given the rewards you believe you deserve. And it's even worse if someone gets a promotion to a higher-paid position or to one which you believe you are better equipped to handle.

It can be difficult to control that envy and prevent it from affecting your work. The question 'What's the point?' is likely to be asked. That is understandable and the fact that a senior manager believes somebody else is better equipped for the task needs to be addressed. It may seem unfair, it may be a case of poor judgement by that manager, but the fact is that it cannot be denied.

So what is the problem? There are several possibilities:

1 You do not put yourself forward or display your strengths

Those around you might have skills and strengths that you are not aware of. It is possible that they are more highly qualified than you think. If an individual is particularly adept at displaying his/her strengths the manager will, understandably, be very aware of those skills. Co-workers may have been proactive, expressed interest and had discussions on career progress that you weren't privy to.

So do you put yourself forward? How? When? Or are you waiting to be discovered?

You need to improve your ability to display your strengths. If you have correctly assessed your skills as being superior to those who are being given upgrades that you believe you're entitled to perhaps it is time to examine your ability to make people aware of your accomplishments. But it must not be done in a bragging way or in a way that makes you look like a shameless self-promoter. It is important to make those in positions of power aware of the work you are doing.

2 You know your manager has poor judgement

Mistakes happen in the world of organisational change and you need to consider it as a possibility.

Going over and over the circumstances of someone else's poor judgement is keeping you stuck. What can you do about it?

Change your frame of reference and stop rehashing past decisions. Look for new opportunities with this manager or with others in the business. Be strong, rise above the politics and demonstrate how brilliant you are. Make that manager, or better still that manager's manager, realise how great you are.

If you ruminate for more than two months make a change. Be proactive to help yourself.

3 You need to objectively assess your performance

Have you received specific feedback on your work? Don't wait for it, ask for it. Get definitive feedback, not vague generalisations. There may be a big gap between your perception of your work and that of your managers or colleagues.

Use 360 degree online assessments. They are not expensive and you can initiate them (see for example Skills Indicators Online).

People who seek feedback and are interested in self development are usually perceived as higher performers and once perceived as a higher performer they are treated accordingly. From that feedback you can see what skills need developing and what under-utilised strengths you can discuss with your manager.

4 Your work is strong but people skills are lacking

This is an important element of frustration, with more senior roles often requiring a more integrated method of working which is heavily reliant on high emotional competence and communication skills. If you are a bit of a loner, preferring not to work with people, it is less likely that you'll be offered a position where you need to swiftly develop communication, networking and presentation skills. Do some work on that. It will pay off the next time you present a business case, sell an idea, influence a decision or go for a job interview and it will help you to do better.

5 Your skills don't match the demands of the new position

So what should you do?

If the position is too demanding and you are constantly stressed find something else or suggest that your manager should reassign the role. If you believe your work output is well in excess of the rewards/appreciation you are receiving and there is no way to improve the situation, so that you are constantly unfulfilled, start looking elsewhere.

No one should be unhappy at work. Take responsibility for your own job satisfaction and career moves.

Source: Eve Ash, psychologist and founder, Seven Dimensions <www.7dimensions.com.au> for SmartCompany <www.smartcompany.com.au>

This Window on Conflict and Negotiation reveals the torrid reality of work in turbulent times. It is an ongoing negotiation over just how much workload people can handle. There is uncertainty in almost every transaction. Time-frames are certainly altered and stress so easily creeps in. Effective managers of people have to be able to help staff take responsibility for balancing their personal needs with those of the workplace because if the people burn out, so too does the organisation's long-term prospects for competing and short-term attractiveness as a place for new workers to join. This is what it boils down to. Organisational behaviour is a discipline aimed at understanding why people join an organisation, why they stay, why they leave, and why they may choose to be productive and collaborative at work. Managers with a good understanding of these things hold the key to the power of human resources.

CASE STUDY

Applying strategy to change: A book industry example

The staff of Wordsworth's Bookstore had been expecting the announcement for some time. They knew their industry was undergoing change but they had no idea how they were going to be affected. They were told there would be a special meeting after the store closed on Tuesday night and they would be addressed by Grant Howden, a new Board member who had come from a department store chain. The announcements were to be made simultaneously by Board members at each of the six stores in the eastern states of Australia.

Wordsworth's staff are generally people who are passionate about books. They love discussing them with customers and make recommendations to the buying team as to what the market wants in the field of quality literature.

The meeting at the South Melbourne store was like a funeral. They were told that the business was no longer growing and they were going to move to stocking more popular books to generate turnover and the more specialist books would be available to order online for delivery or as eBooks for downloading.

The stores were going to be redesigned to provide greater display areas for the popular books and the counter area would be streamlined to allow customers to pay for their purchases more in line with a supermarket than the current system which caused people to bunch around the one small counter and encouraged discussion and delays.

When asked if there were any questions, Nancy Curtis put up her hand. 'Does this mean we'll only be dealing with customers who want the latest bestsellers, and all our regulars will have to go online to find their books?'

'Yes, generally,' responded Grant, 'our regular customers usually know what they want. They belong to book groups, they are Internet-savvy, they usually only come in to have a chat and buy something they have already decided on. Quite often we have to order those books in anyway so they might as well order them online or download them. If we have a good display of attractive and popular books we can attract passing traffic and generate impulse buys. We can free up some space to stock magazines. These people won't take up your time chatting and they'll be able to find what they are looking for. Overall, we'll be able to save on staffing in our stores. But don't worry, the staff not required in our stores will be located to our State Distribution Centres where they can still be involved with handling queries from customers and dispatching the orders that come via the Internet.

'We have a great brand name that you've all helped build and with that we should be able to attract more business if we stock the sort of products that people want.'

Nancy and some of her colleagues went out for a drink afterwards. 'I thought the worst case scenario was going to be redundancies and us shrinking down to smaller specialist shops dealing only with quality books,' she said to the group. 'Now it looks like we'll either be dealing with the rubbish end of the market or stuck behind a computer in a warehouse seeing our regular customers' orders whiz by on the screen.'

'Well, I suppose it's all about staying in business, all about money.' Ron Butler was a long-term staff member who was close to retiring. 'I don't think we have much choice.'

'Don't worry Ron, you'll get your superannuation next year,' said Nardia, another team member, sarcastically, 'but we'll be stuck in dead-end jobs, if we have any at all.'

The next week in the South Melbourne store was not pleasant. Staff from other stores confirmed they had been told the same story but as people started to discuss it further they weren't sure the numbers added up. They could see how their jobs might be redundant if there was no personal service required but they could not see how the Distribution Centres could absorb the redundant staff. They already had staff there who

handled dispatch and if the ordering system worked like other web-based businesses there wouldn't be much call for staff advising customers. They came to the conclusion it would end up being the worst of both worlds: redundancy or a boring job selling what they considered the lower-quality end of the market.

'Let's see what Howden says when we put that to him,' Nancy said to the team over lunch one day. 'Why don't we sound out Fran first?' asked Ron. Fran McDonald was the store Manager, she was well respected for her knowledge of books and the book industry but she seemed to be no better advised than the rest of the team at this stage. However, she had recently had some separate managers' meetings with the Board.

Fran's response was disappointing but what they expected. 'I don't know any more than you do. They haven't told me what staff numbers will be needed or even asked me what I think we need. I can't see how it will work and I've given up caring.'

CASE STUDY QUESTIONS

1 What factors do you think brought about this plan for change?
2 What did Grant Howden do that you thought was positive?
3 Using Lewin's force field analysis model, identify the enabling and constraining factors present in the case study.
4 Using the first two stages of Pettigrew's model, expand on how Grant Howden and the rest of the Board could have improved their chances of a successful project.
5 If this restructuring project was implemented as the Board plans, how would you ensure that it was made sustainable? Refer to 'freezing' in the Lewin model and stage four in the Pettigrew model.

CONCLUSION

This book has taken an integrative approach to the examination of organisational behaviour. The later chapters progressively refer to material covered in earlier chapters. Recurring themes are explored through the Windows on Communication, Decision-making, Conflict and Negotiation, and Ethics which reveal the intrinsic nature of these issues. On the topic of change management in the current chapter, it is a culminating field that embraces all others in organisational behaviour. Managing people can be like herding cats; control is not as reasonable as guidance, coercion is not as successful as intrinsic motivation, and planning is not as sustainable as monitoring and being responsive. It is established that competitive advantage depends on innovation, and that depends on people being willing to learn and continuously improve their practices. Natural resistances mean that this can be easier said than done and there is often more rhetoric than reality, for example when it comes to finding a genuine learning organisation. Understanding the forces for change, the types of change, and people's normal responses to the context of change puts the manager in a position to apply some of the models of change management. The cultural web, the Pettigrew Model and force field analysis are among the well-documented approaches, but there are others too. Change management is a field well serviced by consultants who are very willing to share their insights for a fee. Ultimately, the quest to ensure human resources are empowered to contribute to the creation and maintenance of competitive advantages, and to do so without burning out, is the essence of effective people management.

KEY POINTS

This chapter has

- described the prevailing forces that drive organisational change
- discussed the cyclical nature of stability, change and learning
- explained some of the prominent models of change management
- discussed change as innovation for competitive advantage
- explained the impact of change management on work–life balance.

KEY TERMS

CULTURAL WEB
A diagrammatic view of the components of organisational culture as developed and promoted by Johnson (1988, 2008).

FORCE FIELD ANALYSIS
An analysis developed by Lewin (1951) to diagnose and evaluate the enabling and restraining forces that have an impact on change processes.

INCREMENTAL CHANGE
A type of change that is marginal, careful and measured.

PETTIGREW MODEL
A step-by-step view of organisational transformation developed by Pettigrew (1985) that is quite succinct and yet captures the full range of practical issues that can emerge for managers.

POSTMODERNISM
The understanding that objectivity may not be possible; it proposes that all we know is really a social construct and can be challenged for accuracy.

RADICAL CHANGE
A type of change that is transformative, rapid and turbulent.

STUDY AND REVISION QUESTIONS

Q *Why is planning for change almost an oxymoron?*

Q *What does it mean to say that change has an organic rhythm?*

Q *Describe the main elements of force field analysis and discuss what you think may be its limitations when applying it to the implementation of a change initiative (you may wish to refer to a specific example in your answer).*

Q *The cultural web presents as a nice summary of the main elements of organisational culture. Discuss why this model has instead been presented in this chapter about change.*

REFERENCES

Agboola, A., & Salawu, R. (2011). Managing deviant behavior and resistance to change. *International Journal of Business and Management*, 6(1), 235–42.

Creed, A., Zutshi, A. & Swanson, D. (2008). Power and passion: Remoulded teamwork in a plastics factory. *Team Performance Management*, 14(5–6), 196–213.

de Geus, A. (2002). *The living company*. Boston: Harvard Business School Press.

Erwin, D., & Garman, A. (2010). Resistance to organizational change: Linking research and practice. *Leadership & Organization Development Journal*, 31(1), 39–56.

Fincham, R., & Rhodes, P. S. (2005). *Principles of organizational behaviour*. Oxford: Oxford University Press.

Fisser, S., & Browaeys, M. (2010). Team learning on the edge of chaos. *The Learning Organization*, 17(1), 58–68.

Furneaux, C. W., Tywoniak, S. & Gudmundsson, A. (2010). Selection-adaption-retention dynamics and variety in organisational routines. In: *Annual Meeting of the Academy of Management—Dare to Care: Passion and Compassion in Management Practice & Research*, 6–10 August 2010, Montreal.

Grundy, A. N. (1994). *Strategic learning in action*, Maidenhead, UK: McGraw Hill.

Hamilton, E. (2011). Entrepreneurial learning in family business: A situated learning perspective. *Journal of Small Business and Enterprise Development*, 18(1), 8–6.

Hassard, J. (1994). Postmodern organizational analysis: Toward a conceptual framework. *Journal of Management Studies*, 31(3), 303–24.

Hewison, R., Holden, J. & Jones, S. (2010). *All together: A creative approach to organisational change*. London: Demos.

Johnson, G. (1988). Rethinking incrementalism. *Strategic Management Journal*, 9(1), 75–91.

Johnson, G. (2008). *The cultural web*. White paper, Strategy Explorers, available 28/02/2011 at <www.strategyexplorers.com/whitepapers/Culture-Web.pdf>

Lewin, K. (1951). *Field theory in social science: Selected theoretical papers*. New York: Harper & Row.

Lewis, A., & Juravle, C. (2010). Morals, markets and sustainable investments: A qualitative study of 'champions'. *Journal of Business Ethics*, 93(1), 483–94.

Liao, S. H., Chang, W. J. & Wu, C. C. (2010). An integrated model for learning organization with strategic view: Benchmarking in the knowledge-intensive industry. *Expert Systems with Applications*, 37(1), 3792–8.

McClelland, P., Liang, X. & Barker III, V. (2010). CEO commitment to the status quo: Replication and extension using content analysis. *Journal of Management*, 36(5), 1251–77.

McKendrick, & Wade, (2010). Frequent incremental change, organizational size, and mortality in high-technology competition. *Industrial and Corporate Change*, 19(3), 613–39.

Morgan, G. (2006). *Images of organization*. Thousand Oaks, CA: Sage Publications.

Pettigrew, A. M. (1985). *The awakening giant: Continuity and change in Imperial Chemical Industries*. Oxford: Blackwell.

Schon, D. (1971). *Beyond the stable state*. London: Temple Smith.

Senge, P. (1990). *The fifth discipline: The art and practice of the learning organization.* London: Currency Doubleday.

Stace, D., & Dunphy, D. (2005). *Beyond the boundaries: Leading and re-creating the successful enterprise.* Sydney: McGraw-Hill Australia.

Taylor, R. (2011). Continuity and change: The yin yang of leadership. *Business Leadership Review*, 7(1), 1–9.

Thompson, J. (2010). Understanding and managing organizational change: Implications for public health management. *Journal of Public Health Management & Practice*, 16(2), 167–73.

Zutshi, A., Creed, A. & Sohal, A. (2009). Child labour and supply chain: Profitability or (mis)management. *European Business Review*, 21(1), 42–63.

Actualised power

Potential power made active. Power is actualised when influence is enacted.

Architecture

The structure of an organisation—the way that work is arranged, departments are established and processes are articulated—collectively represent the architecture of the workplace.

Atmosphere

The collective manifestation of people and resources for a purposeful strategy is expressed as an atmosphere.

Attention

The taking possession by the mind of one out of several simultaneously possible objects or trains of thought. It involves withdrawal from some things in order to deal effectively with the things chosen for attention.

Attitude

A subjective evaluation about objects, people or events that manifests as a combination of thoughts, feelings and behaviours.

Behavioural learning theories

The collection of theories that suggest learning expresses itself through changes in behaviour.

Behavioural theory

Any of the leadership theories that focus upon observations of leadership styles which can be changed by the leader, autonomously or by training.

Behaviour modification

This is the process of shaping the behaviour of others through positive reinforcement, negative reinforcement, punishment or extinction.

Bounded rationality

The fact that incomplete (bounded) information is applied in making any decision.

Classical conditioning

The first formalised theory of conditioning in which it was discovered by Ivan Pavlov that reflexive responses could be altered with different kinds of stimuli.

Cognitive dissonance

Leon Festinger's theory that a mismatch between expectations and reality will be handled by individuals, changing their behaviour in ways that try to minimise the dissonance.

Cognitive learning theories

The collection of theories that suggest learning is expressed through changes in thinking or cognition.

Conditioned stimulus (CS)

In conditioning theory a conditioned stimulus is one that has been linked by experience to the generation of a response. In the example of Pavlov's dog, the ringing sound became the conditioned stimulus once it was able to elicit salivation in the absence of the meat.

Conditioned response (CR)

In conditioning theory a conditioned response is one that has been linked by experience to a certain stimulus. In the example of Pavlov's dog, the occurrence of salivation merely at the ringing sound became the conditioned response.

Content theory

A motivation theory that describes the contents of human needs.

Cultural web

A diagrammatic view of the components of organisational culture as developed and promoted by Johnson (1988, 2008).

Culture

One of the key components of overall organisational atmosphere. It is the net expression of all of the physical, mental and emotional contributions of individuals, groups and resources in the organisation.

Delphi Method
A way of building consensus on a course of action by repeatedly applying a series of questionnaires to collect data from a panel of selected experts on the issue.

Emotional intelligence
The ability to be sensitive to the feelings of others and to pick up on and be responsive to social cues.

Empowerment
Providing staff with the power to show initiative.

Equity theory
A process theory that identifies not only the comparisons individuals make about their jobs inside and outside their organisation but also the options for behavioural responses to those comparisons.

ERG
Short for Existence-Relatedness-Growth: the three levels of human needs identified by Alderfer.

Expectancy theory
The theory that people approach their work with expectancies about individual performance, organisational rewards and personal goals; and the nature of the effort–performance relationship, performance–reward relationship and the rewards–personal goals relationship that help determine the level of individual motivation.

Expectation (E)
A factor in expectancy theory that measures a person's expectation about whether individual effort will lead to successful performance of the task.

Explicit cultural factors
The things a worker or any observer encounters as they engage or enter the space occupied by a particular organisation. Explicit culture is a blend of language and stories, behavioural norms and rituals, and designs (involving patterns of colour, sound and smells).

Fixation
The psychoanalytic term for becoming rigid and inflexible.

Force field analysis
An analysis developed by Lewin (1951) to diagnose and evaluate the enabling and restraining forces that have an impact on change processes.

Frustration-regression principle
Alderfer identifies the frustration-regression principle whereby if a higher-level need remains unfulfilled, the person may revert to trying to satisfy lower-level needs that appear easier to address.

Fundamental attribution error
People tend to overestimate the control that others have over their behaviours and therefore default to being quite judgmental and discriminatory towards those others.

Group
A collection of individuals working on achieving similar goals.

Groupthink
When the views of the more dominant members of a group become accepted as the consensus.

High-context culture
A culture in which lots of communication between people occurs beyond verbal discussion, that is, implicit things like body language, facial expressions and other unspoken behaviours, including the broader context of power relationships, are applied and interpreted in the course of normal interactions.

Implicit cultural factors
The largely invisible values and attitudes of the people working in the organisation making the most of its architecture and processes.

Impression management
The conscious planning and control of the balance between real and perceived outcomes, in relation to oneself as well as others.

Incremental change
A type of change that is marginal, careful and measured.

Instrumentality (I)
A factor in expectancy theory that measures how confident a person is that performance of a task will lead to an appropriate reward from the organisation.

Job characteristics theory (JCT)
An integrated theory of job design that bridges concepts from the areas of motivation, individual differences, group dynamics, power and leadership.

Job enlargement
Adding a greater variety of tasks to the job that a person currently does.

Job enrichment
A strategic version of job enlargement that aims to give people work that fulfils their higher-level needs for a sense of meaning, achievement and belonging.

Job rotation
The opportunity to try a completely different job, thus enabling the expansion of skill sets across a number of workers and allowing people to develop a more integrated understanding of the ways different jobs come together in the organisation.

Job simplification
The process of streamlining the work flow of a task, or removing some aspects of a person's job. The aim is to maximise efficiency and sometimes the effect is to enhance role clarity, which has a positive effect on overall job satisfaction.

Judgment heuristics
Judgment patterns formed from previous decision outcomes which can act as guides for future decisions.

Learning
Identifiable changes in thinking, relating and behaving established by individuals or groups in response to internal or external stimuli.

Learning organisation
A kind of ideal culture in which all the people and systems of the organisation are oriented to an open and continuous shared learning cycle as a way to remain competitive and adaptive.

Locus of control
The extent of our feelings about the level of control we have over the world.

Low-context culture
A culture in which explicit written or spoken words are relied on to convey meanings to each other.

Machiavellian
Said of someone given to self-interested political actions.

Management
Planning, organising, leading and controlling the variables of time, money, physical resources and people (human resources).

Motivation
The energy and the processes that provide individuals and groups with direction and perseverance towards their goals.

Multi-skilling
The collection of experiences and training that enables workers to become proficient at more than one job or skill set.

Neural network
A metaphor of the contemporary workplace in which the individuals, groups and organisations simulate the way a brain and nervous system operate.

Nominal Group Technique
A face-to-face method to balance participation, apply different processes for different phases of creative problem solving, and reduce possible errors in aggregating individual judgments into group decisions.

Operant conditioning

A conditioning theory acknowledging the behaviour-shaping capacity of the environment. Skinner suggested that positive reinforcement, or providing something pleasant as a consequence of behaviour that is desirable, will strengthen that behaviour and increase the chances that it will be adopted more permanently. The inverse is also true; that is, remove any response that is unpleasant and the likelihood of repeating the behaviour increases.

Organisation

An organisation comprises people and other resources brought together with a design and strategy directed towards a common purpose.

Organisational behaviour

The study of individual and group characteristics and behaviour in the context of workplace structures and strategies.

Organisational justice

The overall perception of what is equitable in the workplace.

Outsourcing

The decision taken to contract some aspect of an operation out to an external organisation, often offshore.

Paradox of perception

The fact that we are each likely to perceive the same situations in sometimes markedly different ways.

Personality

The combined expression of individual values and attitudes through the actions and reactions the individual experiences with others.

Personal power

The power that comes from one's own individual characteristics and skills. The two broad factors that contribute to personal power are referent and expert.

Pettigrew Model

A step-by-step view of organisational transformation developed by Pettigrew (1985) that is quite succinct and yet captures the full range of practical issues that can emerge for managers.

Position power

The power that comes from occupying key positions with formal lines of authority and accountability. It derives its strength from control of rewards and perceptions of legitimacy.

Postmodernism

The understanding that objectivity may not be possible; it proposes that all we know is really a social construct and can be challenged for accuracy.

Potential power

The latent power that is capable of affecting the ways that others think, feel and behave once it is actualised.

Power distance

Hofstede's term for the extent to which the less powerful members of organisations and institutions accept and expect that power is distributed unequally.

Process theory

A motivation theory that describes the processes that are observed in people's minds and emotions.

Projection

The psychoanalytic term for attribution of one's intentions and feelings to others.

Psychoanalysis

Developed originally by Sigmund Freud as a practical tool for exploring aspects of personality, more specifically dysfunctions in personality development at different stages of life.

Psychological contract

The agreement workers make in their minds with organisations when they accept a position. An expectation is established about what energy will be spent and which duties the worker will be comfortable carrying out. In return, the organisation has expectations about the resources and support they will provide for the worker.

Radical change

A type of change that is transformative, rapid and turbulent.

Rationalisation

The psychoanalytic term for overly complex explaining away to cover up true motives.

Reinforcement

Any kind of feedback that encourages a certain learned behaviour to be repeated.

Regression

The psychoanalytic term for reverting to behaviours learned in childhood.

Relational ethics

An ethical field that focuses on the relationships between people with factors such as processes of communication, the methods for finding rapport with others, and techniques for being respectful at work.

Ringelmann effect

Also known as social loafing; when a person relies on the hard work of others to carry them through.

Self-efficacy

A sense of confidence about one's ability to complete a task.

Self-managing team

A team that draws on the skills and experience of each member and delivers high quality outputs by a collaborative synchronisation without needing a single defined leader.

Situational theory

Situational theories factor in the situations such as relationships between leaders and followers, preferred leader styles, and other situational variables to try to explain successes and failures in achieving organisational objectives.

Social learning theories

The collection of theories that suggest learning is expressed through changes in relationships via mechanisms such as role modelling, parenting, mentoring and general social experiences.

Social loafing

Also known as the Ringelmann effect; when a person relies on the hard work of others to carry them through.

Synergy

High levels of effectiveness and efficiency that sometimes cannot be explained by just breaking down the aspects of the processes that created the event. Synergy is when the whole becomes greater than the sum of its parts.

Team

A collection of individuals working interdependently with shared vision and cohesion on achieving jointly agreed goals.

Trait theory

A group of theories any of which aim to identify and define key traits that leaders exhibit, ideally but not always universally.

Two-factor theory

Herzberg's theory that two separate categories of human needs create motivator and hygiene effects. The two factors are based on the observation that the opposite of job satisfaction is actually no satisfaction and, on an entirely separate continuum, the opposite of dissatisfaction is no dissatisfaction.

Unconditioned stimulus (UCS)
In conditioning theory an unconditioned stimulus is one that elicits a reflexive response. In the example of Pavlov's dog, the meat is the unconditioned stimulus when in the first instance it creates reflexive salivation in the dog.

Unconditioned response (UCR)
In conditioning theory an unconditioned response is a reflex in relation to a certain stimulus. In the example of Pavlov's dog, the meat is the unconditioned stimulus which leads to the unconditioned response of salivation in the dog in the first instance.

Uncertainty avoidance
Hofstede's term for the extent to which a culture programs its members to feel either uncomfortable or comfortable in unstructured situations.

Valence (V)
A factor in expectancy theory that measures the expectation that organisational rewards are aligned with the personal goals a person has in mind.

Values
Basic convictions about means and ends. The Global Sullivan Principles are examples of values.

absenteeism   14–15
actualised power   181–2
Adams, John Stacey   108–9
aggression–calmness   212
Alderfer, Clayton   100–1
American Express   220–1
architecture
    definition   3
    of high-performance teams   140–4
    strategic, effectively managing the   22
architecture of work   17–22
    effectively managing the strategic architecture   22
    organisational structure basics   17–22
Aristotle   36, 155
aspect of diversity   41–2
atmosphere
    definition   3
    of high-performance teams   140–4
    themes affecting the   7
atmosphere of work   7–16
    effective management and globalisation   13–16
    external factors   7–8
    internal factors   10–13
attention and learning   42–5
attitudes and personality   68–72, 73
attitudes and values (cultural factors)   206–8
Australian Public Service   207–8
authority and power   104, 187

Bandura, Albert   36, 52, 79
behaviour, individuals   75–6
behaviour modification   50–1
    definition   38
    and reinforcement   46–52
behavioural learning theories   37
behavioural theories (leadership styles)   158–60
    managerial grid   158–9
    Michigan and Ohio State studies   158
behavioural theory   158
Belbin, Meredith   141

Belbin's team roles   141
Bettelheim, Bruno   188
Blake, R.R.   158–9, 160
Blanchard, K.   163–5
Bloom, Benjamin   36
book industry (case study)   275
bounded rationality   136
Britton, Camilla   30–1
Bruner, Jerome   36
BSI Pty Ltd (case study)   16–17
bullying, workplace   42, 104–5
    case study   87–8

Cafe Vamp   42
calmness–aggression   212
case studies   xiii
case study mapping grid   xiv–xv
change   257–76
    cycles of   260–1
    forces for   258
    incremental   259
    and innovation   270–1
    leadership of cultural learning and   221–2
    learning to   55–7
    people's resistance to   55
    planned   259
    radical   259
    unfreezing, changing, refreezing   267
    unplanned   260
    and work-life balance   271–4
change management models   262–6
charisma and the leadership of change   169–70
China   217–18
classical conditioning   48
cognitive dissonance   45
cognitive learning theories   37
cohesiveness and team spirit   141–2
collaboration and competition   219
communication   6–7, 212, 218
    interpersonal   20, 41, 140

communication *cont.*
    and labour contracting   53
    pathways   52
    personal   81
    window on   xxiv, 24, 42, 86, 99–100, 132, 167, 185, 207, 233, 263–4
competition and collaboration   219
competitive advantages   270–2
conditioned response (CR)   49, 50
conditioned stimulus (CS)   49
conditioning
    classical   48
    operant   49, 50
conflict   6–7, 135
    intergroup   142
    interpersonal   260, 266
conflict and negotiation, window on   xxiv, 54, 70–1, 112, 134–5, 159–60, 182–3, 217–18, 243, 273–4
conflict, interpersonal (case study)   266
conservatism–innovation   210
constructive leadership   59
content theories   96, 97–104
continuous reinforcement   51
Cooper, Wendy   254–5
critical psychological states   239
CSR   271–2
cultural web   258, 262
culture   205–24
    aggression–calmness   212
    definition   206
    and design   213–14
    and ethics   219
    explicit factors   209–14
    global   215–18
    growth–stability   213
    high-context   212
    implicit factors   206–8
    innovation–conservatism   210
    language and stories   209

    and learning   53–5
    and leadership   221–3
    low-context   212
    national   83, 215, 216, 224
    norms and rituals   209–13
    observable   209–14
    organisational   82–4
    overview   206
    precision–imprecision   210
    relationship orientation–task orientation   211–12
    values and attitudes   206–8
    work-life balance   220–1
    workplace   82–4
customer (case study)   170–1
cycles of change and learning   260–1

D'Arcy, Rita   176–7
decision-making, window on   xxiv, 6, 19, 44, 74, 105–6, 135–8, 164, 194, 210–11, 247–9, 268–70, 275
Delphi method   136
Delta Select Chemicals Ltd (case study)   191–2
design and culture   213
Designer Taps (case study)   56–7
Dewey, John   36
discrimination against older workers   70–1
diversity
    aspect of   41–2
    organisational   82–4
    see also modern diversity
DJs   112

emotional intelligence   79–81, 86, 88, 154, 166–8, 169, 172
employee–employer relationship   10–13
employment interviews   210–11
empowerment   95, 111–13, 180, 186–7, 221
ERG theory   100–1
equity
    organisational   82–4
    and performance appraisal   242–3

equity theory   108–9
ethical leadership   168–9
ethics   6–7, 22, 50, 168–9, 196–7, 206
    case study   196–7
    continuum of   188
    and culture   219
    and evil in organisations   187–92, 195
    in organisations   187–91
    and power   196–7
    relational   218
    and trust   13–14, 25
    window on   xxiv, 12, 58, 82–3, 103–4, 128, 156–7,
        189–90, 220–1, 241, 271–2
evil in organisations   187–91
expectancy theory   106–8
expectation (E)   107
expectations and learning   45–6
explicit cultural factors   209–14
external factors of work   7–8
extinction   50–1

Facebook   16, 159–60
Festinger, L.   45
Fiedler, Fred   161–2, 169
Fiji Water   194
Fincham, R.   37, 154, 162, 163, 264
five-factor model of personality   78, 156
force field analysis   258, 265–6
forces for change   258
forces for stability   258–9
Fraser-Kirk, Kristy   112
Freud, Sigmund   75
frustration-regression principle   101
fundamental attribution error   41

genetic testing (case study)   74
George Davis and Associates (case study)   84–5
Gersick, C.   130
Gilbreth, F.B.   43
global culture   215–18
Global Sullivan Principles   69–70

globalisation   13–15
goal-setting theory (Locke)   105–6
Graen, G.B.   161
Greener Parks Pty Ltd (case study)   266
group(s)
    definition   126
    energy, capitalising on   135–8
    overview   126
    vs teams   126–39
    types   128–30
groupthink   131–2, 137
growth-stability   213

Harrison, Jessica   64–5
Hawthorne Effect   43, 128
health and flexible work design   245–9
Heidegger, Martin   36, 51, 55
Hersey, P.   163–5
Herzberg, Frederick   101–4
hierarchy and span of control   18, 20
high-context culture   212
Hofstede, Geert   83–4, 216
House, R.   160–1, 169
human relations   4–6
    and management   4–5
    and organisation   5
    and organisational behaviour   5–6
Hutchinson, Tom   200–1

immigrant employees (case study)   165–6
implicit cultural factors   206–8
imprecision   210
impression management   193
incremental change   259
individual
    behaviour   75–6
    expectations   106–8
    and organisational learning   52–3
individual vs organisational power   182–3
industrial relations   182–3

influence, techniques of   195
innovation and change   270–2
innovation–conservatism   210
instrumentality (I)   107
intelligence
    emotional   79–81, 86, 88, 154, 166–8, 169, 172
    social   154, 166–8, 249
intelligence quotient (IQ)   80
internal factors of work   8–13
interpersonal conflict (case study)   266

Jaakson, K.   207
James, William   42–3
Jensen, Louise   120–1
job characteristics, core   239
job characteristics theory (JTC)   238–9
job design, integrated   237–41
job enlargement   236
job enrichment   236–7
job performance   210–11
job responsibility (case study)   234–5
job rotation   237
job satisfaction   15, 71–2
    and motivation   95–116
job security   10
job simplification   236
jobs, staff turnover in boring   110
Joyce, Alan   182–3
judgment heuristics   136
Jung, Carl   75–6

Kant, Immanuel   36
Klahsen, Leanne   92–3

language and stories (culture)   209
leadership
    of change and charisma   169–70
    contemporary   165–71
    constructive   59
    of cultural learning and change   221–2
    ethical   168–9

    and Fred Fielder   161–2
    Hersey and Blanchard   163–5
    learning and reinforcement through   113
    in the neural network   171–2
    managerial grid   158–9
    Michigan and Ohio State studies   158
    overview   154
    path–goal theory   160–1
    situational theories   160–5
    styles (behavioural theories)   158–60
    theories   154, 160–5
    Theory X and Theory Y   155–6, 158, 212
    trait theory   154
    traits   154–7
    universal traits   155–6
learning
    aspect of diversity   41–2
    and attention   42–5
    to change   55–7
    cultural learning and change   221–2
    and culture   53–5
    cycles of   260–1
    definition   37–8
    and emotional (social) intelligence   166–8
    and expectations   45–6
    and job design   249–50
    nature of   36
    overview   36
    reinforcement and behaviour modification   46–52
    and reinforcement through leadership   113
    relativity of perception   39–41, 73
    social   52–9
    theories   37–8, 249–50
learning organisation   55
Lewin, K.   55, 57, 285, 266, 267
Locke, Edwin   105–6
locus of control   79
low-context culture   212
Lucas, Vin   228–9

McClelland, David   104
McGregor, D.   155–6, 212
Machiavelli, N.   189
Machiavellianism   139, 189, 245
management
    definition   4
    and human relations   4–5
    impression   193
    and reinforcement   51–2
    strategies   xxiv
Management by Objectives (MBO)   105
management style (case study)   213–14
managerial grid   158–9
Maslow, Abraham   76, 97–100, 155, 207
matrix organisational structure   20–2
media releases   105–6
Michigan study (leadership style)   158
Milford Construction (case study)   114–15
Milgram, Stanley   104, 187
moderators   240
modern diversity   67–90
    attitudes and values   68–72
    conclusion   88–9
    foundational ideas   75–81
    overview   68
    personality   72–81
    socialisation   81–8
mothers working from home (case study)   244
motivation
    Adams (equity theory)   108–9
    Alderfer and ERG   100–1
    case study   114–15
    comparison of satisfiers and dissatisfiers   102
    and content theories   96, 97–104
    definition   95
    different kinds of   114–15
    does satisfaction limit   96–7
    and job satisfaction   95–116
    Locke (goal-setting theory)   105–6

McClelland and acquired needs   104
Maslow's hierarchy of needs   97–100
needs-based   97–104
overview   96
process theorists   105–10, 113
situation-based   105–10
theories   96
two-factor theory   101–4
Vroom (expectancy theory)   106–8
work–family balance   113–15
Mouton, J.S.   158–9, 160
multi-skilling   237
Myers-Briggs   76–7

National Appliances (case study)   87–8
national culture   83, 215, 216, 224
needs hierarchy   97–100, 207
negotiation   6, 242–3
    and conflict, window on   xxiv, 54, 70–1, 112, 134–5, 159–60, 182–3, 217–18, 243, 273–4
neural network   22–4, 38, 52–3
    and leadership   171–2
Nominal Group Technique   136
norms and rituals (culture)   209–13
Northern Territory   44–5

Ohio State study (leadership styles)   158
operant conditioning   49, 50
organisation
    definition   3, 5
    and human relations   5
    learning   55
organisational behaviour
    absenteeism and turnover   14–15
    atmosphere, themes affecting the   7
    definition   3, 5–6
    and human relations   5–6
    job satisfaction and productive work   15
    psychological foundations of   35
    task vs relationship   14

organisational behaviour *cont.*
  trait theory   155–6
  trust, ethics and agreements   13–14
organisational culture   82–4
  aggression–calmness   212
  case studies   213–14, 222–3
  growth–stability   213
  innovation–conservatism   210
  norms and rituals   209–13
  precision–imprecision   210
  relationship orientation–task orientation   211–12
  see also culture
organisational equity   82–4
organisational justice   109
organisational learning and the individual   52–3
organisational structure basics   17–22
  control and coordination   18–19
  technology and scale   17–18
organisational structure matrix   20–1
organisational vs individual power   182–3
organisations
  ethics and evil in   187–91
  and the neural network metaphor   22–4
  power and politics   57–9, 189–90, 192–5
  power structure of   18–19
outsourcing   10–11

paradox of perception   40
parental leave, paid   11
path–goal theory (leadership)   160–1
pay and discrimination   11–12
Pavlov, Ivan   48
people, diversity and perceptions   7–8
perception, relativity of   39–41, 73
perceptual paradox   40
performance appraisal   242–3
Perry, Neil   233
personal appearance (case study)   84–5
personal power   183–4

personality
  and attitudes   68–72
  definition   67
  factors   72
  five-factor model   78, 156
  foundational ideas   75–81
  influence of environment or heredity   73–5
  and modern diversity   72–81
  Myers-Briggs Indicator   76–7
  and socialisation   81–8
  and values   68–72
Pettigrew model   258
Pfeffer, Jeffrey   189–90
philosophers on the nature of learning   37
Piaget, Jean   36
planned change   259
Plato   36
politics and power   57–9, 189–90, 192–5
position power   184–6
postmodernism   260
power
  acquiring and maintaining   189–90
  actualised   181–2
  and authority   104, 187
  case study   196–7
  and ethics   196–7
  ethics and evil in organisations   187–91
  exercise of   186–97
  how to get   183–6
  individual vs organisational   182–3
  organisational   182–3, 192–5
  overview   180
  and politics   57–9, 189–90, 192–5
  position   184–6
  potential   181
  sources of   180–3
  structure of organisations   18–19
  techniques of influence   195
power distance   83, 216, 224

precision–imprecision   210
process theorists   105–10
process theory   113
productive work   15
projection   75
psychoanalysis   75
psychological contract   233
punctuated equilibrium   130–1
punishment   50

Qantas   182–3

racism (case study)   8–9
radical change   259
rationalisation   75
regression   75
reinforcement
    and behaviour modification   46–52
    definition   38, 51
    as a management tool   51–2
relational ethics   218
relationship design   249
relationship orientation–task orientation   211–12
relativity of perception   39–41, 73
Rhodes, P.S.   37, 154, 162, 163
Ringelmann, Max   134, 135
Ringelmann effect   134
rituals and norms (culture)   209–13
RLG Tools Ltd (case study)   196–7
Rossini Fine Foods (case study)   139
Rothwell, Nicolas   44–5

self-efficacy   79, 111
self-managing team   142
Senge, Peter   55
situational leadership theories   160–5
    and Fred Fielder   161–2
    Hersey and Blanchard   163–5
    path–goal theory   160–1
situational theory   160
situation-based motivation   105–10

Skinner, B.F.   49
Sleepy Bed Linen (case study)   47
social intelligence   154, 166–8, 249
social learning
    and the complex workplace   52–9
    theories   37, 52
social loafing   133–5, 137
socialisation   81–8
Southern Doors Limited (case study)   143–4
space design   245–6
stability   257–76
    forces for   258–9
stability–growth   213
staff turnover in boring jobs (case study)   110
Stanford Prison experiments   104, 187
stories and language (culture)   209
Strickland, R.A.   207
synergy   132–3

task vs relationship   14
task orientation–relationship orientation   211–12
Taylor, Frederick   17, 43, 134, 245
team(s)
    architecture and atmosphere of high-performance
        140–4
    Belbin's team roles   141
    definition   126
    development sequence   128–30
    vs groups   126–39
    leadership and control   142–4
    overview   126
    performance   130–1
    self-managing   142
    spirit and cohesiveness   141–2
team meetings (case study)   143–4
technology and scale   17–18
Telstra   164
Theory X and Theory Y   155–6, 158, 212
Thodey, David   164
Thomas Brewer Partners (case study)   244

Thompson Components (case study)   110–11
time design   246–7
Toy Deals on Line (case study)   165–6
Toyota   86
trait theory   154, 155–6
Trident Support (case study)   8–9
trust, ethics and agreements   13–14
Tuckman, B.W.   129
turnover   14–15
two-factor theory   101–4

Uhl-Bien, M.   161
uncertainty avoidance   83, 216, 224
unconditioned response (UCR)   49
unconditioned stimulus (UCS)   49
unplanned change   260

valence (V)   107
values and attitudes (cultural factors)   206–8
values and personality   68–72, 73
Vaughan, S.K.   207
Victoria Furniture Designs Ltd (case study)   170–1
Virgin Blue   12
Vroom, Victor   106–8

Woodward, Rebecca   150–1
work
    different approaches to the design of   236–7
    design, flexible   245–9
    designing   232–4
    outcomes, individual   239
Work Choices   54
workers, discrimination against older   70–1
work–family balance   13, 113–15
work–life balance   220, 245–9, 272–4
working from home (case study)   244
workplace
    bullying   42, 104–5
    culture   82–4
    manager–subordinate relations   112–13
    respect and trust   88

social and relational needs   113–14
and social learning   52–9
violence   99–100

Zimbardo, Philip   104, 187